Wreath Layer or Policy Player?

The Presidency and Public Policy

Series Editor: Alan Shank, SUNY–Geneseo

Books in this series take a close look at the American presidency from various angles: executive power, leadership, public policy, foreign policy. In addition to in-depth studies of figures close to the president— such as the vice president and presidential advisors— investigations of past, current, and future trends in presidential decision making will give shape to the state of the American presidency at the start of the twenty-first century.

The Presidency and the Middle Kingdom: China, the United States, and Executive Leadership, by Michael P. Riccards

Wreath Layer or Policy Player? The Vice President's Role in Foreign Policy, by Paul Kengor

Wreath Layer or Policy Player?

The Vice President's Role in Foreign Policy

Paul Kengor

LEXINGTON BOOKS
Lanham • Boulder • New York • Oxford

LEXINGTON BOOKS

Published in the United States of America
by Lexington Books
4720 Boston Way, Lanham, Maryland 20706

12 Hid's Copse Road
Cumnor Hill, Oxford OX2 9JJ, England

Copyright © 2000 by Lexington Books

All rights reserved. No part of this publication may be reproduced, stored in a retrieval system, or transmitted in any form or by any means, electronic, mechanical, photocopying, recording, or otherwise, without the prior permission of the publisher.

British Library Cataloguing in Publication Information Available

Library of Congress Cataloging-in-Publication Data

Kengor, Paul, 1966–
  Wreath layer or policy player : the vice president's role in foreign policy / Paul Kengor.
    p.   cm.
  Includes bibliographical references and index.
  ISBN 0-7391-0174-9 (cloth : alk. paper) — ISBN 0-7391-0218-4 (pbk. : alk. paper)
  1. Vice-Presidents—United States. 2. United States—Foreign relations—1945–1989. 3. United States—Foreign relations—1989– I. Title.

JK609.5 .K46   2000
327.73'0092'2—dc21   00-042123

Printed in the United States of America

⊖™ The paper used in this publication meets the minimum requirements of American National Standard for Information Sciences—Permanence of Paper for Printed Library Materials, ANSI/NISO Z39.48–1992.

Contents

List of Tables	vi
List of Figures	vii
Preface	ix
1 Introduction and Methodology	1
2 The Evolution of a Reform: The Vice President in Foreign Policy	13
3 A Path-Breaking Vice President: Richard M. Nixon (1953-61)	41
4 A Political Vice President: Walter Mondale (1977-81)	83
5 A Crisis-Managing Vice President: George H. W. Bush (1981-89)	125
6 A "War-Time" Vice President: J. Danforth Quayle (1989-93)	165
7 A "Presidential" Vice President?: Al Gore (1993-)	213
8 Conclusion: Lessons Learned and Policy Recommendations	261
Bibliography	307
Index	321
About the Author	327

Tables

Table 4.1	U.S. Representatives at Camp David Talks	105
Table 8.1	Policy Recommendations for the Vice President vis-à-vis Foreign Policy	262

Figures

Figure 2.1	Level of Foreign Policy Involvement by VPs	30
Figure 2.2	The President's Foreign and Security Policy Inputs	32
Figure 4.1	Carter Administration Foreign and Security Policy Structure	90

Preface

When you tell people you are researching the vice presidency they often give you a puzzled look. "The vice presidency?" they ask. "Why? Who cares?" When I add that my focus is the vice president's role in foreign policy, semi- to well-informed observers are quickly confused and skeptical: "Doesn't the vice president just travel overseas to lay wreaths and fake tears at the funerals of foreign dignitaries he has never met?"

I first became interested in this subject as a student in the master's program at the School of International Service at The American University. Oddly enough, I was struggling to come up with a term paper topic for Yehuda Lukacs' course on Arab-Israeli relations. At the time, the *Washington Post* was running a series of in-depth articles by ace reporters David Broder and Bob Woodward on Vice President Dan Quayle. I had always felt a bit sorry for Quayle because of the unrelenting abuse he received. As an undergrad, I read Richard Fenno's book and was intrigued by what it said about this rising star in the Senate. Later, during his vice-presidential years, I was fascinated by the tendency to brush him off as an intellectual lightweight and incompetent. Nowadays, the line is that Quayle earned that reputation as a result of numerous gaffes and malaprops. While he certainly bears some responsibility, that line is not totally true: The shelling began the moment George Bush chose him to be his running mate. Moreover, I was always incredulous that anyone who could be continuously reelected by landslides to the U.S. Congress, not to mention reach the heights of a vice-presidential candidacy, could be so supposedly lacking in intellect.

It was in this context that the Broder and Woodward article caught my attention. Here, alas, was a fair and serious article on Quayle by a nonconservative, mainstream news source. Among the aspects of the article that caught my attention was an item about Quayle's November 29, 1990, speech at Seton Hall University. The speech spelled out the administration's position and objectives regarding the Persian Gulf crisis. I remembered reports on the speech at the time, including one that centered on whether Quayle had written it. (Broder and Woodward confirmed that Quayle alone had crafted it.) As I recalled, the speech seemed impressive and well done. Being that one of my key interests was the Persian Gulf conflict—the first and only real war I ever "experienced," albeit from the comfort of my living room—I decided to retrieve a copy of the speech. After reading it, I felt it offered the most compelling case I had read on what the Bush administration's objectives were in the conflict and what was truly at stake. It even clearly defined such fuzzy administration concepts as the president's New World Order. And, of course, dummy Quayle wrote it.

It was at that point that I began to formulate a term paper idea for Dr. Lukacs' class: How about the role of Vice President Quayle during the 1990-91 Persian Gulf crisis? Lukacs liked the idea and encouraged me to tackle a subject that appeared completely unique. Since neither of us were experts, nor even remotely knowledgeable, on the subject of the vice presidency, we decided I should ask American University's top resident-local expert on the presidency and foreign-policy decision making. The professor was an affable, quiet guy who liked the work I did in his class. In the past, he had written some nice letters of recommendation on my behalf. I telephoned him: "I'm doing a term paper on the role of the vice president during the Persian Gulf crisis. Do you know of any scholars on the vice presidency?" "No!" he answered sternly. I persisted: "Do you know of anything that has been done on the subject?" "No!" he again replied tersely. "Why not?" I asked naively. "Because," he angrily asserted, "no one cares about the vice presidency!" He slammed down the phone without saying goodbye. End of conversation. In retrospect, I think he was probably angered that a promising student would stray off the path of sanity and undertake such a fruitless endeavor as the American vice presidency.

It was not the first time I would get such a response. Many view the study of the vice presidency as being as "useless" as the institution itself. Arthur M. Schlesinger, Jr., called the vice presidency a "useless appendage."

To shorten my story, I buried myself in American University's library and read everything I could on the vice presidency. I found it fascinating. Ironically, I also realized a potential gold mine in the angry professor's comments: If I became a "scholar" on the vice presidency, which seemed appealing intellectually, would I not have somewhat of a niche for myself—or, at least, be doing something that only a small group of others were doing? In Washington, D.C., I was one of thousands of scholars studying U.S. defense and foreign policy, but might be one of only two or three who knew the vice presidency. Perhaps I optimistically had in mind Robert Frost's words: "Two roads diverged in the wood and I, I took the one less traveled by, and that has made all the difference."

The term paper ended up being very enjoyable. Lukacs loved it and gave me an "A." The paper also ended up being my first accepted and published journal article.

My interest and pursuit of the subject continued throughout the years. Among the items I realized in my studies was an issue that developed into this work. Specifically, there has been a phenomenon in the post-World War II era in which the vice presidency has witnessed much greater foreign-policy activity by its occupants. The increased foreign-policy involvement was prodded primarily by changes made by President Harry S Truman and later by the foreign-policy activities of five key vice presidents—Richard Nixon, Walter Mondale, George Bush, Dan Quayle, and Al Gore. I felt this matter merited a full-time research effort, even if many others disagreed. This document is the product of that effort. The study illuminates the active foreign-policy roles of those five vice presidents. More importantly, it explores lessons learned from their foreign-policy experiences. The often successful foreign-policy activities of these men has prompted a number of scholars and analysts to suggest enhanced foreign-policy roles for future vice presidents. Yet, while these five vice presidents were actively involved in White House foreign policy, did their involvement qualitatively effect (positively or negatively) each administration's foreign policy? Did it make a difference? If so, or if not, can lessons be drawn from their experiences that may serve as useful policy recommendations for future administrations? Is there good reason to approve or reject an enhanced foreign-policy role for future vice presidents? How, specifically, might the vice president be used, or not used, in foreign-policy making?

This research may also provide insight to other matters. First, simply by exploring the foreign-policy roles of the five vice presidents, the study produces original research. It should be of interest to presidential scholars, historians, and political scientists—perhaps even the general public. Second, the study's focus on policy implications is unique and perhaps useful, examining suggestions made by others (in a less comprehensive fashion) that the vice president can be helpful in improving White House foreign policy. It should be of special interest to policymakers.

Importantly, as stated, my purpose is to illuminate foreign-policy roles and activities of vice presidents. The intent is not to offer my opinion on the personal foreign-policy views of the five vice presidents, nor of the general foreign policy of particular administrations. For instance, I do not attempt to judge whether the invasions of Grenada and Panama were wise missions. I try to avoid offering my opinion of Al Gore's views on population control. I don't assert that Gore was correct, in my view, for pushing NAFTA. I don't express my gratitude to Gore for helping to pass NAFTA, regardless of the fact that the trade accord has become a keen area of research for me. Again, my goal is to shed light on roles and activities and only to offer judgment on the specific issue of how the vice president can be useful in foreign policy.

That said, there is one exception to my insistence in keeping out my opinion on the views and beliefs of the vice presidents profiled in this book. That exception is Gore's environmental views as expressed in his book, *Earth in the Balance*. I made an exception because I felt it would be irresponsible to casually note and quote Gore's apocalyptic vision without underscoring its radical nature. Many of the book's statements are so utterly shocking that they require evaluation.

I must note that this book was written in fulfillment of my doctoral requirements at the University of Pittsburgh's Graduate School of Public and International Affairs (GSPIA). Then, it contained the straightforward but bland title, *The Role of the Vice President in Foreign Policy: Lessons Learned and*

Policy Recommendations. Thus, it is a dissertation—only slightly modified from the original draft for which I received credit. As a result, it reads like a dissertation in every respect—style, theory, structure. This is immediately evident in the first few pages, where I go out of my way to explain the work's "contribution" to various fields and subfields. The first chapter is tedious in explaining and justifying not only the book's "contribution" but its organization as well. The first chapter also spends a lot of time explaining the study's methodology. As someone with a background in freelance journalism and op-ed writing, I personally find much of the style dry and depressing. I hope most readers do not fully agree. If they do, perhaps they can look beyond the style and hopefully find insight and value in the book as a policy document, a work of political science, and (perhaps) a contribution to historical knowledge. I also hope I've made the five case-study chapters interesting, enlightening, and maybe even somewhat entertaining.

Before the reader moves to chapter 1, I would like to thank a number of people for their assistance in this project. While their input was crucial, any mistakes herein are mine alone.

I would like to briefly thank Dick Bishirjian of CMP International Consulting, Inc., and Bill Taylor of the Center for Strategic and International Studies for helping me in trying to get interviews with key former vice-presidential staff members. Among those who sat patiently for very stimulating interviews were Bill Kristol, Jon Glassman, Carnes Lord, Joe DeSutter, and Tony Motley. Key aspects of this study benefit from their keen intellect. Thanks also to my wife, Susan, for her edits and help on all those tedious footnotes—and for leaving me alone for countless hours in front of the word processor. Additionally, thanks to Jerry Bowyer and Jake Haulk of the Allegheny Institute for Public Policy for not pushing me too hard during a three-four month period in the summer of 1996, when my work for them often had to take second stage to my work on this study.

Finally, I would like to thank the members of my dissertation committee: Gratitude goes to Brian Ripley, one of the better *teachers* I've ever had. His easy-going nature and respect for students was refreshing and appreciated. My first draft "research proposal" for this study was done as a semester-long project in his course. Although the final research proposal was substantially different from the first, his input was instrumental in getting me to the point that I ultimately needed to reach.

Thanks to Don Goldstein, whose knowledge of history has been an asset to my research and will certainly help even more as I proceed. He took the time after my review-committee presentation to try to put into words some of the tips I had received and needed to incorporate. Dr. Goldstein also allowed me to research Vice President Gore during one of his summer courses. That introduced me to some of the research areas I would need to cover in fully developing accurate profiles of the various vice presidents' roles in foreign policy. After some further work on the piece, it was accepted for publication in *Presidential Studies Quarterly*. His knowledge and our discussions of the "Williwaw war" and Pittsburgh Pirates' baseball also helped get me through the doctoral program with a measure of sanity.

Thanks to Phil Williams, who was my program advisor at GSPIA, without whom I may not have been accepted to Pitt's doctoral program. (Ironically, I believe that one of the things that convinced him to allow me entrance into the program was a prepublished version of the Quayle-Persian Gulf piece that I had written at American University.) Phil helped me hone my research skills and aptly warned me when a paper I wrote for him got carried away at times. (He called it a "diatribe.") After following his suggested revisions, the piece was good enough to merit inclusion in the University of Virginia's Miller Center's oral-history series on the Clinton presidency. Phil always had a knack for reining me in when necessary. He also always enjoyed raking me over the coals, particularly during my "defense" of this work.

Finally, appreciation goes to my dissertation advisor, Dr. Paul Hammond, who always knew how to handle me perfectly: Give me the freedom to develop my own ideas and express them on paper, and then gently straighten me out when I've gone too far off course. This has always been the case, including with a paper I did for him on Eisenhower and Reagan that was ultimately published. In my first semester at the University of Pittsburgh he allowed me to do a lengthy research paper on the role of post-World War II vice presidents in foreign policy. That paper gave me the insight I needed to make a decision to further pursue the issue as a dissertation topic. He was particularly helpful in bouncing ideas back and forth in the final chapter of this study, as well as pushing me to the crucial step of undertaking this research with a more critical eye. He also was willing to accept a major last-minute revision of my proposal. Other advisors might have been overly rigid in that regard, but Dr. Hammond, as usual, handled it splendidly. And special thanks to Dr. Hammond for patiently indulging (what he termed) my "obsession with the vice presidency."

Much more recently, thanks to two Grove City College students—Sean Ammirati and Steve Harkleroad—for their assistance in formatting, indexing, and generally preparing this book for the publisher. Sean is a miracle worker. Obvious appreciation also goes to Lexington Books, including Kelli Kobor, Serena Leigh, Steve Wrinn, Ginger Strader, Dorothy Bradley, Collette Stockton, and others.

Lastly, special thanks to Alan Shank and Richard Pious for including this work as part of Lexington's series on the American presidency.

Chapter 1
Introduction and Methodology

"The prestige, if not the power, of the office [of the vice presidency] has grown since World War Two. When Harry Truman succeeded FDR, he didn't know about the A-bomb and needed a crash course to deal with the major decisions facing him in the final days of World War Two. That experience led later presidents to keep their vice presidents informed about the White House decision-making process."
George Bush, Looking Forward, *1987*

Objective

There has been a post-World War II phenomenon in which the vice presidency has seen much greater foreign-policy activity among its occupants. Vice presidents are no longer merely laying wreaths at the funerals of foreign dignitaries they've never met. Pushing this increased foreign-policy involvement have been statutory changes made by President Harry S Truman and the extensive foreign-policy activities of five key vice presidents—Richard Nixon, Walter Mondale, George Bush, Dan Quayle, and Al Gore. This study will illuminate the foreign-policy roles of these five vice presidents. More importantly, the study will explore lessons learned from the foreign-policy experiences of these five men. Valuable policy insights can be gained concerning how the vice president may be used to improve or better assist White House foreign-policy making. At the same time, lessons may be learned on how *not* to use the vice president in foreign policy.

While most of the examples of foreign-policy missions and tasks cited in this study reflect positively on the vice presidents profiled, I went out of my way to find and feature negative cases. The reason is that—when it comes to using the vice president in foreign policy—much, if not more, can be learned from negative examples. These include Nixon's Indochina remarks in 1954 and his reaction to Fidel Castro; Mondale's assignment on South Africa; Bush's representation of the administration during talks with King Fahd as well as possibly some of his Central America duties; Quayle's verbal blasting of Mikhail Gorbachev; and the potentially controversial work of the Gore-Chernomyrdin Commission. Some of these involved serious gaffes and diplomatic turmoil. In featuring these examples, particularly those on Bush and Mondale, I hope to provide a sense of restraint from often knee-jerk suggestions that a vice president is a natural fit in almost any foreign-policy situation. There seems to be a kind of "clientitis" by some vice-presidential scholars, by which they are eager to toss their guy into almost any situation that enhances his resume. Like a number of the policy recommendations aimed to bolster the use of the vice president, not all of the past foreign-policy duties of the second-office holder have been perfect, suggesting that both the pros and cons be fairly assessed.

Whether the vice president can help White House foreign policy is a matter of debate. An enhanced foreign-policy role for the vice president has been suggested by a number of recent scholars and analysts. Yet, such recommendations have not received the necessary scrutiny of a careful, systematic study. A review of the literature on such matters reveals a somewhat superficial treatment by those making suggestions. These scholars also tend to focus exclusively on the positive examples of vice-presidential involvement in foreign policy, while not looking for (or ignoring) the negatives. This has surely contributed to overly optimistic recommendations. This study investigates various policy recommendations—some old, some new. In many ways—from the foreign-policy roles it illuminates to the policy recommendations it explores—the book generates original research.[1]

The study has significance in a number of other respects. The research topic focuses on a neglected area of research within the fields of public policy and political science: the vice presidency. It may fill a research void of interest not only to social scientists but also to historians. In so doing, it also sharpens the focus of research on vice presidents by analyzing it within a foreign-policy context. Moreover, in focusing on the vice presidency it inevitably deals closely with the institution of the presidency and the interaction between occupants in each office—thereby being of special interest to a long-list of contemporary scholars of the presidency. The topic is also timely in that it deals with a continuing and developing situation that includes the most recent and current occupant. Recent occupants, such as vice presidents Dan Quayle and Al Gore, will likely remain in the political arena for years to come, making information included in the study highly relevant to future policy debates.[2] "I would like to be president one day," Gore states candidly.[3] If Gore loses in 2000, there's reason to believe we'll see him running again in 2004 or 2008. Quayle considered a 1996 run for the presidency before opting out, and is now running for 2000. Quayle, too, admits: "Would I like to be president? Of course."[4] In the chapters on these two vice presidents, their basic foreign-policy beliefs become abundantly clear. For instance, after reading chapter 7, it is easily discernible how a President Gore might act in the Balkans if he assumed the presidency tomorrow or in 2001.

Additionally, the subject matter relates to practical situations. As illustrated in the above quote from George Bush, as well as the following pages, post-World War II presidents have kept their vice presidents more involved in foreign policy in large part because of the potential negative consequences that can arise when the latter are not well-informed of crucial policy developments. The information assembled in this study will serve to remind future executive-branch officials of the importance of this matter. The research herein also advises future presidential nominees to be cautious in selection of running mates and to consider the beneficial role that the vice president can at times provide to an administration's foreign policy.[5] On the other hand, the study may find that certain policy recommendations that encourage greater use of the vice president may actually be unnecessary and even hurtful, despite appearing innocuous on the surface. Either way, the study may provide the chief of staff of the office of the president or the office of the vice president with a checklist of areas of foreign-policy activity in which the vice president should or should not be included—(hopefully) for the better of U.S. policy.

On the policy aspects of the vice president, an increased foreign-policy role for the occupant has been suggested recently by three scholars, each of whose suggestions are examined in this work.[6] Kevin V. Mulcahy proposes that the vice president chair major NSC committees, such as the SALT verification panel or the Senior Review Group during the Reagan administration.[7] C. Boyden Gray, counselor to Vice President Bush, recommends a coordinating role for the vice president and an increased foreign-policy role in assisting the State Department.[8] Ben W. Heineman, Jr., says all vice presidents should be elevated to a "senior advisor" role, along the lines of how Vice President Mondale was used during the Carter years.[9] It truly is fair to say that these suggestions—though logically made and often based on personal policy-making experience—have not been given a rigorous examination.

Within the general aspects of the literature on the vice presidency, the study joins a small number of contributions. The issue of greater post-World War II vice-presidential involvement in foreign affairs has been touched upon by Marie D. Natoli, who did so in an article on Truman and other published materials.[10] Similarly, Paul C. Light, in analyzing the institutional role of the vice president, notes that the vice president's increased policy role begins with the increased institutional support the office has received since Mondale's tenure.[11] A small group of scholars have mentioned or analyzed the foreign-policy activities of certain vice presidents. These include pieces on Vice President Nixon by George Sirgiovanni, Ralph De Toledano, and Earl Mazo and Stephen Hess; my works on vice presidents Quayle and Gore; and Finlay Lewis and Steven Gillon on Mondale.[12] Of these, only the studies by myself and Gillon are footnoted and written in a scholarly style. To my knowledge, aside from his own work, no profiles have been done on the foreign-policy roles of vice presidents Bush, Quayle, and Gore. As far as he knows, this is the only systematic study of the five most foreign-policy active vice presidents, particularly with the intention of learning lessons from their experiences.

Lastly, on an almost side note, the study also provides a contribution that at first glance is not evident, but becomes apparent as the reader traverses the chapters: The study inevitably provides a chronology of U.S. foreign policy and geo-strategic interests in the post-World War II period. It does so by displaying the activities of five vice presidents who were at times prominently used in each administration's foreign policy. This takes the reader through a journey from the Eisenhower administration's policies in Latin America to Carter's Middle East initiatives to Reagan's Soviet strategies to Bush's Gulf War management to the Clinton administration's broad definitions of "security" and "foreign policy." The book moves from the heat of the Cold War years to the ambiguity and uncertainty of the post-Cold War period. In this sense, the study may offer a useful historical treatment of postwar U.S. foreign and security policy.

Primary Issues to Be Explored: Addressing Policy Recommendations

In light of those objectives, there are two central themes in this study: (1) how the vice president fits into the president's foreign-policy framework; and (2) recommendations on how or whether the vice president can be used to enhance White House foreign policy. Both issues should be of special interest to policymakers. The study analyzes the vice president within the broader White House foreign-policy framework, exploring how and where the occupant fits into that structure, and how he may or may not be used in possibly altering it. An overview of this matter is provided in the next chapter. On the second issue, the study's focus on policy implications is unique and hopefully useful, examining suggestions made by others that the vice president can be helpful in improving White House foreign policy.

Can the vice president be used to better manage, coordinate, and positively influence an administration's foreign policy? If so, how? A number of successful examples among the five most active vice presidents in foreign policy—Nixon, Mondale, Bush, Quayle, and Gore—has emboldened certain scholars and analysts to suggest various ways in which the vice president can assist an administration's foreign policy. Many of the recommendations, however, have been made with a paucity of detail and typically do not list any prospective negatives that might accompany such a shift, even though they are made by informed scholars and policymakers. For instance, it is not uncommon in the literature for a scholar to take a particular vice president's foreign-policy mission—such as, say, Mondale's role in South Africa policy, or Bush's Western Europe tour of 1983—and cite it as an example of the potential untapped benefits of using the second-office holder in foreign policy. However, the articles that have been written on such matters usually provide only a few paragraphs, that is, a cursory treatment, of the cases they cite as evidence for their assertions. Rarely does the scholar actually dig into an in-depth examination of the case with a skeptical or investigatory eye. This study aims to ameliorate this lack of rigor by adding more flesh to the cases. After all, the recommendations being made do not entail simple changes made in a vacuum.

Consider just one example. Kevin Mulcahy details the parochialism and incoherence that can plague White House foreign policy due to the number and variety of departments and interests within the foreign policy-making apparatus. He contends that there is a need for a presiding official who transcends both existing loyalties and organization interests. He suggests this duty be delegated to the vice president. The vice president, he maintains, could chair major NSC committees, such as the Senior Review Group or SALT verification panel during the Reagan administration. He suggests an executive order to accomplish this recommendation.[13]

On the surface, this suggestion sounds perfectly fine. In general, it has the benefit of giving the vice president valuable training in the event he must assume the presidency. Certainly, few can argue with the advantages that could bring to the nation. Danny M. Adkison asserts that the realization that the vice presidency has propelled so many individuals toward the White House indicates a principal "indirect" function of the institution: training a person to be president. Adkison has thus referred to the vice presidency as a kind of internship or apprenticeship. "What better way, it is argued, for training someone to take over the reins of government?" Adkison asks. "This has been a major defense for preserving the office when proposals for abolishing the office are made."[14] It is difficult to argue with this logic.

However, the aforementioned suggestion, as well as others considered later, go far beyond Adkison's laudable rationale. It asserts that the vice president can provide a valuable role in White House foreign policy by chairing major NSC committees, which would entail a coordinating, managing, and even advisory role. Advocates of this notion maintain that the vice president is the only member of the president's foreign-policy team that has no department or agency that he must represent or be responsive to. Such departments and agencies can cause some players to have dual, clashing interests, i.e., the secretaries of state and defense must often uphold the interests of their departments as much as those of their president—or, at the least, they often must play a delicate balancing act of trying to adequately serve two masters. On the contrary, some argue, the vice president serves only one interest: the president. Hence, unfettered to any bureaucratic-parochial or selfish interests, he is a perfect candidate for being employed in a number of NSC-related functions. This sounds good, and logical. It is well intentioned. But is it a smart idea? Not necessarily. For instance, it is doubtful that the vice president does not have his own parochial interests. One chief of staff to a recent vice president maintains that the vice president is less accountable than other presidential staff:

> In principal, in my view, you want staff people to the president to be in control of those [groups]. You know, vice presidents also have their own agenda. . . . They have electoral futures. If I were the president, or the chief of staff to the president, I would want someone working for the president who is "fireable" by the president, and accountable to the president in the way a staff person is, not the way the vice president is.[15]

Also, of course, many vice presidents are chosen because of purposes of winning an election. This may involve appeals to a disgruntled party faction, age, geography, religion, ethnicity, and so on. The reason may or may not be ideological and almost certainly is not based on total agreement on foreign-policy issues. Presidential candidates rarely select running mates based first and foremost on their foreign-policy views. One might also add that a vice president is rarely chosen because of his policy coordination and management skills, an obvious prerequisite for chairing an NSC committee or crisis-management group. For these skills, the president-elect chooses a national security advisor.

In addition, vice presidents are concerned with their own political fortunes. Five of the last twelve vice presidents have assumed the presidency and most make quite clear their desire to run for the presidency in the future. When it comes to carrying out a certain foreign-policy task, a politically driven vice president may act in a manner that helps him but hurts the administration. If this is difficult to conceive, then I forewarn the reader to pay close attention to the chapters on vice presidents Nixon, Mondale, and Bush. Despite being generally model vice presidents, their political interests were at times their Achilles heel. Additionally, imagine a situation where the president *is* forced to relieve the vice president of his duties, due to the fact that the latter has failed to perform adequately in managing something as important as a major NSC committee. Such a move may produce a political fallout among the party faction the president initially sought to pacify when he selected his vice president as a running mate during the election campaign. Obviously, in this case, the president would have made a poor decision in deciding to use the vice president as he did.

This is only a sample of the potential problems with one recommendation. Keep in mind that there are many other recommendations, each possessing many positives and many negatives. Much more examination of these recommendations will come in the following pages, culminating in the final chapter of the study. But the main point is obvious: *Clearly, recommendations on how to better use the vice president for the purpose of improving White House foreign policy must be carefully considered.*

Structure of Chapters

In exploring these themes and arriving at conclusions, this work follows a specific format: This chapter informs the reader of the objectives of the study and its structure.[16] The second chapter provides pertinent background matter on the subject at hand, showing how the office of the vice president has evolved to its current point. Here is the format for chapter 2:

> Chapter 2: The Evolution of Reform: The Vice President in Foreign Policy
> a) the VP's formal duties in foreign policy and in general
>   1. constitutional
>   2. statutory—the National Security Act of 1947
> b) the VP as part of the president's foreign- and security-policy framework
> c) the Harry S Truman lesson and influence
> d) the trend toward broader VP involvement in FP since World War II

The next five chapters (3-7) profile the foreign-policy roles of the five vice presidents examined. The structure of each of these chapters is identical, covering the following topics for each specific vice president (in between the introduction and conclusion): (1) the vice president's selection and role definition; (2) the president-vice president relationship; (3) the vice president's place within the administration's defense and foreign-policy structure; and (4) the vice president's foreign-policy role. The following is an outline:

> Chapters 3-7: Particular Vice President
> a) introduction
> b) the vice president's selection and role definition
> c) the president-vice president relationship
> d) the vice president's place within the administration's defense and foreign-policy structure
> e) the vice president's foreign-policy role
> f) conclusion

Understandably, the fifth section in each chapter—"the vice president's foreign-policy role"—involves the most space for each of the five "profile" chapters, and typically brings in research not previously compiled. Additionally, it is the only one of all six sections that includes subheadings. The primary subheadings typically feature a vice president's role in, say, Middle East policy, or aspects of Soviet policy, or nuclear nonproliferation. These broader foreign-policy "cases"—usually anywhere from five to thirty pages in length—are preceded by brief descriptions (roughly two to six paragraphs) of more general foreign-policy "tasks." These tasks, the headings of which are indented and underlined, typically include general roles that involve aspects of foreign policy, such as the vice president's duties as a "foreign-policy spokesman" or "congressional liaison." Sometimes, however, the tasks are unique to the vice president at hand; these include, for example, a section in the Mondale chapter called "The Political Mondale in Foreign Policy" and those in the Bush chapter titled "Foreign Policy Crisis Committee" and "Task Force on Terrorism." Discussion of these tasks sets the stage for understanding the larger foreign-policy cases that follow, the headings of which are flush left and italicized. (The Quayle chapter is the most unique and organizationally difficult in terms of what falls under the umbrella of the vice president's foreign-policy role. That is because it looks simply at one long, extended case study—his role in the Persian Gulf crisis.)

Most importantly, for organizational purposes, the crucial issue of "lessons learned and policy insights" derived from the profiles of each vice president is saved until the final chapter (8), in which all of the information on all of the vice presidents is synthesized. Of course, the reader will undoubtedly pick up on many of the lessons to be learned as he or she reads the five chapters preceding the concluding chapter.[17] *Thus, I warn the reader to keep this in mind as he or she traverses the five "profile" chapters, which are often fairly "straight faced" and generally historical and informational. These chapters are intended to inform the reader of the various vice presidents' foreign-policy roles, less so than assessing and analyzing them. The majority of analytical and empirical material is saved until the final chapter.*

Finally, it is worth briefly explaining why this work focuses only on the five vice presidents who had active foreign-policy roles and does not provide chapters on those who were inactive. This is because the study's central question is based specifically on those who *were* involved and whether their involvement made a difference or created problems or both. (As will be further noted, it focuses on the post-World War II era because of changes during that period that make the vice president's involvement in foreign policy so different from other eras.) While excluding analysis of those who were not involved may invite certain constraints, dealing with those who were not involved may not help answer the questions I'm exploring. For instance, consider the following: The six post-World War II vice presidents not featured in this study had very limited roles in foreign policy. From a length perspective, I would be hard-pressed to find ten pages of worthy material on their roles. On the contrary, I struggled to keep the five vice presidents profiled herein within 50-page chapters. There is easily 50 pages of material on Vice President Quayle's role in the Persian Gulf alone.

Take the case of Vice President Johnson, whose foreign-policy role was quite insubstantial. During the Cuban Missile Crisis, LBJ played a minor to nonexistent role, despite regularly sitting in on the NSC Executive Committee, where the administration's responses to the nuclear threat were debated. In Graham Allison's *Essence of Decision*, the classic on the inner-workings of the Kennedy administration during the crisis, Vice President Johnson is mentioned in the book only once for a speech he gave a year earlier. By comparison, there were more references to the Carnegie School, Milton Friedman, and Robert Frost.[18] Later, as president, Johnson would not treat his vice president much better.

As a further illustration of the futility of focusing on vice presidents who were not highly active in foreign policy, consider a key policy recommendation investigated in this study: the vice president should chair the White House crisis-management committee or a major NSC group. Examining vice presidents Bush and Nixon is instructive in addressing this recommendation, since Bush headed up the former and Nixon was considered but rejected for the latter. Lessons can be learned. On the other hand, there appears no evidence that even a thought was given regarding such a role for vice presidents like Spiro Agnew, Hubert Humphrey, and others. Hence, little benefit would be derived from profiling them vis-à-vis the study's primary questions.

The next chapter provides an overview of the historical role of the vice presidency, looking at the occupants' general role, foreign-policy role, constitutional duties, and place in the White House foreign and security-policy structure. It also helps explain how the office has evolved to its current point, providing crucial background information on the pre-World War II and post-World War II experiences. Following chapter 2 are the various individual profiles.

Notes

1. This study also opens a number of questions—the answers to which, at times, are beyond its scope. Some cannot be adequately addressed without confusing or diverting the reader from the intention of the study. Sometimes such open questions are noted directly in the text, but often they are noted parenthetically or by footnote. Examples of the latter are footnote 53 in chapter 4 and footnotes 27 and 44 in chapter 8.

2. Before Gore and Quayle, four of the last five vice presidents who were eligible ran for the presidency.

3. Peter J. Boyer, "Gore's Dilemma," *The New Yorker*, November 28, 1994, Vol. 70, No. 39, pp. 100-03.

4. Paul Bedard, "Talking Like Candidate, Quayle Starts Book Tour," *The Wash-*

ington Times, May 6, 1994.

5. Of course, political considerations will continue to play a dominant role in the selection of vice presidential nominees. Indeed, Louis Hatch hit the nail on the head sixty years ago when he stated: "It is difficult to find even one vice presidential nomination that was not made primarily from the standpoint of its utility in carrying a doubtful state or region, or in satisfying a disgruntled faction of the party." Louis Clinton Hatch, *History of the Vice Presidency of the United States*, revised by Earl L. Shoup (Westport, Conn.: Greenwood Press, 1934, 1970), p. 415. This study does not purport to change that reality. Nonetheless, all things being equal, perhaps it may at least raise a presidential candidate's awareness of how his or her selection of a running mate could have implications for how foreign policy is run in his or her administration.

6. Actually, as we shall see, there have been more than these three scholars making suggestions. These three, however, are among the most far reaching and perhaps even most influential.

7. Kevin V. Mulcahy, "Presidents and the Administration of Foreign Policy: The New Role for the Vice President," *Presidential Studies Quarterly*, Vol. XVII, No. 1, Winter 1987, p. 129.

8. C. Boyden Gray, "The Coordinating Role of the Vice Presidency," in James P. Pfiffner and R. Gordon Hoxie, eds., *The Presidency in Transition* (New York: Center for the Study of the Presidency, 1989), pp. 425-29.

9. Ben W. Heineman, Jr., "Some Rules of the Game: Prescription for Organizing the Domestic Presidency," in Pfiffner and Hoxie, op. cit., pp. 45-53.

10. Marie D. Natoli, "Harry S Truman and the Contemporary Vice Presidency," *Presidential Studies Quarterly*, Vol. XVIII, No. 1, Winter 1988.

11. Paul C. Light, "The Institutional Vice Presidency," *Presidential Studies Quarterly*, Vol. XIII, No. 2, Spring 1983, p. 198.

12. George S. Sirgiovanni, "Dumping the Vice President: An Historical Overview and Analysis," *Presidential Studies Quarterly*, Vol. XXIV, No. 4, Fall 1994; Paul Kengor, "The Role of the Vice President during the Crisis in the Persian Gulf," *Presidential Studies Quarterly*, Vol. XXIV, No. 4, Fall 1994; and Paul Kengor, "The Foreign-Policy Role of Vice President Al Gore," *Presidential Studies Quarterly*, Vol. XXVII, No. 1, Winter 1997, pp. 14-38.

13. Mulcahy, op. cit., p. 129.

14. Danny M. Adkison, "The Vice Presidency as Apprenticeship," *Presidential Studies Quarterly*, Vol. XIII, No. 2, Spring 1983, p. 212.

15. Interview with William Kristol, chief of staff to Vice President Dan Quayle, May 28, 1996.

16. In regard to the methodology employed, the research study employs the comparative method of case study analysis. See Kenneth D. Bailey, *Methods of Social Research*, 4th edition (New York: The Free Press, 1994), pp. 11 and 300-01; and Alexander L. George and Timothy J. McKeown, "Case Studies and Theories of Organizational Decision Making," *Advances in Information Processing in Organizations*, Vol. 2 (1985), pp. 21-22 and 24-25.

17. For instance, it would simply be overly repetitive to address Kevin Mulcahy's policy recommendation each time an opportunity presented itself in chapters 3 through 7. Instead, the recommendation is reviewed once in chapter 8, vis-à-vis the findings in chapters 3 through 7.

18. Jules Witcover, *Crapshoot: Rolling the Dice on the Vice Presidency* (New York: Crown Publishers, 1992), p. 168; and Graham T. Allison, *Essence of Decision: Explaining the Cuban Missile Crisis* (Glenview and London: Scott, Foresman and Company, 1971), pp. 331-33.

Chapter 2

The Evolution of a Reform: The Vice President in Foreign Policy

"My country has in its wisdom contrived for me the most insignificant office that ever the invention of man contrived or his imagination conceived. . . . I can do neither good nor evil."
John Adams, the nation's first vice president, 1789-97

"I personally believe the vice president of the United States should never be a nonentity. I believe he should be used. I believe he should have a very useful job."
President Dwight D. Eisenhower, 1955

Introduction

Vice President Lyndon Johnson recalled that "every time I came into [President] John Kennedy's presence, I felt like a goddamn raven hovering over his shoulder."[1] Johnson felt it would take the death of the president to allow him to play a significant role within the administration. Yet, it seems those days may be over, as vice presidents are being given greater roles in administration policy—foreign policy included. The prior three vice presidents—Quayle, Bush, and Mondale—were among the most influential and busiest in history. The current occupant, Gore, has continued that recent tradition. In the area of foreign policy, each had (and has) roles more substantive than previous vice presidents. Key steps along the road were taken by presidents Truman, Eisenhower, Carter, and Reagan. As President Eisenhower said of his vice president: "Mr. Nixon's willingness to perform a variety of tasks, at my request, and his presence at all important policy meetings, assured that in the event of my death or disability, his own knowledge and understanding of the changing world and domestic situations would have no gaps."[2] Assigning foreign-policy duties to a vice president may be wise not only for reasons of succession but also for assisting an administration's day-to-day foreign policy, regardless of whether he is called upon to replace the commander in chief.

To casual observers of recent vice presidents, these assertions likely come as no surprise. Indeed, the layman might view it has common sense that vice presidents be included in White House foreign policy in order to be kept abreast of key developments and to have some "training" in the event succession is necessary. However, such phenomena are the result of a situation that has only developed in the post-World War II period. As most scholars of the vice presidency would attest, the notion of a vice president who is active in foreign affairs is a historical novelty. For instance, Vice President Truman assumed the presidency with no knowledge of the nation's development of the hydrogen bomb, nor of the nature of FDR's discussions with Churchill and Stalin—that lack of knowledge may have hampered his negotiations at Potsdam and elsewhere. He needed a crash course to handle important decisions facing him in the final days of the war.

There is an added, very important point that underscores this chapter and study as a whole: As will be shown, President Truman began the somewhat "permanent" change in the role of the vice president in foreign policy. Yet, the changes made by Truman are, technically speaking, reversible—even though they would require a dramatic and totally unforeseen (and uncalled for) amending of the National Security Act of 1947. (More on this later.) Still, the point is that the evolution toward the current bolstered foreign-policy role for the vice president is reversible, depending upon the particular president, his team, and his vice president. In all likelihood, however, we have reached a point where the vice president will continue to remain informed in foreign policy, especially compared to his pre-World War II status, and (in the majority of cases in coming years) probably receive occasional substantive roles in foreign policy.

This chapter briefly traces the history of the vice presidency vis-à-vis foreign policy, and how it has evolved to its current state. The benefits and successes stemming from the increased evolvement are largely responsible for sparking recent reform suggestions by scholars and analysts. Between this introduction and the conclusion, the chapter contains the following subheadings:

- the vice president's general historical and constitutional role
- the vice president's historical role in foreign policy
- the reason for the recent increased foreign-policy role of vice presidents
- the Harry Truman lesson and influence
- the trend toward broader vice-presidential involvement in foreign policy since World War II
- "levels" of foreign-policy involvement by vice presidents
- the vice president as a component of the president's foreign-policy structure

This chapter sets the stage for chapters 3 through 7 on specific vice presidents.

The Vice President's General Historical and Constitutional Role

On December 1-2, 1803, Delaware Senator Samuel White made the following prophetic statement during debate on enactment of the Twelfth Amendment providing for the separate election of the president and vice president: "The Vice Presidency will either be left to chance, or what will be much worse, prostituted to the barest purposes; character, talents, virtue, and merit will not be sought after in the candidate. The question will not be asked, is he capable? is he honest? But can he by his name, by his connections, by his wealth, by his local situation, by his influence, or his intrigues, best promote the election of a President?"[3] In a sense, that has happened. According to Gerald M. Pomper, the most significant criteria in selecting a vice-presidential nominee include: (1) a candidate who unifies or satisfies as large a segment of the party as possible; (2) the conciliation of a party faction or defeated candidate's followers; (3) the emphasis of a specific issue; (4) to elicit wider appeal from the electorate by balancing the ticket in terms of geography, issues, age, ethnicity, gender, religion, or personal characteristics; and (5) a candidate who will not lose votes for the ticket.[4]

In short, notes Marie Natoli—one of the top vice-presidential scholars—the vice-presidential candidate must, at best, help win the presidency and, at worst, not contribute to its loss.[5] Louis Clinton Hatch hit it on the head sixty years ago when he stated: "It is difficult to find even one vice presidential nomination that was not made primarily from the standpoint of its utility in carrying a doubtful state or region, or in satisfying a disgruntled faction of the party."[6] In the early 1970s, Robert J. Sickels added that the typical vice-presidential nominee "is at best a necessary evil from the president's point of view. After the election he is a threat to the president unless he can be kept in the background—the older tradition—or bound to loyalty and acquiescence in the performance of apprentice—the recent tendency."[7]

Yet, it was not the constitutional purpose of the vice presidency to help the presidential nominee win elections. Harry C. Thomson notes that when the Founding Fathers drafted the U.S. Constitution in the summer of 1787 they gave much thought to the nature of the presidency but very little thought to the nature of the vice presidency. The vice presidency came mainly as an afterthought. Throughout the first three-fourths of the sessions of the Constitutional Convention there was no mention of a vice president. Discussion of the subject took place only near the end of the convention when delegates debated a proposal for electing the president. The president was to be elected by electors designated for that purpose by each state. Each presidential elector had to vote for two persons, one of which had to be a resident of some other state. The purpose of the procedure was to prevent electors from taking a parochial view and to force them to look beyond their own state boundaries. The person receiving the highest number of electoral votes was to be the president and the person receiving the next highest tally was to be vice president.[8]

The framers of the Constitution granted the vice president essentially one duty: to be "President of the Senate," under which he "shall have no Vote, unless they [legislators] be equally divided. In reference to succession of the president, Article II, Section 1 of the Constitution states: "In Case of the Removal of the President from Office, or of his Death, Resignation, or Inability to discharge the Powers and Duties of the said Office, the Same shall devolve on the Vice President." The issue was further detailed in the 25th amendment, which made additional provisions for selecting a vice president when the presidency is vacated.

Oddly, on this issue, Arthur M. Schlesinger, Jr. has received a tremendous amount of attention for a piece he did on the vice presidency that seems to be grounded in inaccurate assumptions. Looking at the vice presidency today, said Schlesinger, we assume it was created for reasons of succession. To the contrary, he argues, it is a product of the double-vote system. Hence, Schlesinger has concluded: "The vice presidency entered the Constitution not to provide a successor to the president—this would easily have been arranged otherwise—but to insure the election of a *national* president." Partly as a result of this fact, Schlesinger has advocated that the vice presidency be abolished because he feels it is not an essential institution of the U.S. government, unlike the presidency, Congress, or judiciary.[9] Yet, as noted above, the vice presidency entered the Constitution not simply because of the double-vote system but also because of the need to provide a successor to the president.

Still, this has not stopped one of the leading experts in the study of the vice presidency from apparently granting Schlesinger's assumption before tackling its deficiencies. Natoli argues that Schlesinger neglects a significant point: the vice presidency ensures continuity within the U.S. government. Since the Founding Fathers created a constitutional basis for the office of the vice president, the need for the vice president to succeed to the presidency has occurred eight times as a result of presidential death and once as a result of presidential resignation. "Thus the statistical yardstick which the past has provided is that there is a one-in-five chance that vice presidential succession will occur," Natoli writes. "Is it possible, therefore, to hold that the institution which provides for the immediate succession to the presidency is not performing a vital function of government?"[10]

As noted earlier, Adkison agrees, noting that the realization that the vice presidency has propelled so many individuals toward the White House indicates a principal "indirect" function of the institution: training a person to be president. Adkison has thus referred to the vice presidency as a kind of internship or apprenticeship. "What better way, it is argued, for training someone to take over the reins of government?" Adkison reasonably asks. "This has been a major defense for preserving the office when proposals for abolishing the office are made."[11]

With Schlesinger's point in mind, former President and Vice President George Bush writes that the "modern vice presidency is the most misunderstood elective office in our political system. People either make too little or too much of it." He notes that some view the vice presidency as a "useless appendage."[12] This view is held by such men as Schlesinger and former Senator Eugene McCarthy.[13] At the other end of the spectrum, says Bush, are those that perceive the vice president as a kind of "surrogate president." This groups grants modern vice presidents constitutional and political powers that they don't actually possess. Bush cites the news media as adherents to the surrogate view of the vice presidency:

> One of the recurring questions I've had from reporters, almost from the day I became vice president has been: "Well, we know that's the official administration position on the issue, but what's *your* position?" My answer has always been the same: a vice president can hold a different opinion from a president on an issue and express it while the White House decision-making process is going on. But once the president makes his decision, the matter is settled. That answer doesn't always satisfy inquiring reporters and columnists, but consider the alternative: A president takes a position on a foreign policy objective. Unhappy with that position, the vice president goes public with his views in a major speech or interview. Here at home he may become a hero to those opposed to the president's policy. He may even be editorially praised (by the president's editorial opponents) for his "independence." But overseas, any division at the highest level of American government can only be perceived by potential adversaries as a vulnerable area to exploit, through diplomacy and propaganda.[14]

Bush maintains that the last thing a president needs is a vice president "with his own agenda, grinding his own political ax." He continues, "it's fundamental that the country can only have one president at a time. On the day a disgruntled, self-serving vice president declares civil war on the White House by publicly challenging a president, our system of government will be in serious trouble."[15] Bush's own vice president, Dan Quayle, understood the importance of this point. "I like to give [the president] my ideas in private," said Quayle. "When we're in a large group where it's probably going to get out, I try to be somewhat circumspect. . . . I try to be somewhat judicious so people can't read it that the president feels this way, but the vice president feels that way."[16]

Part of the frustration of the vice presidency is what some have referred to as the "paradoxical nature" of the position. The vice president has a privileged seat, closer than anyone to the center of power. Yet because he (by definition) has no specific area that is strictly his own, he can maneuver only in the margins of most important policy matters.[17] The position has been referred to as a "high office without power."[18]

Compared to his years in the Congress, commented Vice President Quayle, the vice presidency was a "much more confining job. You don't have your own agenda. Your agenda is the president's agenda. . . . Wherever I might go, somebody has primary jurisdiction, and that's one of the problems with being vice president. . . . Anything you do, you're going to be getting into somebody else's domain." Former Bush administration Secretary of Defense Dick Cheney agreed: "It's an uncomfortable position to be in. The vice president is there sort of as an overall generalist. . . . He's there as the president's understudy, in a sense."[19]

Such is the frustration of the vice presidency. But the good news for future occupants is that the office has grown in stature over the past fifty years, including the foreign-policy realm. As Natoli notes, "While the constitutional job description for the vice president has not changed, the growth in real terms has been extraordinary."[20] The next section also takes a historical view of the office, looking specifically through the prism of foreign policy.

The Vice President's Historical Role in Foreign Policy

The vice president has no constitutional role in foreign policy. Yet, in a twist of historical irony, considering the early limited role of vice presidents in foreign policy, had it not been for the action of a vice president the president would today need the consent of the Senate to remove his chief foreign-policy operator, the Secretary of State. The nation's first vice president, John Adams, cast the deciding vote in a tied Senate on July 18, 1789, to retain in the bill creating the Department of State a provision recognizing the right of the president to remove the secretary of state without the consent of the Senate. Obviously, without that ability, the president's capacity to handle the direction of foreign policy might be limited.

Perhaps this was Adam's revenge. Once described by Vernon L. Parrington as "the most painstaking student of government, and the most widely read in political history, of his generation of Americans"[21]—not to mention one of the nation's greatest experts on the U.S. Constitution—Adams would come to loathe the office of the vice president. "I am Vice President," wrote Adams in a letter to his wife Abigail. "In this I am nothing, but I may be everything." Vice President Adams, who sarcastically referred to himself as "His Superfluous Excellency," somberly added: "My country has in its wisdom contrived for me the most insignificant office that ever the invention of man contrived or his imagination conceived . . . I can do neither good nor evil."[22] Mark Twain may have had in mind Adams' frustrations when he used tell the joke about the two brothers: one went to sea and the other became vice president. Neither was ever heard from again.

Some early vice presidents were offered *opportunities* to play big roles in foreign affairs, but usually only upon possible succession to the Oval Office. For instance, Thomas R. Marshall, vice president from 1913 to 1921, in being informed of the extent of President Woodrow Wilson's stroke in 1919, declined to take the constitutional steps to assume responsibility of the Oval Office, out of fear he would be labeled a usurper. Marshall was reportedly sympathetic to the Senate amendments to the Treaty of Versailles. Wilson refused to accept the amendments, thus destroying the treaty's ratification chances and U.S. participation in Wilson's dream, the League of Nations. Ironically, in retrospect, if Marshall had assumed presidential powers and compromised with the Senate by approving the amendments, Wilson's dream might have come to fruition.[23]

Vice presidents' roles in many key White House developments—not to mention foreign policy—were often almost non-existent. The lack of importance and prestige of the office was demonstrated by the fact that on a number of occasions throughout American history the office had been left vacant and caused little worry.[24] The short-sightedness of this reality became in part evident due to the frequency of the potential for succession.

In the post-World War II era three vice presidents—Truman, Johnson, and Ford—have been elevated to the presidency by the death or resignation of the president. In the same period, presidential illnesses or assassination attempts raised the prospects of the succession of three others—Richard Nixon (three times, upon the sicknesses of President Dwight Eisenhower), George Bush (twice, once resulting from an assassination attempt and later from cancer surgery of President Ronald Reagan), and Dan Quayle (once resulting from tests which President Bush underwent as a result of potential heart problems). Since World War II, five of the last ten presidents first served as vice president, and in seven of the last eight presidential elections one or both of the major-party presidential nominees served as vice president. In 1968, both Democrats and Republicans turned to former vice presidents, Hubert Humphrey and Richard Nixon, as their party nominations for the presidency. The modern era even witnessed the demise of the "Van Buren jinx," as George Bush in 1988 became the first vice president to be elected president since Martin Van Buren in 1836.[25]

The reality that so many vice presidents had become president, particularly through emergency-succession situations, began to expose the salience of the need to get the vice president more involved in foreign policy.

The Reason for the Recent Increased Foreign-Policy Role of Vice Presidents

This study does not seek to provide a complete, unassailable explanation of *why* the vice president has become more involved in foreign policy in recent years. Inevitably, however, it is necessary that the study briefly address some key contributing factors.

For instance, the realization that the vice president often becomes president has led many post-World War II chief executives to better prepare their understudies in key areas of foreign policy. As will be seen in chapter 3, President Eisenhower was especially cognizant of, and concerned with, historical deficiencies in the succession process. His own battles with illness led him to personally take quick steps to get his vice president more involved. He developed a formal policy of succession that had far greater detail than that spelled out in Article II of the Constitution. Ike's reforms actually presaged changes instituted by the 25th amendment.

The Eisenhower example is symptomatic of an underlying theme throughout this study. This theme, more than any other, explains why certain vice presidents were (or were not) used in foreign policy and the level to which they were involved or influential. A term that comes close to fitting this theme is James Rosenau's "individual variable," which is one among four types of "independent variables" he defines. Rosenau explains that individual variables are those unique aspects of a policymaker's background, values, and talents that are not part of his official role and may vary from one occupant of the position to another.[26] Each president has his own unique aspects—or, what might be termed "idiosyncrasies"—that effect the way his administration operates and performs. This has important ramifications for how the vice president is used by a president. This study makes clear that the foreign-policy role of a particular vice president is dependent upon the unique set of circumstances in which he finds himself. Key among those circumstances are the idiosyncrasies of both him and his president. Moreover, I would like to extend Rosenau's definition to include the unique aspects of not only the vice president and the president but also the administration he serves. Thus, the vice president is also affected by the idiosyncrasies of the other members of the administration he interacts with, such as, among others, the secretary of state. How each vice president is used depends upon these idiosyncratic factors. This "idiosyncratic variable" is especially fitting in understanding how presidents like FDR, Eisenhower, and Clinton used, or did not use, their vice president, and how the second-office holder's utility could depend in large part on whether the administration's secretary of state was Cyrus Vance, James Baker, or Warren Christopher.

Additionally, the greater foreign-policy role of the post-World War II vice president also derives from the expanded physical size of the office. Paul C.

Light argues that the vice president's policy role begins with the institutional support needed to give advice. That support, he contends, grew markedly in the 1970s. "From an office with too many payrolls, too many locations, and not enough staff, the Office of the Vice President of the United States now has a distinct institutional identity," Light writes. "It is now very much a part of the Executive Office of the President." The vice president's office moved from less than twenty staff members in 1960 to seventy permanent positions by the early 1980s. During the same time period, it went from an office with no executive budget to its own line with an annual budget of $2 million. The vice president's office is now a replica of the president's office, with a press secretary, national security advisor, domestic staff, chief of staff, counsel, scheduling team, and administrative staff.[27] As will be noted in chapters 3-7, the addition of foreign-policy and national-security advisors in particular has enabled vice presidents to take on foreign-policy projects and issues that they more than likely would not have been involved in without the input of such aides. Specifically, this will be seen in the case of Vice President Quayle in Latin America, as well as Vice President Gore in the Balkans and in the Clinton administration's retaliatory strike against Saddam Hussein as a payback for the dictator's assassination attempt on President Bush.

Finally, the onset of the Cold War after World War II and the subsequent dangers of nuclear war gave foreign policy a heightened emphasis in U.S. policy, demonstrated by changes ushered in by the National Security Act of 1947 and NSC-68, the nation's first comprehensive national security policy and strategy.[28] The prominence of foreign policy during the Cold War period may have impacted the second-office holder's role in foreign policy. The advent of the nuclear age raised the stakes and likely led to a heightened emphasis on the vice president. Vice President Quayle, for example, states that the office has "evolved" in foreign policy since Truman due to "sheer necessity in the nuclear age, to a point where the vice president's awareness of national security matters [is] kept on a par with the president's."[29] Upon assuming office, President Carter was stunned to learn that the secretary of state, rather than the vice president, was designated as second in the chain of command of a nuclear strike. He immediately changed the policy.

In addition, changes in the general size and scope of the U.S. government since and before World War II has simply led to a situation where the president cannot handle everything himself and needs assistance, some of which often gets passed to his vice president. Before FDR and World War II in particular, the government was vastly smaller and simpler. In a physical sense, the Old Executive Office Building housed most facilities. There was no Pentagon or State Department building. There was no NATO, SEATO, CENTO, or UN. At the risk of oversimplification, foreign policy until that period was dominated by three main concepts/policies: staying out of European "entanglements," the

Monroe Doctrine, and the Open Door Policy. The president could easily "run" foreign policy himself, as did Teddy Roosevelt and James Polk. Lincoln had much more time to write his own speeches. During much of this pre-World War II period, there was no radio, let alone a television, Internet, or Associated Press. In sum, the whole edifice has now become so immense that there is more need to delegate to a vice president.

Yet, the largest impetus for the foreign-policy boost was the FDR/Truman experience.

The Harry Truman Lesson and Influence

President Franklin Delano Roosevelt was reputed to have never included his three vice presidents in major policy considerations, including foreign policy.[30] FDR's first vice president, former Texas congressman John Nance Garner, was so enamored with the position that he once assessed it as not worth "a pitcher of warm spit."[31] His second vice president, Henry A. Wallace, likewise did not receive much of a role in foreign policy.[32] Wallace's successor was also exempted from the administration's foreign policy-making team. Incredibly, Harry Truman saw the president only eight times during the time he occupied the vice presidency.[33]

As Natoli makes clear, that lack of preparation hindered Truman's abilities upon assuming the office under emergency circumstances.[34] "It takes time," Truman mordantly noted in his memoirs, "for anyone to familiarize himself with a new job. This is particularly true of the presidency of the United States."[35] But, amazingly, during his brief tenure as vice president, Truman received no information regarding the conduct of the war, the development of the atomic bomb (despite, as a senator, chairing the Committee on War Preparedness), nor on the conversations FDR had with Churchill and Stalin. And yet Truman was handed responsibility for dealing with all of these issues. He had to quickly work extensively with Roosevelt staff members to gain insight on policies that would decide the war and literally shape the post-World War II world. He had to find out about decisions reached with Churchill and Stalin, such as what happened at Yalta, among other things.[36] Later, General Harry Vaughan, a confidant of Truman who became his chief of staff in the White House, made the following comment:

> [Truman] talked to everybody that had been to Yalta; everybody that had been to Tehran and everybody that had been to Casablanca, to any of those conferences; he talked to Mrs. Roosevelt and even talked to Anna Roosevelt, the President's daughter, because she had accompanied the President. I'm sure she wasn't in any of the conferences but he thought

she might have overheard some casual conversation that might give him some pointers. It was a terrific job to try to prepare himself because the Potsdam Conference was scheduled. . . . I can recall meetings at the Potsdam Conference where some item would come up and Mr. Churchill said, "Now, Mr. Roosevelt promised he would do so-and-so." Well, you don't want to doubt Mr. Churchill's word, but Mr. Churchill is a man who is dedicated to . . . the interests of the British Empire. I'm sure he demonstrated that sufficiently. Mr. Joe Stalin would say, "Now the President [Roosevelt] promised that he would. . . ." Everybody within the sound of his voice suspected that it was a lie from start to finish but how could you prove it?[37]

Of course, you couldn't "prove it." Vaughan's remarks demonstrated a clear shortcoming in the structure of the presidential-vice presidential relationship. The FDR/Truman debacle underscored the shameful inadequacies in vice-presidential succession. One can only speculate on the consequences of Truman's being uninformed. But the potential for damage was significant. "I discovered that he actually hadn't been informed of the vast bulk of the foreign policy decisions that were in progress," recalled Ambassador Robert D. Murphy, who accompanied Truman to Potsdam. "Nor did he really know the president's planning for the future. Thus when Mr. Roosevelt died on the eve of the conference, it was extremely difficult for the new president who had nothing to do with it before."[38]

Consider the vital issues taken up at Potsdam: the administration of defeated Germany, the demarcation of the boundaries of Poland, the determination of reparations, the further prosecution of the war against Japan, and the definition of the Soviet Union's role in Eastern Europe. These issues would literally shape postwar global boundaries. They were discussed throughout the war, from Casablanca and Cairo to Tehran and Yalta, confidentially among FDR, Churchill, and Stalin. Potsdam was the meeting where lingering, critical questions were wrapped up. For Truman to go into the meeting without any knowledge from FDR of what had transpired previously is disgraceful. "Truman's first days and months were spent . . . learning to be president," writes Mary Natoli. "In this respect, Franklin Roosevelt . . . had done his vice president and the nation a great disservice."[39] Adds R. Gordon Hoxie, Truman took to Potsdam, "a simplistic, albeit refreshing, view of world affairs."[40]

Consider the issue of the atomic bomb. Some historians maintain that one reason for Truman deciding to use the bomb was that it allowed the United States to end the war in Japan without Soviet assistance, thereby keeping the Soviet Union from attempting to occupy Japan after the war.[41] At Potsdam, Truman informed Stalin that the United States had developed the bomb and was intending to use it on Japan. Suppose Stalin had retorted by insisting that FDR promised him the Soviet Union would be allowed to permanently place forces in Japan after the war. Thankfully, Stalin tried nothing of the sort. However, if he did, how would Truman have been able to prove otherwise? Additionally, the definition of the Soviet Union's role in Europe was clarified at Potsdam. Previously, the issue had been taken up at Yalta. After the Yalta agreements were made public in 1946 they were harshly criticized. This was because, as events turned out, Stalin broke his promise that free elections would be held in Poland, Czechoslovakia, Hungary, Romania, and Bulgaria. Instead, communist governments were established in those countries. With such a track record, it would hardly be unfair to suggest that Stalin may have exploited Truman's being uninformed at Potsdam as a means to further delude the allies and acquire greater gains in Europe. Again, one can only speculate.

Clearly, it is very important that the vice president be kept informed of foreign policy. But why the vice president? Could the president simply not relay key information, such as that on Potsdam or nuclear-weapons strategy, to another high-level U.S. official? Sure. But the vice president is the number-two person in the U.S. government, behind only the president in terms of succession. If the president if forced to give up office, the vice president is the person assigned to fill the chair. As a result, the vice president—more than any other administration official—needs to be kept intimately informed of crucial foreign-policy situations.

As a result of such experiences, President Truman vowed that no vice president would ever again come to the office so ill-prepared in foreign policy. He thus initiated a number of reforms, statutory and informal, that began the evolution to the modern office. He sought and earned congressional approval of a bill including the vice president as a statutory member of the National Security Council, via an August 1949 amendment to the National Security Act.[42] As a result of Truman's experiences and efforts, the vice president also now sits with the president's cabinet. Truman also began a critical practice that has continued throughout the contemporary vice presidency: the president keeping the vice president fully briefed on a daily basis.[43] "Truman's succession from the vice presidency to the presidency can be considered a turning point," writes Marie Natoli. "Truman's determination to keep future vice presidents better prepared to assume the presidency set the stage for the growth that was to follow."[44]

For his vice president, Truman in 1948 selected seventy-year-old Kentucky Senator Alben Barkley, who also served as the Senate majority leader. Barkley managed to be an effective and energetic campaigner, traveling throughout the nation in a chartered airplane, and became affectionately known as "the Veep."[45] In a memo considering Barkley for the vice presidency, President Truman stated that Barkley was "an honorable man. He won't give me the double cross, I am sure."[46]

In keeping with his experiences and changes, President Truman sought to make greater use of his vice president than FDR had made of him. He aimed to keep him more informed of events, particularly in foreign policy. That role allowed Barkley to participate in the major foreign-policy decisions of Truman's full term, including action to gain a United Nations mandate to try to halt North Korea's aggression against South Korea and the subsequent commitment of U.S. troops to Korea under the mandate. He also provided some input into Truman's hugely controversial decision to relieve General Douglas MacArthur of his duties for insubordination. Truman telephoned Barkley to solicit his opinion on MacArthur during the closing hours of his decision. Given all that had happened, Barkley concluded reluctantly, a compromise was out of the question and MacArthur had to go.[47]

All of this notwithstanding, one should not view Vice President Barkley as one of the most foreign-policy active vice presidents in history. Natoli notes how Barkley—an able, likable, grandfather-type figure—failed to take greater advantage of the statutory changes intended to widen the vice presidency.[48] Moreover, the "among-the-most-active" role has been usurped by vice presidents Nixon, Mondale, Bush, Quayle, and Gore. Identifying a key moment of departure, Natoli has aptly noted, "Extensive vice presidential activity would have to wait for the next and perhaps the most dramatic turning point, the Nixon vice presidency."[49] At the same time, however, Barkley was likely one of the most foreign-policy active vice presidents in history, especially up to that time.

In part, then, it may seem contradictory that Truman—the president most responsible for initiating the vice president's enhanced foreign-policy role—selected a vice president who did not maximize his new latitude. The author speculates that the following may be a suitable explanation for this seeming contradiction: Truman was, first and foremost, looking to keep his vice president fully informed in foreign policy in order to prevent a repeat of what happened to him and FDR. In this sense, he succeeded with Barkley. However, any available foreign-policy enhancements for Vice President Barkley were up to him. Apparently, Barkley did not pursue such "freelancing" opportunities. While Truman may not have been adverse to an activist vice president in foreign policy, *a la* Nixon or Gore, he at least wanted an informed vice president in foreign policy, and got that much out of Barkley.

In general, the Truman administration was instrumental in establishing a defense policy and strategy that would dominate U.S. foreign policy throughout the 40-plus years of the Cold War, formulating NSC-68, the Truman Doctrine, containment policy, and creating such institutions as the National Security Council and the Central Intelligence Agency, among others. One can chalk up Truman's use of his vice president as another foreign-policy innovation. Many scholars have credited the Eisenhower administration with giving rise to the enhanced role of the vice president. It is true that the Eisenhower administration did play a major role. In reality, however, that mantle should be at least shared with the Truman administration.

Chapter 2

The Trend toward Broader Vice-Presidential Involvement in Foreign Policy since World War II

As a result of lessons learned from the FDR-Truman incident, many later presidents and vice presidents were careful not to repeat the same mistakes. One can find numerous references from past presidents and vice presidents—including those in this study—asserting that a key reason for the increased role of the vice president in foreign policy was the lesson of FDR-Truman. "The prestige, if not the power, of the office [of the vice presidency] has grown since World War Two," explained George Bush. "When Harry Truman succeeded FDR, he didn't know about the A-bomb and needed a crash course to deal with the major decisions facing him in the final days of World War II. That experience led later presidents to keep their vice presidents informed about the White House decision-making process."[50]

Many of Truman's predecessors therefore ensured that the vice president play a greater role in foreign affairs. President Richard M. Nixon, himself a vice president, later stated that the most critical duties for the vice president were: "his participation in the deliberations of the [NSC], his participation in the deliberations of the cabinet; and then the increasingly greater use of the vice president as a trouble-shooter and as a representative of the president in the field of foreign policy."[51] Until the time of his death, Nixon would instruct on-lookers of the vital importance of assigning the vice president substantive duties in the foreign-policy apparatus, particularly in regard to NSC and cabinet meetings.

Some might argue that while there has been increased foreign-policy involvement by post-World War II vice presidents, such involvement still depends upon the president, as do all duties of the second-office holder. "The president can bestow assignments and authority and can remove that authority and power at will," stated former Vice President Hubert Humphrey. "I used to call this Humphrey's law—'He who giveth can taketh away and often does.'"[52] As Joel K. Goldstein notes, the activities of the vice president depend upon presidential generosity.[53] Hence, there is a critical, underlying presidential-style factor (also referred to herein as the idiosyncratic variable) that must be kept in mind when studying the foreign-policy roles of various vice presidents. The style element can make a big difference in how the vice president is involved in foreign policy. Consider the cases of President Eisenhower and his vice president, Nixon, and President Johnson and his vice president, Humphrey. While Vice Presidents Nixon and Humphrey were both involved in White House foreign policy to a degree, thanks to Truman's statutory and informal changes, the ultimate level of their involvement depended heavily upon the president they served. Contrast, for example, the following two views:

"I personally believe," said Dwight Eisenhower, "the vice president of the United States should never be a nonentity. I believe he should be used. I believe he should have a very useful job." As a result, Eisenhower met with Nixon before the 1952 campaign to discuss what was expected to be—and in practice, became—a more active role for the vice president.[54] On the other hand, LBJ did not treat his vice president with the same degree of respect. Humphrey found himself in trouble with LBJ when he spoke out on Vietnam. Al Haig, in his book *Caveat*, includes an account from the time he served on the NSC staff in the Johnson administration: "In at least one White House meeting that I attended, with members of the NSC and congressional leaders present, President Johnson allowed the loquacious Hubert H. Humphrey five minutes in which to speak ('Five minutes, Hubert!'); then Johnson stood by, eyes fixed on the sweep-second hand of his watch, while Humphrey spoke, and when the Vice President went over the limit, pushed him, still talking, out of the room with his own hands." Humphrey's outspokenness against Vietnam policy had cost him within the administration. He found himself not invited to regular weekly lunches where war policy was discussed. George Ball, undersecretary of state, remarked: "I think the president felt that if the vice president was going to raise any arguments, he didn't want him around. He treated him pretty much the way the Kennedys treated [LBJ] when he was vice president. I would have thought that Johnson, having been through the miserable experience himself and being excluded from most things, would have leaned over backwards to treat Humphrey differently, but he didn't."[55]

Clearly, presidential style and preferences make a difference in the vice president's foreign-policy role within any administration. Might it follow, then, that a modern vice president can still be left in the dark on foreign-policy matters if a president so chooses? Not really. Sure, it is still ultimately up to the president whether or not the vice president has a *substantive* foreign-policy role. Yet, that fact notwithstanding, the modern vice presidency has evolved to where it is extremely unlikely that contemporary occupants will be totally alienated in foreign-policy matters, despite the president's actions or preferences. Among other reasons, this is due to President Truman making the vice president a statutory member of the NSC as well as the second-office holder now having his own national-security advisors (since Vice President Mondale). These factors should continue to exist irrespective of the president's style or wishes. The president can ignore his vice president's input in foreign policy and not give him any substantive duties whatsoever, but, due to Truman's changes, the latter will never be totally ignorant of basic developments in international affairs. Additionally, it has become customary since Vice President Nixon that the second-office holder receive copies of all the paper that goes to the president on foreign policy and all other issues.

The evolvement[56] toward greater foreign-policy involvement by post-World War II vice presidents can be demonstrated by a number of factors. By and large, presidents now understand the need to have the vice president receive copies of all paper and memoranda related to foreign policy, sit in at all NSC meetings, and even have his own foreign-policy advisors—all of which are post-World War II novelties. This is a significant step up from the pre-1945 vice presidency, when the occupants' "foreign-policy" roles were essentially limited to ceremonial trips abroad—what I term "wreath-laying missions." Modern vice presidents' foreign-policy missions usually include fact-finding duties that involve a debriefing by the president upon their return. Some vice presidents, such as Nelson Rockefeller, chose to concentrate on domestic issues rather than foreign policy.[57] Nonetheless, often the vice president has the option of spreading his wings somewhat in foreign policy, and there is no doubting the fact that the institution itself allows room for increased involvement in foreign affairs, assuming such action is desirable.

The heightened foreign-policy role for modern vice presidents have, in my opinion, been forged primarily by six key figures: Truman (as president), and Vice Presidents Nixon, Mondale, Bush, Quayle, and Gore. Truman heeded critical lessons from his own experience of being kept completely in the dark on vital foreign policy matters. He vowed that no vice president would ever again be so ill-informed, and took formal actions to make the vice president an active foreign-policy player. The increase of the stature of the office in foreign policy would magnify under Nixon, who used it as a stepping stone to become a definitive foreign-policy president.[58] Under Mondale, the modern vice presidency began to take shape in staff size, as he was the first occupant to have his own foreign-policy advisors.[59] Bush's role as an experienced foreign-policy voice was exploited by President Reagan, who tapped him to head up the administration's crisis-management team—a significant increase in foreign-policy leadership for a vice president. Quayle maintained the momentum of Mondale and Bush, and participated in a series of intriguing tasks during the conflict in the Persian Gulf. Gore may have taken it to another level. In September 1993, Vice President Gore and Russian Prime Minister Viktor Chernomyrdin initiated a joint commission designed to facilitate U.S.-Russian cooperation on a variety of issues, including: space cooperation, trade and business development, defense conversion, science and technology, and energy, nuclear safety, and the environment.[60] As far as I know, the Gore-Chernomyrdin commission was the first and only example of a vice president forming a major, bilateral foreign-policy commission with a top foreign-policy leader.

"Levels" of Foreign-Policy Involvement by Vice Presidents

This research study defines "greater foreign-policy involvement" by vice presidents via six levels, each of which represents progressively higher levels of involvement by the vice president in foreign policy. Level zero will be defined as little to no foreign-policy involvement, which essentially reflects the pre-1945/Truman vice presidency. Level one signifies a vice president who, in line with President Truman's changes, receives copies of all paperwork relating to foreign affairs and is a sitting member of the NSC. At this level, the vice president can participate in daily or weekly national security briefings. Quayle, for example, met every morning at 8:15 with President Bush, National Security Advisor Brent Scowcroft, and CIA briefers for a 30-minute national security briefing.[61] (In contrast, recall that the last pre-World War II vice president, Truman, saw the president only eight times during the time he occupied the vice presidency.[62]) Essentially, all vice presidents since Vice President Truman have reached at least level one. To a degree, this allows a vice president to "participate" in the decision-making process on administration foreign-policy issues. This does not, however, ensure that the vice president is active nor taken seriously in such deliberations. Vice presidents Humphrey and Johnson, for example, were not taken seriously—in contrast to Vice President Gore. "You can search but you won't find one major policy decision in this administration that President Clinton made without discussing it with the vice president," said Clinton presidential assistant Mark Gearan. "Just doesn't happen."[63]

A "level two" vice president can serve as a foreign-policy spokesman within the administration—particularly during crises—by publicly announcing its goals and objectives. This role often entails acting as the president's "attack dog" by taking on critics of his policies, as was done by both Vice President Spiro Agnew during the Vietnam War and Quayle during the Persian Gulf crisis.[64] Level three entails traveling abroad as an emissary to meet with foreign officials or announce key administration policy objectives. This includes duties beyond the ceremonial, often for fact-finding purposes, and typically involves a debriefing by the president upon return. An example of such a mission was Vice President Johnson's trip to Berlin to announce a major administration foreign-policy objective.[65] The third level also includes vice presidents who acted as a liaison to the U.S. Congress to discuss with members critical foreign-policy initiatives or deliberations, as Quayle did during the Gulf crisis.[66]

A "level four" vice president has his own national-security and foreign-policy advisors. This applies to all vice presidents after and including Mondale. Level five represents vice presidents who negotiated with foreign-policy leaders on behalf of the administration. Examples of such missions are Quayle's trips during the Gulf crisis to Argentina, Saudi Arabia, and Venezuela, where, respectively, he negotiated with foreign leaders over issues such as stopping missile transfers to Iraq, allocating more financial assistance for U.S. intervention in the Gulf, and increasing oil production;[67] Gore's trips to Russia, among other missions;[68] and Vice President Nixon's 1959 meeting with Fidel Castro, where he was instructed to assess how the administration should interpret and react to the Cuban leader.[69]

Finally, level six is defined as the highest attainable level for vice-presidential involvement in foreign policy. It entails a vice president who heads up or participates in key foreign-policy committees at home or abroad. This includes Vice President Bush chairing an administration foreign-policy crisis committee and Gore's co-sponsorship of the Gore-Chernomyrdin commission with the Russian prime minister. The six levels have been constructed in a manner that encompasses all broad categories of vice-presidential activity in foreign policy that have taken place up to the current occupant of the office (Gore).

The five vice presidents profiled in this study each achieved a level five.[70]

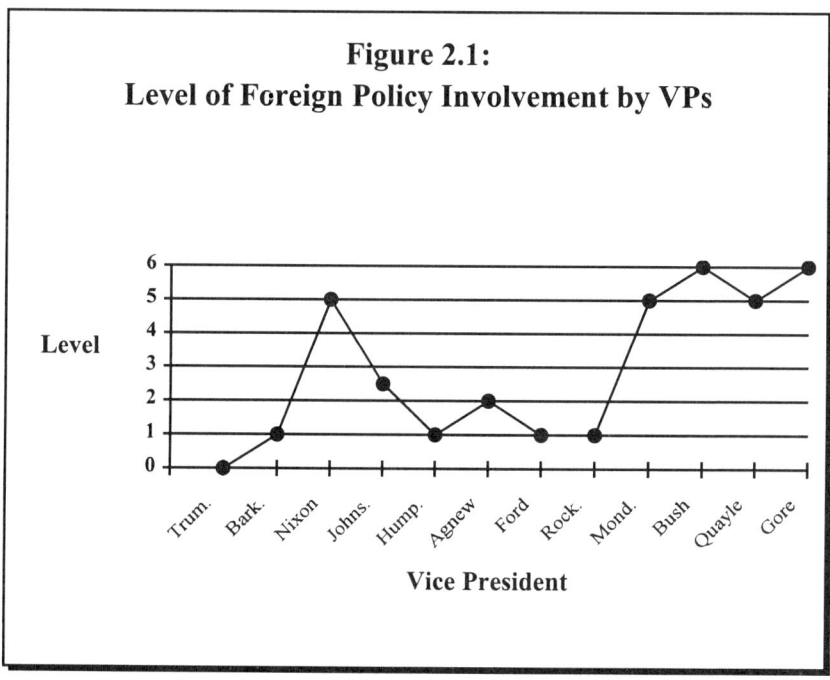

Source: Paul Kengor, "The Role of Post-World War II Vice Presidents in Foreign Policy," Graduate School of Public and International Affairs, University of Pittsburgh, December 1994.[71]

The degree to which a particular vice president engages in such activities will help determine the level of his involvement in administration foreign policy. These are all largely new phenomena. Not until after World War II have vice presidents been given such substantive roles within White House foreign policy. This study will illuminate the roles of five of those post-World War II vice presidents—all level five or higher—as well as exploring the issue of whether their experiences provide insights into better improving White House foreign policy.

The Vice President as a Component of the President's Foreign-Policy Structure

Part of the reason for the modern vice president's increased involvement in foreign policy stems from his elevated place within the White House's foreign-policy structure. The contemporary foreign-policy structure is heavily influenced by legislation during the Truman administration. "The structure for national security and foreign policy production is partially dictated by a statute," notes Ralph C. Bledsoe, "the National Security Act of 1947, and subsequent amendments." The act established the NSC, chaired by the president, and consisting of the vice president and secretaries of state and defense. Additional cabinet members may be added by the president. The chairman of the Joint Chiefs of Staff, director of Central Intelligence, and others serve as ex officio advisors. Typically, substructures are established under the NSC, including interagency groups and various executive-level committees.[72] Obviously, various chief executives have played with this structure. By and large, however, it has provided a basis of consistency through the post-World War II period.

The vice president is now a "member" of the president's foreign policy-making team simply by virtue of the fact that he is a member of the National Security Council, in addition to the president, secretary of state, secretary of defense, and national security advisor. In this sense, he is at least assured *somewhat* of a "foreign-policy role." Figure 2.2 expresses these realities and structure in a rather generic manner. The various chapters of the larger study itself will delineate the specific structures used by each administration.

Figure 2.2: The President's Foreign and Security Policy Inputs

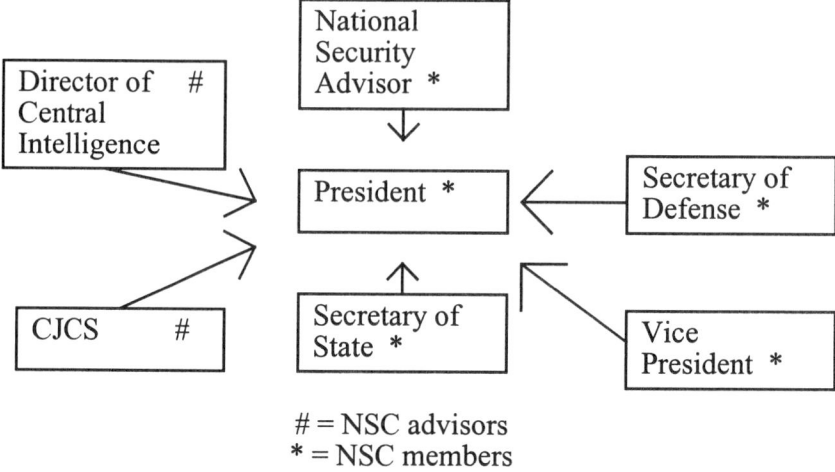

\# = NSC advisors
* = NSC members

The degree of input and influence in large part depends upon the president, although all are ensured a certain degree of influence by the fact that they are NSC members or advisors. Source: Adapted from Amos A. Jordan and William J. Taylor, Jr. *American National Security: Policy and Process* (Baltimore and London: The Johns Hopkins University Press, 1981). pp. 94, 134 & 202.

There is a limited literature on how to best incorporate the vice president into the broader NSC structure or a president's foreign-policy apparatus. Yet, when it comes to the separate (and large) literature on how the president might best improve the operation of his NSC or use of his National Security Advisor (NSA), many scholars—despite unending suggestions—usually fall back to a similar conclusion that may have implications for using the vice president: the president should do what works best for him, although a degree of structure is important. For instance, when asked to rank recent NSAs in order of effectiveness, former Carter NSA, Zbigniew Brzezinski, responded:

> No, I won't do that. I think that the security advisor is so much an extension of the president that the way he functions is very much determined by the president's political style and the role he chooses for himself in the area of foreign policy. In other words, you cannot transpose the national security advisor from one president to another. If, for example, I were to say that Scowcroft was good under Ford, it doesn't follow that he would

have been good under Nixon or Kennedy or Carter.[73]

Brzezinski, of course, has been criticized for how he ran the NSC in the Carter White House. However, the language establishing the foreign- and security-policy system, encapsulated in the National Security Act of 1947, in part reflects this philosophy. Duncan L. Clarke argues that the act, which also made the vice president a statutory member of the NSC, gives the president "maximum flexibility to use (or not use) the NSC as he sees fit." He argues that, in retrospect, an outstanding featuring of the NSC has been its reflection and responsiveness to the personal styles and preferences of successive presidents.[74] The act, in creating the NSC, brought together with the president and vice president the senior foreign and defense policy and intelligence officials for the purposes of policy coordination, integration, and advice. The act states: "The function of the Council shall be to advise the President with respect to the integration of domestic, foreign, and military policies relating to the national security so as to enable the military services and the other departments and agencies of the Government to cooperate more effectively in matters involving the national security."[75]

Still, many who share this perspective understand that despite the president's preferences, there are certain steps that he should take in running his NSC. "Close observers of the NSC process agree that there is no 'ideal' system," writes Clarke. "No system is acceptable unless it conforms to the president's style and needs.... But whether a president opts for a formal, highly structured process or a more informal one, *some* structure is essential."[76] Philip A. Odeen agrees with Clarke's assessment:

> There is no ideal system for managing national security policy. Each president will tailor a system to reflect his unique needs and style. In some cases he may desire a very structured system; in others a highly informal approach. Nonetheless, a degree of planned structure is essential in any president's national security system, regardless of his philosophy.[77]

There may be similar manifestations of this when it comes to how the president uses his vice president in foreign policy. President Reagan decided to have Vice President Bush head up the administration's crisis-management team, which is usually a duty assigned to the NSA. But Reagan made such a move for two reasons. First, he felt it was a way to get the vice president involved in key aspects of administration policy formulation rather than being, as Reagan quotes Vice President Rockefeller as saying, "standby equipment." Second, Secretary of State Al Haig did not like and could not work with NSA Richard Allen. Thus, Reagan, along with Michael Deaver, Ed Meese, and James Baker, decided it would be best to have Bush take on the crisis-management role.[78] There is a lesson in this example for how the vice president may or may not fit into the president's foreign-policy apparatus, and it is one that is often drawn by observers of the NSC system: President Reagan and his team felt it was best to step out of the "formal" national-security system structure in order to implement a process that they believed would work best for their administration's foreign policy. At the same time, however, Reagan's NSC lacked structure, appeared undisciplined, and likely facilitated the Iran-Contra debacle.[79] Hence, as scholars maintain, a system needs both flexibility *and* structure.

Perhaps not surprisingly, occasional chaos within the NSC process has provoked some scholars of the vice presidency to look to the NSC in applying their suggestions on how to use the second-office holder to improve White House foreign-policy management and coordination. For instance, Kevin Mulcahy argues that the vice president has no bureaucratic-parochial interest—unlike other cabinet-level foreign-policy players—and can thus serve as a neutral foreign-policy voice, particularly in administrations with activist NSCs. Even the sometimes unfortunately politicized NSA may have an agenda. The NSA is supposed to concentrate on broader foreign-policy interests, but often represents the interests of an increasingly independent National Security Council. As Robert E. Hunter and others have noted, the NSC system was created in 1947 to transcend the trappings of departmentalism.[80] In reality, however, the opposite has at times prevailed, as demonstrated by infighting among various NSAs and secretaries of state—such as Zbigniew Brzezinski and Cyrus Vance within the Carter administration, and ostensibly Anthony Lake and Warren Christopher in the Clinton administration[81]—as well as the usurpation of many of the secretary of state's foreign-policy duties by NSA Kissinger during the early Nixon administration, and chaos within the NSC during the Reagan administration. Hence, Mulcahy argues that the vice president could step in as a neutral foreign-policy voice to the president.[82] Unlike other cabinet members, he avers, the vice president has no parochial interests except for serving the president.

Conclusion

As the following pages purport to show, post-World War II vice presidents have become components of the formal White House defense and foreign-policy structure merely as a result of Truman's statutory changes. Additionally, as noted earlier, while President Truman began the somewhat "permanent" change in the role of the vice president in foreign policy, his changes are technically reversible —albeit by a move as dramatic and unexpected as an amending of the National Security Act of 1947; there is no movement afoot for such a change. Likewise, the foreign-policy activism beyond the basic changes by Truman—and embodied by the five vice presidents in this study—is not structural nor permanent. Proof of the reversibility of the activism is obvious. For instance, the momentum built up by presidents Truman and Eisenhower and Vice President Nixon was quickly snuffed out during the next four administrations, especially the JFK-LBJ era. The trend toward greater involvement *was* reversed and was not rekindled until Vice President Mondale—although, again, all along these vice presidents were at least *informed* in foreign policy. In sum, the vice president can still be cut out of the foreign-policy process by the president. The vice president is the president's creature, as is the NSC.

Having said that, we seem to have reached a point where the vice president will continue to remain informed in foreign policy, especially compared to his pre-World War II status, and (in the majority of cases in coming years) probably receive occasional substantive roles in foreign policy. There may still be Humphreys and Agnews, but another vice president as ill-informed and free of substantive duties as Truman is very unlikely. Also, as of 1999, Truman's statutory changes appear permanent in a *de facto* sense, even if they can in fact be technically reversed. And, at the very least, the fact that the vice president is now a sitting member of the NSC ensures him at least a modicum of foreign-policy influence beyond that granted to vice presidents before Truman's changes. Yet, the ultimate level to which a particular vice president is influential within that structure depends, as always, primarily upon himself and the president he serves. The next five chapters will illuminate those and other factors.

Notes

1. Quoted in Doris Kearns, *Lyndon Johnson and the American Dream* (New York: Harper & Row, 1976), p. 164.

2. Dwight D. Eisenhower, *Waging Peace: The White House Years, 1956-1961* (Garden City, N.Y.: Doubleday, 1965), p. 631.

3. Jules Witcover, *Crapshoot: Rolling the Dice on the Vice Presidency* (New York: Crown Publishers, 1992), p. xiii.

4. Gerald M. Pomper, et al., *The Performance of American Government: Checks and Minuses* (New York: Free Press, 1972), as cited by Marie D. Natoli, "Vice Presidential Selection: The Political Considerations," *Presidential Studies Quarterly*, Vol. X, No. 2, Spring 1980.

5. Natoli, "Vice Presidential Selection," p. 165.

6. Louis Clinton Hatch, *History of the Vice Presidency of the United States*, revised by Earl L. Shoup (Westport, Conn.: Greenwood Press, 1934, 1970), p. 415.

7. Robert J. Sickels, *Presidential Transactions* (Englewood Cliffs: Prentice Hall, 1974), p. 50.

8. Harry C. Thomson, "The Second Place in Rome: John Adams as Vice President," *Presidential Studies Quarterly*, Vol. X, No. 2, Spring 1980, p. 171.

9. Arthur M. Schlesinger, Jr., "The Vice Presidency: A Modest Proposal," appen-

dix to *The Imperial Presidency* (Boston: Houghton Mifflin, 1973, 1974).

10. Marie D. Natoli, "Abolish the Vice Presidency?" *Presidential Studies Quarterly*, Vol. IX, No. 2, Spring 1979, p. 203.

11. Danny M. Adkison, "The Vice Presidency as Apprenticeship," *Presidential Studies Quarterly*, Vol. XIII, No. 2, Spring 1983, p. 212.

12. George Bush, with Victor Gold, *Looking Forward* (New York: Doubleday, 1987), p. 225.

13. Martin D. Tullai, "Speaking of the Vice Presidency . . . " *American History Illustrated*, Vol. 19, January 1985, pp. 10-15.

14. Bush, op. cit., pp. 226-27.

15. Ibid.

16. David S. Broder and Bob Woodward, "Facing Limitations in an 'Awkward Job,'" *The Washington Post*, January 8, 1992, pp. A1, A14.

17. Ibid., p. A14.

18. Lance Morrow, "The Strange Destiny of a Vice President," *Time*, May 20, 1991, p. 23.

19. David S. Broder and Bob Woodward, op. cit., p. A14.

20. Marie D. Natoli, "The Vice Presidency in the Third Century," in James P. Pfiffner and R. Gordon Hoxie, eds., *The Presidency in Transition* (New York: Center for the Study of the Presidency, 1989), p. 414.

21. Vernon L. Parrington, *Main Currents of American Thought* (New York: Harcourt, Brace, 1930), Vol. I, p. 307.

22. C. F. Adams, ed., *The Works of John Adams*, 10 vols. (Boston: 1850-1856), 1: 460.

23. Witcover, op. cit., p. 11.

24. Marie D. Natoli, *American Prince, American Pauper* (Westport, Conn.: Greenwood Press, 1985), p. 138.

25. Van Buren served four years as President Andrew Jackson's vice president. Since Van Buren was elected president in November 1836, thirty-four men preceded Bush as vice president. Incredibly, not a single one accomplished what Van Buren and two of his predecessors, John Adams and Thomas Jefferson, did.

26. James N. Rosenau, *The Study of Political Adaptation* (New York: Nichols, 1981), p. 80n.

27. Paul C. Light, "The Institutional Vice Presidency," *Presidential Studies Quarterly*, Vol. XIII, No. 2, Spring 1983, p. 198.

28. Richard Smoke, *National Security and the Nuclear Dilemma* (New York: Random House, 1987), pp. 59-62.

29. Dan Quayle, *Standing Firm: A Vice-Presidential Memoir* (New York, N.Y.: HarperCollins, 1994) p. 87.

30. George S. Sirgiovanni, "Dumping the Vice President: An Historical Overview and Analysis," *Presidential Studies Quarterly*, Vol. XXIV, No. 4, Fall 1994, p. 775.

31. In reality, Garner referred to a different bodily fluid. The anecdote has been cleaned up for high school civics classes. Morrow, op. cit., p. 23.

32. Wallace had unusual foreign-policy views. He was reportedly hopelessly naive about Stalin's Russia and outright sympathetic to communism. This brought him occasional disfavor within some Democratic party ranks. Jules Witcover writes: "Wallace's ideas about the oppressive nature of capitalism toward the working man and his utopian

The Evolution of a Reform 37

dreams of a society more deeply committed to the cares and needs of 'the common man' found much common ground with the Great Experiment being conducted from Moscow. He gave speeches comparing the plight of American workers with the downtrodden Russian people; not even the reports of Stalin's pogroms or the devious Ribbentrop-Molotov nonaggression pact that cleared the way for the Nazi invasion of Poland in September 1939 seemed to cool Wallace's pro-Soviet ardor. Once Hitler turned on Russia in 1941, Wallace was able to give full voice to his sentiments, even to the point of comparing American business magnates to Nazism's fascists leaders, calling them 'midget Hitlers who continually attack labor.'" Witcover, op. cit., p. 82. Such sentiments stand in marked contrast to Wallace's successor. On June 22, 1941, Senator Truman responded to Hitler's double-cross and attack of Russia by stating: "If we see that Germany is winning we ought to help Russia, and if Russia is winning we ought to help Germany, and that way let them kill as many as possible." David McCullough, *Truman* (New York: Simon & Schuster, 1992), p. 262.

33. Harry S Truman, *Year of Decisions* (New York: Doubleday, 1955), p. 194.

34. Marie D. Natoli, "Harry S Truman and the Contemporary Vice Presidency," *Presidential Studies Quarterly*, Vol. XVIII, No. 1, Winter 1988, pp. 81-82.

35. Truman, op. cit., p. 194.

36. Natoli, "Harry S Truman and the Contemporary Vice Presidency," p. 82.

37. Harry Vaughan, Oral History Interview, Harry S Truman Library, Independence, Missouri, p. 36, as cited by ibid., pp. 82-83.

38. As quoted in, R. Gordon Hoxie, *Command Decision and the Presidency* (New York: Reader's Digest Press, 1977), p. 337.

39. Natoli, "Harry S Truman and the Contemporary Vice Presidency," pp. 82-83.

40. Hoxie, *Command Decision and the Presidency*, p. 337.

41. For research on this matter, see Gar Alperovitz, *Atomic diplomacy: Hiroshima and Potsdam; the use of the atomic bomb and the American confrontation with Soviet power* (New York, NY: Vintage Books, 1967, 1965); Gar Alperovitz, with assistance of Sanho Tree, *The decision to use the atomic bomb and the architecture of an American myth* (New York, NY: Knopf, 1995); Thomas B. Allen and Norman Polmar, *Code-name downfall: the secret plan to invade Japan and why Truman dropped the bomb* (New York: Simon & Schuster, 1995); Robert James Maddox, *Weapons for Victory: the Hiroshima decision fifty years later* (Columbia: University of Missouri Press, 1995); John Hersey, *Hiroshima* (New York: A. A. Knopf, distributed by Random House, 1985, 1946); and Masuji Ibuse, trans. John Bester, *Black Rain* (New York: Bantam Books, 1985, 1969).

42. R. Gordon Hoxie, *Command Decision and the Presidency*, p. 337; R. Gordon Hoxie, "The National Security Council: Introductory Survey," in James P. Pfiffner and R. Gordon Hoxie, eds., *The Presidency in Transition* (New York: Center for the Study of the Presidency, 1989), p. 198; and Ralph C. Bledsoe, "Policy Management in the Reagan Administration," in Pfiffner and Hoxie, eds., p. 58.

43. Natoli, "Harry S Truman and the Contemporary Vice Presidency," p. 83.

44. Natoli, "The Vice Presidency in the Third Century," p. 414.

45. A remark by Barkley before Truman embarked on his famous whistle-stop train led to the president's popular campaign slogan "give 'em hell, Harry." As the train was about to leave Washington's Union Station on the first coast-to-coast trip in mid-

September, Barkley instructed the president to, "Go out there and mow 'em down." To which Truman replied: "I'll mow 'em down, Alben, and I'll give 'em hell." Witcover, op. cit., p. 104.

46. Ibid., p. 103.

47. McCullough, op. cit., pp. 104 and 839-40; and Alben W. Barkley, *That Reminds Me* (Garden City, N.Y.: Doubleday, 1954), pp. 105-14.

48. Natoli, *American Prince, American Pauper*, p. 138.

49. Natoli, "The Vice Presidency in the Third Century," pp. 414-15.

50. Bush, op. cit., p. 7.

51. Birch Bayh, *One Heartbeat Away* (New York: Bobbs-Merrill, 1968), p. 87.

52. Hubert H. Humphrey, "Changes in the Vice Presidency," *Current History*, Vol. 67, 1974, pp. 58-59.

53. Joel K. Goldstein, *The Modern American Vice Presidency* (Princeton, N.J.: Princeton University Press, 1982), p. 135.

54. Marie D. Natoli, "Perspectives on the Vice Presidency," *Presidential Studies Quarterly*, Vol. XII, No. 4, Fall 1982, pp. 598 and 602; and William Costello, *The Facts about Nixon* (New York: Viking, 1960), p. 229.

55. Witcover, op. cit., p. 197.

56. It is accurate to describe the increased role of the vice president in post-World War II foreign policy as an "evolvement." Indeed, the level of involvement has increased, albeit not in a consistently upward slope, from vice presidents Barkley to Gore. Whether or not the evolution has reached its peak is another question, but there has been an evolving, increased involvement throughout the post-World War II era.

57. Marie D. Natoli, "The Vice Presidency: Gerald Ford as Healer?" Guest Editorial, *Presidential Studies Quarterly*, Vol. X, No. 4, Fall 1980, p. 664.

58. Sirgiovanni, op. cit., p. 775.

59. Light, op. cit., p. 199.

60. "Fact Sheet: Gore-Chernomyrdin Commission," *U.S. Department of State Dispatch*, Vol. 5, No. 1, January 3, 1994, pp. 2-3.

61. Broder and Woodward, op. cit., p. A14.

62. Natoli, "Harry S Truman and the Contemporary Vice Presidency," pp. 81-82.

63. Ann Devroy and Stephen Barr, "Gore Bucks Tradition in Vice President's Role," *Washington Post*, February 18, 1995, p. A8.

64. Goldstein, op. cit., p. 104; Maureen Dowd, "Quayle Aims at Protests, A la Agnew," *The New York Times*, January 24, 1991, p. A13; and Paul Kengor, "The Role of the Vice President during the Crisis in the Persian Gulf," *Presidential Studies Quarterly*, Vol. XXIV, No. 4, Fall 1994, pp. 796-98.

65. Witcover, op. cit., p. 168.

66. Kengor, op. cit., pp. 795-96.

67. Ibid., pp. 793-95, and; Michael Duffy, "Is He Really That Bad?" *Time*, May 20, 1991, p. 22.

68. Karen Breslau and Bob Cohn, "Al Gore: Talk a Lot, and Carry a Big Stick," *Newsweek*, October 31, 1994, pp. 30-32.

69. Jeffrey J. Safford, "The Nixon-Castro Meeting of 19 April 1959," *Diplomatic History*, 1980 4 (4), pp. 425-31.

70. Vice President Nixon did not have his own "defense and foreign-policy advisors" in the contemporary post-Mondale sense. He did, however, have "aides" that per-

formed similar tasks. Such aides to a vice president were unprecedented at the time. More on the difference between Nixon's aides and modern vice-presidential advisors is explained in the next chapter on Vice President Nixon.

71. As an added "source," the information required to formulate this figure has also been taken from the research in this study.

72. Bledsoe, op. cit., p. 58.

73. Michael R. Beschloss and Allen Weinstein, "The Best National Security System: A Conversation with Zbigniew Brzezinski," *Washington Quarterly*, No. 1, 1982, p. 71.

74. Duncan L. Clarke, *American Defense and Foreign Policy Institutions* (New York: Harper & Row, 1989), p. 3.

75. National Security Act of 1947, 50 U.S.C. Sec. 402(a).

76. Clarke, op. cit., p. 3.

77. Philip A. Odeen, "Organizing for National Security," *International Security*, Vol. 5, No. 1, Summer 1980, p. 112.

78. Ronald Reagan, *Ronald Reagan: An American Life* (New York: Simon & Schuster, 1990).

79. See Clarke, op. cit., pp. 7-9; Lawrence E. Walsh, *Iran-Contra: The Final Report* (New York: Times Books, Random House, 1994), p. 452; and Frank Carlucci's remarks in Kenneth W. Thompson, "The Reagan Presidency: Interview with Frank Carlucci," *Miller Center Journal*, Vol. 2, Spring 1995, p. 45.

80. Robert E. Hunter, *Organizing for National Security* (Washington, D.C.: Center for Strategic and International Studies, 1988); and Clarke, op. cit., pp. 3-10.

81. As reported by Elizabeth Drew, "Meet the Press with Tim Russert," *NBC-TV*, October 30, 1994.

82. Kevin V. Mulcahy, "Presidents and the Administration of Foreign Policy: The New Role for the Vice President," *Presidential Studies Quarterly*, Vol. XVII, No. 1, Winter 1987, p. 129.

Chapter 3
A Path-Breaking Vice President: Richard M. Nixon (1953-61)

> *"Persons familiar with the vice president's helpful activities have told this correspondent that they consider them unique in the records of his high office."*
> Arthur Krock, The New York Times, *1953*

Introduction

This is the first of five chapters that directly profile the foreign-policy roles of the various vice presidents featured in this study.[1] In that sense, it is fitting that the first chapter examine the vice presidency of Richard Milhous Nixon. Thanks to his own abilities and the innovations of the president he served, Dwight D. Eisenhower, Nixon's vice presidency was truly revolutionary. In the realm of foreign policy in particular, he performed path-breaking duties that no vice president before him undertook. Not until the vice presidencies of Walter Mondale and George Bush some twenty to thirty years later would a vice president again play such a strong role in foreign policy. Perhaps it is appropriately "Nixonesque" that, to this day, no vice president has completed a foreign-policy mission that matched the drama of Vice President Nixon's 1959 trip to Moscow—immortalized in the "kitchen debate" with Soviet Premier Nikita Khrushchev—or his life-threatening (literally) tour of South America in 1958. In keeping with the peaks and valleys and love and hate that characterized Nixon's career, and those who either admired or despised it, his vice presidency was not conventional.[2]

While profiling Nixon's general foreign-policy role and place within the Eisenhower administration's foreign- and security-policy framework, this chapter provides a number of examples of his duties abroad. Among these, it focuses primarily on two cases: the vice president's role in Soviet policy, which includes his 1959 Moscow mission and various jousts with Khrushchev, and his duties in Latin America policy. The latter includes not only his 1958 South America trip but also the impressive duties he was given regarding Castro and Cuba.

However, concerning Castro and Cuba, the Nixon experience is also instructive in a somewhat negative manner. Overall, his duties in this assignment were carried out in a salutary fashion. Yet, his later actions concerning how the administration should react to the Cuban dictator may have been motivated by his own personal political fortunes. As this study shows, this is the first of similar, repeated examples that also took place with the politically obsessed Mondale and with Vice President Bush. This reality flies in the face of the premise by many scholars that the vice president can be a valuable asset in foreign affairs because he allegedly lacks selfish-parochial interests. Modern vice presidents seem as tied to selfish-political interests as much if not more than any cabinet member dedicated to his or her department, or service chief to his military branch.

As will also become evident in this study, each vice president profiled took away something unique from his experiences as vice president. Among the most fascinating elements of Nixon's two terms as vice president is the manner in which he used them to educate himself about foreign policy and to eventually make himself known—positively or negatively—as a definitive foreign-policy *president* and the nation's often-stated "elder statesman." In studying Nixon's vice-presidential years, it becomes abundantly clear that they were especially formative in turning him into the foreign-policy animal he would remain throughout his life.

Finally, as stated previously, the Nixon vice presidency, not unlike those of the other four vice presidents profiled on the following pages, provides crucial lessons when it comes to policy recommendations related to the vice president's role in foreign policy. While some of those lessons may become evident as one reads through this chapter, a complete evaluation of them is not provided until the final chapter of the study, in which all five of the vice presidents' experiences are considered comprehensively vis-à-vis the various policy recommendations.

Nixon's Selection and Role Definition

Key to understanding Nixon's use in foreign policy is the issue of why Eisenhower selected him in the first place. Before the 1952 GOP convention, Nixon was the junior Republican senator from California. He was an ambitious thirty-nine year-old Navy veteran of World War II barely two years into the Senate after a highly visible career as a communist-hunter who cracked the celebrated Alger Hiss case.[3] He had a reputation as a very bright, young, and ambitious politician.

The Hiss case, in particular, really established Nixon as a national player and household name. In fact, the Hiss case both helped and hurt him. For every lifetime supporter it earned him, it also gained him an eternal enemy.[4] Nixon recalled conversations with two friends after the 1960 election. "If it hadn't been for the Hiss case, you would have been elected president of the United States," said one. The other friend replied: "If it hadn't been for the Hiss case, you never would have been vice president of the United States or candidate for president." Nixon concluded: "Ironically, both of my friends may have been right."[5] Both were partly right.

Nixon's performance in the Hiss case deeply impressed Eisenhower. According to Ike, he chose Nixon as his running mate for three principal reasons. First, the political philosophy of the two men was similar. Second, the general viewed his age as a potential liability, and thought he "should take the opportunity to select a vice-presidential candidate who was young, vigorous, ready to learn, and of good reputation." Finally, said Ike, the question of "communist infiltration and proper methods for defeating it in our country" had become a hot issue. What most impressed Eisenhower was not so much that Nixon had exposed Hiss, but that he had done so fairly and persistently. "Not once had he overstepped the limits prescribed by the American sense of fair play or American rules applying to such investigations," said Eisenhower. "He did not persecute or defame. This I greatly admired."[6]

Nixon realized what the Hiss case had done for his political career, including his selection as vice president. He recalled that when Eisenhower introduced him as his running mate to the Republican National Convention he described Nixon as "a man who has a special talent and an ability to ferret out any kind of subversive influence wherever it may be found, and the strength and persistence to get rid of it."[7] Ike, however, wanted more than just a red hunter.

Importantly, Eisenhower wanted his vice president to be a player. "I personally believe," he said, "the Vice President of the United States should never be a nonentity. I believe he should be used. I believe he should have a very useful job."[8] With this in mind, Eisenhower met with Nixon prior to the 1952 campaign to discuss what they expected would be a much more active role for the vice president.[9] Immediately after Ike was nominated for the presidency in 1952 he summoned Nixon into his hotel suite. He recalled how FDR had failed to inform Truman on many basic, critical decisions and the serious situation this created when Truman was elevated to the presidency in 1945. It was vital, said Ike, that this never happen again. As a result, he would ensure that Nixon participated in all policy-making meetings. Additionally, Nixon would be given assignments to prepare him for the possibility that he might suddenly become president.[10] Eisenhower kept his promise.

The President-Vice President Relationship

Among the items that have distorted our image of the Eisenhower-Nixon relationship was a famous (or infamous, in Nixon's view) August 1960 press-conference remark by the president. At the time, Nixon was the Republican nominee for the presidency. A reporter sarcastically asked Ike: "I just wonder if you could give us an example of a major idea of [Nixon's] that you had adopted." Eisenhower angrily replied: "If you give me a week, I might think of one. I don't remember."[11]

Eisenhower's comment damaged Nixon's 1960 presidential campaign and placed a dark spot on his political image. The historic remark is not of casual insignificance. It was a blistering blow to Nixon during a very tight presidential race—the closest in American history. (John F. Kennedy won the election by a mere 144,000 votes. For hours, the election was too close to call.) The ripple effects from Ike's comment may have, literally, cost Nixon the presidency. Eisenhower's remark, however, was made out of frustration with the press. Ironically, he likely meant the opposite of what some journalists, Nixon biographers and critics have always presumed. Immediately after making the remark, Eisenhower realized how terrible it sounded. As soon as he got to the Oval Office he telephoned Nixon to apologize and expressed his regret. Years later, up to the time of his death even, Eisenhower continued to apologize to his vice president for the remark.[12] Hearing President Lyndon Johnson drudge up the old remark in November 1966 incited an angry Ike to call Nixon from Eisenhower's home in Gettysburg, Pennsylvania. "Dick, I could kick myself every time some jackass brings up that goddamn 'give me a week' business," Ike allegedly told Nixon.[13] The way he treated Nixon in both private and public, and the significant duties he assigned him, belies the view that Ike was unimpressed or displeased with his loyal vice president. As will become evident, his foreign-policy responsibilities alone were unprecedented at the time for a vice president.[14]

An early thorn in the side of the Nixon-Ike relationship was injected during the early days of the 1952 presidential campaign. As Ike's running mate in 1952, Nixon was reported to have maintained an $18,000 "slush" fund to be used to pay the incidental expenses of his congressional office. The California representative took to the television airwaves to combat the charges in a famous thirty-minute address now known as the "Checkers speech." In the speech—made before the largest television audience in history to that time[15]—he acknowledged the existence of the fund but denied it was used for personal expenses. Nixon also admitted in the speech to having accepted a cocker spaniel puppy as a gift to his family, which his daughter Tricia named "Checkers." He said he could give up his place on the ticket, but he would never give up the children's dog. The response to the speech was overwhelmingly positive, as Republicans contacted campaign headquarters and exhorted that Nixon be kept on the ticket.

The two men recovered from the incident, striking up a successful working relationship and rapport. Stephen Ambrose writes: "In their three years together . . . Eisenhower appreciated Nixon for his obvious qualities—he was extremely hardworking, highly intelligent, loyal, devoted to Eisenhower and the Republican Party, an effective campaigner who could take the low road, allowing

Eisenhower to stay on the high road." On January 25, 1956, in a press-conference briefing, Ike told Press Secretary James C. Hagerty that "it would be difficult to find a better vice president."[16] In general, he appears to have liked, trusted, and respected Nixon, as well as appreciated his abilities. He essentially proved it by making Nixon the most active vice president in history up to that point, sending him on weighty foreign-policy missions, giving him substantive roles, and seeking his advice on issues and leaders from Castro to Khrushchev.[17]

According to Nixon, Ike told him: "There has never been a job I have given you that you haven't done to perfection as far as I'm concerned. The thing that concerns me is that the public does not realize adequately the job you have done."[18] Various sources seem to confirm Eisenhower's view in this regard. "I was confident that Dick Nixon was highly qualified to take over the duties of the Presidency on a moment's notice," stated Eisenhower after a number of illnesses almost led to such a situation. Shortly before the 1956 election, a time in which pressure mounted in some quarters to "dump Nixon," Ike pacified the vice president by reaffirming his "high regard for him" and appreciation of "all the effective work you've done at my request during the past four years."[19] Ralph De Toledano reported that Ike said privately: "Dick is the most valuable member of my team."[20] William Costello alleged that Eisenhower and Nixon "established an unprecedented intimacy." They saw each other three times a week while Congress was in session, in addition to cabinet and NSC meetings.[21]

As a demonstration of his trustful relationship with Nixon and respect for the vice president's abilities—as well as Ike's innovations regarding the vice president—Eisenhower was the first president to formalize a process for vice-presidential takeover during a period of incapacitation by the commander in chief. The U.S. Constitution does, of course, address the issue of presidential disability and vice-presidential succession. Specifically, Article II, Section 1, Clause 5 of the Constitution states: "In case of the removal of the President from office, or of his death, resignation, or inability to discharge the powers and duties of the said office, the same shall devolve on the Vice President, and the Congress may by law provide for the case of removal, death, resignation, or inability, both of the President and Vice President, declaring what officer shall then act as President, and such officer shall act accordingly, until the disability be removed, or a President shall be elected." However, both Eisenhower and Nixon were troubled by the ambiguity of this clause. "[W]ho decides when the President is unable to discharge the powers and duties of his office?" asked Nixon, "just what devolves upon the Vice President, the 'powers and duties' or the 'office' itself? Can the President resume office once he has given it up? Who decides if the President is well enough to resume his office, if he can at all?" Nixon understandably said that he personally could conceive of "two dozen troublesome contingencies" which might become involved in a process of transition.[22]

As a result, the two men sought a more formal succession process, aside from that in the Constitution. The real prodding behind the initiative to reform the process was Eisenhower, who because of his recent illnesses in particular felt a sense of urgency in addressing the problem. "I felt I should not wait for legislative or amendatory action [by Congress]," Ike stated. "So I decided at once to set up a plan that, for my case would be satisfactory."[23] After studying the problem closely, he decided to write a four-page letter that began "Dear Dick" and spelled out a process. He gave copies for review to Nixon, Attorney General William Rogers, and John Foster Dulles. "With the exception of our very minor suggestions," writes Nixon, "the letter was wholly Eisenhower's in concept and drafting, and it was a masterpiece. Leaving the White House, Bill Rogers remarked that Eisenhower would have made an outstanding lawyer, for the letter handled the contingencies of a very complex problem from every angle and was as good a drafting job as any constitutional expert could have done."[24]

The letter, completed in 1958, set historical precedent. As Stephen W. Stathis notes, Ike had firmly decided when a president's disability warranted the assumption of presidential powers and duties by the vice president. His model was followed by succeeding presidents until the adoption of the 25th amendment, which was fully ratified in February 1967.[25]

Those political scientists and historians who are familiar with Eisenhower's style and impressive organizational processes will not be surprised that he was the first president to set up a formal process for succession. In fact, his tendency toward formalistic machinery is also evident in his general foreign- and security-policy structure.

Nixon's Place within Eisenhower Administration Foreign- and Security-Policy Structure

The linchpin of the Eisenhower administration's foreign- and security-policy framework was the National Security Council. Throughout the years, many scholars have complemented the Eisenhower system. In 1958, Walter Millis commented that Ike "reactivated NSC and infused into it a greater responsibility than it had enjoyed under Truman."[26] He did so by formalizing, developing, and expanding the structure and procedures of the NSC and in effect creating an NSC *system*. In 1964, Stanley L. Falk commented on how Ike successfully institutionalized policy formulation and integration through the NSC.[27] Twenty-five years later, Duncan L. Clarke cited it as among the best-operated NSC systems.[28]

Robert Cutler, Ike's special assistant for national security, worked during the post-election transition on a task force studying ways of reorganizing the NSC. He completed his blueprint before the preinauguration cabinet meeting. Following a modification after a 1953 trial run, the plan was institutionalized for the life of the administration. The NSC was highly articulated in its formal operating procedures, behind which Ike skillfully worked informal procedures. Fred I. Greenstein reports that Eisenhower evolved more systematic formal machinery than that used in any other presidency to shape cabinet agendas and to ensure that participants had advance briefings.[29] Ike's NSC system, like many successful structures, reflected his personal style and preferences. Stanley Falk maintains that the NSC machinery provided an extremely effective means of developing national security policy and the one best suited to the ideas and methods of Eisenhower. "By 1960," states Falk, "the NSC had developed into a highly complicated but nonetheless smoothly operating machine, with clear lines of authority and responsibility and elaborate yet systematized staff work."[30]

The structure of the NSC system was as follows: The council itself met regularly on Thursday mornings and was comprised of five statutory members: the president, vice president, secretaries of state and defense, and the director of the Office of Civil and Defense Mobilization. In addition to the statutory members, others might also be present. Meetings typically included the Budget Director and Secretary of the Treasury. Depending upon the issue, attendees might also include the Attorney General, the administrator of NASA, the chair of the Atomic Energy Commission, the Secretary of Commerce, and various invited private citizens. The CJCS and DCI were there as advisors. Finally, regular observers included a number of undersecretaries and close presidential assistants. As chairman of the council, Eisenhower was directly supported by two White House staff members, the Special Assistant for National Security Affairs and the Special Assistant for Security Operations Coordination. The former was much more important. He was the principal supervisory officer of the NSC. He advised the president on the council agenda and briefed him before each meeting. The Special Assistant for National Security Affairs also presented issues for consideration at each meeting, appointed special committees and consultants (with the president's approval), and supervised the executive secretary in the direction of the NSC staff. He also chaired the council's two principal subgroups: the Planning Board and the Operations Coordinating Board.[31]

Robert Cutler described the NSC structure in the following fashion. The NSC was at the top of the "policy hill." Policy recommendations moved up one side of the hill, through the Planning Board, where they were "thrashed out." After that, the recommendations made by the Planning Board moved up the hill to the NSC, where they were submitted to the president for approval. Following presidential approval, the new policy traveled "down the other side of the policy hill to the departments and agencies responsible for its execution." A short distance down the slope was the OCB, to which the president referred the new policy for coordination and operational planning with the relevant departments and agencies. (Below these two main subgroups were the Interdepartmental Intelligence Conference, the Interdepartmental Committee on Internal Security, and other special ad hoc committees.)[32]

The Planning Board of the NSC met regularly on Tuesday and Friday afternoons. The membership was comprised mainly of officials at the assistant secretary level. Advisors from JCS and CIA were usually present, as were observers from other interested agencies.[33]

Once Eisenhower made his decision, it was the OCB's function to coordinate and integrate the activities of those departments and agencies responsible for executing the new policy. While the OCB had no authority to direct or control those activities, it provided a means for allowing the responsible departments and agencies to consult and cooperate with one another. The OCB's primary functions were limited to advising, expediting, and following up on previous policy decisions and actions. However, most OCB members were on the undersecretary level, meaning each had enough authority within their own agencies to ensure the board's wishes were carried out. The board acted as the coordinating and integrating arm of the NSC for all aspects of the implementation of national security policy. It met regularly on Wednesdays at the State Department.[34]

As a statutory member of the NSC, Vice President Nixon was assured some level of foreign-policy involvement within Eisenhower's foreign- and security-policy framework. As the following pages show, the NSC presence did increase his ability to influence the administration's foreign-policy process. Yet, Nixon's role in the administration's framework could have been exceptionally more prominent from a historical point of view, further bolstering his foreign-policy role. For instance, at the beginning of the second Eisenhower term, Herbert Hoover, Jr., an undersecretary of state who chaired the OCB, was planning to resign his chairmanship. Protocol established that the next undersecretary of state, Christian Herter, would automatically fill the position. Nixon's internal supporters pushed to have the vice president take over the seat. Herter was willing to waive his rights to the position in favor of Nixon. This started a minor skirmish within the administration. Eventually, Ike and Dulles decided against Nixon taking over the post.[35]

There are a number of questions that can be asked about this incident, although a lack of complete information makes many of these questions primarily speculative. For instance, did Ike or Dulles find Nixon too aggressive in seeking the greater role? Did Ike and Dulles clash with Nixon over the OCB issue? If not, why not? Dulles, in particular, could be quite territorial at times. The answers are not clear.

Yet, judging from the limited amount of evidence on this subject, the president's decision on this matter seemed to be based upon a fairly simple premise: Ike, who had been extremely open in allowing Nixon a strong foreign-policy role, felt that taking over the OCB was simply beyond the scope of what the vice president should do. "The vice president has statutory constitutional duties," he said. "It would be impossible as a matter of practice to give, within the executive department, the vice president specified duties because if you happen to have a vice president who disagrees with you, then you would have ... an impossible situation. ... I don't know of any vice president that has ever been given the great opportunities to participate in difficult decisions, conferences, and every kind of informative meeting that we have than Mr. Nixon. But I decided as a matter of good governmental organization that it would not be correct to give him a governmental position in the executive department."[36] In clarifying Ike's rationale on this matter, the citation is instructive regarding the "vice-president-who-disagrees-with-you" point. Ike likely feared a scenario where a potential "firing" of his vice president from an OCB chairmanship could backfire against the president politically by possibly alienating Nixon's considerable constituency. These issues and Eisenhower's reasoning on them will be revisited in the final chapter on lessons learned and policy recommendations.

The preceding analysis of Nixon's place in the foreign- and security-policy structure provides hints into how he would be used in general in the area of foreign policy.

Nixon's Foreign-Policy Role

During his two terms as vice president, Nixon regularly attended all meetings of the cabinet and the National Security Council. Eisenhower had Nixon preside over all cabinet and NSC meetings in his absence (not just during times of illness). He made this change at the very start of the administration. This was a major break from tradition. Previously, the secretary of state had assumed the responsibility of presiding over NSC meetings in the president's absence.[37] Nixon presided over nineteen cabinet meetings and twenty-six NSC meetings.[38] He read the president's daily intelligence reports and had access to all secret information.[39]

The vice president would ultimately travel some 160,000 miles to fifty-five countries as Eisenhower's emissary.[40] Some of these trips, of course, were ceremonial. In many such instances, however, the vice president fulfilled a role as a foreign-policy spokesman for the administration, as will be seen in the many examples listed below.[41] Moreover, by and large the Eisenhower administration believed Nixon was an astute and intelligent member of the foreign-policy team and usually tried to set up substantive duties when he made trips that originated with a ceremonial purpose. Ike felt that the vice president "had a special talent for understanding and summing up the views of others."[42] Evidence of this will be seen in the cases below on Castro and Khrushchev, in particular. This view of the vice president gained currency as the administration went on.[43]

A truly revolutionary example of the stepped up foreign-policy role given two Nixon was established in a two-page memo sent to him by Eisenhower on September 3, 1957. Earl Mazo and Stephen Hess accurately maintain that the memo "for the first time in history assigned a vice president a major role in foreign policy." The memo stated:

> My basic thought is that you might find it possible—and intriguing—to be of even more help in our whole governmental program dealing with affairs abroad than you have been in the past. By your extensive travels you have been of inestimable assistance to the Secretary of State and to me. In addition you have gained an understanding of our foreign problems that is both unusual and comprehensive. My belief is that this knowledge and comprehension, supplemented by your special position of having one foot in the legislative branch, can be advantageously used in helping to lay out advanced programs and schedules.[44]

The memo from Eisenhower outlined additional responsibilities he wanted the vice president to assume in trade policy, foreign aid, mutual assistance, and monetary and defense policies. It is likely no coincidence that Vice President Nixon's three most significant foreign-policy activities—his meeting with Castro and trips to Latin America and the Soviet Union— all took place after this memo.

As a further indication of Nixon's increased role in foreign policy—as well as the nature of the hostile, complex, and "nonisolationist" times—he was later provided with two national security aides. In 1957, Admiral Arthur Radford, chairman of the Joint Chiefs of Staff, arranged for the vice president to have military aides—making him the first second-office holder in history to have such assistants.[45] He was assigned two junior officers from the Pentagon: Major J. D. Hughes, who served the vice president as appointments secretary, and Marine Colonel Robert E. Cushman, who acted as assistant for national security matters.

Nixon's foreign-policy tasks translated into influence. A reading of any account of Eisenhower administration deliberations on foreign and security policy issues usually features the vice president providing input into the advisory process, often influencing the president's decisions.[46] Nixon participated actively in NSC and cabinet discussions.[47] On foreign policy in general, Ike said that he "often talked" with the vice president about his ideas "and he had helped me to put them into practice."[48] Ike personally referred to Nixon as one of his "principal advisors," who "never hesitated . . . to express his opinion in terms of recommendations as to decision. . . . Mr. Nixon has taken a full part in every principal discussion."[49]

The substantive duties Eisenhower granted Nixon in the area of foreign policy were impressive and unprecedented at the time. This, mind you, was a time when vice presidents had low expectations and were not taken seriously by pundits, the public, and even high-level officials. It is a credit to both Eisenhower and Nixon that the vice president became so involved in foreign policy during the latter 1950s. Listed below are some of Vice President Nixon's foreign-policy activities. First provided are brief descriptions of some of his foreign-policy tasks, followed by two lengthy examples: Latin America and Soviet policy. The broader foreign-policy "tasks"—emissary abroad, foreign-policy spokesman, campaign attack dog, and congressional liaison—often featured duties that involved domestic issues as well. For instance, the vice president acted as a spokesman and congressional liaison on both domestic and foreign issues. The below examples focus on cases in which these tasks crossed into foreign policy.

Emissary Abroad: First Trip Overseas

Ike utilized Nixon as an emissary to foreign nations, a role he relished and that helped turn him into the guru of foreign policy he became. In 1953 the vice president made a 38,000-mile, 72-day round-the-world trip—his first overseas mission—that began in the Far East. The trip was intended to underscore the administration's foreign-policy goals. "His task had been to help convince our Asian friends that the United States was as fully concerned about their needs and dangers as we were about Europe," recalled Ike. "It had been a highly successful mission. Through his observations and conferences, the Vice President had acquired knowledge and understanding of the areas visited, valuable to us in the formulation of our policies."[50] Nixon, who had been plagued by poor showings in the opinion polls ever since he joined the Eisenhower ticket, believed that his "stock soared" after the trip.[51]

Foreign-Policy Spokesman: The Indochina Speech

The emissary role is a bit more advanced than the foreign-policy spokesman role. The former tends to involve some discussion with high-level officials abroad, fact-finding duties, and sometimes even negotiating, whereas the latter usually entails giving a speech or announcing a key foreign-policy objective.

Typically, a major mission overseas will involve both elements, as seen below in Nixon's Moscow mission. This Indochina incident would fall under the spokesman role, in which the vice president was at home giving his view on a particular global situation—and a sensitive one at that.

As Ike himself stated, by all accounts Nixon's foreign-policy tasks were performed exceptionally in terms of executing the administration's goals and the vice president's duties. One exception was a series of remarks he made concerning Indochina in 1954. Although he made only a brief misstatement, his remarks rightly caused quite a stir.

Nixon gave a number of speeches that afforded him opportunities to speak up on major foreign-policy issues. One example in which he almost wrongly committed the administration was an April 16, 1954 off-the-record remark made after a speech before the American Society of Newspaper Editors, where Nixon was asked whether he thought the United States should send troops to Indochina if the French decided to withdraw from the area. He replied that if sending U.S. troops was the only way to avoid communist expansion in Asia, "I believe that the executive branch of the government has to take the politically unpopular position of facing up to it and doing it, and I personally would support such a decision."[52] (The media, possibly believing the comments were too important, decided to report them anyway.)

The statement was greeted by uproar.[53] Nixon did not mention the participation of Congress nor allies, thus seemingly representing a major shift in U.S. policy.[54] The administration had to smooth over the misstatement by Nixon.[55] Secretary of State Dulles sought to quell anxieties by saying that such action by U.S. troops was "unlikely." There were suspicions that the administration had asked Nixon to make the remarks as a trial balloon to test public reaction, although such assertions were denied.[56] Most accounts suggest that Nixon had stepped out of bounds and made a mistake. As shall be seen in the proceeding chapters—including those on Mondale, Bush, and Quayle—vice presidents are susceptible to foreign-policy mishaps, perhaps stemming from their lack of training in the art of diplomacy.

Campaign Attack Dog on Foreign-Policy Issues

Another popular vice-presidential role that almost falls under the umbrage of the foreign-policy spokesman is that of campaign "attack dog," particularly when the attack-dog role involves foreign-policy issues, as it often does. As Joel K. Goldstein notes, the most common activity of the vice president during presidential campaigns is to blast the president's political opponents; this can include international issues, especially unseemly ones that the president might be "reluctant" to turn into a "campaign issue." Subsequently, the vice president is often chosen for that role, as opposed to the president or presidential nominee, who refrains from such activities for the purpose of appearing statesmanlike.[57] In this vein, Nixon, as Ike's running mate, assumed this sort of "attack dog" role during campaigns.

In 1952, the vice-presidential nominee hammered away at the "mess in Washington" and legacy of "communism, Korea, and corruption" that President Truman had allegedly left and was being picked up by the Adlai Stevenson-Democratic ticket. Foreign policy was a major campaign issue, especially Truman's policies in Korea and China. The spread of communism was so high on the campaign agenda that Nixon even concluded his historic "Checkers" speech with a reference to communism: "Just let me say this last word: Regardless of what happens, I am going to continue this fight. I am going to campaign up and down America until we drive the crooks and Communists and those that defend them out of Washington." During the 1954 midterm elections, Nixon continued to attack the Democrats as the party of Korea, communism, and corruption. He traveled 26,000 miles through ninety-five cities in thirty-one states.[58] Ambrose writes that Ike appreciated the fact that Nixon was "an effective campaigner who could take the low road, allowing Eisenhower to stay on the high road."[59]

Congressional Liaison on Foreign-Policy Issues

The vice president was helpful to Eisenhower in ways beyond his attack-dog and spokesman duties. His congressional experience allowed him to serve Ike in a unique way also. Nixon was automatically included among all White House meetings with legislative leaders.[60] He attended the weekly meetings with the congressional leadership.[61] As Ralph de Toledano notes, Nixon was the only cabinet member who had been a member of Congress. As a result, other members looked to him to assess the legislative and domestic political prospects of White House policy matters. Also, constitutionally, the vice president presided over the Senate. This all combined to allow Nixon to serve as the administration's representative in the Senate and as the Senate's ambassador to the White House. "When legislation important to the administration was up before the Senate," writes de Toledano, "and passage was a touch-and-go matter, Nixon got to work."[62]

In *Eisenhower: The Inside Story*, Robert J. Donovan stated that it was in the political field, particularly in his maneuvers involving Congress, that Vice President Nixon's help was most sought by the president and his staff.[63] "The president," wrote Donovan, "welcomes Nixon's judgment on how certain proposals will be received in Congress. Occasionally someone at the White House will telephone Nixon at the Capitol and say that the president would like to know what he thinks about a measure under consideration." In the cabinet and NSC the president looked to Nixon "to reflect the Congressional viewpoint and raise a red flag" when a policy recommendation did not adequately consider the political ramifications or roadblocks it might face.[64] Ike referred to Nixon as a "troubleshooter" on the politics of issues (much like, as will be seen, the role fulfilled by Mondale in the Carter administration, although to a lesser degree by Nixon).

To further illustrate the level of Nixon's foreign-policy involvement, the following pages illuminate his role in two separate cases: administration policy in Latin America, including with emerging Castro forces in Cuba; and White House policy toward the Soviet Union, which involved a very personal and unorthodox role for Nixon in dealing with Nikita Khrushchev. Additionally, as will be seen, these two larger case studies often featured the duties just discussed. (This format—in which the aforementioned help set the stage for specific foreign-policy assignments discussed in greater detail below—applies for all the "profile" chapters.)

Latin America Policy and Cuba

Cuba

Before examining Nixon's role in broader administration policy in Latin America, this section first considers the intriguing duties performed by the vice president regarding the administration's crucial and delicate handling of Fidel Castro's emergence in Cuba.

The administration had been deeply concerned about communist influence in Latin America. One location in which the establishment of a communist influence could not be tolerated was Cuba, an island only seventy miles south of Key West, Florida. For some time, the corrupt leadership in Cuba had been pro-American. Now, however, that nation's dictator, Fulgencio Batista, was being undermined by a dynamic young rebel leader named Fidel Castro. The Eisenhower administration was concerned about what Castro might do once he became the leader of Cuba. At the worst, it feared the island becoming a Soviet satellite.

Many in the United States were becoming enamored by the rebel leader, romanticizing him as a Third World revolutionary who would bring social justice to the tiny island. Eisenhower, Nixon, and others in the administration, already skeptical, became even more bothered when Castro in February 1958 announced a two-year postponement of the election he previously promised. On March 26, Allen Dulles reported to Ike that "the Castro regime is moving toward a complete dictatorship. Communists are now operating openly and legally in Cuba. And though Castro's government is *not* communist-dominated, communists have worked their way into the labor unions, the armed forces, and other organizations." The president, continually irked by what he viewed as kid-glove treatment of Castro by the U.S. media, became even more irritated when he learned that the American Society of Newspaper Editors had invited the rebel leader to come to Washington to give a speech at the National Press Club on April 17.[65]

In this context, Eisenhower gave to his vice president a crucial foreign-policy responsibility that should not be underestimated in its importance: Nixon would meet with Castro during his U.S. visit and try to gain insight into the Cuban leader's true intentions and personal views. Why did Ike give such a key assignment to his vice president? Was it because it was important or distasteful? The president's memoirs do not make clear precisely why he assigned to Nixon such an important task.[66] However, Ike did seem to perceive the meeting as important, even if he did or did not view it as a "distasteful" (my word) assignment. In my view, Ike may have delegated this job to the vice president because, as he said, he felt Nixon had always been especially adept at "understanding and summing up the views of others." The subsequent, below-listed memo written by Nixon on his meeting with Castro reflects the view that the vice president personally felt his goal was to assess and sum up the intentions, mindset, and general philosophy of the Cuban leader. Also, as noted earlier, Ike was impressed by Nixon's ability to carefully and fairly dissect and assess people and situations. Recall that in choosing Nixon as his running mate the president commented thusly regarding how Congressman Nixon had handled the Alger Hiss case. For these reasons, perhaps, Ike chose Nixon to carry out the Castro task. Moreover, of course, it is clear that Ike would not hand such an important assignment to his vice president unless he had a very high degree of confidence in his abilities.

Whatever Ike's motivation, Nixon held a three-hour meeting with Castro on April 19, a Sunday afternoon. No staff members or photographers were present.[67] Of all the meetings that Castro had during his Washington visit, Jeffrey J. Safford aptly notes that the one he had with Vice President Nixon was "the most significant of these meetings."[68] The meeting and Nixon's subsequent assessment of Castro would be highly influential in forming the administration's official view of the rebel leader and the fate of his revolution on the Caribbean island.

Following the meeting, Nixon wrote a confidential memorandum for distribution to the CIA (directed to DCI Allen Dulles), the State Department (John Foster Dulles and Christian Herter), President Eisenhower, and Senate Majority Whip Mike Mansfield.[69] In the memo, Nixon admits to being somewhat ambivalent and confused by Castro's statements during the meeting. The vice president actually seemed somewhat sympathetic to Castro. He was, however, convinced that the rebel leader was "either incredibly naive about communism or under communist discipline."[70] "My own appraisal of him as a man is somewhat mixed," wrote Nixon in the memo. "Whatever we may think of him he is going to be a great factor in the development of Cuba and very possibly in Latin American affairs generally." The vice president concluded: "He seems to be sincere, he is either incredibly naive about communism or under communist discipline—my guess is the former and I have already implied his ideas as to how to run a government or an economy are less developed than those of almost any world figure I have met in fifty countries. . . . The one fact that we can be sure of is that he has those indefinable qualities which make him a leader of men."[71] Eisenhower later acknowledged Nixon's contribution, asserting that, "Subsequent events more and more confirmed the Vice President's opinion."[72]

While many scholars have since interpreted Nixon's memorandum as seeming to endorse a nonhostile approach to dealing with Castro, the fact is that he became rather hawkish in believing that the Cuban leader should be overthrown. The vice president understood that such a position "was a minority one within the administration and particularly so within the Latin American branch of the State Department." Specifically, the vice president advocated and steadfastly pushed Eisenhower to accept a plan to allow the CIA to provide arms, ammunition, and training for Cubans who had fled the Castro regime and were now in exile in the United States and elsewhere in Latin America. Nixon said that he had pushed for such a policy for nine months before it was endorsed in early 1960.[73] K. S. Karol credits Nixon's assessment of Castro as triggering a shift in the Eisenhower administration from accommodation to hostility.[74]

Importantly, however, Historian Stephen Ambrose perceives a political motivation in the vice president's policy preference. He says that Nixon, like many Republican leaders at the time, was desperate for administration action against Castro before the November 1960 presidential elections—which, of course, featured Nixon as the GOP's nominee. Nonetheless, Eisenhower refused, fearing a backlash throughout Latin America if the administration were perceived to be trying "to accomplish our aims [in Cuba] by force . . . we would see all of [the Latin American countries] tending to fall away and some would be communist within two years. . . . If the United States does not conduct itself in precisely the right way vis-à-vis Cuba, we could lose all of South America."[75] (It is not clear if Ike minded the disagreement with Nixon on this issue, nor how he dealt with it. Apparently, however, the president did not seem to agonize over the disagreement with Nixon.) Ike was, however, ready to move covertly against Castro.

Nixon's moves here are instructive for how the vice president is used in foreign policy. While his initial duties in assessing Castro seemed to have been carried out as ordered by Ike, his later actions regarding how the administration should react to Castro may—as Ambrose argues—have been heavily motivated by his own personal political fortunes. This stands in contrast to the premise by many scholars that the vice president can be a valuable asset in foreign affairs because he allegedly lacks selfish-parochial interests. While the vice president may be a valuable asset in foreign policy, it is foolish to argue that such is the case because he is uncorrupted by selfish interests. In reality, politics drives the actions of some vice presidents.

Yet, the vice president's policy prescription for dealing with Castro also presented an interesting problem for Nixon politically. We typically perceive the vice presidency as an effective stepping stone to the presidency—which it is, as proven by the fact that ten of the last twelve presidential elections has witnessed a former vice president as one of the two parties' nominee for president. However, sitting vice presidents who are running for the presidency often face constraints on which aspects of administration policy they can speak about or comment upon on the campaign trial.[76] A prominent example of this was Vice President Hubert Humphrey's inability to lash out at the Johnson administration's Vietnam policy during the 1968 presidential race, to the chagrin of himself and his supporters.[77] In the Castro-Cuba situation, Nixon faced a similar problem. "This issue is an excellent illustration of the disadvantage that confronts a candidate who also represents an incumbent administration," Nixon rightly acknowledged.[78]

As noted, the vice president had long urged a stronger policy against Castro within the administration after his April 1959 meeting with the rebel leader, and had succeeded in gaining one. However, the program he supported for eliminating Castro was covert. Although the program had been in operation for six months before the 1960 campaign got underway, the vice president was not allowed to speak a word about it. As a result, Democratic presidential nominee John F. Kennedy was able to talk tough about how to control Castro and Cuba, while Republican nominee Nixon could only quietly sit by and listen. "I knew we had a program under way to deal with Castro," states Nixon, "but I could not even hint at its existence, much less spell it out. . . . Under no circumstances could it be disclosed or even alluded to."[79] Hence, Kennedy looked assertive on the Cuba issue while Nixon appeared passive and weak. It must have been killing Nixon inside to remain silent on a policy that he was out in front on.

Latin America

The administration viewed Cuba primarily through a Cold War lens that placed the island as a key location within the bipolar struggle between the United States and the Soviet Union. In turn, it applied such a perspective toward Latin America in general.

According to Nixon, of all the trips abroad he made as vice president he was (initially) least excited about a request that he visit South America in 1958. He felt the projects he was working on in Washington at the time were more important and interesting, particularly after hearing the initial rationale for his visit. Early in March that year, Roy R. Rubottom, Jr., the assistant secretary of state for Latin American affairs, approached Nixon and asked him to represent the United States at the inauguration of Arturo Frondizi as the new president of Argentina. A number of dignitaries from all over the globe would be present for the occasion. Rubottom presented to the vice president the following reasons why he should attend:

- South America needed U.S. recognition at the highest level
- Argentina was a symbol of a possible changing tide toward democracy in the region
- Juan Peron had been among the most iron fisted of dictators and had been overthrown
- it was the first free election in twenty years in Argentina

Rubottom, said Nixon, felt the vice president should go to dispel the widespread impression in Latin America that the United States had sympathized with Peron. The vice president rejected the request. "I told Rubottom that I could see the merits of his arguments but I could not spare the time for a trip outside the country because of my current heavy work load in Washington," Nixon explained. "Also, I did not believe that a 'purely protocol' trip which Rubottom had described, where I would be one of sixty or seventy dignitaries from foreign countries, would afford enough of an opportunity for serious constructive conversation with the new government leaders to justify my leaving my duties in Washington." Apparently, Rubottom was not satisfied and began looking for ways to sweeten the kitty. The next evening, said Nixon, John Foster Dulles unexpectedly dropped in at the vice president's home to argue that it was "essential" for the administration's foreign policy not only for the vice president to appear at Frondizi's inauguration but also to arrange an extensive tour of several key Latin American countries. The next day, the president, after a cabinet meeting had ended, asked Nixon to stick around for a few minutes and step into his office. He mentioned that he had been speaking to Secretary of State Dulles and his brother, Milton Eisenhower, and they felt a tour of Latin America at that time by Nixon would be of considerable long-range benefit to the nation.[80]

By the time Rubottom's behind-the-scenes lobbying had finished, the vice president was suddenly faced with a very interesting mission that involved duties well beyond the ceremonial. Soon added to the list were all the nations in South America except Brazil. A large group of reporters, ambassadors, and other figures would accompany Nixon. The vice president spent the next few weeks boning up on the region via volumes of memoranda and papers and countless briefings by the State Department, CIA, and various experts. Allen Dulles informed Nixon of intelligence estimates on possible anti-American demonstrations in two or three of the capitals he was to visit, "But there were no intimations of any possible violence." In reality, this piece of advice would be the most flawed, understated, and dangerous of all the information Nixon received in preparing for his mission. As the following demonstrates, the trip turned out to be an abject failure on the intelligence side.[81] "No journey ever started out in a less exciting way and ended more dramatically than this one to South America," he later recalled.[82]

The first official stop of Nixon's eighteen-day visit was Montevido, Uruguay, where the vice president would get his first minor taste of what would intensify into greater hostility as he went from country to country. The communist movement in Latin America had eagerly awaited Nixon's visit and pulled out all the stops. They made plans in each city for disruptions, protests, jeering, and even violence against the vice president.[83] As a result, the Nixon team was constantly updating its plans in a manner that eluded communist agitators and did not give them time to set up. Whenever possible, the location and times of his appearances were kept secret so, according to Nixon, the "hard core of communist agitators would have no advance of my coming." In part, this was fine with Nixon anyway. One of his greatest political tactics, evident in every foreign trip he made, was to pull off in his limousine and make an impromptu appearance among unexpected crowds he came across. This gave him an opportunity to talk to people one on one and usually (it appears) left a terrific impression with everyday people.[84]

On the next morning, the vice president's motorcade was moving toward the airport when it approached the local university. Nixon saw a number of students on the grounds and ordered the car stopped. Along with Mrs. Nixon, the ambassador, Colonel Vernon Walters (along as Nixon's interpreter), and a secret service agent, the vice president headed for the law school. "Events worked out as I had hoped they would," Nixon remembered. "Word that I was there spread like wildfire through the school. Students swarmed around, asking for autographs, shaking hands as I moved into one of the law school classrooms." The vice president then told the students assembled that he was ready and willing to answer all questions they had about U.S. policy toward Uruguay and other Latin American countries. "For almost an hour they questioned me about alleged U.S. imperialism, unfair trade practices, economic exploitation, and support of dictatorships in South America," Nixon recalled. He asserted: "No problem between the United States and Uruguay, real or imagined, was overlooked or bypassed, and because of my intensive briefing, I was able to answer each one directly and honestly." One report describes how the vice president "easily bested" a twenty-six-year-old communist leader who debated him from the audience.[85]

Nixon contends that the stop was a rousing success, not only because he allegedly left to a standing ovation but because the communists were taken by surprise and failed to adequately disrupt the meeting. "The Communists, of course, could not take this lying down and toward the end of the session they got in some of their typical questions," Nixon remembered. "But they had not had time to pack the audience." The communist leaders quickly marshaled their forces and were able to distribute some of their literature while shouting anti-American slogans as Nixon exited. But, claimed the happy vice president, "they ran into a hornet's nest of opposition. The students were so overwhelmingly on our side that they tore up the pamphlets, shouted down the hecklers and called out at the tops of their voices in Spanish, 'Long live United States and Uruguayan friendship.'"[86] Nonetheless, the vice president would never again be so lucky.

Nixon left Uruguay for a fairly uneventful trip to three other countries. He then went on to Lima, Peru, where he intended to speak at San Marcos University. "It was apparent that the Communists," says Nixon, "after the failure of their efforts to disrupt my tour in Uruguay, Argentina, or Bolivia, had decided to make an all-out effort to embarrass me and the United States at San Marco University." While attempting to speak at San Marcos University in Lima, a mob of students organized by local communist leaders pelted him with stones as his car drove away. Throughout the previous night anti-American crowds protested outside his hotel.[87]

The context for his talk at the university began like his Uruguay discussion. He stepped out of the car in an impromptu fashion and instructed a pleasantly surprised group of students that he would like to talk to them and answer any complaints they had against the United States. At first, said Nixon, the strategy seemed to again take hold. "Some of the younger students started to quiet down," Nixon recalled. "But the older ones in the rear, the ringleaders, saw what was happening. They tried to whip up a frenzy again, egging the younger students on. . . . They shouted insults at those who shook hands with me. There were only a few leaders—the usual case-hardened, cold-eyed Communist operatives." This time, the ringleaders won.[88]

As members of Nixon's crew began getting hit in the head by rocks, they decided to back out, get in the car, and drive away. In what must have been a sight to behold, Nixon, with the American ambassador bracing his legs, stood up on the rear seat as the car moved away. The vice president then shouted, with Vernon Walters translating in rapid-fire Spanish, "You are cowards, you are afraid of the truth! You are the worst kind of cowards." The vice president felt a sense of victory in that no one had been seriously injured and the incident proved that the communists had to stoop to violence to prevent a free discussion of ideas.[89]

The situation could have been much worse. Nixon's visit to Peru had been marred by expectations of severe mob violence aimed at the vice president at San Marcos. The threats were so serious, and local police protection so bad, that a number of the vice president's staffers felt he should decline the invitation. Yet, Nixon and some staffers felt that refusing to show up would give the communists a moral victory and send a signal to the world that the United States, in

Nixon's words, was "putting its tail between its legs and running away from a bunch of communist thugs." The vice president decided to do the speech. He later stated: "I gave little thought to the possibility of personal injury to myself not because I was 'being brave' but because such considerations just were not important in view of the larger issues involved."[90] In the end, of course, Nixon survived, but not without a good scare.

As impossible as it may sound, Nixon's final stop in Caracas, Venezuela, was even worse than Lima. Nixon arrived amid CIA reports of rumors that communists planned to assassinate him.[91] Yet, the vice president was assured that the situation was safe. He stated: "Right up until our arrival . . . the Venezuelan officials reported that everything was completely under control." The Nixons were greeted by a hostile mob at the airport. They descended the staircase abutting the plane and were subject to loud boos. "I was very surprised in one respect," Nixon told Earl Mazo and Stephen Hess, in a biography of his pre-presidential political career. "I expected placards, but I was surprised that they allowed the airport to be completely dominated by the Commies and their stooges." The Venezuelan chief of security, sensing Nixon was worried, assured him, "Oh, they are just kids. They are harmless." As Nixon and his wife stood for the playing of the Venezuelan anthem, crowds standing at the observation deck showered them with spit and garbage. After American agents were able to clear a path, Nixon got into the first car with the foreign minister, while his wife, Pat, got in the other car. In travel to their destination, they viewed altered placards which, once stating, "Fuera [go home] Nixon," had been painted over to tellingly read, "Muera [death to] Nixon."[92]

About four blocks from their first destination, the vice president's car got stuck in a traffic jam in the city. Hundreds of people suddenly came storming at the car and pelted it with stones and horse dung, hammered it with pipes and sticks, rocked it back and forth, and tried to turn it over. Amazingly, as soon as the mob became visible, the Venezuelan escort, police, and security detail fled the scene, leaving the U.S. secret service alone to fight the mob. Nixon described the drama:

> [T]he first rock hit the car window, lodging itself in the glass and spraying us with tiny slivers. One sliver hit the Foreign Minister in the eye, and he started to bleed heavily. He tried to stop the blood, moaning over and over, "This is terrible. This is terrible."
>
> I saw a thug with an iron pipe work his way up to the car. He was looking right at me as he began trying to break the window. Once again the glass held, but flying slivers hit Walters in the mouth. Both Sherwood and I caught some in the face. Suddenly the car began to move, and the idea that we had somehow broken free gave me a surge of relief. Then I realized that the crowd was rocking the car back and forth—slower and higher each time. I remembered that it was a common tactic for mobs to

turn a car over and then set it on fire.

I believe that at that moment, for the first time, each of us in the car realized we might actually be killed. . . .

Suddenly Sherwood pulled out his revolver and said, "Let's get some of these sons of bitches." I told him to hold his fire. Once a gun went off the crowd would go berserk and that would be the end of us.[93]

Mazo and Hess dramatically reported that the principal objective of the mob was to open the car doors and rip the vice president apart limb by limb, which is considered the most degrading death possible by Venezuelan standards. Nixon later commented that he had never before seen such hate in the eyes of people: "This was a killer mob. They were completely out of hand, and I imagine some were doped up to a certain extent."[94] Luckily, the press truck out front managed to clear open a path and the vice president's vehicle was able to break free and drive off to the embassy. The next move by Nixon was extremely fortunate. As they headed for their first destination, a wreath-laying ceremony, Nixon decided to abandon the plan and route altogether and ordered a quick right-turn detour. He figured that the previous event may have been an indication that the organizers of the ruckus had probably found out about his route and that even worse trouble might lay ahead. He later found out that his hunch was right.

"That decision," said Mazo and Hess, "saved his life and Mrs. Nixon's." Indeed, the first incident was merely intended to wet the appetite of the planners. At a plaza not far ahead, a well disciplined crowd awaited with a plan and mission in place to kill Mr. and Mrs. Nixon. First, a large group of 100 or more was to barrage the cars with rocks and fruit. A unit of hardened experts was then to follow through with homemade bombs. Venezuelan investigators later procured a full copy of the murder plot while searching the home of a female communist functionary near the plaza. Officials found a cache of about 400 Molotov cocktails under the steps of the functionary's home, stacked neatly and primed for reissue.[95]

The situation was still not resolved. The vice president's team decided to hole up in the embassy and figure out how to escape back to the airport as soon as possible. Mazo and Hess commented on how the Venezuela trip was quickly transformed into a "commando operation." At the White House, Ike was furious. Nothing like this had ever happened before. He ordered the Pentagon to prepare for action.[96] Ike later noted how Nixon's confrontation with the "howling and ugly mob" incited him to order a thousands troops flown to Guantanamo Bay and Puerto Rico, "ready to move in and rescue the Vice President and Mrs. Nixon if necessary." (Ike said that he commented to his wife Mamie that evening: "Maybe I should be digging out my uniforms to see whether they still fit.")[97] The marines were readied, as were Air Force jet-bomber, fighter and fighter-bomber units in a plan with the code name "Operation Poor Richard."

"By nightfall," wrote Mazo and Hess, "America's military might was poised for the liveliest and most bizarre rescue mission of all time." In the end, Nixon was able to escape without a large-scale military effort, although his extraction did not come easy. The next day the Venezuelan government had to use tear gas to vacate the streets in order to clear a route for the vice president back to the airport.[98]

As far as I'm aware, no other vice president in the history of the United States has ever been subjected to such harsh treatment abroad—certainly not any of the other four in this study. Obviously, no other ever came under such a physical assault.[99]

The original intention of Nixon's trip was overshadowed by the aforementioned drama. Nonetheless, when he returned he offered a number of insights and policy recommendations. On the former, he obviously had come away with a heightened understanding and appreciation of how strongly certain forces were working in the region on behalf of communism. This he successfully intimated to Eisenhower and others. Ike felt the trip "brought home to all of us the clear truth that . . . the threat of communism in Latin America is greater than ever before."[100] Nixon also felt that the people and government of the United States had been taking Latin America for granted, and that his trip would be a real wake-up call in that respect: "Caracas was a much-needed shock treatment which jolted us out of dangerous complacency. . . . The Caracas crisis was so sharp and so dramatic that it could not be brushed away so easily."[101] Specifically, here are some of the vice president's policy recommendations:[102]

- "We should not appear to give dictators, of either the right or the left, the same moral approval that we gave to leaders who were trying to build free and democratic institutions."

- "American government personnel abroad must do a more effective job of reaching the opinion-makers of Latin America. It is no longer enough simply to know and talk to top government officials and the elite among the financial and business communities. Students, teachers, newspaper editors, reporters, labor leaders—these are the people who are exerting massive influence in the Latin American countries, and we must find a way to get our story across to them more adequately. Person-to-person contact is the most effective way to accomplish this. USIA broadcasts and giving publicity to public statements by U.S. officials, are generally ineffective."

- "We must develop an economic program for Latin America which is distinctly its own. Latin Americans do not like to be classed like the undeveloped countries of Asia and Africa. They believe they are in a special position and are therefore entitled to special consideration, because of their geographical proximity to the United States, and their long record of friendship for this nation. There must be a new program for economic progress for the hemisphere."

- Argentina: "When I returned to Washington I recommended all-out cooperation with Frondizi and his government. As I flew from Argentina to Paraguay, I realized that Rubottom had been right. My four days in Argentina alone had been worth the trip."

On the policy side, the vice president's trip allowed him to engage in substantive meetings with high-level officials and to provide a number of policy recommendations upon his return. Many of the recommendations suggest that the harsh treatment he received affected him. While Nixon the vice president said that some were "implemented," he does not specify which.[103] Again, however, Ike's writings illustrate that he internalized a number of lessons from the trip. Moreover, Mazo and Hess contend that, "In the six months after his 1958 trip there was more positive action than ever before in United States relations with its southern neighbors." Indeed, there were many changes that put into place what Nixon recommended. Emphasis was placed on cultivating influential elements in universities and labor unions, promoting economic development, and pointing the impact of United States information projects and propaganda at the worst sore spots of misunderstanding.[104] Specifically, the student exchange program was doubled. After years of reluctance, the United States joined the international agency for stabilizing coffee prices. The Export-Import Bank was authorized to lend an additional $2 billion. Loans and grants were speeded up.[105] There were a number of other changes. Nixon's trip had affected policy.

Politically and personally, rather than hurting the vice president, the trip carried him to an all-time high in popularity. The shaky overseas incidents allowed him to display a braveness and toughness that was hailed by most Americans, as reflected in opinion polls.[106] Ike felt the trip was a success and especially appreciated the vice president's boldness in the face of such humiliation and apprehension.[107]

Soviet Policy and Khrushchev

A trip that took place not long after the Latin America mission, and also gave the vice president a chance to participate in substantive meetings, analysis and evaluation, not to mention yet another flare for the dramatic, was Nixon's Moscow mission of 1959. Many of the vice president's trips overseas constituted fact-finding missions that involved him assessing key foreign-policy situations and being debriefed by President Eisenhower upon his return.[108] This trip was all of that and much more. As Jules Witcover notes, the trip would provide the vice president with "near celebrity status."[109] (Nixon had generally been a quite unpopular vice president among the public, and a liability to Eisenhower as a whole, until his second-term trips to Latin American and the Soviet Union.)

The principal justification for the vice president's trip was to open the first United States "exhibition" ever held in the Soviet Union, on July 24 in Sokolniki Park in Moscow. The exhibition was a main feature of a broader cultural exchange program which had been adopted in the "spirit of Geneva" as an attempt to thaw out relations between the two countries. Seven months earlier, Nixon had presided at the opening of the Soviet Union's exhibition in New York. The Soviet exhibition had featured a model of the new Sputnik, boasted about the nation's technological advances, and heavily emphasized the Kremlin's military prowess. The American exhibition in Sokolniki Park, the brainchild of a Los Angeles businessman, stressed U.S. consumer goods in the hopes of dramatizing the difference in the standards of living between the two nations. It was in that light that the "kitchen debate" would take place, as an angry Khrushchev, bitterly reproaching Nixon, simply could not believe that an American home would actually have the type of simple features evident in the exhibition model.[110]

The more important aspects of the trip, however, had to do with what Nixon could learn from Khrushchev to help U.S. policy. Nixon remarked: "My visit would also afford an opportunity for high-level talks with Khrushchev in which I could make clear the United States' position on world issues and, at the same time, obtain for President Eisenhower and our policymakers some firsthand information as to Khrushchev's attitudes and views on the points of difference between the United States and the USSR." Recall, after all, the context of the times: Khrushchev was a relatively new Soviet leader whom we knew little about. Nixon first and foremost hoped to find "a new and fresh approach on how to talk to Nikita Khrushchev," as well as (as Ike put it) "changing some of Khrushchev's misconceptions about America."

Both Eisenhower and John Foster Dulles agreed on all these objectives. "[Dulles] believed I could hold my own in conversations with Khrushchev and he thought the conversations might provide some additional insight into Khrushchev's tactics and strategy which could be helpful in any meeting he might have with the president at a later date," wrote Nixon. The secretary of state also believed that Nixon might be able to use the forum of the exhibition to expose some segments of the Russian people to the reasonableness and justice of the American position on global issues. Among the topics the vice president prepared to discuss were: the Berlin problem, East-West trade, atomic testing, the long-missing U.S. airmen who had been shot down in a C-130 transport plane by Soviet fighters, the possible lifting of travel restrictions, censorship, opening of consular establishments, the jamming of radio broadcasts, and permission for a list of over 100 Soviet relatives of U.S. citizens to leave the USSR to live with their families in America.[111]

Lastly, on the eve of his departure, the vice president had a final session on the trip with President Eisenhower. For some time, Nixon, Ike, and others in the White House had discussed the pros and cons of inviting Khrushchev to America. While they were concerned that a tour by the premier would lend a certain degree of respectability to the Soviet leader and allow him to spread propaganda among the American people, they felt the United States stood to gain a great deal more by convincing Khrushchev of the size, strength, and spirit of the United States, which he would inevitably gain simply by traversing the landscape. In that vein, Ike decided to invite the Soviet leader and authorized Nixon to discuss it with him privately.[112]

Clearly, the vice president was about to engage in a substantive foreign-policy mission. "We hoped that his going would represent more than a mere courtesy call," Ike stated blandly. "It seemed . . . that some encouraging results might well flow from it."[113]

Like the Latin America trip, the vice president also extensively prepared for this mission, but far more so. For months before the trip he spent "every spare moment" studying reports and recommendations from the State Department, the CIA, the Joint Chiefs of Staff, and the White House. The difficulty in preparing for the Moscow mission focused on one item in particular: Soviet Premier Nikita Khrushchev. Yes, says Nixon, he had been warned that the Soviet premier would be unlike any other leader he had met, and the warnings were correct.[114]

The vice president spent hours with every person he could find in Washington who had met and knew Khrushchev and was briefed on more than 100 different issues the Soviet leader might bring up. He spoke to Averell Harriman and Hubert Humphrey, as well as journalists who met the Soviet leader, such as William Hearst and Walter Lippman. In *Six Crises*, Nixon details the varying counsel he received on the Soviet premier. The advice that seemed to influence him the most came from John Foster Dulles (a Nixon mentor who at this point was four days from death) and Harvard professor of government, William Yandell Elliott (who ended up accompanying the vice president on his Moscow mission). Elliott's advice, expressed to the vice president in a detailed memorandum, was very similar to that of Dulles:

> Khrushchev doesn't need to be reassured that we are for peace, and that we do not threaten him with aggression. He knows this. It is he who is threatening aggression and advocating revolution around the world. He should be told that we are ready to negotiate on equal terms but will not be bullied; we are willing to enter into peaceful competition between our two economic systems; that we are confident that we will win, but that we

are ready to fight to defend our rights if necessary.[115]

Likewise, Dulles said: "Khrushchev does not need to be convinced of our good intentions. He knows we are not aggressors and do not threaten the security of the Soviet Union." The advice of Elliott and Dulles seemed to be what Nixon was looking for, affirming his thinking on communism and the Soviet Union, which was well evident in statements he had made as far back as the Alger Hiss case in 1948. He internalized the counsel.[116]

Yet, despite all the preparation, nothing could prepare Nixon for the daunting task of taking on Khrushchev. Before his trip, he had even talked to two of the top men who occupied the Soviet hierarchy, Mikoyan and Kozlov, during their visit to Washington shortly before the vice president's trip. "But meeting Khrushchev, after talking with them," said Nixon, "was like going from minor to major league pitching. He throws a bewildering assortment of stuff—blinding speed, a wicked curve, plus knucklers, spitters, sliders, fork balls—all delivered with a deceptive change of pace." Later, when the two met, Nixon was struck by the brashness and rudeness of the Soviet leader, who actually seemed to relish in what was obviously a perfected art of insult. The vice president had made hundreds of visits with high government officials around the world, "but never before had a head of government met me with a tirade of four-letter words which made his interpreter blush as he translated them into English."[117]

Such was the tone of the meeting from the outset, as Nixon first met Khrushchev in his office for a brief courtesy call. The Soviet leader immediately railed against the United States about the Captive Nations Resolution passed by the U.S. Congress on July 6. The resolution designated the third week in July as a period in which Americans would pray for the "enslaved peoples" behind the Iron Curtain. The resolution outraged Khrushchev. (This would be the first of countless times he would bring it up.) In a long harangue directed at Nixon, the Soviet leader in a high-pitched voice declared that the Soviet government regarded the resolution as a very serious "provocation." He repeatedly pounded the table in order to drive home his anger. Nixon tried to respectfully and diplomatically answer his assertions point by point and slowly attempted to skillfully change the subject. In part, he was probably remembering Ike's advice that he "be positive in his conversations" with the Soviet leader. Khrushchev, however, would not relent. "This resolution stinks! It stinks like fresh horse sh—!," he shouted, continuing to pound the table. He concluded with a fury of four-letter invectives that the translator embarrassingly shuddered to interpret. "His attack at this early stage of my visit had been a surprise," said Nixon. "His vehemence and choice of language had been a shock." He surmised: "[W]hen God created Khrushchev (something Khrushchev would deny), He broke the mold."[118]

Not long after this initial encounter with the brash Soviet leader came the "kitchen debate." As noted earlier, the vice president traveled to Moscow to open the first American exhibition ever held there as part of a cultural exchange program with the Soviet Union. As it turned out, the main feature of the exhibit ended up being a feisty "debate" started by the showy Khrushchev over the virtues of communism and capitalism. The two men came upon an American model home, from which they entered via the kitchen. They two men then took to arguing over the comparative merits of Soviet and American washing machines. The vice president—not wanting to appear as the aggressor or disrespectful to the Soviet leader—played defense to Khrushchev's offensive. Looking to cool down the rhetoric, Nixon asserted: "Isn't it better to be talking about the relative merits of our washing machines than the relative strength of our rockets? Isn't this the kind of competition you want?" In reply, wrote Nixon, "jamming his thumb into my chest, [Khrushchev] shouted: 'Yes, that's the kind of competition we want, but your generals say we must compete in rockets.'" The "kitchen debate" raged on, with Nixon wisely doing some finger-pointing of his own, thus conveying an image that he was giving Khrushchev a dose of his own medicine.[119] He was also able to coolly shrug off personal insults[120] from Khrushchev while still appearing stern in defense of U.S. values. The vice president received due accolades from the American public for his performance during the debate.[121] Ike was also pleased with Nixon's performance: "[T]he vice president met [Khrushchev] point by point and in my opinion came out considerably even."[122]

Finally, the vice president's last and most important meeting with Khrushchev during the tour was on a Sunday afternoon, when they were to have a private conversation. That conversation began in characteristically belligerent fashion by the Soviet premier, who started by making extravagant claims about his nation's military power. His remarks sparked a point by point rebuttal by Nixon. By the time the five-and-a-half-hour discussion ended, the two men had debated nearly every aspect of Soviet and U.S. defense and security policy. The talks were astonishingly blunt. On the surface, no great tangible issues were resolved. Khrushchev, now in private and away from the cameras, was more pensive and analytical than before. Yet, true to form, he rudely and coldly rejected most statements made at the discussion. He answered "noncommittally" to Nixon's extension of the president's invitation to have Khrushchev visit America.[123]

All of this notwithstanding, Nixon seemed to came away with a weird sort of respect and possibly even admiration for Khrushchev as a politician and person.[124] Throughout his career, Nixon—born dirt poor to a Quaker family in Yorba Linda and who always felt slighted that he could not afford the Ivy League schools, even though he qualified for them—had an obvious resentment toward what he viewed as snobby intellectuals. What seemed to appeal to him about Khrushchev was that the Soviet premier—who had an upbringing much like Nixon's—disgusted the very people that Nixon did not like. To most intellectuals, Khrushchev's audacity was a sign of boorish brutishness. They felt he lacked class, an urbane sophistication, fine manners, elegant culture, etc. To Nixon, however—and this is merely an educated judgment—Khrushchev's behavior may have been merely his modus operandi for the political arena, and it was as much a psychological, Machiavellian technique as it was boorish brutishness. Along with the helpful tips of ambassador Llewellyn Thompson and others, Nixon had come to view Khrushchev's actions during his trip mainly as tactics intended to goad the vice president into rash and impulsive statements.[125] In this vein, he gained a valuable profile of the man that could be of benefit to U.S. policy:

> A picture of Khrushchev, the man, began to form in my mind. Intelligence, a quick-hitting sense of humor, always on the offensive, colorful in actions and words, a tendency to be a show-off, particularly where he has any kind of gallery to play to, a steel-like determination coupled with an almost compulsive tendency to press an advantage—to take a mile where his opponent gives an inch—to run over anyone who shows any sign of timidity or weakness—this was Khrushchev. A man who does his homework, prides himself on knowing as much about his opponent's position as he does his own, particularly effective in debate because of his resourcefulness, his ability to twist and turn, to change the subject when he is forced into a corner or an untenable position. . . .
>
> Despite giving the public impression of being a highly emotional man who might start war in a moment of anger, or when he had too much to drink, Khrushchev had . . . demonstrated to me that when anything of importance was being discussed he is sober, cold, unemotional, and analytical.[126]

Nixon seems to have constructed the profile sought by Ike, Dulles, and others. In retrospect, his profile seems to foretell some of the problems that President John F. Kennedy ran into in his early dealings with Khrushchev, reflected in JFK's infamous quote during the Cuban Missile Crisis, "He [Khrushchev] thinks I don't have any guts." But that's another issue.

All in all, Nixon's activities in Moscow were unprecedented for a vice president. Among the added events that would fall into this category was an August 1 radio-television address by Nixon to the Soviet nation.[127]

The press throughout the world reported, not inaccurately, that the vice president delivered (through an interpreter) many facts never before heard by a Soviet audience. His address was followed by a question-and-answer session with reporters. A number of the exchanges illustrate how Nixon's trip allowed him to move well beyond the tedious ceremonial tasks of so many past vice presidents traveling abroad. One reporter asked if Nixon would recommend to Ike that Khrushchev be invited to the United States. Playing the delicate role of loyal soldier, Nixon replied: "I will give my own opinion as to whether such a visit should be made, but I emphasize that whether such a visit should be made, and when, is the President's decision."[128] The vice president then gave his own evaluation of the pros and cons of a Khrushchev visit, presaging how he'd brief Ike on his return:

> There are a number of factors to be taken into consideration, some on the plus side, some on the minus side. On balance, I believe that at some time Mr. Khrushchev should be invited to come to the United States. I think on such a visit, clearly apart from the discussions he would have with the President on an official basis, the visit would serve other useful purposes. He would have a chance to see firsthand the United States.
>
> In my conversations and those of others who have talked to Mr. Khrushchev from the United States, we have, of course, tried to tell him about our policies, our people, and the attitudes of our Government on various issues. But, in my view, he still has some very real misconceptions with regard to both our policies and the attitudes of our people. And I think that his going to the United States, and seeing it firsthand, would serve to reduce and remove those misconceptions which may exist.[129]

Nixon did brief Eisenhower thusly upon his return. Regarding the point that a Khrushchev visit to the United States might change some of his misconceptions, Ike's memoirs illustrate that he clearly subscribed to the same view Nixon described.[130] Whether or not Ike's view was further influenced by Nixon is unclear, but it is obvious that both men shared a common objective on how the Soviet premier's visit could benefit U.S.-U.S.S.R. relations. This view by Eisenhower, it is reasonable to expect, may have at least been partly influenced by the assessment of his vice president.

By the end of the trip, the vice president had been insulted by Khrushchev over and over again in private and public, but had certainly learned a great deal about diplomacy and tense situations. Most of what took place on the trip involved unprecedented duties for a vice president abroad. This included a television press conference before the Soviet people with Khrushchev and a dramatic debate during which the pugnacious general secretary threatened his adversaries with missiles. The vice president also partook in an extremely candid five-and-a-half-hour debate with Khrushchev covering the whole range of American-Soviet relations.

Regarding specifics, Nixon concluded that he had achieved the following: For one, he had gained insights into Khrushchev's personality, his thinking, and the sort of tactics that the Soviet leader boldly employed. Knowledge of all of these, Nixon rightly believed, could be helpful to Ike. In addition, the vice president believed that his unscheduled walks down the streets of various Soviet cities gave him a chance to talk to the Soviet people firsthand and away from the bureaucrats. This and his radio-television address gave him a unique perspective into the true feelings of the Soviet people (as opposed to the apparatchiks). Nixon felt that this also afforded him a rare opportunity to convince the Soviet people firsthand that Americans desired peace and merely opposed attempts by Soviet leaders to spread communism throughout the world by any means necessary. The former was something he could take home and convey to American audiences. Eisenhower, for his part, declared he was "delighted" with Nixon's trip.[131]

Conclusion

Nixon's Moscow mission was highly unusual for a vice president at that time. Due to this and other tasks, Nixon's role in foreign policy and the vice presidency in general have been recognized for their revolutionary nature. In midsummer 1953, only a few months into the administration, Arthur Krock wrote in *The New York Times* that "persons familiar with the vice president's helpful activities have told this correspondent that they consider them unique in the records of his high office."[132] Those activities expanded greatly in the ensuing eight years. Judging from scores of remarks by scholars and observers, history has responded in kind.

Yet, as will become evident throughout this book, vice presidents who were active in foreign policy must thank the presidents they served as much as themselves. This is especially true in Nixon's case. Scholar George Sirgiovanni argues that President Eisenhower made Nixon, "the first 'modern' vice president," transforming the office "from a 'do nothing' job into one with high visibility and some substantive responsibilities."[133] This especially included foreign policy. Marie Natoli, who agrees that "the Nixon [vice presidential] incumbency was marked by extensive foreign affairs activity," writes that Ike "was undoubtedly responsible for the turning point in the development of the vice presidency." She credits Nixon as being revolutionary among vice presidents, and she points to Ike as the person responsible.[134] She states that the Nixon vice presidency is a "crucial case study" demonstrating how important presidential character and personality are in determining the level of vice-presidential activity.[135] Likewise, Mazo and Hess make the Ike-Nixon connection: "During the Eisenhower administration, with a mandate from the president, Richard Nixon removed the Throttlebottom concept of the vice-presidency from the lexicon of American public life. Never again would the office be without responsibility and importance." They credit Nixon's nonconstitutional duties for having changed the "concept" of the vice presidency.[136] Eisenhower himself felt that he and Nixon had established for the vice president an "unprecedented association—the Vice Presidency had not historically been afforded an opportunity for an extensive use of a man's abilities."[137]

Clearly, the idiosyncratic variable is at work here. The foreign-policy role of the particular vice president is largely dependent upon the unique set of circumstances in which he finds himself. Key among those circumstances are the idiosyncrasies of both he and his president. How each vice president is used depends upon these factors. The idiosyncratic variable is especially apropos for Ike-Nixon. In light of that, what idiosyncrasies made Nixon so involved in foreign policy?

For one, Nixon was a very ambitious vice president who had his eye on the presidency throughout his eight years in office—to the point, obviously, where he ran for and almost won the seat in 1960. (This is contrary to his notable unambitious predecessor, Alben Barkley.) As a result, he wanted to be busy in foreign policy and to receive substantive assignments (and perform them well). Additionally, Nixon was a vice president of keen intellect who developed a sharp interest in foreign policy; this contributed to his ability to perform well in global assignments, leading the president to reward him with an impressive entree of foreign-policy tasks. Also in Nixon's favor was the fact that Ike was a famous delegator, which likely influenced his tendency to pass on tasks to his vice president. At the same time, Ike's management style—which led to such delegation—also led him at times to constrain Nixon in some foreign-policy areas that the vice president would like to have been involved in, such as chairing the OCB.

Here is an added example of how each man's idiosyncrasies and political interests affected Nixon's foreign-policy role: While Nixon's ability to "understand" and "sum up the views of others"—as Ike put it—probably influenced him being chosen to assess Castro's intentions, the political interests of both he and the president probably affected how they ultimately dealt with the Cuban leader. Nixon seemed to have a political interest in wanting to depose of Castro before the 1960 presidential election. Eisenhower, on the other hand, was not facing elective office in 1960 and treated the Cuba situation from more of a long-term perspective of U.S.-Latin American relations, rather than his own political fortunes.

Another reason for Nixon being so involved—also stemming from the idiosyncratic variable—is that, as noted earlier, Eisenhower wanted his vice president to be a player. "I personally believe," he said, "the Vice President of the United States should never be a nonentity. I believe he should be used. I believe he should have a very useful job." With this in mind, Ike met with Nixon prior to the 1952 campaign to discuss what would be a much more active role for the vice president.[138] Ike responded immediately, only to further the vice president's involvement five years later. "By your extensive travels you have been of inestimable assistance to the Secretary of State and to me," Ike told Nixon in a September 3, 1957 memo. His satisfaction was so great that he decided to give Nixon an even larger role. "My basic thought is that you might find it possible—and intriguing—to be of even more help in our whole governmental program dealing with affairs abroad than you have been in the past."[139] Twice, once in a September 1957 memorandum and again after leaving office, Eisenhower commented directly on his vice president's "unusual" grasp of foreign affairs.[140] Ike stated: "Mr. Nixon's willingness to perform a variety of tasks, at my request, and his presence at all important policy meetings, assured that in the event of my death or disability, his own knowledge and understanding of the changing world and domestic situations would have no gaps." He was well aware of the fact that his "use of Vice President Nixon as a member of advisory bodies and as a personal representative in many affairs, both domestic and foreign, created an organizational precedent in American history."[141]

Thanks to Ike and Nixon himself, Nixon's vice presidency established a prototype on effectively using a vice president in foreign policy. There are countless examples of Nixon providing input during NSC and cabinet meetings and other events. He affected policy on many occasions, such as the changes made after his 1958 trip to South America. The high-level discussions he engaged in with men like Khrushchev and Castro show the confidence Ike had in him, not to mention the tremendous upgrade in the foreign-policy responsibilities of a vice president. He also used his foreign-policy trips for personal enhancement as an advisor in the administration and for his own enlightenment, education, and political fortune. As noted, Nixon had generally been a quite unpopular vice president among the public, and a liability to Eisenhower as a whole—until his second-term trips to Latin American and the Soviet Union. Both the trips catapulted him high in the Gallup polls, even pulling him ahead of Kennedy in the presidential race. In the end, he almost won the 1960 presidential election.

Nixon's positive experiences in foreign policy have led many to suggest such an enhanced role for all vice presidents. In many respects, the Ike-Nixon model is a useful prototype. Yet, it is important to bear in mind that Eisenhower drew a line regarding the vice president's responsibilities in foreign and security policy. Specifically, he felt vice presidents should not head up certain executive-level committees, such as the OCB. Ike's rationale has strong implications for such suggestions by Kevin Mulcahy and others. Additionally, on the negative side, Nixon's ultimate policy advocacy regarding how to handle Castro may have been motivated more by his personal political interests, as opposed to the paramount factor of whether or not deposing Castro at the time was good policy for the United States. The Castro example holds key lessons when it comes to employing the vice president in foreign policy.

The policy implications of the Nixon-Ike executive-committee experience (OCB), Nixon-Castro example, the vice president's Indochina remarks, and other matters will be revisited in the final chapter on lessons learned and evaluation of policy recommendations.

Notes

1. Unlike other chapters in the study, this chapter benefits at times from the vice president's own account of his foreign-policy activities, specifically in the sections on Latin America and Kruschev. This is because Vice President Nixon, in two separate books, elaborated extensively on his personal activities, unlike the other vice presidents in this study (Quayle is a minor exception). As a result, I've strived, whenever possible, to confirm Nixon's account with those of more independent (non-Nixon) sources—which is typically achievable. When such confirmation is not available, I've tried to openly qualify the citation.

2. Nixon himself preferred to refer to his career of one of "peaks" and "valleys"—ups and downs—in which he was either riding high or hitting rock bottom. See, for example, chapter 1 of Richard Nixon, *In the Arena: A Memoir of Victory, Defeat and Renewal* (New York: Simon & Schuster, 1990).

3. As someone who had gained notoriety in the Alger Hiss case as a "Red-hunter," one of Nixon's first tasks as vice president was to carefully placate the Communist-hunting senator from Wisconsin, Joseph R. McCarthy. Early in the administration McCarthy sent Eisenhower a letter complaining about British trade with communist China, demanding that the administration spell out its position on the policy. The letter placed the president in an embarrassing position relative to U.S. allies. Soon McCarthy would recklessly attack what he called "Fifth Amendment Communists" in the U.S. Army. An angry Eisenhower assigned Nixon to make a speech on television designed to put McCarthy in his place without actually mentioning him by name. Jules Witcover, *Crapshoot: Rolling the Dice on the Vice Presidency* (New York: Crown Publishers, 1992), p. 124; and Fred I. Greenstein, *The Hidden-Hand Presidency: Eisenhower as Leader* (New York: Basic Books, 1982), p. 197. Also, see Nixon television broadcast, March 13, 1954, *Facts on File*, p. 84.

4. In an op-ed ran shortly after Nixon's death, columnist Robert Novak elaborated on this phenomenon. Among conservatives, Novak maintains that Nixon's prosecution of the Hiss case "created a bond between Richard Nixon and the Right that, whatever his later transgressions, never can be broken." Robert D. Novak, "Nixon and Hiss," *Washington Post*, April 28, 1994.

5. Richard M. Nixon, *Six Crises* (New York: Doubleday, 1962), pp. 1 and 70; and Tom Wicker, "Richard M. Nixon 1969-1974," *Presidential Studies Quarterly*, Vol. XXVI, No. 1, Winter 1996, p. 256.

6. Dwight D. Eisenhower, *Mandate for Change, 1953-1956; The White House Years* (Garden City, N.Y.: Doubleday, 1963), p. 46.

7. Nixon, *Six Crises*, p. 69.

8. Marie D. Natoli, "Perspectives on the Vice Presidency," *Presidential Studies Quarterly*, Vol. XII, No. 4, Fall 1982, p. 598; and William Costello, *The Facts about Nixon* (New York: Viking, 1960), p. 229.

9. Michael Dorman, *The Second Man* (New York: Delacorte, 1968), p. 209.

10. Earl Mazo and Stephen Hess, *Nixon: A Political Portrait* (New York: Harper & Row, 1968), p. 207.

11. Stephen E. Ambrose, *Eisenhower: Volume II, The President* (New York: Simon & Schuster, 1984), p. 600.

12. Ambrose, op. cit., pp. 600-01 and 666-67.

13. Richard M. Nixon, *The Memoirs of Richard Nixon* (New York: Grosset & Dunlap, 1978), pp. 275-76.

14. Marie D. Natoli properly shows that Harry S Truman enabled his vice president, Alben Barkley, to become the first vice president to receive substantive, formal roles in areas such as administration foreign policy. Nixon, however, with the obvious help of Eisenhower, took the role of the vice president to a higher, unprecedented level. Marie D. Natoli, "Harry S Truman and the Contemporary Vice Presidency," *Presidential Studies Quarterly*, Vol. XVIII, No. 1, Winter 1988, pp. 81-82; and George S. Sirgiovanni, "Dumping the Vice President: An Historical Overview and Analysis," *Presidential Studies Quarterly*, Vol. XXIV, No. 4, Fall 1994, p. 775.

15. George F. Will, "Some Bravery, Even More Melancholy," Op-ed, *The Washington Post*, April 24, 1994.

16. Ambrose, op. cit., p. 292.

17. Eisenhower was among history's greatest, and most successful, delegators. (He stated his view on the need to delegate in a 1960 letter to Henry Luce. He pointed out to Luce that "the government of the United States has become too big, too complex, and too pervasive in its influence on all of our lives for one individual to pretend to direct the details of its important and critical programming. Competent assistants are mandatory; without them the executive branch would bog down.") In part, perhaps, his initial assigning of unique foreign-policy duties to his vice president was likely in a function of his penchant for delegation. Yet, by the middle of his second term, Ike was delegating substantive duties to Nixon mainly because the vice president had impressed him and won his confidence. Source: Greenstein, op. cit., p. 81, taken from Eisenhower to Henry Luce, August 8, 1960, Dwight D. Eisenhower, Papers as President of the United States, 1953-61 (Ann Whitman File); DDE Diary Series.

18. Nixon, *Six Crises*, p. 159.

19. Dwight D. Eisenhower, *Waging Peace: The White House Years, 1956-1961* (Garden City, N.Y.: Doubleday, 1965), pp. 6-7 and 235.

20. De Toledano does not provide a source, place, time, or general context for this remark. Ralph de Toledano, *Nixon* (New York: Duell, Sloan and Pearce, 1956, 1960), p. 157.

21. Costello, op. cit., p. 229.

22. Nixon, *Six Crises*, p. 178; and Eisenhower, *Waging Peace*, p. 233.

23. Eisenhower, *Waging Peace*, p. 233.

24. Nixon, *Six Crises*, pp. 178-79. For copies of the text of the letter, see Nixon, *Six Crises*, p. 179, and Eisenhower, *Waging Peace*, pp. 233-35.

25. Stephen W. Stathis, "Presidential Disability Agreements Prior to the 25th Amendment," *Presidential Studies Quarterly*, Vol. 12, No. 2, 1982, pp. 208-15. The 25th amendment at last defined a mechanism for the replacement of a disabled president by the vice president. Also see Herbert L. Abrams, "Shielding the President From the Constitution: Disability and the 25th Amendment," *Presidential Studies Quarterly*, Vol. 23, No. 3, 1993, pp. 533-53.

26. Walter Millis, with Harvey C. Mansfield and Harold Stein, *Arms and the State: Civil-Military Elements in National Policy* (New York: 1958), p. 182.

27. Stanley L. Falk, "The National Security Council under Truman, Eisenhower, and Kennedy," *Political Science Quarterly*, Vol. LXXIX, No. 3, September 1964, p. 417.

28. Duncan L. Clarke, *American Defense and Foreign Policy Institutions* (New York: Harper & Row, 1989). For examples of a contemporaneous defense and attack of the Ike NSC system, see, respectively: Gordon Gray, "Role of the National Security Council in the Formulation of National Policy," delivered to the American Political Science Association, September 1959, in *Organizing for National Security*, II, p. 189; and Senator Henry M. Jackson, "How Shall We Forge a Strategy for Survival," April 16, 1959, *Organizing for National Security*, II, pp. 266-77.

29. Greenstein, *Hidden-Hand Presidency*, p. 125.

30. Falk, op. cit., pp. 418 and 426.

31. Ibid., pp. 419-20.

32. Robert Cutler, "The Development of the National Security Council," *Foreign Affairs*, XXXIV, 1956, p. 448.

33. Falk, op. cit., pp. 420-23.

34. Ibid., p. 422.

35. Costello, op. cit., p. 244-45.

36. Ibid., p. 244-45.

37. De Toledano, op. cit., pp. 151-52; Nixon, *Six Crises*, pp. 148-50; and Sirgiovanni, op. cit., p. 775.

38. On the domestic side, the vice president was made chairman of the president's Commission on Government Contracts and the Cabinet Committee on Price Stability. Mazo and Hess, op. cit., pp. 207-08.

39. Costello, op. cit., p. 247; and Mazo and Hess, op. cit., pp. 207-08.

40. Costello, op. cit., p. 247; and Mazo and Hess, op. cit., pp. 207-08.

41. Among his better foreign-policy speeches was a talk he gave at Guildhall in London in 1958. See Nixon, *Memoirs*, pp. 200-01.

42. Eisenhower, *Waging Peace*, p. 7.

43. Mazo and Hess, op. cit., pp. 207-08.

44. Ibid., pp. 207-08.

45. Costello, op. cit., p. 232. In the literature on the vice presidency it is commonly believed that Vice President Mondale was the first second-office holder to have his own defense and foreign policy advisors. In part, this remains true. Both Nixon and Mondale had "military aides." However, Mondale seems to be the first vice president to have both military aides and general defense and foreign policy advisors, brought in irrespective of the Pentagon's assistance. Moreover, Mondale's defense and foreign policy staff was paid through the vice president's own budget, whereas Nixon's two aides were paid by the Pentagon.

46. Among such examples, not cited in this chapter, see Eisenhower, *Waging Peace*, pp. 337-38 (Nixon on Berlin, Kruschev, and Soviet policy) and pp. 220-21 (Gaither report); De Toledano, op. cit., pp. 158-59, 163, and 203-04; and John P. Burke and Fred I. Greenstein, *Decisions on Vietnam, 1954 and 1965* (New York: Russell Sage Foundation, 1989), pp. 32-33, 78, 85-86, 106, 113-14, and 260. In particular, see pp. 85-86 and 260 of Burke and Greenstein for examples of Nixon pressing Eisenhower and making proposals to him.

47. De Toledano, op. cit., p. 153.

48. Eisenhower, *Waging Peace*, p. 486.

49. Ambrose, op. cit., p. 600.

50. Eisenhower, *Waging Peace*, pp. 6-7.

51. Nixon, *Six Crises*, p. 301. For a detailed treatment of this trip, see Nixon, *Memoirs*, pp. 119-37; De Toledano, op. cit., pp. 161-66; and Costello, op. cit., pp. 246-51.

52. Nixon, *Memoirs*, pp. 152-53.

53. Among other sources on the resulting outcry, see Burke and Greenstein, op. cit., pp. 76-77.

54. It may also be worth noting that Nixon's statement here somewhat presaged his view of war powers, which would lead him into conflict with the legislative branch during his own presidency. This provides another indication of how studying the vice presidency can be useful: it can tell us key information about its occupants and how they might act as presidents. This is important when one considers that most vice presidents eventually run for the presidency or end up occupying it. Marie D. Natoli notes that since the Founding Fathers created a constitutional basis for the office of the vice president, the need for the vice president to succeed to the presidency has occurred eight times as a result of presidential death and once as a result of presidential resignation. "Thus the statistical yardstick which the past has provided is that there is a one-in-five chance that vice presidential succession will occur," she writes. Marie D. Natoli, "Abolish the Vice Presidency?" *Presidential Studies Quarterly*, Vol. IX, No. 2, Spring 1979, p. 203.

55. Ambrose, pp. 180-81.

56. Witcover, *Crapshoot*, p. 125. For more on Nixon and the Indochina War, see Nixon, *Memoirs*, pp. 150-55; and Burke and Greenstein, op. cit., pp. 32-33, 76-78, 85-86, 106, 113-14, and 260.

57. Joel K. Goldstein, *The Modern American Vice Presidency* (Princeton, N.J.: Princeton University Press, 1982), p. 104.

58. Witcover, *Crapshoot*, p. 125.

59. Ambrose, op. cit., p. 292.

60. Eisenhower, *Waging Peace*, p. 7.

61. Mazo and Hess, op. cit., pp. 207-08.

62. De Toledano, op. cit., pp. 152 and 154-56. De Toledano provides a number of examples of Nixon's congressional liaison activities. Also see Kenneth W. Thompson, "Richard Nixon: The Man & the Political Leader," Interview with Bryce Harlow, *Miller Center Journal*, Vol. 1, Spring 1994, pp. 90-91.

63. As we shall see, vice presidents Mondale and Quayle also prominently fulfilled such roles.

64. Costello, op. cit., p. 235.

65. Eisenhower, *Waging Peace*, pp. 522-23.

66. Ibid., p. 7.

67. Mazo and Hess, op. cit., p. 209.

68. Jeffrey J. Safford, "The Nixon-Castro Meeting of 19 April 1959," *Diplomatic History*, Vol. 4, No. 4, Fall 1980, pp. 425-31.

69. While Nixon published portions of the memorandum in his *Memoirs*, the full text was reproduced in Mike Manfield's recently released private papers. For a published version of the full text, see Safford, op. cit., pp. 425-31.

70. Nixon, *Six Crises*, pp. 351-52.

71. Safford, op. cit., p. 431.

72. Eisenhower, *Waging Peace*, p. 523.

73. Nixon, *Six Crises*, pp. 351-52.

74. K. S. Karol, *Guerrillas in Power: The Course of the Cuban Revolution* (New

York: Hill and Wang, 1970), p. 6. For a critique of Karol, see Alan H. Luxenberg, "Did Eisenhower Push Castro into the Arms of the Soviets?" *Journal of Interamerican Studies and World Affairs*, Vol. 30, No. 1, Spring 1988, pp. 47-49.

75. Ambrose, op. cit., pp. 582-84.

76. Marie D. Natoli wrote of this phenomenon. See Marie D. Natoli, "The Vice Presidency: Stepping Stone or Stumbling Block?" *Presidential Studies Quarterly*, Vol. 18, No. 1, 1988, pp. 77-79.

77. Among others, see Carl Solberg, *Hubert Humphrey: A Biography* (New York: W. W. Norton, 1984), pp. 264 and 269.

78. Nixon, *Six Crises*, p. 351.

79. Ibid., pp. 351-52.

80. As told by Nixon: Ibid., pp. 183-84.

81. One reviewer of this chapter speculates that Ike, Dulles, and Rubottom may have "set up" Nixon in Latin America. By this the reviewer means that Ike was having trouble with the Congress in showing that he was sufficiently alarmed about communism after Sputnik (1957). The reviewer wonders if sending Nixon to Latin America—perhaps with the belief that the vice president might be incited to behave provocatively—would be a way for the administration to make waves. While such is interesting (and somewhat cynical) speculation, I know of no evidence which would suggest it to be true.

82. Ibid., pp. 184-87. On whether Nixon adequately heeded intelligence warnings, see Costello, op. cit., p. 255.

83. Among other sources on this, see evidence in Mazo and Hess, pp. 166-69; and Costello, op. cit., pp. 254-59.

84. De Toledano, op. cit., pp. 160-62; and Nixon, *Six Crises*, pp. 185-88. Among the examples of Nixon doing this, see his actions in Poland during a 1959 visit: Nixon, *Six Crises*, pp. 286-87.

85. See Nixon, *Six Crises*, pp. 186-88; and De Toledano, op. cit., pp. 255-56.

86. Nixon, *Six Crises*, p. 188; and De Toledano, op. cit., pp. 255-56.

87. Ibid., pp. 192-95; Witcover, *Crapshoot*, pp. 134-35; and Costello, op. cit., pp. 254-57.

88. Costello, op. cit., pp. 256-57; and Nixon, *Six Crises*, pp. 201-23.

89. See Costello, op. cit., pp. 254-57; and Nixon, *Six Crises*, pp. 201-03.

90. Nixon, *Six Crises*, pp. 197-99.

91. There were at least two serious assassination plans. See Mazo and Hess, op. cit., pp. 168-69.

92. Nixon, *Memoirs*, pp. 188-90; Nixon, *Six Crises*, pp. 211-27; Mazo and Hess, op. cit., pp. 165-73; and De Toledano, op. cit., p. 257.

93. Nixon, *Memoirs*, pp. 189-90; Nixon, *Six Crises*, pp. 211-27; Mazo and Hess, op. cit., pp. 166-67; and Costello, op. cit., pp. 257-59.

94. Mazo and Hess, op. cit., pp. 175-77.

95. Ibid., p. 178.

96. Ibid., pp. 166 and 180-81.

97. Eisenhower, *Waging Peace*, p. 519.

98. Mazo and Hess, op. cit., pp. 179-87; and Witcover, *Crapshoot*, pp. 134-35.

99. Judging from Nixon's account, the antithesis of his Caracas trip was a 1959 visit he made to Poland, where he was greeted by an astonishing crowd of 250,000 chanting "Long Live America, "Long Live Eisenhower," "Long Live Nixon." The response was

even more surprising considering the Polish government officially blacked out the event. (Word of the visit was started by Radio Free Europe.) "So many flowers and bouquets were thrown at us that our driver had to stop the car several times to clear the windshield," wrote Nixon. "I could not believe it. The press corps could not believe it." See Nixon, *Six Crises*, pp. 283-87.

100. Eisenhower, *Waging Peace*, pp. 519-20.

101. Nixon, *Six Crises*, pp. 228-29.

102. He appears to have made at least nine specific recommendations. While some of these apply to broad Latin American policy, he also made country-specific suggestions. Nixon, *Six Crises*, pp. 191-92 and 229-30.

103. Ibid., p. 230.

104. Ibid.

105. Mazo and Hess, op. cit., pp. 208-09.

106. Nixon, *Six Crises*, p. 301; Mazo and Hess, op. cit., p. 187; Costello, op. cit., p. 257; and Witcover, *Crapshoot*, pp. 134-35.

107. Eisenhower, *Waging Peace*, pp. 519-20; and Mazo and Hess, op. cit., p. 187. Moreover, I'm not aware of any evidence that Ike was angry with Nixon or held him responsible for generating the crisis.

108. During the Moscow trip, Nixon kept Ike "intimately informed" throughout. Ibid., p. 410.

109. Witcover, *Crapshoot*, p. 136.

110. Ike refers back to this specific "kitchen debate" item in telling an anecdote that took place during Kruschev's Washington visit a year later. The president and premier happened to be in transit via air during rush hour in Washington. In Moscow, Kruschev had simply refused to believe Nixon's assertion that most American families owned cars. The helicopter trip quickly conveyed to him this reality. Eisenhower, *Waging Peace*, p. 408; and Nixon, *Six Crises*, p. 237. An almost identical situation occurred four decades later between U.S. president George Bush and Soviet leader Mikhail Gorbachev as they helicoptered to Camp David. Pointing below, Gorbachev asked, "What are they, those things down there?" Bush replied, "Well, they're homes." "Homes?" said Gorbachev incredulously. "Well, who owns them?" See Dan Quayle, *Standing Firm: A Vice-Presidential Memoir* (New York: HarperCollins, 1994), p. 167.

111. Nixon, *Six Crises*, pp. 237-38 and 241; and Eisenhower, *Waging Peace*, pp. 408-09.

112. Eisenhower, *Waging Peace*, pp. 408-15; and Nixon, *Six Crises*, pp. 242-43.

113. Eisenhower, *Waging Peace*, p. 408.

114. Nixon, *Six Crises*, p. 236; and Nixon, *Memoirs*, p. 203.

115. Nixon, *Six Crises*, p. 238; and Nixon, *Memoirs*, pp. 203-04.

116. Nixon, *Memoirs*, p. 203. Also see, for example, the vice president's comments in *Six Crises*, pp. 244-45.

117. Nixon, *Six Crises*, p. 236; and Mazo and Hess, op. cit., pp. 189-91.

118. Mazo and Hess, op. cit., pp. 188-89; Nixon, *Six Crises*, pp. 250-53; Nixon, *Memoirs*, pp. 206-08; and Eisenhower, op. cit., p. 410.

119. Witcover, *Crapshoot*, p. 136; Nixon, *Six Crises*, p. 303; Nixon, *Memoirs*, pp. 208-09; Eisenhower, op. cit., p. 408; and Mazo and Hess, op. cit., pp. 190-91.

120. For instance, as the two men walked by a model American grocery store, Nixon commented, "You may be interested to know that my father owned a small gen-

eral store in California, and all the Nixon boys worked there while going to school." The remark in part was likely intended to convey to Khrushchev Nixon's non-"silver spoon" upbringing. But the Soviet leader wasn't sympathetic. He waved his arms and snorted, "Oh, all shopkeepers are thieves." As told by Nixon: Nixon, *Six Crises*, pp. 254-55.

121. The incident helped Nixon's political image at home considerably, presenting him as a major foreign policy player and giving a huge boost to him in the presidential campaign of 1960, which was only months away. The vice president had been trailing Democratic candidate John F. Kennedy in the Gallup Poll by 61 to 39 percent before the trip to the Soviet Union. After the trip, Nixon jumped ahead by a 52 to 48 percent margin, before going ahead in November 53 to 47 percent. From a personal-political standpoint, Nixon called the Khrushchev meeting "a decisive break." Ibid., p. 303.

122. Eisenhower, *Waging Peace*, p. 410.

123. For details, see Mazo and Hess, op. cit., pp. 191-206; Nixon, *Six Crises*, pp. 265-71; and Nixon, *Memoirs*, pp. 209-12.

124. Interestingly, this would not be the last of the verbal boxing matches between Nixon and Khrushchev. Eisenhower relays *three* separate amusing incidents in one Washington visit in which the Soviet premier again assailed the vice president. At a luncheon, recalled Ike, "the Chairman seemed to take particular delight in hurling barbs at the Vice President. Dick replied briskly and pointedly to each of the Chairman's sallies. I was a little astonished that Khrushchev should take advantage of a social occasion to try to make another guest feel uncomfortable." Eisenhower, *Waging Peace*, pp. 436, 438, and 447

125. Nixon, *Six Crises*, p. 252; Nixon, *Memoirs*, pp. 203 and 206; and Mazo and Hess, op. cit., pp. 191-93.

126. Nixon, *Six Crises*, p. 272.

127. Nixon, *Memoirs*, p. 212. In an interesting parallel, the only other vice president to make such a substantial trip to that part of the world, including a televised speech to the Russian people, was Vice President Al Gore—although, admittedly, it paled in significance to the time (and impact) in which Nixon went. The Gore example will be examined in the chapter on Vice President Gore.

128. Transcript of press conference published in: Nixon, *Six Crises*, pp. 442-43.

129. Ibid., pp. 442-43.

130. See Eisenhower, *Waging Peace*, pp. 408-11 and 435-39.

131. Ibid., p. 410.

132. Quote cited in De Toledano, op. cit., p. 156.

133. Sirgiovanni, op. cit., p. 775.

134. Marie D. Natoli, "Harry S Truman and the Contemporary Vice Presidency," p. 83; and Marie D. Natoli, "Perspectives on the Vice Presidency," p. 598.

135. Marie D. Natoli, "The Vice Presidency in the Third Century," in James P. Pfiffner and R. Gordon Hoxie, eds., *The Presidency in Transition* (New York: Center for the Study of the Presidency, 1989), p. 415.

136. Vice President Alexander Throttlebottom was a fictional character invented for a 1930s Broadway musical called *Of Thee I Sing*. Throttlebottom and the perceived uselessness of his office were parodied mercilessly. Mazo and Hess, op. cit., pp. 207 and 219.

137. Eisenhower, *Waging Peace*, p. 7.

138. Dorman, op. cit., p. 209.

139. Mazo and Hess, op. cit., pp. 207-08.
140. Eisenhower, *Waging Peace*, p. 590; and Mazo and Hess, op. cit., pp. 207-08.
141. Eisenhower, *Waging Peace*, p. 631.

Chapter 4
A Political Vice President: Walter Mondale (1977-81)

"In general, Carter rarely, if ever, thought of foreign policy in terms of domestic politics, while Mondale rarely, if ever, thought of it otherwise. . . . I did feel at times that [Mondale] was too much inclined to defer to special domestic interests in fashioning his priorities."
Zbigniew Brzezinski, Power and Principle, *1983*

Introduction

President Jimmy Carter looked to bring his vice president into policy and operational planning, and hoped to make him among history's most active. A contemporaneous account claimed Carter met with mixed success, due in part to the vice president's lack of jurisdictional authority. In a 1980 article in *Presidential Studies Quarterly*, R. Gordon Hoxie wrote:

> Mondale was being acclaimed during the first two Carter years as one of the president's closest advisors; but by the third year he was suffering the fate which every vice president seemed to have experienced . . . [being] cut off from the president's inner advisory circle and relegated to ceremonial and political representations. By the third year Mondale was viewing with disdain Carter's daily meetings with his top assistants where, presumably, key policies were being made. Unimpressed, Mondale usually sent an aide to represent him, and he was not missed.[1]

Judging from evidence, Hoxie's 1980 account was off base. Most scholars writing during the Carter period felt Mondale was the most influential and active vice president up until that time. In the very next issue of *Presidential Studies Quarterly*, Marie Natoli wrote: "Walter Mondale has perhaps been the most influential and active vice president to date—serving in the capacity he himself chose—that of a general 'troubleshooter' and advisor to the president. This troubleshooter role has afforded Mondale the chance to get involved in a multitude of activities and has contributed significantly toward enhancing the image of the second office."[2] She later added: "Mondale became the most active vice president to that point in the history of the office, in both domestic and foreign affairs."[3] Those who have written about Mondale since, backed up by numerous memoirs and other accounts, all agree with Natoli. Alexander Moens wrote: "The vice president's role during the Carter administration was unique, for it was actually made into a crucial advisory role in both domestic and foreign policy." He was a "generalist" advisor who was not afraid to disagree with the president or with the other advisors.[4] From a strictly *advisory* standpoint, Mondale's only equal seems to be Vice President Al Gore.

This chapter will examine Mondale's noteworthy role in the Carter administration's foreign policy. At the same time, it does feature an example—namely, his role in South Africa policy—that reflects both negatively on Mondale and on the notion of using a vice president in certain foreign-policy situations. In that respect, it also touches on an issue that makes Mondale unique among the vice presidents examined in this study: His utter infatuation with the political aspects of policy. Among other aspects, this chapter will explore how his political infatuation squared with Carter the technician. While this infatuation often served the administration in a productive fashion, it also tied to Mondale a selfish-political interest that was at times a detriment to his use in certain foreign-policy situations. This fact (a similar example is given in the next chapter on Vice President Bush) calls into question the premise by many scholars that the vice president can be a valuable asset in foreign affairs because he allegedly lacks selfish-parochial interests.

Mondale's Selection and Role Definition

During the 1976 presidential primaries, Governor Jimmy Carter named three criteria he wanted in a vice president: the person he believed was best qualified to become president if necessary; a person politically and personally compatible with him; and someone from a region other than the South. Mondale fit the bill.[5] He was politically more liberal than Carter and could help the Democratic moderate appeal to leftist segments of the party.[6] He was also more politically savvy to the ways of Washington, a real plus to a southern governor. Carter later wrote:

> I had made only one early decision about the vice president—that it was important for me to choose a member of Congress as my running mate in order to provide some balance of experience to our ticket. Without ever having served in Washington myself, I needed someone who was familiar with the federal government and particularly with the legislative branch. I did not know many of the senators or representatives on Capitol Hill and had not spent much time studying about them.[7]

Carter would choose Mondale as his running mate and they would win the 1976 election. By his own estimate, he never regretted his decision. "During our four and a half years together," said Carter, "I never for a moment had reason to doubt his competence, his loyalty, or his friendship."[8] In particular, Mondale would prove himself invaluable as a link between the administration and Congress. Throughout his four years, Mondale would have a say in just about every Carter decision, including the structure of his vice-presidential role.

The structure of Mondale's role began even before he was picked by Carter. On July 8, 1976, a week before the Democratic convention, Carter invited the Minnesota senator to his Georgian home to be screened as a potential vice-presidential running mate. Mondale wisely followed up on the advice of his top Senate aide, Dick Moe, and crammed for the interview. He read Carter's biography, speeches, and campaign papers. He then came up with a list of the ways in which he could help Carter politically as his running mate. Mondale even went so far as to develop a description of his role as vice president in a Carter presidency.[9] "When Fritz came down to Plains he had really done his homework about me and the campaign," Carter recalled. "More important, he had excellent ideas about how to make the vice presidency a full-time and productive job."[10] When asked by Carter about the type of role he desired, the senator stated unambiguously that he wanted to be an activist vice president, enjoying a level of access that few, if any, previous occupants had attained. Knowing of the often depressing history of previous vice presidents, Mondale did not want to be doomed to the same fate.[11]

Equally important, both Carter and Mondale knew that a President Carter would need a politically astute, experienced legislator who was wise to the ways of Washington. In the July interview before he was selected, Mondale listed this among the salient elements of attraction he could offer Carter. In turn, Carter's list of needs held a vacancy for a politically savvy running mate who could help him inside the Beltway. As this chapter illustrates, this contrast—Carter the rule-bound technician vs. Mondale the politician—seems to have forged the guts of their working relationship, often (but not always) serving to the benefit of the administration.[12]

In December 1976, a few weeks after the election, Mondale met with the president-elect at Blair House, the transition residency of Carter, to again discuss their plans for the vice presidency. Similar to his attempt to sell himself to Carter as a running mate months earlier in Georgia, Mondale was very much prepared for this meeting also. He brought with him a detailed memorandum outlining the role he wanted to play in the new administration. After conducting careful research, including conversations with two of the most recent vice presidents, Hubert Humphrey and Nelson Rockefeller, Mondale had come to the understandable conclusion that the vice president's role had been "characterized by ambiguity, disappointment and even antagonism." He knew of the negative memories Humphrey had and did want to experience them himself. He and Carter recalled the lesson of FDR and Truman.[13]

During the meeting, Mondale commented: "The history [of the vice presidency] is pretty grim. I'd be surprised if this works out any differently." Before he left, Carter assured him: "This time it's going to be different."[14] Carter was true to his word from the outset. "Immediately after we were elected, he came to me with a well-prepared book of suggestions, all of which I accepted," he stated in recalling the meeting at Blair House. "We agreed that he would truly be the second in command, involved in every aspect of governing."[15]

Mondale recommended that the vice president's role should be that of a general advisor to the president. The vice president-elect argued that too often presidents had failed because they neglected independent voices. Using an argument later made by Kevin Mulcahy in recommending an enhanced foreign-policy role for the vice president, Mondale asserted that the vice president is (like the president) the only other member of the administration with broad responsibility unfettered by loyalty to an agency or department. This, he maintained, would allow the vice president to provide independent analysis. To fulfill such a general advisor role, Mondale made a number of demands. He said that as vice president he needed:

- access to the same information as the president, especially the daily briefings from the CIA and other intelligence groups;
- close and frequent access to the president;
- a close relationship with other executive-branch members;
- participation in meetings of key groups; and
- an experienced vice-presidential staff member on both the National Security Council and the Domestic Policy Council.[16]

Carter, unlike some presidents, had no apprehension of allowing his vice president an active role, in part because he feared no political competition from Mondale. (Despite Mondale's significant political aspirations, he apparently never competed against the president.) He agreed that Mondale should attend all cabinet meetings, NSC briefings, and Economic Policy Group discussions, as well as receive copies of the president's intelligence reports and all other papers that went to Carter. Mondale was incorporated into the president's inner circle of advice. Carter extended to Mondale a standing invitation to attend all of his political meetings. They scheduled a regular, private Monday lunch to discuss important business. Mondale had free access to Carter and could attend any meeting he wanted.[17] The vice president was even in charge of long-range planning of Carter's agenda.[18] Carter sums it up: "[H]e received the same security briefings I got, was automatically invited to participate in all my official meetings, and helped to plan strategy for domestic programs, diplomacy, and defense."[19]

An additional change was made that may seem unimportant on the surface but was quite the contrary in practice. In terms of the location of his office, Mondale desired to be "in the loop" with an office in the West Wing of the White House, as opposed to a spot in the Executive Office Building, where most vice presidents were housed. Carter granted the vice president his wish, locating Mondale's office adjacent to his own. Carter noted that the West-Wing move was a first in the history of the vice presidency.[20] Reflecting on this innovation, Mike Berman commented: "The White House operates not by structure but by osmosis. Most of the business is done by floating in and out of each other's offices, bumping into people in the hall, dealing in the White House restaurant. If you are out of the loop, it is very hard to be part of the process."[21] (Jon Glassman, who served Vice President Quayle, also stresses the importance of the vice president being located in the West Wing, for similar reasons that will be examined later.) Brzezinski alludes to how the West Wing location of his and Mondale's offices allowed the vice president to be kept more abreast of foreign affairs issues:

> Our offices in the West Wing of the White House were adjoining, and that made for easy and informal contact. When there was something to talk about, Fritz . . . would simply pop into my office, or I would stick my head into his. . . . [Twenty] or so days after assuming office, I jotted in my journal: "It is quite striking how often Mondale now drops by to chat. . . . For example, today he came in to talk about our relations with Europe."[22]

In a further attempt at ensuring himself influence, Mondale worked to place loyal staff members in sensitive executive-branch positions. Mondale figured that having people loyal to him in critical positions would prevent the president's staff from ever being able to undermine his influence. Eizenstat recalled: "During the transition it was obvious that he had a detailed knowledge of how the bureaucracy worked and how he was going to have an influence on it."[23] One often noted example of the success of his efforts was Carter deciding to appoint David Aaron, Mondale's foreign-policy advisor in the Senate, as his deputy national security advisor.[24]

Mondale's ability to assign (intentionally or unintentionally) loyal staff members within the administration says a lot about his lauded loyalty to the president. While evidence shows him to be a loyal vice president, the fact of the matter is that Mondale could afford to be loyal because he had placed so many allies within the administration. Additionally, of course, this helped assure Mondale not only power but also influence as vice president.

The President-Vice President Relationship

All of these changes and early interaction served to create a very good relationship between Mondale and Carter. Recalled Stuart Eizenstat (in a remark that sounds strikingly like those made about the relationship between President Clinton and Vice President Gore): "What was unique about their relationship was that it was across the board. Carter saw Mondale as his most senior advisor. No one else had that breadth of relationship with the president." His remark is not hyperbole.[25] The relationship between the two was very good.[26] Scholar John Dumbrell writes: "Mondale was not the nation's chief mourner and was worth far more to Carter than a pitcher of warm spit."[27] In a 1977 news conference, Carter estimated that he was spending more time with Mondale than with all his other senior staff advisors combined.[28] "I see Fritz four to five hours a day," estimated Carter, in what seems like an exaggeration. "There is not a single aspect of my own responsibilities in which Fritz is not intimately associated. He is the only person that I have with both the substantive knowledge and political stature to whom I can turn over a major assignment."[29]

The president respected the vice president's opinion and routinely sought it. During meetings, he would often ask Mondale for his assessment prior to making a final decision.[30] Although they at times disagreed, Mondale never publicly rebuked the president—an essential attribute to proper vice-presidential decorum. In the closing days of his presidency, Carter told Lloyd Cutler that the vice president "has been extremely helpful and terribly loyal, even when we disagreed."[31] John Dumbrell agreed: "The Carter-Mondale relationship really does seem to have been devoid of that mutual suspicion and distrust—often a holdover from the nomination race—which often relegates the vice president to the policy-making sidelines."[32]

They also seemingly became close friends. At the final White House staff meeting, Carter said Mondale was "like a brother and a son" to him, and that he "never had [a] closer relationship than with Fritz." In return, Mondale offered similarly effusive praise. "Never before has a vice president been so generously and so kindly treated by his president," Mondale stated. "On a personal level it was a spectacular relationship. His personal generosity toward me and my staff never wavered during the four years."[33] By the end of his incumbency, he observed, "I have been closer to a president . . . than any vice president in history."[34] In many respects, Mondale's remarks were probably accurate. Up to that point, perhaps only President Eisenhower had allowed his vice president a degree of latitude that had remotely approached what Carter bestowed on Mondale. In the end, Mondale believed that he and Carter had established a groundbreaking institutional relationship. Mondale considered the role he played in elevating the stature of the vice presidency his greatest contribution during the Carter years.[35]

A large part of that elevation took place in the realm of foreign policy. Before examining Mondale's foreign-policy role, the following pages will illuminate the Carter administration's foreign- and security-policy structure and Mondale's place in it.

Mondale's Place within Carter Administration Foreign- and Security-Policy Structure

The president's inner core of foreign-policy advisors included Mondale, Brzezinski, Brown, and Vance. Brown aside, the primary group, or the "Big Four," were Carter, Mondale, Brzezinski, and Vance.[36] As one casual example of the dominance of these four in foreign policy, Brzezinski refers to an episode in which an angry Carter warned Vance: "If this goes on I will make my decisions only with Fritz and Zbig and simply not tell anybody else."[37] The Carter administration's National Security Council had two principal committees—the Policy Review Committee (PRC) and the Special Coordination Committee (SCC)—established by Brzezinski and approved by the president on Inauguration Day (see Figure 4.1). The SCC was chaired by Brzezinski and, according to the NSA's plan, would "deal with specific cross-cutting issues requiring coordination in the development of options and the implementation of presidential decisions." The SCC was the group that performed crisis management, as well as coordinating arms-control issues and overseeing sensitive intelligence activities.[38] Mondale on occasion chaired the SCC when necessary. For instance, in February 1979, Mondale held a principals-only meeting of the SCC while Carter, Brzezinski, and Vance were in China meeting with Deng Xiao Ping. The PRC dealt with three broad categories: "foreign-policy issues," "defense policy issues," and "international economic issues." It was chaired by the appropriate secretary, typically the secretary of state, the secretary of defense, and the secretary of the treasury, depending upon the issue.[39]

In addition to these two main committees, there were lower-level interdepartmental groups, chaired by senior agency officials, to deal with matters not requiring the attention of the SCC or PRC. These have also been referred to as the "mini-SCCs," chaired by an official to develop, coordinate, and monitor implementation of certain national-security policies, especially in the areas of NATO and SALT II. Vance, who for many reasons had trouble with the "too frequent" SCC and PRC meetings, found the mini-SCCs to be "highly effective."[40]

FIGURE 4.1: CARTER ADMINISTRATION FOREIGN AND SECURITY POLICY STRUCTURE

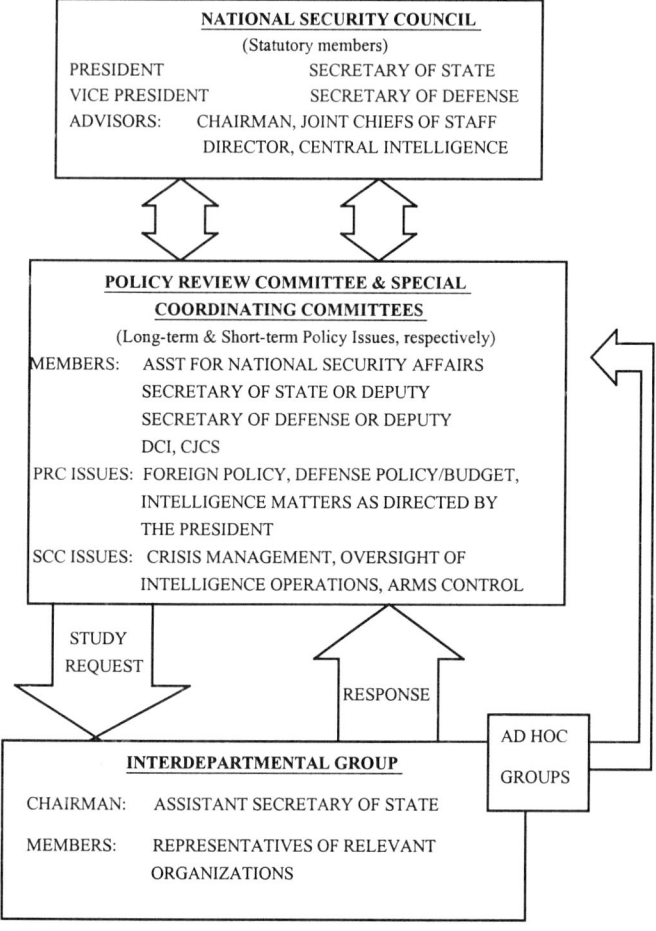

Source: Amos A. Jordan and William J. Taylor, Jr.,
American National Security: Policy and Process
(Baltimore and London: The Johns Hopkins University Press, 1981). p. 134.

The NSC meetings typically included the NSA, president, the vice president, the secretary of state, the secretary of defense, the director of central intelligence, the chairman of the joint chiefs of staff, and sometimes Hamilton Jordan, Jody Powell, or Lloyd Cutler. As election concerns began to become paramount, domestic advisors were included in the meetings more frequently from 1979 on. For example, Cutler, a Washington lawyer and close political advisor to the president, was especially insistent on attending meetings. On truly sensitive matters, however, only the statutory members (vice president included) were permitted to attend. On Carter's style in presiding over the meetings, Brzezinski writes:

> The president would chair the meeting, commenting quite often and quizzing the participants. There was no doubt that he was in charge, and he would make his decisions in a very clear-cut fashion. He would listen very attentively to debates among us, and on one occasion he told me that he particularly enjoyed disagreements between Harold Brown and me, since the debates between us involved such quick and sharp sparring.[41]

Mondale took part in all NSC and cabinet meetings. He chaired NSC meetings in the president's absence. The first informal NSC meeting, held January 5, 1977, was presided over by the vice-president elect. He or someone from his staff attended PRC and SCC meetings.[42] The vice president's place in the foreign-policy apparatus was solidified primarily by two principal means: President Truman's statutory changes of 1947 and the areas of agreement that Mondale and Carter resolved after their Blair House meeting during the transition.

Additionally, the vice president lunched with Carter on Mondays to discuss any matter of interest to Mondale. Hamilton Jordan says this was known colloquially as the "Vice President's time."[43] Each day, Carter had his Presidential Daily Briefing, which brought to the president a highly secret document that was distributed to only five people: the president, vice president, secretaries of state and defense, and the NSA.[44] He had an open invitation to all Oval Office meetings, even those that the president was holding with foreign chiefs of state. Mondale attended the president's weekly breakfasts with foreign-policy advisors. Carter gave instructions that Mondale receive the full paper flow sent to the president's desk.[45]

Mondale participated in the weekly, Friday foreign-policy breakfasts, along with the president, secretary of state, secretary of defense, and the national security advisor. (Mondale was not involved in the other foreign-policy meeting — the foreign-policy lunch held between the president, Vance, Brown, and Brzezinski, a.k.a., the "VBB luncheon.") The breakfast took place at 7:30 A.M. in the Cabinet room. Occasional participants were Press Secretary Jody Powell, Hamilton Jordan, Hedley Donovan, Lloyd Cutler, and Deputy Secretary of State Warren Christopher. Vance called it "a valuable forum for frank discussion.

Issues were aired thoroughly and we were able to consider the interaction between domestic and foreign-policy matters."[46] Brzezinski agreed: "These weekly presidential breakfasts quickly became important executive sessions. . . . Sometimes as many as ten topics would be covered, and the format permitted closer discussion, more intimacy and confidentiality than the formal NSC meetings."[47] Mondale was a vocal contributor at the Friday foreign-policy breakfasts.[48]

The vice president's staff structure testified to his foreign-policy influence.[49] Reflecting the change in emphasis on the vice presidency, Mondale had his own team of foreign-policy advisors—unlike Vice President Johnson, for example, who relied on the State Department and NSC experts. The vice president's staff size grew markedly in the 1970s. Mondale had a staff of between fifty-five and sixty people, compared to an office size of less than twenty in 1960. His staff became a replica of the president's office. "When I went over to visit some of the Mondale people after their first year, I saw something completely different," said an aide to former Vice President Humphrey. "The vice president's staff had come out of the closet. They weren't worried about letting the rest of the White House know who they were." According to Paul C. Light, these changes in staff size offered Mondale a level of independence not previously found in the vice presidency. As a result, Mondale did not have to depend on Carter's staff for political support.[50] Light explains how this helped bolster Mondale's role:

> The vice president's policy role starts with the institutional support needed to give advice. . . . Unlike [Vice President Lyndon] Johnson, who relied on State Department or NSC experts, Mondale had his own team of foreign advisors. Mondale was never forced to depend on Carter's staff for basic political support. That provided a level of independence not previously found in the vice presidency.[51]

Also unique to Mondale was what might be called his "extended" staff. "His staff became integrated with other elements of the White House staff to an unprecedented degree," notes Dumbrell. "Bert Carp of the DPS and David Aaron (Brzezinski's deputy) kept Mondale informed on domestic and foreign issue respectively."[52] Aaron, Mondale's former assistant in the Senate, became deputy director of the NSC. He alerted Mondale to upcoming issues. The vice president frequently walked the few steps to Aaron's office for information. (So close was he to Aaron that Mondale felt comfortable to complain to him about Brzezinski daring to interrupt the vice president at an SCC meeting.)[53] Mondale's staff was active in providing information to him and in helping Carter's staff make and implement policy. Moe, Mondale's chief of staff, and Eizenstat, Carter's assistant for domestic policy, jointly made or coordinated all domestic policy. Mondale's incorporation of his own foreign-policy advisors enhanced his role in foreign policy. "His staff provided him with independent analyses of foreign-policy issues," writes Moens, "which enabled Mondale to make substantial recommendations on policy options during the PRC and SCC meetings."[54]

Mondale's secure stature within the administration's foreign-policy structure, not to mention the placing of his former Senate friends within that framework, helped to provide the vice president with a quite active role in foreign policy in the Carter White House.

Mondale's Foreign-Policy Role

Mondale got his first taste of argument over a "foreign-policy issue" early on during the election campaign, notably during a key debate exchange with Republican vice-presidential candidate Robert Dole.[55] Mondale and Dole, the two vice-presidential candidates, met in Houston's Alley Theater on October 15, 1976 for the first vice-presidential debate in history. A question was posed to Dole about a comment he made in 1974, saying that Ford's pardon of Nixon was premature and a mistake. Dole angrily replied that Watergate was not a good campaign issue "any more than the Vietnam War would be, or World War I or World War II or the Korean War—all Democrat wars, all in this century. . . . I figured up the other day if we added up the killed and wounded in Democrat wars in this century, it would be about 1.6 million Americans." It was a remark that Dole would clearly later regret, but not before Mondale was able to insert an incisive rejoinder: "I think that Senator Dole has richly earned his reputation as a hatchet man tonight. Does he really mean to suggest that there was a partisan difference over our involvement in the fight against Nazi Germany?"[56]

Yet, Mondale's foreign-policy activities would not be confined to vice-presidential debates. Making good on his promise to involve Mondale in foreign policy, Carter right away took the extraordinary step of signing an executive order that made the vice president second in the chain of command for the control of nuclear weapons. Historically, the secretary of state had served as the deputy commander in chief, resulting from Congress passing the National Security Reorganization Act in 1958. "I was astounded to learn that former vice presidents had never been involved in this process," remarked Carter. "It was obvious to me that in a nuclear exchange, the president might well be incapacitated, and the vice president, as the new commander in chief, had to be fully qualified to assume his duties."[57]

This would be an early indication of the quantum leap in vice-presidential involvement in foreign and defense issues sparked under Carter and Mondale. As an illustration of his emerging influence, during the transition period Mondale took part in key foreign-policy appointments. He, Carter, and Jordan worked together in the selection of the cabinet. Mondale, along with Carter, interviewed Brzezinski for the NSA job and agreed with Carter in his selection. Years later, Mondale was also in on the decision in choosing Vance's successor as secretary of state. He, like Hamilton Jordan, may have preferred Warren Christopher, but conceded that Ed Muskie would be a popular public and political choice.[58]

Not much time passed before Carter publicly expressed his tremendous confidence in Mondale on foreign policy. In the fall of 1977, he told Jack Nelson of the *Los Angeles Times*: "On thirty minutes' notice, I would be perfectly willing to say, 'Fritz, I can't go to the Soviet Union because of some reason, would you go and do the final arrangements in the SALT negotiations with Brezhnev?' He has complete knowledge of the subject and of my position."[59]

Mondale did, in fact, have knowledge of all foreign-policy positions. Major presidential speeches on foreign policy were prepared under NSC supervision and were submitted to Mondale, Brown, and Vance before final approval.[60] Likewise, memos on key foreign-policy issues were run by Mondale. Hamilton Jordan mentions a memo he prepared on how the administration could modify its position in order to better the White House's chances of getting the hostages out of Iran. He described the new position as a "significant change" in administration policy on the hostages. Carter, in a typical response, returned the memo with the following handwritten instructions: "Good ideas. Discuss with Fritz, Cy, and Zbig." A special meeting was then arranged between Jordan, Carter, Mondale, Vance, and Brzezinski to discuss Jordan's memo. There, in essence, is a prototypical example of how Mondale was casually but automatically considered among the big four players in foreign policy.[61]

Mondale, as a senator, had been a champion of liberal Democratic ideas. As a result, liberals hoped he would keep Carter administration domestic policy staked to the left. He was seen as someone who could pacify traditional Democratic constituencies. Ironically, notes Steve Gillon, "Mondale's greatest accomplishments came in foreign policy."[62]

Gillon, in publishing one of the few profiles done on a vice president's role in foreign policy, details a number of areas in which Mondale played a key role. In the Middle East, he claims, Mondale had a "sustained role" in developing administration strategy and in constructing domestic political support for new initiatives. According to Gillon, Mondale's 1978 trip to Israel, especially his private discussions with Menachem Begin, "represented an important step toward Carter's greatest foreign-policy triumph—the signing of the Camp David Accords." In keeping with his concern for human rights, the vice president focused public attention on the plight of the boat people and the brutality of Vietnamese policy.[63] Gillon says Mondale's 1979 negotiations with Chinese leaders helped ease Sino-American tensions and form a more solid friendship between the two nations.[64] He also allegedly played a strong role in procuring Senate passage of the Panama Canal treaties—one among many duties that allowed him to fulfill a critical liaison role to the Congress. Nonetheless, writes Gillon, Mondale "had little impact on the two problems that eroded public support for Carter's foreign policy: the administration's confused approach toward the Soviet Union and his response to the hostage crisis in Iran."[65] Lastly, as shall be shown, there were instances in which Mondale's foreign-policy activities caused problems with other members of the foreign-policy team, such as the secretary of state—suggesting, of course, that using the vice president in foreign policy is not always as "squeaky clean" and problem free as some might believe.

Some of these items will be explored over the following pages. Before going into the larger foreign-policy cases examined below, the next several pages cover three general foreign-policy tasks performed by Mondale. An examination and appreciation of these tasks helps set the stage for the larger cases. For instance, the third task—"The Political Mondale in Foreign Policy"—is imperative to gaining an understanding of how domestic politics play a premium in the larger foreign-policy cases that involved the vice president.

Foreign-Policy Spokesman

Right off in the administration, Mondale began a foreign-policy spokesman role, taking the first of many overseas trips that extended far beyond the ceremonial wreath-laying missions of many past vice presidents. A few days after the inaugural ceremonies, Mondale took off for a nine-day trip to Europe and Japan. Carter scheduled the trip as a sign of his desire to consult with U.S. allies on important issues. Lest there been any doubt about the importance of the trip to the administration and the vice presidency in general, Carter remarked: "the leaders of other nations . . . recognize that Fritz indeed speaks for me. I doubt that this has ever been the case in the history of our nation with another vice president."[66] While the latter of these may or may not be true, Carter's remarks clearly confirm a foreign-policy spokesman role for Mondale.

The vice president's objectives for the trip were substantial. He served as the first Carter administration foreign-policy voice heard by European and Japanese leaders, offering an early pronouncement of White House commitments on cooperation and consultation with allies. He discussed the administration's foreign-policy plans.[67] The vice president himself immodestly called it "an unprecedented . . . diplomatic mission so early in a new administration." Among those Mondale consulted with during the trip was the NATO Council, where he told representatives that Carter's promised defense cuts would not effect the U.S. commitment to the Atlantic alliance. The next day he made a symbolic visit to the Berlin Wall, following a two hour meeting with West German Chancellor Helmut Schmidt, in which he spent two hours unsuccessfully lobbying him to halt the export of nuclear technology to Brazil.[68] While many of Mondale's efforts during the trip constituted affirmations of the Carter administration's intentions abroad, thus fulfilling his spokesman-abroad role, the Schmidt meeting demonstrated how the vice president actually *negotiated* with foreign officials.

The negotiating-abroad role is a historical rarity that seems to have been present only among a few vice presidents.

Either way, by most accounts, Mondale's trip was a success. "By handling many sensitive issues with skill and grace," writes Gillon. "Mondale emerged from his maiden voyage as a forceful spokesman for the administration."[69] Bernard Weinraub of the *New York Times* dubbed the trip "symbolism turned into substance" and asserted that Mondale had "emerged as a forceful spokesman for the administration and an adept diplomat." He quoted a NATO official in Brussels as saying: "He never put a foot wrong. He said all the right things, and he said them eloquently." The trip "made clear" to European and Japanese leaders what was on the mind of the new administration. Weinraub credited Mondale not only with "healing some diplomatic cracks" and "calming the fears" of some allies, but also with sending a signal "that the private and secretive diplomacy of Henry A. Kissinger would no longer dominate foreign policy." Pointing to Mondale's emphasis on "coordination and consultation with allies," one of the vice president's aides asserted that he was "exorcising the ghost of Henry Kissinger."[70]

Before going into the vice president's area-specific foreign-policy activities, here are two added crucial roles he played in foreign policy: congressional liaison and political watchdog. The reader will notice the salience of these two roles throughout the chapter.

Congressional Liaison on Foreign-Policy Issues

Mondale fulfilled a valuable congressional-liaison role between the White House and Capitol Hill. "Almost daily, Mondale made suggestions for improving relations with his former colleagues on the Hill," writes Gillon. "He recommended that the president hold more frequent meetings with congressional leaders, establish informal contacts between the White House staff and Congress, cultivate leaders in both houses who could make the difference on close votes." Jordan recalled that Carter "listened to Fritz because he knew his attitude was dominant among Democrats and Congress."[71]

One example of the vice president's congressional duties occurred during the Panama Canal debate. In the later summer of 1977 the Carter administration completed negotiations aimed at returning the Panama Canal. The negotiations led to two treaties—one that allowed for mixed control of the canal until 1999 and one that spelled out U.S. rights to defend the canal afterward. Both treaties required congressional approval. Securing the votes of key senators became a difficult battle in which Mondale played a key role as a congressional liaison.

Much like Vice President Quayle's role over a decade later during the Gulf War, Mondale made full use of his Senate contacts in lobbying former colleagues to support the president. He helped coordinate the administration's lobbying effort. During debate over the second treaty, Mondale spent at least one day per week on Capitol Hill working on wavering senators. To cite just one example of his daily efforts, Mondale brought one key senator, S. I. Hayakawa, a California Republican, to the vice president's Capitol Hill office, where they called the president and allowed Carter to personally press his case. During the phone call, Hayakawa changed his mind and agreed to vote for the treaty.[72]

In discussing the Panama Canal issue during administration meetings, Mondale explored the possibility of calling the Senate into special session if the treaty was voted down.[73] That, however, proved unnecessary, as the White House won both votes. Gillon writes: "Mondale was satisfied that by successfully translating his years of service and personal connections in the Senate into votes for the administration, he had helped the president score an impressive legislative victory."[74] More on Mondale's congressional role will be provided later.[75]

The other often (but not always) valuable service the vice president provided to the administration's foreign policy came via his political judgment.

The Political Mondale in Foreign Policy

Bill Kristol, Vice President Quayle's chief of staff, asserts that vice presidents do in fact have parochial interests, contrary to some claims. These parochial interests are political and involve advancing the vice president's fortunes.[76] In the case of Vice President Mondale, this is especially fitting. Believing that "my personal and political success is totally tied to yours," Mondale told Carter at Blair House that he wanted to break the perpetual frustration that had plagued the vice presidency. A key reason for Mondale becoming active in foreign policy was the lack of options in domestic affairs, in part (allegedly) imposed by stagflation. Moreover, the excitement and boldness of some foreign-policy initiatives were enticing. Steve Gillon writes: "Mondale, ever the astute politician, was hardly blind to the political advantages to be gained by bolstering his foreign-policy credentials."[77]

Vice President Mondale desperately wanted to be president someday. As a result, he had a built-in political barometer. Hence, he could always be counted on to place (literally) every Carter administration issue, foreign policy included, into a political framework—one that sized up both the administration *and* himself. As shall be seen throughout the cases in this chapter, Mondale was always looking at foreign-policy issues with a political eye. Brzezinski noted: "In general, Carter rarely, if ever, thought of foreign policy in terms of domestic politics, while Mondale rarely, if ever, thought of it otherwise." There were indisputably positive payoffs from Mondale's political focus. "Mondale's most important substantive contribution was his political judgment," writes Brzezinski. "He was a vital political barometer for the president, and Carter respected his opinion on the domestic implications of foreign-policy decisions. I also felt that Mondale had a good sense of political timing." In the end, Brzezinski felt that Mondale "complemented Carter both as a person and as a politician. Together, they made a team that was much more effective than either of them would have been by himself."[78]

The vice president applied his political barometer not simply to specific foreign-policy issues but also the administration's broader foreign policy in general. A spring 1978 memo to Carter demonstrates Mondale's political angle on foreign policy, not to mention his influential relationship with the president. In the memo, Mondale assessed the administration's development of foreign policy as lacking "strategic political thinking." "I have long sensed an attitude among the foreign-policy advisors," he wrote, in a subtle reference to Brzezinski, "that there is something suspect about looking at a foreign-policy problem in the context of the political environment in which it must be fought. I couldn't disagree more profoundly with this attitude, and I think we must do everything possible to reverse it." He later complained that Carter frequently made his decisions in a political vacuum: "A lot of these foreign-policy things used to come shooting in on a memo to the president and it didn't seem to me there was any thought about whether they were domestically sellable." In a direct reference to the NSA, Mondale later told Steve Gillon that, "Politics is a bad word for Brzezinski."[79]

Brzezinski admits that he shared with Carter a "predilection" to focus on national-security concerns without much attention to domestic politics, and that his experience in the White House "gradually educated me to a much higher awareness of the importance of domestic politics to our effectiveness." In that respect, he credits Mondale with providing "a needed corrective" to him and Carter. However, the NSA says that he "did feel at times that [Mondale] was too much inclined to defer to special domestic interests in fashioning his priorities. He probably felt that I was excessively insensitive to such matters."[80]

In some respects, Brzezinski here is merely being diplomatic and putting the best face on a sensitive situation. But he is also being forthright: He probably did learn from his experiences that totally divorcing foreign policy from domestic politics is not a stable recipe for a successful presidency. On the other hand, he was probably correct in viewing Mondale as being overly dictated by political interests, sometimes to the detriment of sound foreign policy. Surely, these remarks illuminate an occasional touchy relationship between Mondale and the NSA when it came to the political priority of some international issues. This occasional tension will become very obvious in the section on Mondale's role in Middle East/Israel policy.

A third observer, Robert Hunter, a former member of the Carter NSC, later recalled: "Zbig tended to look at things from a strategic and foreign policy perspective leaving mostly to other people the question of the politics of getting things done. Mondale always thought in terms of the politics within which things happen."[81] Hunter viewed Mondale's political perspective as an asset. In a 1989 interview, he told Alexander Moens:

He brought in particular a political perspective which was not always appreciated. The president was less political. I use "political" as a good word, not a bad word. Unless you can sell something to Congress and to the American people, you don't have a policy. . . . He had a genuine instinct for integrating politics and everything else. He was a tremendous asset to the process.[82]

In general, however, Mondale's attention to politics seemed to usually help the administration. For example, it allowed him to have a good feel for the administration's support for the Panama Canal treaties and (as will be seen) the mood of the American Jewish community during a time of sensitive administration policy regarding Israel-Egypt relations. But the political dynamic also seemed to cloud the vice president's judgment and actions, to the point where his personal presidential aspirations often seemed to be dictating his efforts. This was very likely a key reason why he abandoned his commitment to the politically dangerous South Africa issue.

Again, the aforementioned congressional and political roles of Mondale will become evident in the proceeding sections. The following pages cover specific areas of foreign-policy activity by Mondale. Due to space constraints, some areas had to be exempted, such as the vice president's impressive duties in Southeast Asia and China. Primarily, the chapter focuses on three cases: (1) Mondale's role in the Middle East/Egypt-Israel matter; (2) South Africa, and; (3) the Soviet Union and SALT II. Each case shows the lengths and limits of his involvement. There are also crucial policy insights that can be drawn from Mondale's experiences.

Middle East and Egypt/Israel

Middle East policy was an area in which Vice President Mondale's subservience to the political element put him on a path counter to administration policy. More specifically, it put him at odds with Carter, Brzezinski, and Vance. "From the beginning," writes Finlay Lewis, "Mondale often found himself playing a dissenter's role in the formulation of Middle Eastern policy."[83] Brzezinski, who had a generally positive relationship with Mondale and often agreed with him on policy, states that the most significant difference between him and the vice president involved the administration's Middle East efforts. A passage from the NSA's journal reads:

> During the day I had a sharp disagreement with the vice president. He was beating up on [NSC Middle East specialist] Bill Quandt over some relatively tough language that we are proposing to put before the Israelis and Egyptians. The thrust of the tough language will be critical of the Israelis.

The vice president was insisting that this be softened, and as a result he and I had a rather sharp exchange. I told him flatly that if he wants to change the presidential strategy he ought to discuss it with the president.[84]

Of the Big Four, Mondale came off as being the most pro-Israel, in large part because he was especially sensitive to the domestic-political implications of U.S. policy, namely in its impact on the American Jewish community.[85] In this sense, it seems that Israelis and American Jews likely viewed Mondale as their best ally among the inner core of him, Carter, Brzezinski, and Vance. (As will be shown later, this situation is strikingly parallel to how American and Israeli Jews perceived Vice President Quayle as their man in the Bush-Baker White House. Quayle's pro-Israel stand, however, was dictated more by hawkish security concerns, strategic-defense issues, and his strong Judeo-Christian roots, as opposed to domestic politics.) Indeed, as Brzezinski notes, this allowed Mondale to fulfill somewhat of a liaison role between President Carter, the Israeli embassy in Washington, and the Israeli leadership abroad.[86]

As one example of Mondale's views on the Arab-Israeli issue, as well as his White House influence, consider the following: Secretary of State Vance sent to Carter a copy of a speech he was preparing to deliver to the United Nations in late September 1978. The vice president, who was permitted to review all such material, was dissatisfied with language in the text that he felt might alarm the Israelis. Mondale argued unsuccessfully with Vance and Brzezinski for milder language. They refused. He then took his complaint to Carter, who had already approved the draft. Mondale convinced the president to make the changes. Carter later recalled the incident:

> One evening—I think it was probably nine-thirty, ten o'clock—Fritz called me on the phone and said he wanted to appeal my decision, and asked me to reexamine it. I think I was in a movie theater with a group of guests. . . . I left the theater and went up to my study and reread the text to look at Fritz's comments and I agreed with Fritz. I called Vance in New York and told him to modify the text. And I might say that both the Arabs . . . and the Israelis accepted the revised text with a great deal of appreciation.[87]

In general, the Carter administration adopted a Middle East policy at odds with much of Israeli leadership. When it came to territorial claims, the administration demanded not only a Palestinian homeland but that Israel return essentially to its pre-1967 borders. On the security side, Israel, which usually received fairly open dibs on U.S. weapons exports, was excluded from the list of allies given priority on U.S. weapons purchases. Additionally, Carter canceled the Ford administration's promise to sell Israel concussion bombs.[88] In an article in *Commentary*, Steven Spiegel suggests that the Carter policy in practice portrayed Israel as the greatest obstacle to peace in the region.[89] For such reasons, the administration was always willing to publicly criticize Israel.

Mondale felt that the administration was wrong on a number of fronts. He believed that Carter's statements on a Palestinian homeland, his seeming proclivity to recommend Israeli sacrifices while making only vague references to Arab concessions, and his commitment to a U.S. solution for the area would all combine to alienate skeptical Jewish voters and make the peace process more difficult. On June 10, 1977, Mondale expressed his concerns to Eizenstat, worrying that Carter "has gone too public and hasn't brought along the Jewish community." He feared that the White House would "be in bad shape politically" if it pursued a policy that alienated American Jews.[90]

In June, Mondale planned a major speech at the Northern California World Affairs Club in San Francisco, in which he hoped to quell Jewish concerns about Carter policy. In his briefing notes, Mondale noted that the address would offer "a good occasion for a public statement on our Middle East policy that can be helpful domestically." Yet, what Mondale hoped to say was toned down during weeks of haggling over the speech's language with the State Department. Additionally, although Mondale wanted to announce new administration objectives that might placate Israel, the president demanded that the speech merely clarify existing policy. In vain, the vice president sternly objected to Carter.[91] Making it even worse for the vice president was the fact that Brzezinski began pushing the president to have Mondale publicly speak out in complete agreement with administration policy, "thereby showing that the administration is united on the subject and that any successor to the president would pursue the same policy." Brzezinski said that he "kept pushing for this, in spite of Mondale's understandable reluctance to risk his standing with the Jewish community."[92]

In the end, Mondale gave a speech that simply towed the administration line, sparking the *New York Times* to aptly call it "a reaffirmation of the basic American policy that had aroused Jewish and Israeli concerns." The speech prompted a point-by-point rebuttal by New York Senator Jacob Javits, who called it "unrealistic." Javits' rebuttal included many of the points Mondale had hoped to make.[93] Needless to say, the speech was a bust from Mondale's perspective. (Interestingly, as shown below, the original intent of the Mondale speech was similar to one given by Vice President Quayle on June 11, 1990 to the American Israel Public Affairs Committee, AIPAC, on the anniversary of the 1967 Israeli victory. In Quayle's speech, he managed to say everything he wanted, even boldly referring to the occupied West Bank and Gaza Strip as Judea and Samaria, thereby ignoring long-standing U.S. policy. While the vice president's remarks delighted the Jewish lobby they infuriated the White House, the Baker State Department, and Arab allies. In short, Quayle seemed to get away with what Mondale could not!)[94] The speech also angered Mondale's activist Jewish friends, prompting many of them to (quite accurately) begin comparing his plight on the Middle East to Vice President Humphrey's lonely, silenced voice of opposition to Vietnam policy in the Johnson administration.[95]

However, partial relief and somewhat of a moral victory would come to Mondale only three weeks after the June 17 speech, as President Carter spoke to about forty prominent American Jewish leaders at the White House. The president pleased them by saying that a future Palestinian homeland should not be created as an independent state and had to be tied to the moderate Jordanian regime. A satisfied Israeli supporter who attended Carter's talk visited with Mondale shortly after and happily conveyed the details of the presentation. The vice president angrily responded: "Goddamn it, that's what I wanted to say in my San Francisco speech but they wouldn't let me."[96]

Despite Mondale's misgivings over the administration's approach, time would subsequently prove that the White House had acted wisely. Carter would eventually find himself presiding over historic negotiations that would culminate in the Camp David Accords, seemingly vindicating the president's policy. Mondale would play an active role in the Middle East peace negotiations up to and including the Camp David talks.

A big move by Mondale was his summer 1978 trip to Israel and Egypt. The vice president proposed the trip during a time of considerable turmoil. Despite Anwar Sadat's dramatic visit to the Knesset in November 1977, relations between the two nations remained strained due to a number of military maneuvers during the ensuing months. The vice president's trip was publicly billed as a commemoration of the 30th anniversary of Israeli statehood. In truth, Mondale used the trip to bridge the communications gap between Israeli Prime Minister Menachem Begin and Carter, in addition to discussing specific proposals aimed to rekindle the peace process. The vice president believed that Carter was genuinely committed to a strategy that he thought was best for the Israeli people, regardless of his sometimes harsh statements. Mondale hoped to convey to Begin that he should also trust Carter. He also hoped the trip might allow the administration to heal wounds it had with the American Jewish community.[97]

When the vice president arrived at Ben-Gurion International Airport he was greeted by Prime Minister Begin and his entire cabinet. Mondale made a number of symbolic appearances, including a meaningful visit to the Wailing Wall in East Jerusalem, a part of the Holy City seized by the Israelis in 1967. The wall was situated in a area regarded by the U.S. government as occupied territory, and thus off-limits to official U.S. representatives, if accompanied by an Israeli host. Over State Department objections, Mondale visited the wall anyway, stating that he was doing so as a personal visit by an American tourist. He was accompanied by Jerusalem Mayor Teddy Kollek in a limousine from which the customary American flag was noticeably missing. Not surprisingly, a number of Israelis were very excited by the Mondale gesture.[98]

Yet, the most important aspect of Mondale's trip was the time he spent lobbying Begin to trust President Carter. The vice president held a private, hour-long talk with the prime minister shortly before leaving for his meeting with Sadat in Egypt. In an interview with Finlay Lewis, Mondale recalled the meeting: "I made a strong plea that he trust Carter. . . . I tried to interpret Carter to him. I believe I made an impact on him because I think he was beginning to doubt us in our commitment to Israel."[99]

Likewise, Mondale seemed to have somewhat of an effect on the Egyptian leader, Anwar Sadat. The vice president flew from Israel to Egypt to meet with Sadat. The two men had a brief meeting. At the end of the meeting Sadat had accepted an invitation by Mondale to send the Egyptian foreign minister to London for the first face-to-face political talks between Egypt and Israel in six months. Sadat, in a joint press conference with Mondale, stated: "Let's hope this move will break the ice."[100]

Not surprisingly, the vice president regarded his trip a success, telling Carter upon his return that "there was substantially more flexibility privately from Begin and Sadat than anyone would ever suspect publicly." Mondale also told the president, in a rather prescient and ironic statement, that he was "especially convinced that Sadat was willing to go a long, long way to bring about a settlement."[101] By the time the vice president's trip had ended, he had persuaded Begin and Sadat to resume negotiations in London. While the talks in London did not produce an immediate breakthrough, they did prove that the signs of deadlock were easing. On his return, Mondale provided Carter with a memo arguing that the time was ripe for direct peace talks between Begin and Sadat, but only in an environment free of outside pressures—partly presaging the Camp David talks. He said that lower-level contacts between the two parties would not work.[102]

Oddly, Vance and Carter did not share Mondale's enthusiasm about his trip. The secretary of state, who had been against the vice president's trip from the outset, dubbed it "unnecessary" and "not very helpful." The president, in his memoirs, also played down the trip, strangely asserting that Mondale had come back with "a very discouraging report" on his discussions with Begin and Sadat. Carter noted that the two sides still remained far apart on key issues.[103] Steve Gillon, however, persuasively argues that Vance and Carter underestimated the impact of Mondale's trip. He points to two achievements. First, the vice president did help narrow the communication gap between Carter and Begin. Begin himself told Mondale's National Security Advisor Denis Clift that the vice president's visit represented "a turning point for the better in previously strained U.S.-Israeli relations." The Israeli leader said "that he was deeply impressed by the vice president's statement on the importance America attaches to good U.S.-Israeli relations made during their forty-five-minute ride from the airport to Jerusalem." Eizenstat said that Jewish leaders who accompanied Mondale saw a noticeable change in Begin's attitude after the visit, stating: "In Mondale, Begin saw someone who he knew had the best interests of Israel at heart. I don't think he was ever sure [that] Carter did."[104]

As a second achievement, Mondale helped regain crucial Jewish domestic support. "Mondale is a great and natural politician," Eisenstat wrote in his notes at the time. "Mondale really changes views of Jews on the plane." Gillon states that the Jewish leaders found Mondale to be a reassuring presence and concluded the trip more convinced of the administration's sincerity. Many were moved by the invitation to join the delegation. Gillon quotes one of the members, Hyman Bookbinder, as saying: "To be there as an official member of the vice president's delegation in the Jewish homeland, having him address the Knesset and giving expression to the American understanding of what Israel means to world Jewry was a moment unequaled in my public life."[105]

Understandably, Mondale believed that his efforts had resurrected the stalled negotiations. At that point, ironically, he began to make a number of policy proposals, all of which were rejected by either Carter, the State Department, or both.

Mondale was rightly concerned that the State Department might undermine his efforts. The vice president said that a negotiating paper prepared by Vance for the Leeds Conference contained, in Mondale's words, "every buzz word," including a canned statement about "legitimate Palestinian rights." He complained that the draft was a product of "Arabists in the State Department" and pushed to get it changed. He told the president that such continued public statements were creating hostility among Israelis. Mondale tried to convince Carter of the need to avoid making such public statements and to instead shift the debate to private forums. "We've got to get it off the public dialogue," he said. "If there's a public debate over this stuff, if we're exchanging papers that get into the press, we'll never get this thing settled." Believing it would be impossible to keep the issue out of the papers, the vice president made a bold proposal. He suggested Carter appoint former Secretary of State Henry Kissinger as a special negotiator in the region. This, he hoped, would not only increase bipartisan support but would also make use of Kissinger's negotiating skills, which Mondale admired. Further, said Mondale, appointing a special negotiator would remove responsibility from the State Department, which was mistrusted by both he and the Israelis. Although the president was reportedly receptive to the idea, he refused it. Vance agreed, stating: "I felt the Middle East was something that the Secretary of State had to be involved in every day."[106]

Another critical policy recommendation by Mondale was that Carter move slowly with any negotiations between the United States, Egypt, and Israel, because the congressional elections were only a few months away. Mondale, the consummate politician, did not want to anger Jewish voters. Carter, along with Hamilton Jordan, disagreed, believing that the only way the administration could win over Jewish voters was to get a peaceful settlement. Carter also desired a summit in Washington to bring him, Begin, and Sadat together for face-to-face negotiations. Mondale strenuously opposed the idea, feeling that such a situation would be a fireball that could blow up the whole process. As noted six weeks earlier in his memo on his trip to Israel and Egypt, Mondale favored discussions between Begin and Sadat. Yet, he was leery about involving the president at that time. Privately, Mondale questioned the wisdom of Carter's idea. Carter, on the other hand, decided "it would be best, win or lose, to go all out."[107] In July, Carter invited the two men to meet with him at Camp David in the fall.

Table 4.1: U.S. Representatives at Camp David Talks

NAME	TITLE
Jimmy Carter	President
Walter Mondale	Vice President
Cyrus Vance	Secretary of State
Zbigniew Brzezinski	National Security Advisor to the President
Hamilton Jordan	Staff of the President
Jody Powell	Press Secretary of the President
Harold Saunders	Assistant Secretary of State for Near East Affairs
Alfred Atherton	Ambassador at Large
Hermann Eilts	Ambassador to Egypt
Samuel Lewis	Ambassador to Israel
William Quandt	Staff of National Security Council

Source: Jimmy Carter, *Keeping Faith: Memoirs of a President* (Toronto and New York: Bantam Books, 1982), p. 326.

Nonetheless, the vice president was able to effect a crucial policy change in the weeks leading up to the talks. Already fearing that the summit could turn out to be a dismal failure, further sinking the president politically, Mondale was alarmed to discover that one of the American proposals forwarded during preliminary negotiations called for substantial Israeli withdrawal from the occupied West Bank. The vice president successfully killed the proposal by going directly to Carter and arguing that attempting to dictate such a solution to the Israelis would be fatal to the entire peace process. Mondale convinced the president that the administration had to come to the table with a clean slate and allow the solution to evolve via face-to-face bargaining between Israel and Egypt.[108]

In general, however, the vice president's advice had mixed results. In hindsight, it was a good thing Carter rejected Mondale's proposals about the timing of the talks, involving Kissinger, and excluding Carter from the direct, one-on-one Begin-Sadat talks the vice president recommended. The Camp David summit, of course, turned out quite well. The success, in large part, resulted from

Carter's timing and personal involvement.

In September, the three leaders met. According to the original plan, Mondale was supposed to stay in Washington to serve as acting president in Carter's absence, rather than attending the summit. Carter, realizing the unique help that Mondale could offer because of his personal rapport with Begin and Sadat, asked the vice president to come to Camp David to help him in what had thus far been fruitless dealings.[109] In particular, the president felt Mondale could be helpful in trying to move the Israeli leader. In an interview, Mondale told Steve Gillon how he pressed Begin to accept the conditions of the U.N. resolution that called for Israeli withdrawal from the Sinai:

> Mr. Begin, [said Mondale], this is not Judea and Samaria, this is not Jerusalem. We're on the brink of an historic breakthrough here. I know how painful this is but this is just land and buildings and brick. We can resettle these people. We should not let a couple of blocks of real estate stand in the way of this historic settlement.[110]

Although others on the U.S. team were advancing the same argument, Carter looked to Mondale because of the respect he had gained from the Israelis.[111] Yet, despite Mondale's exhortations, Begin made few concessions.[112] Still, in the end, the three sides reached a much-ballyhooed agreement. Many, however, Mondale included, felt that Sadat had sacrificed much more than Begin. The vice president feared that the Egyptian leader had jeopardized his personal safety. "When we left Camp David, I was certain Sadat was going to be killed and I was certain he knew it," admitted Mondale.[113]

The actual merits of the final accord is a matter to be debated elsewhere. In reaching the agreement, Carter's skill, timing, and determination was pivotal in allowing the breakthrough. Mondale recognized Carter's achievement. At the same time, Mondale took great satisfaction in his own role.[114] Brzezinski notes that the vice president was involved intensely in all negotiations, strategy sessions, framework papers, and so on.[115] The record adequately bears that out. Certainly, from the administration's perspective, it can be argued that Mondale made an impact. From the view of the vice presidency, he gained an undeniable accomplishment: Mondale attained a level of foreign-policy involvement that few of his predecessors ever achieved: direct, one-on-one negotiations with top foreign leaders in reaching a historic international agreement. Finlay Lewis is quick to underscore the benefits of the vice president's role:

> Mondale's [Middle East] visit was recalled months later as the participants in the Camp David summit were congratulating each other on what appeared to have been a diplomatic breakthrough. As he was preparing to leave . . . Begin told a small group of Americans that the vice president had been singularly responsible for the apparent success. The process

started, Begin said, with Mondale's arrival in Israel aboard Air Force II.[116]

In essence, Mondale was able to play an effective role in Carter administration policy regarding Egypt and Israel, including the policymaking and execution side. All along, he had an advisory role. Yet, throughout the process, his influence on administration Arab-Israeli strategy was hamstrung by the fact that his views were often opposed by the other three members of the inner core. He exhibited a decided inability to personally bring others to his point of view. That notwithstanding, the vice president's trip to Israel did seem to make a difference, as comments by Begin, Eizenstat, and Bookbinder attest—even though Carter and Vance stated otherwise. He also bargained with Begin during Camp David talks. And at the very least, Mondale's policy views were heard and respected, unlike Vice President Humphrey during Johnson administration discussions on Vietnam, not to mention other past second-officeholders.[117]

Lastly, and perhaps most importantly from the perspective of this study, is what this example says about potential differences and conflicts of interest between the vice president and other administration foreign-policy players, such as the NSA and secretary of state. Regarding the latter, there are many examples in which Mondale and the State Department came into conflict. For instance, in the speech at the Northern California World Affairs Club, Mondale hoped to quell American-Jewish concerns about Carter policy in the Middle East. But what he hoped to say was toned down during weeks of haggling with the State Department over the speech's language. Later on in the peace process, after which Mondale believed his efforts had resurrected stalled negotiations, he began to make a number of policy proposals, all of which were rejected by either the State Department, or Carter, or both. Mondale was rightly concerned that the State Department might undermine his efforts. As noted, the vice president complained that a negotiating paper prepared by Vance for the Leeds Conference contained "every buzz word," including the statement about "legitimate Palestinian rights." It was, in his view, a product of "Arabists in the State Department." Thus, as stated, Mondale pushed to get it changed. There was also the Kissinger issue. Vance objected to all of these issues advocated by the vice president.

As shall be shown in the final chapter, the conflicts of interest in this example have implications for reform recommendations on how to use the vice president in foreign policy. In a different sense, the following chapter on South Africa also offers crucial policy lessons.

South Africa

An area where Mondale's desires were translated into greater authority and influence was South Africa policy. South Africa was a hot topic on the agenda of the White House in large part because of its human-rights component. Neither Mondale nor Carter could ever be accused of not emphasizing human rights as a foreign-policy priority. During a September 10, 1976 campaign appearance at Notre Dame University, Mondale asserted that a Carter White House would work for the "restoration of a foreign policy that will enable Americans to see the best of themselves reflected in our actions abroad." He called his speech a "very significant" attempt to outline differences between Republican and Democratic approaches to foreign relations.[118] Lest anyone have trouble interpreting this language, the vice-president elect was stressing the importance of a foreign policy that placed human rights on a pedestal. The Carter administration hoped to separate itself from its predecessors by placing human rights at a level equal to or higher than military-strategic interests. South Africa would be a prime testing ground for that policy and a hallmark of the administration's human-rights commitment. Secretary of State Vance, in noting the administration's "commitment to human rights and democracy," stated: "President Carter and I were not willing to seek political advantage by presenting opposition to Soviet influence or radicalism as the foundation of American policy toward Pretoria."[119] The administration wanted to make a point with South Africa: Not all foreign policy, it felt, had to be viewed (and made) through the lens of communism and the East-West struggle; human rights could be elevated to an equal, if not higher, footing than the great rivalry with Moscow.

The administration was pressuring South Africa's prime minister, John Vorster, to end the nation's policy of apartheid and grant independence to Namibia. This would include a significant role for the vice president. On March 7, 1977 Carter announced he was placing Mondale *in charge* of the administration's Africa policy. Obviously, this was an impressive foreign-policy role for a vice president, especially because of what the region represented for the administration. Mondale, for his part, was concerned that being given such specific policies might tie him down and limit his ability to serve as a general advisor to the president, which was his original wish.[120] Nevertheless, an issue that situated black nationalists struggling for freedom against an oppressive white-minority government was an irresistibly intriguing assignment to a civil-rights liberal like Mondale. He happily took the job.

Mondale's role and influence in South Africa policy was especially impressive for a vice president; it was historically unique as far as the institution itself is concerned. However, as this section shows, his political self interests and lack of diplomatic experience may have hurt the administration in terms of South Africa policy. Hence, this case may provide an example of why some foreign policy should be left to diplomats and others, rather than vice presidents.

A month after the president's announcement, Mondale asked Carter if he could present the administration's case in a private meeting with Vorster. Carter agreed. Over the following weeks, Mondale buried himself in details about the history and politics of South Africa, meeting with scholars, State Department experts, and reading CIA-written psychological profiles of Vorster. He prepared for discussions with Vorster, learning how to avoid getting stuck in the prime minister's style of negotiating. Mondale felt that he was facing an extremely difficult task. He commented to Steven Gillon that trying to get South African leaders to end apartheid, stop destabilizing other nations in the region, and comply with United Nations resolutions on Namibia "was like trying to make Adolf Hitler a western liberal." They eventually met on May 19, 1977 in the Hofburg Palace in Vienna.[121] Gillon characterizes the somewhat dramatic exchange:

> Early in the meeting, Vorster challenged the vice president's moral authority by suggesting Africa's racial record was similar in many respects to America's treatment of Indians. Mondale retorted that Americans had learned from their experience that attempts to exclude groups from mainstream society were bound to fail. If it did not change course, South Africa would learn that same painful lesson. Vorster proceeded to justify his apartheid policy by claiming that divisions in South Africa were not just between black and white but between and among numerous tribal and national groups. "The only way to look at your problem," Mondale countered, leaning slightly forward in his chair for emphasis, "is that you have four percent of the population running everybody else and you're going through all these definitions to try and avoid that reality. We can't accept that and we will not accept that."
>
> Having dismissed most of Vorster's self-serving justifications, Mondale assumed the offensive. He warned that future relations would depend on Pretoria's actions and attitudes toward political and racial change in southern Africa, including the beginning of a progressive transformation of Southern African society away from apartheid. He underscored that, in sharp contrast to previous American policy in the region, the new administration's approach was rooted in concern for human rights, not anti-communism. Mondale said the United States was prepared to work closely with South Africa in pursuit of better relations, but he made clear that failure to address injustices would force Carter to support mandatory sanctions.[122]

From the view of the vice presidency, the exchange demonstrated a clear diplomatic/negotiating role for a second-officeholder. Such a dramatic overseas role for a vice president might not have taken place since Nixon's "kitchen debate" with Khrushchev. Yet, what Mondale actually accomplished from the exchange is less clear. While he may have won somewhat of a private moral victory, the vice president confessed during a cabinet briefing back home that he was not optimistic about his discussions with Vorster. He was not successful in changing South African behavior, although such a goal was admittedly beyond the realm of what Mondale likely hoped to effect anyway. He did get favorable reviews from sources like the *Washington Post*.

However, some critics charged that Mondale's recent actions were becoming symptomatic of the Carter administration's neglect of the complexity of international issues and showed a marked lack of *realpolitik*. Some opponents, such as Ronald Reagan, asserted that in its zeal to address new issues like human rights the administration was ignoring the most basic threat to U.S. security: the power and influence of the Soviet Union. These critics may have had a point. For instance, the administration's chief concern in the region, as demonstrated by Mondale's agenda, seemed to be that South Africa end its policy of apartheid and grant independence to Namibia. The memoirs of Cyrus Vance illustrate such priorities.[123] However, there were many other serious concerns in the region that directly affected the bipolar struggle of the Cold War. For example, a Cuban proxy backed by the Soviet Union had helped establish a Marxist regime in Angola. The same scenario was taking place in Ethiopia. There was suspicion that Rhodesia was next. Reagan and others charged that the White House was slighting these concerns and Mondale's trip was an indication.

In defense of the vice president, Vance said that Mondale's meeting was intended to underscore "the fact that our policy was rooted in our view of human rights and was not solely based on anti-communism."[124] Mondale shrugged off accusations of focusing on human rights at the expense of other more traditional security concerns. At a March dinner in honor of New York Senator Daniel Patrick Moynihan, he condemned "any definition of this country's national interest which fails to include a definition of our commitment to human rights." Three months later, he told the graduating class at the Naval Academy: "We've survived for 200 years as a free people because we've had a strong defense and because we've never . . . lost our commitment to human rights."[125]

Yet, there was a more specific criticism of Mondale's meeting with Vorster, one that showed the vice president's lack of foreign-policy experience and his ability to be driven by political self interests, and may have implications for how the second-office holder is used in global affairs. The Carter administration favored a "one-man, one-vote" policy in which each black in South Africa was permitted to vote along with each white, a stance totally at odds with South African leadership. Realizing the sensitivity of this matter, the administration decided to bite its tongue in pushing the issue at the current time, out of fear of sabotaging the early discussions. However, when asked by a reporter at a press conference following his meeting with Vorster, Mondale asserted that "every citizen [in South Africa] should have the right to vote and every vote should be equally weighted," thus endorsing the one-man, one-vote policy. Not only did Vorster respond angrily to Mondale's suggestion, but he also used the comment to rally white support and hinder reform.[126] Mondale trespassed the fine line between bargaining and telling a nation what to do. Although the president himself, only two to three months before the Mondale-Vorster meeting, had told the United Nations in a major human-rights speech that none of its members "can claim that mistreatment of its citizens is solely its own business," the White

House did understand the sensitivity of dictating to a nation like South Africa about its own internal affairs. Finlay Lewis seemed to hit it right when he wrote:

> Inexperienced in the subtleties of diplomacy, Mondale had crossed an invisible line. For the last day and a half, he had been telling Vorster with earnest directness what would happen to relations between the two countries if South Africa failed to heed black demands for political reform. Now he was dictating a solution to an embattled but sovereign nation whose politicians were notoriously sensitive about outside meddling. When it was his turn at the microphone, Vorster said pointedly, "If there is a choice and if that is the only choice—whether I want to be free and independent or whether I want to be recognized throughout the world—then naturally I opt for freedom and independence." By advocating universal suffrage for South Africans of all races, Mondale in effect was demanding that Vorster's group commit political suicide. The repercussions were felt for months afterwards, as American diplomats labored to assure the Vorster government that the United States had no intention of telling them how—in specific terms—they should solve South Africa's racial troubles.[127]

In the end, Mondale disavowed his own earlier statement. In an October interview with a leading South Africa newspaper, the vice president asserted: "I believe that the crucial step is to begin the dialogue among all segments of society. If there is one central suggestion that I made, it was that the leaders of the South African government meet with the legitimate nonwhite leaders of South Africa and develop with them the reforms which made sense to all South Africans." That Mondale message, Lewis contends, was "far different . . . from an unyielding insistence on a one-man, one-vote formula as the only basis for restructuring South African society."[128]

Mondale's misstatement had undermined two of the administration's chief goals in the Vorster talks. Cyrus Vance explicitly stated these objectives: "We agreed that our message must be worded so that South Africa could not misunderstand the attitude or intentions of the new administration. At the same time we sought no public confrontation with the South Africans." Of course, the Mondale message on the one-man, one-vote policy was worded in a manner that allowed the South Africans to interpret the administration's policy in a way the White House had not intended, which in turn created a public confrontation with the South Africans. Although Vance personally believed that Vorster misinterpreted and overreacted to Mondale's remarks, he acknowledged the subsequent damage the incident caused.[129]

While the vice president's remark may seem like an unfortunate slip of the tongue, it was a serious diplomatic mistake that may in large part have explained why the Carter administration, and Mondale himself, were unable to make much headway in future efforts with South Africa. This case may provide an example of the limits of using the vice president in foreign policy, particularly negotiations. While any U.S. official can make a casual but critical misstatement, the chances of such occurring may be higher when the negotiator—in this case a vice president thrust into a tough bargaining situation—is inexperienced in international diplomacy. On the other hand, a trained diplomat or State Department official might be more skilled in the nuances of such matters.

Mondale faded from view on South Africa policy after the Vorster meeting, despite having originally helped Carter lay out the grand design for the administration's Africa policy. Not surprisingly, the detailed, day-to-day execution was handed over to professional diplomats and area specialists. Moreover, there was another reason why Mondale abandoned the issue: The deepening turmoil on the continent, including the ugly situation in Rhodesia, was turning Africa into a political "tarbaby" (Mondale's words), and hence a no-win issue. According to Finlay Lewis, the astute politician "felt he had no more to contribute and a great deal to lose by a continuing political association with an inherently intractable problem."[130] Not wanting to hurt his future political standing, the vice president bailed out. Mondale's decision in this regard demonstrates that vice presidents do sometimes have their own selfish, parochial interests in mind—especially on the political side—when conducting foreign policy, contrary to the statements of scholars who maintain otherwise.

Soviet Union and SALT II

While South Africa was important to the Carter administration, another topic high on its agenda was Senate ratification of the SALT II treaty. Negotiations on the treaty with the Soviets stalled over a number of issues. The major disagreement in the administration involved linkage. The Soviets had been especially active in exporting communism, particularly in Africa. Understandably, there were calls from many corners to link negotiations to Soviet behavior in Africa and elsewhere. The implementation of linkage had split the Carter administration. Brzezinski wanted to use SALT to constrain Soviet adventurism. Vance disagreed, not wanting to jeopardize the agreement because of Soviet actions in Africa.[131] Some analysts were critical of the perceived "softness" of the Vance-Carter approach. Paul Nitze, who argued against the SALT accord, stated: "The Soviet leaders respect people of character, wisdom, and strength. . . . I do not believe that the way to improve one's relations with the Soviets is to enter into arrangements that are one-sided in their favor." He called the treaty "really worrisome."[132]

While Mondale was sympathetic to Vance's view, he appreciated the political implications of appearing soft on the Soviets. The vice president later complained that Vance never seemed to grasp the importance of going easy on Kremlin actions. "In order for us to make the inevitable concessions in negotiations with the Soviet Union," he told Steve Gillon, "we first had to be seen honestly by the American people, and by our allies as being tough. . . . [T]he public had to know we were hardminded if they were going to give us the confidence to get [SALT II] done." The vice president, always mindful of the political fallout, also pressed this case to Carter.[133]

Throughout the Carter years, Mondale served as a valuable congressional liaison, as shown in the Panama Canal example. This was also true for the SALT II debate. A group of ninety-five Republican senators, congressmen, and state office holders took positions solidly against the administration.[134] The vice president's visits to the Senate proved to him that a tough battle was in store for the president. Many conservative senators took a view similar to that of Nitze. A large number sided with Utah's Jake Garn, who argued that the treaty was "so one-sided in favor of the Soviets" that it posed a threat to the nation's security. Garn promised, "This is going to be a full-dress debate on a real foreign-policy issue. You'll see a deep and complete analysis of the treaty and its consequences." Yet, Republican leader Howard Baker said he doubted if there were twenty-five senators fully committed one way or the other.[135] Hence, this left a lot of room for lobbying, and the vice president would play a key part. Surveying the trouble on the right and the left, Mondale judged that about thirty conservatives would follow Washington Democrat Henry Jackson in not voting for the treaty under any circumstances. On the other hand, giving ground to conservatives invited opposition from liberal senators like George McGovern, who threatened to vote against the treaty if it was "weakened" to appease conservatives. Gillon writes:

> Throughout the summer, Mondale worked as an integral part of the SALT task force designed to convince wavering senators to support the agreement. While helping to plan administration strategy, Mondale met privately with individual senators and established himself as their prime contact on SALT. The president hoped that the close friendships Mondale maintained in the Senate, and the reservoir of respect that still existed there for him, could win valuable votes. In some cases, the vice president's congressional liaison believed that Mondale was the only person in the administration with the credibility to make a convincing case.[136]

Drawing on internal White House documents, Gillon offers examples of how critical Mondale was in working on fence-sitting senators. Regarding Paul Sarbanes of Maryland, the vice president was informed by his staff: "You are probably the only one in the White House who can talk to him anymore." Likewise, he was told of Oregon Republican Bob Packwood: "You are the one person in the administration for whom he has the kind of respect that would cause him to listen to substantive arguments." In the case of New York's liberal senator, Daniel Patrick Moynihan, Mondale was told that his "personal relationship and credibility with him could be crucial in keeping him from . . . making anti-Russian statements and otherwise gumming up the works."[137]

The vice president stepped out of his Capitol Hill office to put pressure on key senators in their home states. In July, he visited seven states—California, Oregon, Kansas, Nebraska, South Dakota, Tennessee, and Pennsylvania—which, not by coincidence, accounted for fourteen uncommitted senators. Mondale's schedule included seven major speeches to groups like the League of Women Voters and the various World Affairs Councils, four editorial conferences, seven press conferences, twelve "exclusive" television interviews, and a number of other appearances.[138]

Upon his return, the vice president briefed Carter on his efforts. Again, Mondale was true to the political eye that allowed him to serve as probably the administration's most astute judge of what was domestically workable. Consider another example within the SALT debate: In an overture intended to improve the SALT II situation, Carter would later move to placate conservatives by supporting an MX-missile system, advocated by Secretary of Defense Brown and the Joint Chiefs of Staff. The vice president argued that the idea was doomed politically because no state governor—pressured from environmental and peace groups, lawyers, etc.—would favor "a fifty mile race track down the center of his state [that would be] the target for all the bombs in the world." Recalling the mood of politicians and the public during his seven-state visit, Mondale felt that some administration members—such as Harold Brown and the Joint Chiefs of Staff—had come up "with a plan that was a political impossibility and all we got was trouble. That was typical of the sort of thing that bothered me."[139]

In the SALT II negotiations, the vice president played the role of a key congressional liaison, a general presidential advisor, an administration insider who framed White House recommendations within a broader framework of political feasibility, and an administration spokesman who lobbied for the president's policies. Ultimately, however, many of his efforts and the positions he took would be undermined by Soviet activities in Afghanistan, which prompted Carter to postpone the SALT negotiations.

The Soviet invasion of Afghanistan sparked a whole new dynamic. The administration was already struggling to move forward with SALT II. Yet, Soviet moves against Afghanistan—in addition to those in Vietnam, Cuba, Africa, and elsewhere—were, in Brzezinski's words, "to put it mildly, less than helpful."[140] By the end of March 1979, Brzezinski and Brown wanted to formally register the administration's concern with the Soviets, and eventually prevailed upon a less enthusiastic Vance and Warren Christopher. In the months that followed, the NSC adamantly pushed for a more vigorous U.S. reaction to Soviet activities, while the State Department reluctantly went along.[141] In April 1979, Brzezinski pushed through the SCC a decision to "be more sympathetic to those Afghans who were determined to preserve their country's independence." Mondale supported Brzezinski, despite State Department complaints. "Mondale was especially helpful in this," writes Brzezinski, "giving a forceful pep talk, mercilessly squelching the rather timid opposition of David Newsom, who was representing the State Department."[142] Mondale was in large part motivated by the fact that the administration was reacting too meekly to Soviet activities. The vice president understood that the issue was hurting the White House in the opinion polls.

Interestingly, Mondale's stance on Soviet policy and SALT talks seemingly wavered from dovish to moderate to hawkish throughout his four years as vice president. For instance, a firm Mondale unilaterally ordered U.S. intelligence activities directed at Cuba to be stepped up in the hope that the administration could get a clearer picture of Soviet activities there.[143] Typically, however, where Mondale stood usually depended upon how the issue was affected by politics. Consider the following examples:

His position on SALT II was primarily formed by two political factors: (1) if the administration was too hard on the Soviets, it could jeopardize Carter's chances of reaching an agreement with the Kremlin, thus hurting politically with American liberals; and (2) if the administration was too soft on the Soviets, it risked reaching an agreement that benefited the Kremlin at American expense, thus hurting politically with U.S. conservatives. Hence, Mondale teetered back and forth, seeing the merit in each side.

The vice president was at times willing to suggest bold symbolic moves to protest Soviet actions. For example, he was the first administration member to raise the issue of possible U.S. abstention from the Moscow Olympics. But Mondale's desire to register administration complaints with the Soviets reversed itself when the grain embargo was debated. To Brzezinski's surprise, at a December 30 NSC meeting even Vance came out in favor of a deep cut in U.S. grain deliveries to the Soviet Union. Mondale, however, pointed out that an embargo could be damaging to the forthcoming presidential primary in Iowa, and convinced Carter to at least defer his decision on the matter. "Mr. President, we need to be strong and firm," said Mondale, "but that doesn't mean you have to commit political suicide."[144] Despite Mondale's temporary victory, a couple of weeks later Carter dismissed the vice president's concerns and decided to go with the embargo, due primarily to the strong support for it by both Vance and Brzezinski.[145] "The vice president was not convinced by my explanation," admitted Carter.[146]

But Mondale did continue to play the loyal vice-president role. Carter stated: "[W]hen I could not be dissuaded, he was loyal in backing my decision. As he traveled through the Midwestern states on the campaign trail, he defended my action to anxious farmers."[147] Mondale also continued to lobby for it throughout the campaign. As the 1980 presidential campaign heated up, challenger Massachusetts Senator Ted Kennedy assailed the grain embargo. Kennedy made the case that the embargo was punishing American farmers more than the Soviets. With Carter devoting most of his time to trying to resolve the

Iranian crisis, he sent Mondale to challenge Kennedy. The vice president flew to Iowa and allegedly raised the ire of his long-time friend by accusing him of being driven by "the politics of the moment."[148] Mondale was biting his tongue. Before heading off to the June 1980 Economic Summit in Venice, he again recommended to Carter that the grain embargo be lifted, pointing to GOP presidential candidate Reagan's successful exploitation of the issue. Again, Carter rejected the request.[149]

In sum, this account of Mondale's role in Soviet policy and the SALT debate reflects all of his manifestations in Carter administration foreign policy: a generalist advisor whose position was often dictated by political interests, an astute judge of political realities, a very loyal spokesman who put aside his own disagreements in order to publicly pitch Carter's positions, a forceful and vocal participant in Oval Office debates, and a valuable congressional liaison.

Conclusion

As always, when discussing the role played by a vice president, an integral component is the president himself. A point made in this study over and over is that while all vice presidents are now guaranteed somewhat of a foreign-policy role simply as a result of Truman's statutory changes, the degree to which a particular vice president is involved or has influence is ultimately up to the president he serves. Mondale was fortunate to have a sympathetic and innovative president who allowed him to maximize the vice president's possibilities in foreign policy. In this case, both the president and vice president had big eyes regarding how the vice presidency could be expanded. Carter, for instance, spoke of his own "ideas for a greatly expanded role for the vice president," and they were compatible with Mondale's "excellent ideas about how to make the Vice Presidency a full-time and productive job." Immediately after the election, says Carter, Mondale came to him with a well-prepared book of suggestions on how to better use the vice president, and Carter accepted all of them.[150] In the Carter-Mondale situation, the idiosyncrasies of each man contributed to the bolstered foreign-policy role of the latter. "The president deserved much of the credit for [the] relationship's success," concedes Steven Gillon. "Defying precedent, he readily accepted Mondale's proposals for strengthening the vice presidency. He always solicited Mondale's opinion and carefully weighed his advice."[151] Marie Natoli adds that "Carter was fully comfortable with, willing to, and interested in having his vice president play a full role."[152] Both Gillon and Natoli are exactly right.

Mondale played a unique and impressive role in foreign policy, especially at that time. However, one must be careful not to exaggerate his role. Gillon correctly notes:

Though he served as the administration's first emissary, Mondale did not play a major role in developing Carter's ambitious foreign-policy agenda. ... Since he lacked experience in foreign policy and had greater interest in long-neglected domestic problems, Mondale planned to let Brzezinski and Vance develop a strategy appropriate to the new approach. His foreign-policy activity may have lacked the sustained day-to-day involvement that characterized his interest in domestic politics, but the vice president established himself as a link in the foreign-policy apparatus.[153]

That said, Mondale's foreign-policy role was unquestionably extensive in scope and revolutionary in nature. Never before had a vice president had his own defense and foreign-policy advisors—not until Mondale. The vice president had never been officially listed as the second in the chain-of-command for responsibility for a nuclear exchange. That, too, changed under Mondale. He was intimately involved in all major foreign-policy discussions and decisions, even if his ability to influence them was constrained. In particular, the Middle East/Camp David example shows his strong but limited influence. He also played a valuable political and congressional liaison role throughout the administration's foreign policy, as seen also in the case of the Panama Canal and SALT II treaties. These two roles were tailored to Mondale specifically and, it seems, might not have been carried out by any other administration member as well as him. At the least, as many accounts attest, he was invaluable in offering such attributes to a president who was weak in the area of congressional relations and in understanding the political implications of foreign-policy issues.

Finally, on the negative side, his often-valuable political barometer was also at times a liability to the White House. For instance, the vice president was initially given control of foreign policy for an entire region—Africa. His duties there did not fulfill their promise in part because of Mondale's own selfish-political interests, which may have often clouded the vice president's judgment and actions to the point where his personal presidential aspirations seemed to dictate his efforts. This was very likely a key reason why he abandoned his commitment to the politically dangerous South Africa issue. This reality flies in the face of reformers who suggest that the vice president be used extensively in foreign policy because he, allegedly unlike other administration players, is unfettered by selfish-parochial interests. As the Mondale example in South Africa indicates, this is not necessarily true. This issue has policy implications which will be reexamined in the final chapter. Likewise with many of the issues discussed in this chapter.

Notes

1. R. Gordon Hoxie, "Staffing the Ford and Carter Presidencies," *Presidential Studies Quarterly*, Vol. X, No. 3, Summer 1980, p. 390.
2. Marie D. Natoli, "The Vice Presidency: Gerald Ford as Healer?" Editorial, *Presidential Studies Quarterly*, Vol. X, No. 4, Fall 1980, p. 664.
3. Marie D. Natoli, "The Vice Presidency in the Third Century," in James P. Pfiffner and R. Gordon Hoxie, eds., *The Presidency in Transition* (New York: Center for the Study of the Presidency, 1989), p. 421.
4. Hamilton Jordan, *Crisis: The Last Year of the Carter Presidency* (New York: G. P. Putnam's Sons, 1982); and Alexander Moens, *Foreign Policy under Carter: Testing Multiple Advocacy Decision Making* (Boulder, Colo.: Westview, 1990), pp. 44-45.
5. Jules Witcover, *Crapshoot: Rolling the Dice on the Vice Presidency* (New York: Crown Publishers, 1992), p. 299.
6. Finlay Lewis, *Mondale: Portrait of an American Politician* (New York: Harper & Row, 1980), pp. 1-4.
7. Jimmy Carter, *Keeping Faith: Memoirs of a President* (Toronto and New York: Bantam Books, 1982), p. 35.
8. Ibid., p. 39.
9. Lewis, op. cit., pp. 1-4.
10. Carter, op. cit., p. 37.
11. Lewis, op. cit., pp. 1-4.
12. Ibid., and Carter, op. cit., pp. 36-37.
13. Ibid., p. 232; Carter, op. cit., p. 39; and Steven M. Gillon, *The Democrats' Dilemma: Walter F. Mondale and the Liberal Legacy* (New York: Columbia University Press, 1992), pp. 165 and 180. Steven M. Gillon's book is based on scores of interviews with Carter administration officials, including many with Mondale himself. He also had access to personal notes written by officials, including Mondale's briefing notes for the Monday lunches with Carter and the Friday morning foreign-policy breakfasts. More than any other chapter in this study, this one on Vice President Mondale benefits greatly from the research of Gillon.
14. Lewis, op. cit., p. 232.
15. Carter, op. cit., p. 39.
16. Gillon, op. cit., p. 180.
17. Zbigniew Brzezinski, *Power and Principle: Memoirs of the National Security Advisor, 1977-1981* (New York: Farrar, Straus, Giroux, 1983), p. 68; Carter, op. cit., p. 55; Paul C. Light, *Vice-Presidential Power* (Baltimore: Johns Hopkins University Press, 1984), p. 80; and Jordan, op. cit., p. 185.
18. Witcover, op. cit., p. 299.
19. Carter, op. cit., p. 39; Brzezinski, op. cit., pp. 33-35; Jordan, op. cit., p. 77; and Light, *Vice-Presidential Power*, pp. 76, 154, and 177.
20. Carter, op. cit., p. 40; Brzezinski, op. cit., pp. 33-35; Jordan, op. cit., p. 77; and Light, *Vice-Presidential Power*, pp. 76, 154, and 177.
21. Gillon, op. cit., pp. 181-82.
22. Brzezinski, op. cit., p. 33.
23. Gillon, op. cit., p. 182.
24. Brzezinski argues that he chose to have Aaron as his deputy NSA and that

Aaron was not "imposed" on him by Mondale, as "was later often alleged in Washington." Aaron was the transition chief for the NSC. Brzezinski, after working with him during the transition, asked him to remain and even become his deputy "without either consulting Mondale or being pressed by him." Hence, Mondale was not so influential as to hand pick Brzezinski's deputy, but he would at least benefit from his presence. Brzezinski, op. cit., p. 76.

25. Gillon, op. cit., p. 181.

26. Jordan, op. cit., p. 68; and Moens, op. cit., p. 45.

27. John Dumbrell, *The Carter Presidency: A Re-Evaluation* (Manchester and New York: Manchester University Press, 1993), p. 38.

28. Lewis, op. cit., p. 241.

29. *The New York Times*, September 29, 1977.

30. Lewis, op. cit., p. 242. Also see Jordan's book for references that illustrate this point.

31. Jordan, op. cit., pp. 391-92.

32. Dumbrell, op. cit., p. 38.

33. Gillon, op. cit., p. 291.

34. *The New York Times*, December 21, 1980.

35. Gillon, op. cit., p. 291.

36. Numerous accounts show Harold Brown to be an important player. However, his status did not seem to equal the level of the Big Four. In particular on this issue, see Moens, op. cit., p. 44.

37. Brzezinski, op. cit., p. 30.

38. Cyrus Vance, *Hard Choices: Critical Years in America's Foreign Policy* (New York: Simon & Schuster, 1983), pp. 36-38.

39. Brzezinski, op. cit., pp. 59 and 412.

40. Vance, op. cit., pp. 36-37.

41. Brzezinski, op. cit., p. 67.

42. Ibid., p. 51.

43. Ibid., p. 68; Carter, op. cit., p. 55; Light, *Vice-Presidential Power*, p. 80; Jordan, op. cit., p. 185.

44. Carter, op. cit., p. 55; Gillon, op. cit., p. 217; and Brzezinski, op. cit., p. 224.

45. Witcover, op. cit., p. 299; and Dumbrell, op. cit., p. 38.

46. Vance, op. cit., p. 39.

47. Brzezinski, op. cit., pp. 67-69.

48. Dumbrell, op. cit., p. 38.

49. Marie D. Natoli, "The Vice Presidency: Gerald Ford as Healer?" p. 664.

50. Paul C. Light, "The Institutional Vice Presidency," *Presidential Studies Quarterly*, Vol. XIII, No. 2, Spring 1983, pp. 198-99; and Moens, op. cit., p. 44.

51. Light, "The Institutional Vice Presidency," pp. 198-99.

52. Dumbrell, op. cit., p. 38.

53. Brzezinski, op. cit., pp. 33-34; Light, *Vice-Presidential Power*, pp. 76, 154, and 177; and Moens, op. cit., pp. 44-45. A subject for future research might explore exactly how Mondale's "extended staff" helped him in regard to the administration's foreign policy. There is a considerable lack of research on this subject. Moreover, it would be interesting to know how the staffs of Mondale, Nixon, and other vice presidents interacted with the White House team, and what bureaucratic conflicts resulted. I touch on this latter subject in my research on Quayle and Gore. A separate study, however, might

be worthwhile.

54. Moens, op. cit., p. 44-45.

55. Further proof of the post-World War II surge of the vice presidency is that the first vice-presidential debate in history did not take place until 1976 between Mondale and vice-presidential nominee Dole.

56. *New York Times*, October 16, 1976; *Washington Post*, October 16, 1976; and Witcover, op. cit., p. 297. In turn, the Carter campaign began to view the Mondale/Dole contrast as a winning issue. Carter ran television ads everywhere except the South. As the TV screen relayed pictures of the two men, a voice chimed in: "What kind of men are they? When you know that four of the last six vice presidents have wound up as presidents, who would you like to see a heartbeat away from the presidency?" Gillon, op. cit., pp. 176-77.

57. Carter, op. cit., p. 40.

58. Jordan, op. cit., pp. 46, 171, and 282.

59. Lewis, op. cit., pp. 240-41.

60. Brzezinski, op. cit., p. 72.

61. Jordan, op. cit., pp. 121-22 and 125.

62. Gillon, op. cit., p. 228.

63. For an intriguing account of the substantive role played by Vice President Mondale in his twelve-day trip to Southeast Asia in May 1978, see Gillon, op. cit., pp. 228-32. The trip allowed Mondale to negotiate with foreign leaders and act as an emissary and spokesman. Finishing his trip with an emotional July 19, 1979, speech in Geneva, Mondale spoke eloquently on the plight of the Vietnamese boat people. Cy Vance called the speech "one of the most significant acts of the Carter administration." Vance, op. cit., p. 126.

64. Brzezinski was not alone in calling Mondale's 1979 visit to China "a great success." He referred to it as the "high point" in the administration's "stratagem of 'trip diplomacy.'" For information on Mondale and China, see Brzezinski, op. cit., pp. 417-25; Vance, op. cit., p. 390; and Gillon, op. cit., pp. 244-49.

65. Gillon, op. cit., p. 293.

66. *New York Times*, January 23, 1977.

67. Brzezinski, op. cit., p. 292.

68. David S. Broder, "Mondale Begins Tour in Brussels," *Washington Post*, January 24, 1977, p. A1; and "Vice President Mondale Visits Europe and Japan," *The Department of State Bulletin*, Vol. LXXVI, No. 1967, March 7, 1977, pp. 181-97. Also see *New York Times*, January 24-31, 1977; and *Washington Post*, January 24-31, 1977.

69. Gillon, op. cit., p. 216.

70. Bernard Weinraub, "More Open U.S. Diplomacy Is Message of Mondale's Trip," *The New York Times*, February 1, 1977, p. A3; and Broder, op. cit., p. A1.

71. Gillon, op. cit., pp. 193 and 203.

72. Ibid., pp. 223-26.

73. Brzezinski, op. cit., p. 138.

74. Gillon, op. cit., pp. 224-25.

75. In another example of his working the Congress on foreign policy, during a February 1978 trip to the Philippines—which involved bargaining with Ferdinand Marcos—Mondale telephoned congressional liberals from Manila to try to persuade them against cutting aid to the Philippines while the administration was negotiating an extension of its lease on the Subic Bay naval base. Dumbrell, op. cit., p. 185.

76. Interview with Bill Kristol, May 26, 1996. Kristol's point will be examined in greater detail in the final chapter.
77. Gillon, op. cit., pp. 180 and 228.
78. Brzezinski, op. cit., pp. 34-35.
79. Gillon, op. cit., pp. 227 and 239-40.
80. Brzezinski, op. cit., p. 35.
81. Gillon, op. cit., p. 239.
82. Moens, op. cit., p. 45.
83. Lewis, op. cit., p. 257.
84. Brzezinski, op. cit., p. 35.
85. Carter, on the other hand, gave little attention to the domestic political aspects of Israeli policy. Brzezinski writes: "Occasionally Carter would say that he would be willing to lose the presidency for the sake of genuine peace in the Middle East, and I think he was sincere." Ibid., p. 97.
86. Ibid., p. 92.
87. Lewis, op. cit., pp. 238-89.
88. Brzezinski, op. cit., pp. 84-90, Carter, op. cit., pp. 273-80; Vance, op. cit., pp. 159-95; and Gillon, op. cit., p. 221.
89. Steven Spiegel, "Carter and Israel," *Commentary*, July 1977, pp. 35-40.
90. Gillon, op. cit., p. 222.
91. Ibid., p. 222; and Lewis, op. cit., pp. 257-58.
92. Brzezinski, op. cit., p. 96.
93. Gillon, op. cit., p. 222; *New York Times*, June 18, 1977; and *Washington Post*, June 18, 1977.
94. "Text of Remarks by the Vice President to the American Israel Public Affairs Committee on June 11, 1990," *American-Arab Affairs*, Summer 1990, No. 33, p. 167; and Michael Duffy, "Is He Really That Bad?" *Time*, May 20, 1991, p. 22.
95. Lewis, op. cit., p. 258.
96. Ibid.
97. Gillon, op. cit., pp. 232-33.
98. Lewis, op. cit., pp. 256-57.
99. Ibid., p. 259.
100. "Vice President Mondale's Address to the Israeli Knesset," *The Department of State Bulletin*, Vol. 78, No. 2017, August 1978, pp. 33-37; and Gillon, op. cit., p. 234.
101. Gillon, op. cit., pp. 234-35.
102. Lewis, op. cit., pp. 258-59.
103. Carter, op. cit., p. 315; and Gillon, op. cit., pp. 234-35 (based on interviews with Mondale and Vance).
104. Gillon, op. cit., p. 235.
105. Ibid., p. 235.
106. Ibid., pp. 235-56.
107. Lewis, op. cit., pp. 258-60; and Gillon, op. cit., pp. 236-37.
108. Lewis, op. cit., pp. 259-60.
109. Ibid., p. 260.
110. Gillon, op. cit., pp. 236-37.
111. Lewis, op. cit., p. 260.
112. Vance, op. cit., p. 199.
113. Gillon, op. cit., p. 237.

114. Ibid.

115. See Brzezinski, op. cit., pp. 238-39, 242-44, 246, 249, 256, 258, 260, 265, 267-68, 271, and 279-81.

116. Lewis, op. cit., p. 257.

117. Humphrey found himself in trouble with LBJ when he spoke on Vietnam. Alexander Haig, in his book *Caveat*, includes an eyewitness account from the time he served on the NSC staff in the Johnson administration: "In at least one White House meeting that I attended, with members of the NSC and congressional leaders present, President Johnson allowed the loquacious Hubert H. Humphrey five minutes in which to speak ('Five minutes, Hubert!'); then Johnson stood by, eyes fixed on the sweep-second hand of his watch, while Humphrey spoke, and when the Vice President went over the limit, pushed him, still talking, out of the room with his own hands." See Witcover, op. cit., p. 197.

118. Warren Brown, "Mondale Assails Foreign Policy As Tainted by 'Watergate Era,'" *Washington Post*, September 11, 1976, p. A3.

119. Vance, op. cit., p. 263.

120. Gillon, op. cit., p. 218.

121. Lewis, op. cit., pp. 251-52; and Gillon, op. cit., pp. 219-20.

122. Gillon, op. cit., pp. 219-20. Also see Lewis, op. cit., pp. 252-53.

123. Vance, op. cit., pp. 262-63.

124. Ibid., p. 265.

125. Gillon, op. cit., p. 221.

126. "Vice President Mondale Visits Europe and Meets with South African Prime Minister Vorster: Remarks during the Visit and News Conference Following His Meeting with Prime Minister Vorster," *The Department of State Bulletin*, Vol. LXXVI, No. 1982, June 20, 1977, pp. 659-66; Lewis, op. cit., pp. 252-53; Gillon, op. cit., p. 220; and Vance, op. cit., p. 265.

127. Lewis, op. cit., pp. 253-54.

128. Ibid., p. 254.

129. Vance, op. cit., pp. 263-66.

130. Lewis, op. cit., p. 254.

131. Vance, op. cit., pp. 46-60 and 91-92; and Brzezinski, op. cit., pp. 178-83.

132. David Butler, "SALT II: And Now for the Battle," *Newsweek*, May 21, 1979, Vol. 93, No. 21, p. 43.

133. Brzezinski, op. cit., pp. 34-35; and Gillon, op. cit., pp. 240-41.

134. Peter Goldman, "The Hard Salt Sell," *Newsweek*, February 19, 1979, Vol. 93, No. 8, pp. 32-33.

135. Butler, op. cit., p. 37.

136. Gillon, op. cit., p. 242.

137. Ibid.

138. Ibid., pp. 242-43.

139. Ibid., pp. 243-44.

140. Brzezinski, op. cit., pp. 354-55.

141. Of course, a dramatic manifestation of the administration's unhappiness with the Soviet Union was Carter's 1978 speech in Annapolis, which prompted a vitriolic, detailed, 5,000-word response from the Kremlin, published in *Pravda* and all other Soviet daily newspapers. See Don Oberdorfer, "U.S. Studies Soviet Attack: Vance May Reveal Reaction," *The Washington Post*, June 18, 1978, p. A16; and "Excerpts from

Pravda Commentary on Relations between Soviet and the United States," *The New York Times*, June 18, 1978, p. A10.

    142. Brzezinski, op. cit., pp. 426-27 and 433.
    143. Vance, op. cit., p. 359.
    144. Jordan, op. cit., p. 100.
    145. Brzezinski, op. cit., pp. 427-31
    146. Carter, op. cit., p. 476.
    147. Ibid.
    148. Witcover, op. cit., p. 302.
    149. Brzezinski, op. cit., pp. 460-61.
    150. Carter, op. cit., pp. 37-39.
    151. Gillon, op. cit., pp. 291-92.
    152. Marie D. Natoli, "The Vice Presidency in the Third Century," p. 421.
    153. Gillon, op. cit., pp. 216-17.

Chapter 5
A Crisis-Managing Vice President: George H. W. Bush (1981-89)

"Bush had not conveyed any firm, clear message about Central America or the Contadora treaty. [B]oth Venezuela and Colombia would interpret his silence as U.S. agreement with their having gone along with Mexico."
NSC staffer Constantine Menges, on Bush's alleged mishandling of a delicate foreign-policy task in Latin America

"During Grenada, Bush was superb."
Menges, on Bush's first crisis-management experience

Introduction

The scene was the 1988 Democratic National Convention. The Democrats were readying for a November showdown between their guy, Michael Dukakis, and the Republican presidential nominee, George Bush. Amidst the hoopla of the convention, Massachusetts Senator Ted Kennedy roused the party faithful into a frenzied chant of "Where was George?!" Cheerleader Kennedy would name a key Reagan administration event—positive or sometimes even negative, depending upon which purpose he was trying to serve. He would then ask rhetorically, "Where was George?!," implying that former Vice President George Bush was (1) a "do-nothing" lackey who made no difference whatsoever during his two terms or (2) someone who was very busy doing no good.

Obviously, Kennedy's charges were motivated by partisan politics. Ironically, however, the first of his aspersions was slightly more justified than maybe even he realized. Bush was a very quiet vice president who assumed a faithfully low profile. To a degree, Kennedy could be forgiven for not noticing him. But only to a degree. "George" was often in many places during the Reagan administration. In the area of foreign policy in particular, he performed some very impressive, positive roles that were little noticed—a tribute to Bush's silent demeanor. He participated in some highly successful negotiating trips abroad, such as in his role in the INF-Euromissile deployment in Western Europe.

The vice president's counselor, C. Boyden Gray, was not off the mark when he asserted that "Bush has continued and indeed strengthened the Office of the Vice President as a strong and integral part of the executive branch.... [A] review of both the vice president's record and the ever-increasing demands of the presidency strongly suggest that the nature of the vice presidency has been permanently altered."[1] He continued the strong roles established by vice presidents Nixon and Mondale. Bush, however, took it to another level by being the first vice president to head up a major interagency foreign-policy committee.

By all objective measures, Bush was a model vice president who performed well in his foreign-policy capacities. An examination of most of his duties should partly comfort those who suggest an enhanced foreign-policy role for the vice president. However, Bush's record is marred by at least one foreign-policy mission in which he did not seem to adequately fulfill his tasks. One involved King Fahd of Saudi Arabia and the other (possibly) Central America policy in August 1984. Both were important, delicate foreign-policy missions; they are highlighted in this chapter. The vice president's poor performance in at least the Saudi case suggests that while no one is perfect, it may not always be a wise idea to hand over crucial foreign-policy responsibility to an untrained negotiator or to someone who has selfish political interests, as most vice presidents do. This brings to mind Vice President Mondale's misstatements regarding South Africa policy and Vice President Nixon's on Indochina.

Bush's Selection and Role Definition

Reagan's choice for vice president had the potential to impact his foreign-policy decision-making process far beyond what most know or could conceive. For instance, the two leading contenders to serve as Reagan's running mate in 1980 were Bush and former Republican president Gerald Ford. The Reagan-Ford combo was referred to in some quarters as a GOP "dream ticket." Had Ford been chosen, it could have affected Reagan's foreign-policy structure significantly. Consider that on the afternoon of June 16, 1980 during the Republican convention—the presidential balloting and vice-presidential choice would be made that night—a group of former Ford administration officials, including Henry Kissinger, Alan Greenspan, William Brock, and Jack Marsh met with top-level Reagan staffers to kick around plans for a Reagan-Ford ticket. Shockingly, according to reports, Kissinger and the others were trying to work out an arrangement in which a President Reagan would be in charge of domestic and economic policy and a Vice President Ford, presumably with Kissinger's help, would be responsible for foreign and defense policy. Ford himself alluded to such an ordering during an interview that evening with Walter Cronkite.[2] Obviously, had such a silly arrangement been secured, Reagan's vice president would have had extraordinary powers in foreign policy—certainly the most influential such role in the history of the vice presidency.

As it turned out, Reagan's vice president—George Bush, not Gerald Ford—would take on impressive duties in foreign policy. Of course, the outcome would not be nearly as revolutionary as the Ford consideration. Still, Bush would substantially enhance the vice president's foreign-policy role. Part of the reason for that role related to the confidence Reagan had in Bush's abilities in foreign policy, stemming from his past experiences.

Bush finished second to Reagan during the heated 1980 presidential-primary race. As a result, Reagan felt his selection of Bush would help solidify GOP splits caused by a "competitive and sometimes rough primary battle." But, said Reagan, "I had always liked [Bush] personally and had a great respect for his abilities and breadth of experience; and I know he had a lot of support within the party."[3] Interestingly, Reagan, probably more than any other president in history, insisted on a strict ideological test for appointees. He was, however, more tolerable of Bush, a moderate rather than conservative Republican. This is not a contradiction when one considers why modern presidents have typically chosen their vice presidents, compared to other appointees. Reagan did not pick Bush for ideological agreement but instead for factors that had to do with winning the election, in addition to necessary personal-compatibility issues.

Although George Bush was chosen by Ronald Reagan as his running mate largely as an overture to the moderate wing of the Republican party, there was little doubt that Reagan appreciated his running mate's background in foreign policy.[4] Bush was a former ambassador to the United Nations (1971-73), U.S. ambassador to China (1974-75), CIA director (1975-76), national party chairman, and a congressman (1967-71). Because of this impressive back-ground, it was often said that he had "the best resume in politics."[5]

Ultimately, the glorified resume that impacted Reagan's decision to select Bush as his running mate would also influence how he used him as a vice president. This included the foreign-policy realm. Langhorne A. (Tony) Motley, an ambassador and assistant secretary of state who accompanied Bush on numerous foreign-policy trips, recalled how Bush's previous experience made him an asset in foreign policy as a vice president. "George Bush really understood international politics," said Motley. "You didn't have to 'spoon feed' him on foreign policy. As a vice president involved in international politics, he was a delight to work with."[6]

Reagan, following Carter's cue, invited his vice president to take a West Wing office. As in the Mondale chapter, one will notice how this seemingly minor adjustment helped bolster Bush's role. He also encouraged an expanded job description for the vice president.[7]

Also helping to enhance the vice president's role was the fact that Reagan brought some Bush people onto his own staff. Especially important among these people was James Baker, who formed a key part of the triad surrounding the president—Ed Meese, Michael Deaver, and Baker. In 1982, Bush commented on how, "One area that needs exploring is the relationship of the vice president to the president's staff. This is a major thing. For me, it's working well."[8] As noted in the previous chapter, Vice President Mondale also heavily benefited from the presence of his former staffers being on the president's staff.

Chapter 5

The President-Vice President Relationship

The selection of Bush and his early role definition say a lot about the roots of his relationship with Reagan. As a presidential candidate, Bush had some hefty public disagreements with Reagan during the 1980 presidential primaries. One of his more notorious slings was when he referred to the supply-side economics advocated by Reagan as "voodoo economics" (later called "Reaganomics").[9] Once in office, however, Bush became a model vice president. That meant that he would carry out the wishes of the Oval Office and not speak out publicly against the president or administration policy. In part, this would later explain the lack of knowledge about his role or stance on particular Reagan policies or crises, despite being chairman of the president's crisis-management team. As will be very evident throughout this chapter, Bush was very cautious not to publicly offer his views on policy. He quickly came to understand the nature of the second office and adapted accordingly by consistently defending the president and arguing forcefully in favor of White House policy—almost always.[10]

"Loyal, self-effacing and hard-working, Bush time and again demonstrated his ability to work as a 'team player,'" writes Marie Natoli, "something which Reagan valued quite highly, and which earned Bush the respect of the Reagan staff."[11] Indeed, Reagan on many occasions referred to Bush as the "best" vice president in history, saying so often throughout the 1984 campaign and during the televised presidential debates with Walter Mondale.[12] And the vice president especially benefited from his terrific relationship with President Reagan.

Bush said that once Reagan made his decision on the vice presidency, he viewed the Reagan-Bush ticket not simply as a convenient political alliance but as a "partnership," saying, "We would run and serve together as team." Bush carefully added that there was never any doubt which of the two was the senior partner. "But as president," wrote Bush, "Ronald Reagan—more than any president before him—broke down the barriers between the nation's two highest elective offices. . . . He [went] out of his way to bring his vice president inside the White House circle, and our trust and friendship had grown each passing day."[13]

The vice president had tremendous access to the president. Bush said that he had "plenty of opportunities to chat privately with the president and to quietly offer advice." He added that he was "clued in on all the meetings I want to be informed about—all."[14] Just as Carter regularly met with his vice president for substantive meetings, so, too, did Reagan meet with Bush.[15] Bush and Reagan saw each other daily for national security briefings.[16] On Thursday of each week Bush and Reagan would meet alone for lunch, usually in either the Oval Office, a small adjoining office, or (weather permitting) on the south lawn terrace. While these meetings were informal, Bush would later refer to them as "the most productive sessions I had with the president." "There was no formal agenda," he recalled. "At times he'd ask me about a specific project I was working on, or if there was an upcoming overseas trip on my schedule, we'd discuss what message he wanted to deliver to my foreign hosts. The lunches were relaxed, the conversation wide-ranging, from affairs of state to small talk."[17]

All of these factors shared by Bush and Reagan—the positive personal relationship; the respect, trust, and loyalty; the regular daily and weekly access—ensured the vice president at least somewhat of an influence in White House foreign policy. That influence would be bolstered by his unique role within the administration's foreign- and security-policy structure.

Bush's Place within Reagan Administration Foreign- and Security-Policy Structure

To a large degree, Bush was ensured a place within the structure because of his access and relationship with the president. Additionally, like Vice President Mondale before him, Bush (who had a staff size of seventy people) became only the second vice president in history to have his own defense and foreign-policy advisors. These staff members helped keep him abreast of key foreign-policy developments.

But the vice president also had a spot within the more formal framework that ran White House foreign policy. An extra prod was provided by President Truman decades earlier when he made the vice president a statutory member of the NSC—a seat that Bush filled. Bush also took part in the meetings of the tightly restricted National Security Planning Group (NSPG), a key White House-level unit which involved the president and his cabinet-level foreign-policy advisors.[18] To briefly cite just one example of his inclusion in the NSPG, in March 1984, as Reagan sensed the administration might be able to develop a long-range arms-reduction plan with the Soviets, the president confined discussion on the issue to a small group within the NSPG that included only Bush, Secretary of State George Shultz, Secretary of Defense Caspar Weinberger, and NSA Bud McFarlane. Clearly, Bush was playing an important policymaking role on a significant issue.[19] Within the entire NSC structure were sixteen subgroups. The following is a breakdown in hierarchical order: Information Policy/Security Review, Crisis Management Support and Planning, European and Soviet Affairs, African Affairs, Political-Military Affairs, Legislative, Asian Affairs, Public Affairs, Latin American Affairs, International Communication and Information, International Economic Affairs, Defense Programs and Arms Control, Near East and South Asia Affairs, Intelligence Programs, Arms Control, and Defense Programs.[20]

The president's National Security Council system appeared infamously undisciplined, likely facilitating the Iran-Contra debacle.[21] The vice president at times occasionally helped oversee the system—although such was not his duty. Frank Carlucci, in describing the chaotic NSC system he took over, gives an example of Bush in that capacity:

> When I moved into the national security job, I found an organization, quite frankly, that no one could have run. There were two deputies; everybody seemed to report to the top; management was done by computer; and Ollie North had an office that was called Political Military Affairs, which seemed redundant because the entire National Security Council deals with political military affairs. That was, in effect, a hunting license for him to do what he pleased. I ended up reorganizing the whole thing. There was no general counsel. I put in a general counsel with total liberty to attend any meeting he wanted, and I ended up firing about half the staff. At one point, George Bush said to me, "The president is getting a little nervous about all these people you are firing, Frank."... [But the president] allowed me to go ahead and shape the organization as I saw fit.[22]

However, Bush's place within Reagan's foreign- and security-policy structure was prominent for one key reason in particular. He became the first vice president in history to head up a major administration interagency foreign-policy committee—the Special Situation Group. The group was designated as the administration's crisis-management committee, and it was run by Bush. The significance of this cannot be ignored. Never before, or since, has a vice president been given such immense responsibility in foreign-policy decision making. This allowed Bush to serve as a vital link in the administration's handling of global crises. (More on the vice president's role as a crisis manager will be provided in the next section.)

These factors contributed to allow Bush a place within the foreign- and security-policy structure. Martin Anderson, a top Reagan economic advisor, refers to what he called Reagan's "foreign-policy directorate." During the first Reagan administration, the directorate was made up of nine people: Bush, Secretary of State Al Haig, Weinberger, DCI William Casey, NSA Richard Allen, Ambassador Jeane Kirkpatrick, Meese, Baker, and Deaver.[23]

But a more important question might be the following: What was the vice president's *influence* within the Reagan administration's foreign- and security-policy structure? The answer is difficult to gauge. This is especially true for the always restrained Bush.

Bush's style was to interact quietly during NSC meetings in order to avoid the impression that he and Reagan differed or that he was attempting to upstage the president. (Bush's vice president, Quayle, took the same approach.) "In the vice president's role," said the vice president, "sometimes it is better to quietly express your differences to the president rather than to command attention at the cabinet meeting or an NSC meeting. It is a question of style, because you don't want to be putting the president on the spot or make him choose between the vice president and the cabinet officers."²⁴ In this vein, he added: "I have taken a very low profile. Because I think the way you become an effective vice president—have something substantive to do—is to have the confidence of the president."²⁵

This style prompted observers to often pressure Bush for his personal views. He stated:

> One of the recurring questions I've had from reporters, almost from the day I became vice president has been: "Well, we know that's the official administration position on the issue, but what's *your* position?"
>
> My answer has always been the same: a vice president can hold a different opinion from a president on an issue and express it while the White House decision-making process is going on. But once the president makes his decision, the matter is settled.
>
> That answer doesn't always satisfy inquiring reporters and columnists, but consider the alternative: A president takes a position on a foreign-policy objective. Unhappy with that position, the vice president goes public with his views in a major speech or interview. Here at home he may become a hero to those opposed to the president's policy. He may even be editorially praised (by the president's editorial opponents) for his "independence." But overseas, any division at the highest level of American government can only be perceived by potential adversaries as a vulnerable area to exploit, through diplomacy and propaganda.²⁶

Bush maintains that the last thing a president needs is a vice president "with his own agenda, grinding his own political ax." He continues, "it's fundamental that the country can only have one president at a time. On the day a disgruntled, self-serving vice president declares civil war on the White House by publicly challenging a president, our system of government will be in serious trouble."²⁷ On many occasions, Bush informed reporters that he voiced disagreement with the president only in private. As early as 1981, he asserted: "There is no point in the vice president playing into the hands of the speculators around Washington with stories that 'the vice president is known to differ with the president' on this or that. I just won't do that."²⁸

At times, this low-key approach was interpreted negatively. Sometimes, the interpretations were politically motivated witness Ted Kennedy's convention remarks. Other times, however, it led even Bush allies in the Reagan White House to question his leadership and initiative. For instance, Jeane Kirkpatrick, the former Reagan U.N. ambassador stated, "Strange as it may sound, after four-and-a-half years of serving on the Reagan administration's senior foreign-policy team and being in meetings with the vice president, I don't feel I know what he feels about most issues in the world, and I don't feel I know where he stands. And that bothers me."[29] When it came to the formulation of major Reagan covert operations designed to undermine the Soviet Union, including the Solidarity initiative with the Vatican, Richard Pipes recalled, "George Bush never said a word. I used to sit behind him, and I never knew what his opinions were."[30] "He did not . . . speak up at NSC meetings," said a national security aide.[31]

On the contrary, former NSA Richard Allen asserted (years after he left office): "The idea that George Bush hasn't contributed to the substance of this administration is preposterous." Martin Anderson added: "[Bush] went to all the important meetings, met regularly with the president for private weekly lunches, and was intimately tied to the entire foreign-policy community. He was everywhere, but he left few visible tracks, sometimes not even fingerprints."[32] Those remarks seem close to Reagan's. The president called Bush "a part of everything we've been doing."[33]

Why the widely divergent assessments? I do not want to dismiss the remarks by Kirkpatrick and Pipes. However, a careful, open look at the broad scope of remarks from all parties reveals that the statements of Kirkpatrick and Pipes likely do not give a fully accurate portrayal. The reason for this, and thus true answer, probably comes back to Bush's quietness: Nowhere was Bush more of a model vice president than in the area of loyalty to the commander in chief. "[B]ecause of the way he has exercised his fealty," aptly wrote Randall Rothenberg of *The New York Times Magazine*, "no one knows for certain how Bush has influenced the president." On specific items of policy involvement, Bush informed Rothenberg in a 1988 interview: "There are just many examples that I'm not gonna share with you, where I know I've shaped what happens." In perhaps the ultimate display of his fealty, Bush evoked snickers for a 1984 commented in which he professed, "I'm for Mr. Reagan—blindly."[34] He simply refused to speak up out of fear of appearing to try to upstage or disagree with the president he served.[35] George Shultz, who in his memoirs offers numerous examples of Bush's activities, had it right when he said that Bush "sometimes would not state his position in meetings on the ground that he owed it to the president to provide his thoughts and recommendations privately."[36] That view was backed by Tony Motley in an interview with the author: "[Bush] rarely spoke up in the meetings with Reagan, reserving most of his comments for private sessions with Reagan, which was his modus operandi. When he had the ball, he advanced it expeditiously in the direction he knew Reagan wanted to go."[37]

Nonetheless, despite the quiet demeanor, Bush demonstrated that he was quite influential in Reagan administration foreign policy. The following section spells out his role.

Bush's Foreign-Policy Role

A cornerstone of Vice President Bush's foreign-policy role was his regular agenda of meetings dealing with global and security issues. As vice president, he sat with the cabinet and NSC. He presided over cabinet meetings in the president's absence. Throughout the administration, he participated in a 9:00 A.M. meeting with President Reagan and top staff members to go over the current agenda and discuss problems that may have arisen in the previous twenty-four hours. At 9:30 A.M., Bush and Reagan stayed on for a briefing by the NSA on what had transpired overnight in world affairs. Frank Carlucci recalls that Bush sat in on all the briefings that the president received from the national security advisors.[38] As noted earlier, Bush had lunch with Reagan on Thursdays, during which the president, said Reagan, "brought him up to date on everything that was going on."[39] He joined Mondale as one of only two vice presidents in history (up to that time) who were privy to full and complete information contained in the Presidential Daily Briefing (PDB), a crucial source of data on foreign policy. Prior to this, vice presidents only received summaries of the PDB.[40]

Bush received important special assignments and was fortunate enough to be designated chairman of the crisis-management team, a special role unique in the history of the vice presidency.[41] He appears to have been a fairly active player on Reagan's foreign-policy team. One controversial area where he may or may not have been involved centers around the Iran Contra affair. Bush's knowledge or participation in this affair may likely never be known.[42]

When it came to policy matters, Bush tended to most often side with Baker and Shultz.[43] He served as an administration spokesman, spreading the Reagan message throughout the world. From 1981 through the spring of 1987, Bush traveled to seventy-three foreign countries on presidential assignments both ceremonial and substantive.[44] There are many examples of the vice president speaking up during cabinet and NSC meetings and offering his view on issues.[45] There are also numerous examples of him negotiating with foreign leaders at home and abroad.[46] Among key areas not covered in this chapter is Bush's role in halting the extraordinary protectionist legislation contained within the Gephardt amendment.[47]

Listed below are a number of brief descriptions of elements of Bush's foreign-policy role. These include his role as a congressional liaison, as chair of the administration's crisis-management committee, and as chair of the president's task force on terrorism. Following that, the section focuses on three greater-detailed cases. While the last of the three cases reflects quite positively on Bush's foreign-policy role, the first two are predominantly negative.

Congressional Liaison in Foreign Policy

Like all of the vice presidents in this study, Bush served as a congressional liaison between the White House and Capitol Hill. Such a role is somewhat of a natural fit for a vice president, since the occupant also presides over the Senate and can break dead-locked votes. Typically, the vice president has an office in the Senate. Add to this the fact that most vice presidents have tended to have backgrounds as congressmen, and one can see how the second-office holder can be very useful to the president as a liaison to Capitol Hill. Often, such activities took place on the foreign-policy side, as was evident in Mondale's working of the hill during debates over SALT and the Panama Canal treaties. Vice President Bush was no exception. He met individually with senators key to certain votes. He made a point to keep in touch with his many former acquaintances on the House side. In general, he did a lot of listening and collecting of "political intelligence" valuable to the White House.[48]

Foreign-Policy Crisis Committee

A big step up from Bush's congressional liaison role was his duty as chair of the crisis-management committee. Reagan became the first president in history to allow his vice president to chair a major NSC committee with considerable authority.

Reagan (in his words) decided to name Bush "chairman of a special group within the NSC that would help me manage affairs during an international crisis."[49] During the March 1981 announcement of the move, White House spokesman James Brady said that Bush, as part of the NSC system, would "coordinate and control all appropriate federal resources in responding to emergency situations both foreign and domestic." In an actual crisis situation, Bush would only chair the team in the absence of the president. Importantly, however, he would "also engage in forward planning for emergency responses, develop options for presidential consideration and take the lead in the implementation of those decisions."[50]

Reagan made the move for two reasons: For one, in the past, the president's national security advisor had generally served as chairman of the White House crisis-management team. But Secretary of State Al Haig didn't like or trust NSA Richard Allen. Said Reagan: "I had discussed the matter with the top three staff people in the White House, Jim Baker, Ed Meese, and Mike Deaver, and we'd come up with the plan giving the responsibility to George Bush." In part, Reagan felt this move would "deal with Haig's unhappiness over Allen." (Haig disagreed with the move for additional reasons.[51]) Also, however, the president made the move because he "thought it was prudent—and important for the country—for the vice president to play as large a role in the affairs of the administration as possible; I didn't want George, in the words of Nelson Rockefeller, simply to be 'standby equipment.'"[52]

The crisis-management group was called the Special Situation Group. It first met on September 1, 1983, as a result of the Soviet shootdown of the Korean Air Lines passenger plane, KAL 007.[53] An example of Bush's crisis-management group in action took place during the Grenada episode. On October 19, 1983, leader Maurice Bishop and five other high-level officials were executed. The executions took place a week after Bishop and others were placed under house arrest. Immediately after the killing of Bishop, a new sixteen-man leftist-military government was installed. The events concerned the administration not only due to the place of Grenada in the larger geopolitical struggle with the Soviet Union—and the connection between the junta and Havana and Moscow—but also because of the fact that 1,000 Americans resided there, including about 700 medical students. Late the next day, on October 20, Reagan asked the vice president to convene a meeting of the Special Situation Group in the White House for the first of a series of important meetings on Grenada coordinated and led by Bush.[54]

Reagan and his new NSA, McFarlane, had scheduled a golf weekend in Augusta, Georgia. A group of reporters was planning to go along. The administration decided not to cancel the trip. It felt that doing so might cue the press into believing a crisis atmosphere was taking place at the White House. To further illustrate a "relaxed" mood in Washington, Secretary of State Shultz went along. Behind the scenes, Reagan, Shultz, and other staff in Georgia stayed in close contact via speaker phone with the Washington group, which was headed up by Bush. In the Situation Room meetings in the basement of the West Wing of the White House, Bush sat in the president's chair at the head of the table.[55]

In a key meeting, Bush, from Washington, participated in an emergency 4:00 A.M. October 22 meeting held between Reagan, McFarlane, and Shultz in the living room of the Eisenhower Cottage. The meeting was convened in response to a request by the Organization of Eastern Caribbean States asking the administration to intervene militarily in Grenada.[56] Shultz was awakened in the cottage at about 2:45 A.M. with the request. He and McFarlane reported the request to Bush at about 3:30 A.M. The vice president, in turn, roused other officials to discuss the plea, including Weinberger, CJCS General Jack Vessey, Tony Motley, Baker, Meese, John Poindexter, and John McMahon. Bush reported back to Shultz and McFarlane that the advisors were eager, at the least, to speed up the planning of an invasion. At 5:15 A.M. Reagan listened to a briefing on the situation from Shultz and McFarlane. He decided he wanted to get the views of Bush and Weinberger firsthand and telephoned them.[57] This interaction continued as Bush commandeered the operation in Washington.[58]

In sum, most reports show Bush, as a crisis manager during the Grenada situation, to be dynamic and proactive. He quickly assembled and coordinated the necessary staff and was able to effectively interact with the president, McFarlane, and Shultz. According to accounts, he proposed, listened to, and evaluated others ideas and ran them back and forth with the president's team in Georgia.[59] While information on the vice president's full activities during this episode is not plentiful, most of the available assessments are laudatory. Constantine Menges, an NSC staffer who worked closely with the vice president and was highly critical of him (as will be seen below), said that, "During Grenada, Bush was superb"—a remark backed by Motley.[60] The vice president's performance during the Grenada crisis led Menges to conclude that a President Bush equipped with a competent staff of experts from outside the career services and using "his own sensible instincts" could preside over an effective foreign policy.[61]

Task Force on Terrorism

The crisis committee was not the only foreign-policy-related group commandeered by Bush. He also spent six months as chairman of a task force created to come up with measures to "combat" terrorism, designated so by President Reagan in early July 1985. Terrorism had, of course, been salient throughout the Reagan administration. The president's inauguration was celebrated with the optimistic release of the fifty-two American hostages who had been held in captivity by Iran in the U.S. embassy for 444 days. That joyous occasion, however, gave way to a darker reality throughout Reagan's two terms. The vice president was given the important task of trying to figure out how to deal with terrorism.

The executive director of the task force was a retired naval admiral. The entire staff was composed of foreign service officers and military personnel. The senior NSC representative was John Poindexter and Oliver North was the day-to-day NSC participant. The task force sprung off into two subgroups, the interagency Operations Sub-Group and the Office to Combat Terrorism. In conducting research for the task force report, Bush personally met with many members of Congress, former cabinet officers, diplomats, airline CEOs, and media executives. The task force in general was briefed by some twenty-five government agencies and 100-plus "statesmen," military officers, scholars, and law enforcement officials. Bush and others traveled throughout the world visiting embassies, military commands, and operations centers.[62]

Constantine Menges said that a number of factors made the vice president a good pick for the job of heading up the task force: Bush had a good relationship with Reagan, and had strong personal attributes, such as "vigor, openness, and political instinct," which "could help him break through the old ways of thinking about terrorism." Most importantly, Bush "was seen by the government agencies as a possible future president, and this added to both his authority and his ability to provide real leadership on a complex political-legal-security issue such as terrorism. After all, he was the *vice president*."[63]

The task force released its findings in February 1986. In one assessment,

Constantine Menges underestimated the task force for being staffed entirely with career government employees and producing "a bland report that had little impact."[64] In part, such an assessment is fair: the report was clearly an affirmation of the status quo. "Our national program is well-conceived and working," wrote Bush in the intro. Yet, among the useful outcomes of the task force was the formulation of a policy on terrorism that led to the 1986 U.S. bombing of Libya in reprisal for Kaddafi-sponsored terrorist activities against Americans.[65]

The last three sections analyzed specific tasks of Vice President Bush—congressional liaison, crisis committee, and task force on terrorism—that often translated into foreign-policy work for him in a number of different areas. The next three sections offer three specific case studies of foreign-policy missions undertaken by the vice president. The first two cases involve possible negatives. The first features a small but crucial mission to Saudi Arabia, in which Bush seems to have made a near-critical foreign-policy gaffe. The second involves a 1984 trip to Central America. In at least one of them, President Reagan apparently had to personally intervene and straighten out the mess created by his vice president. The Saudi case at least—and possibly the Central America one also—calls into question knee-jerk demands that the vice president be quickly thrust into nearly any foreign-policy situation. It is for this purpose in particular that the two cases are being employed in this study. As shown in the Mondale example in South Africa, vice presidents can certainly make foreign-policy mistakes.

The third case is largely positive and demonstrates the highly beneficial role that the vice president can at times play. It looks at Bush's role in Western Europe in lobbying leaders to accept the deployment of President Reagan's Pershing missiles. His actions were impressive.

Bush's Role in Saudi Strategy

As stated, not all the cases of various vice presidents' foreign-policy involvement are positive, as proven by Vice President Mondale's work on South Africa policy. Vice President Bush's trip to Saudi Arabia in early 1986 is a further reflection of that reality.

The trip must be viewed through the prism of the Reagan administration's Soviet/Cold War policy. The administration was participating in a broad policy intended to break the back of the former Soviet Union. In early 1982, Reagan and a few key advisors began mapping out a strategy to attack the fundamental economic and political weaknesses of the Soviet system. "We adopted a comprehensive strategy that included economic warfare, to attack Soviet weaknesses," said Secretary of Defense Caspar Weinberger. "It was a silent campaign, working through allies and using other measures." The goals and means of the campaign were outlined in a series of NSDDs signed by Reagan in 1982 and 1983.[66]

The role of Bush in executing this strategy is quite cloudy. The few sources that provide details on the matter offer little insight, suggesting his role may have been minimal. By most accounts, Reagan made his decisions on this highly sensitive strategy with only two to three advisors present, usually CIA Director William Casey and a top NSC staffer or the NSA. National Security Advisor William Clark maintained: "Few of these initiatives were discussed at cabinet meetings. The president made his decisions with two or three advisors in the room."[67]

One of the few published examples of the vice president providing advice on elements of the strategy was the administration's support of the Solidarity movement in Poland, a major covert action plan authorized by Reagan in the summer of 1982 (NSDD-32). Part of the administration's Soviet strategy included secret directives allowing for covert financial, intelligence, and logistical support to Solidarity in order to ensure the survival of an opposition movement in the heart of the Soviet empire. Arguing for such action at an NSC meeting was Richard Pipes. It was strongly opposed by Secretary of State Haig, who called it "crazy," and Vice President Bush, who agreed with Haig. Bush expressed concerns about inflaming Moscow and counseled against any sort of operation. Reagan liked the idea and went against Bush and Haig. He immediately instructed Casey to draw up a covert operation plan.[68]

The only other available example of Bush's activities in carrying out the administration's covert strategy designed to undermine the Soviet Union related to the vice president's dealings with Saudi Arabia in 1986. And, by and large, the example is not a positive one.

Over the years Bush had developed a close relationship with the Saudis, particularly the director of Saudi intelligence and the royal family in general. He had fostered a number of friendships with these men during his stint as CIA director and during his return to private life in the oil business in the late 1970s. When DCI Casey—who was the architect and primary foot soldier of Reagan's covert plan—was planning a trip to Saudi Arabia to discuss ideas on how to increase the pressure on the Soviets in Afghanistan, he met with Bush first. Casey's host in the country would be Prince Turki al-Faisl, who got along splendidly with Bush as a result of their dealings over the years. The vice president gave Casey some insights, which were reportedly very accurate. Bush then sent the prince a note shortly before Casey left Washington, saying that the DCI would be a good friend of the Saudis and was sympathetic to their concerns and geostrategic position. Bush's assistance proved helpful to Casey.[69]

Saudi Arabia played a key part in the administration's broader framework. Reagan had an excellent rapport with King Fahd of Saudi Arabia. In an amazingly innovative, gutsy, and largely unknown plan, Reagan and Casey convinced Fahd to help the administration hurt the Soviets economically via controls on oil flows. In late 1985, the Saudis agreed to increase oil production dramatically—ultimately raising output from less than two million barrels a day in mid-1985 up to nine million barrels per day by Fall 1985—driving oil prices through the floor. Energy exports represented the centerpiece of Moscow's annual hard currency earnings structure. A dramatic increase in oil production by a country like Saudi Arabia would cause oil prices to plummet worldwide. The administration knew that this would severely damage the hard currency earnings of Moscow, which it did. The Treasury Department calculated that every $1.00 rise in the per-barrel price of oil meant roughly $500M to $1B in extra hard currency for the Kremlin. Conversely, the reverse was true for dropping prices. Ultimately, the price plunged from $30 a barrel in the fall of 1985 to $10 in April 1986 because of the Saudi intervention in the market. There were predictions it could hit $5 a barrel.[70]

The massive drops were killing the Soviets. Hard currency exports from oil sales accounted for an incredible 80 percent of all Soviet hard currency earnings. The manipulation of oil prices destroyed their hard currency earnings in 1985. From 1984 to 1985, the Soviet trade surplus with the West had shifted from a $700 million trade surplus to a deficit of $1.4 billion. That was just the direct, calculable effect on hard currency earnings. The ripple effect may have cost tens of billions of dollars more. Yevgenny Novikov, who served on the senior staff of the Soviet Communist Party Central Committee, recalled: "The drop in oil prices was devastating, just devastating. It was a catastrophic event. Tens of billions were wiped away." Author Peter Schweizer, who profiled this episode in his book, *Victory: The Reagan Administration's Secret Strategy That Hastened the Collapse of the Soviet Union*, asserts: "The calculated annual loss from the price drop was $13 billion."[71]

In the face of an unprecedented drop in currency earnings, a strongly worded letter signed by wary Politburo members was sent to King Fahd in early 1986. Moscow, deeply affected by the drop during a harsh winter, was joined by an angry Libya and Iran. The letter candidly warned against pushing prices lower and proposed secret meetings in Geneva to stabilize prices. Iran made public threats toward the Saudis, as the loss of oil revenue threatened an end to its planned offensive against Iraq.[72]

In light of this, the nervous Saudi leadership sought reassurances that the United States would provide moral support against Soviet protests and physical support if necessary to ensure the security of oil coming from the Gulf, which was now being threatened by Iranian and Libyan attacks. Saudi Arabia was paying a price for helping the United States implement its covert economic war against the Kremlin. Prince Bandar in Washington communicated his concerns to Weinberger and Casey. They reassured him and told him that direct talks on the matter would take place during Vice President Bush's visit to the Arab peninsula in April 1986.[73] Hence, the vice president's trip would be a substantive one involving a very delicate, important matter.

In the spring of 1986, Bush embarked on a highly visible ten-day tour of the Persian Gulf area. In one sense, he would succeed in fulfilling his mission, telling the Saudis that the Reagan administration was "committed to keeping the Strait of Hormuz open" and to maintaining the "stability of the gulf countries." The administration had very recently flexed its muscles in the Mediterranean and wanted to tell the world it would do the same for the seething Arabian peninsula. The vice president became Reagan's messenger for doing so. "With a meaty diplomatic mission," commented one reporter, "Bush made the most of it."[74]

In another sense, however, the vice president betrayed his mission. Bush, a product of Texas oil country, saw danger in the recent dramatic decline in oil prices. There was speculation from many quarters that he feared the effect on his political base in the southwest, which would be crucial in the 1988 presidential campaign. The vice president's subsequent steps were deleterious. Right off, he became uncharacteristically public in expressing dissenting views on the matter. Oddly, as if he knew nothing about *why* prices were down, before leaving for his trip Bush told a Washington press conference on April 1 that "stability in the market is a very important thing, and I will be selling very hard in terms of our domestic interest . . . and thus the interest of our national security. . . . I think it is essential that we talk about stability and that we just not have a continued free fall like a parachutist jumping without a parachute."[75] In an April 3 interview, Bush once again said he would tell Saudi Arabia that the four-month free fall in prices was jeopardizing U.S. security by battering the nation's oil producers.[76]

The comments went against everything the White House had said and done. The administration and Saudi Arabia agreed to publicly state that oil prices were low strictly because of market forces, despite the reality that they had rigged flows and thus prices. A White House spokesman countered Bush by saying that the administration believed, "The way to address stability is to let the free market work," and that Bush would convey this to Fahd.[77]

Only a few days after his press-conference remarks, which confused the already nervous Saudis, Bush spoke to several Saudi ministers in Riyadh. They talked candidly about a number of subjects, including the price of oil. Bush warned that if prices remained low, U.S. oil producers would pressure Congress for tariffs or other protection from the cheap imports. Again, the Saudis were confounded and worried. For months, Reagan, Weinberger, Casey, and other senior administration officials had succeeded in convincing the Saudis into increasing oil production and avoiding any boost whatsoever in prices. The Saudis had placed their necks on the line. Now, the vice president was vocally and persistently arguing the precise opposite, pushing the Saudis in the other direction. Worse yet, Bush headed off to Dhahran for a private talk with King Fahd on April 6. While the vice president rightly reiterated U.S. support to Fahd in the event of an Iranian onslaught, he also told the king puzzlingly that he was looking for "stability in the market." On April 7, recalling his discussion with Fahd, Bush publicly recalled that "the focus of the discussion related to oil prices and production. I described the link we in the United States see between a strong domestic oil industry and the national security. *I reiterated our desire to see market forces work.*" (Emphasis added.) Fahd became visibly upset by Bush's perplexing remarks.[78]

Once he got word of what Bush had said, an angry Reagan took steps to quickly mend the situation with the Saudis. He then turned his attention to Bush. "This clear departure from administration policy was quite unusual for Bush, who had proven to be a loyal, if quiet, vice president during the previous five years of the Reagan presidency," writes Peter Schweizer. "This was his first break from administration rank, but he was making it with a foreign head of state." Reagan felt compelled to take some action. The president did something he had scarcely done before: "He gave Bush a real dressing down," said one ambassador in the region. Reagan told Bush that it did not look good to have the president and senior cabinet officials saying one thing while the vice president was saying the exact opposite.[79] Asking "why on earth did the vice president go so far astray from administration policy?" Rowland Evans and Robert Novak agreed that "Bush's abandonment . . . is all the more startling considering the kind of vice president he has tried to be. For better than five years, he has tailored his views from tax reduction to abortion. Why, then, would he go off the reservation on oil prices?"[80] Bush later conceded on NBC's "Meet the Press" that his remarks had caused "a lot of flak."[81]

The situation was resolved, but not without a number of serious diplomatic fissures. To some, it may be difficult to tell from the evidence if Bush's actions were politically motivated, an act of disloyalty, or motivated by sheer ignorance (maybe based on a lack of communication) of why the oil prices were low in the first place. Yet, Reagan's reaction suggests it was not the latter. Additionally, Secretary of Energy John Herrington had made Bush-like comments on March 31, ripping the Saudis for pumping too much oil. Herrington was reprimanded for his comments. The next day, Bush made the same mistake as the energy secretary. Evans and Novak reported that it was made clear to the Bush staff immediately after his April 1 comments that he had misspoken.[82] Nonetheless, the vice president continued to misrepresent the administration's position on the issue—at home on April 3 and abroad among the highest Saudi officials. Bush was clearly out of whack. Politics may be the best explanation.

One must conclude that as a foreign emissary during his 1986 Saudi trip, the vice president did not perform his tasks properly. In as much as Bush's actions were motivated by future political (presidential) aspirations, this episode (like Mondale in South Africa) suggests that a vice president does have selfish interests that can effect his ability to be leveraged in foreign policy. This factor, missed by many of those who assert the vice president lacks parochial interests, is crucial in considering how the second-office holder may or may not be used in foreign policy.

In reality, contemporary vice presidents seem to be motivated by selfish-political interests as much as any cabinet member dedicated to his or her department, or service chief to his military branch. Vice President Bush during the Saudi oil crisis may have been as concerned about his southern-oil constituency as would be any congressman from Texas. He may have been as willing to go to bat for the oil industry as the top chief of the Air Force might for a fighter plane that had become obsolete and cost prohibitive. Bush very well may have been so motivated by personal political concerns that he was willing to go against the president's policy.

Hence, while the vice president may at times be a valuable asset in foreign policy, it is foolish to argue that such is the case because he is uncorrupted by selfish interests. This reality flies in the face of the premise by many scholars that the vice president can be a valuable asset in foreign affairs because he allegedly lacks selfish-parochial interests. The Bush case, similar to those involving Nixon and Mondale, demonstrates how intently the vice president's actions can be dictated by politics. In light of that, the "lessons learned" from this case will be briefly revisited in the final chapter on lessons learned and policy recommendations.

Bush in Central America Policy

On the contrary, political self interests did not seem to be a detriment to Bush's duties in Central America, although other difficulties may have ensued. He seems to have been a valuable spokesman in that region. As noted earlier, Bush—continuing a trend begun mostly by vice presidents Nixon and Mondale—exploited ceremonial trips abroad as an opportunity to engage in substantive discussions on key issues with foreign officials. The vice president himself explained: "Representing the president overseas—not only at state funerals but on special missions—is another facet of the modern vice presidency."[83] (In that sense, Bush, like Nixon and Mondale, could be grateful to the president he served for allowing him such latitude.)

In that spirit, Bush made many trips to Latin America during his vice presidency, including a key December 1983 trip to Argentina, Panama, and El Salvador.[84] His most sensitive part of the trip was in El Salvador, where his job was to tell President Alvaro Magana and senior Salvadoran political and military leaders that the activity of the government's "death squads" would have to cease and human rights would have to be respected if they expected American aid to continue. "The message had to be delivered forcefully," Bush later recalled, "but in a way that wouldn't offend key allies in the fight against the spread of Marxist-Leninism in Central America." Bush made his pitch at a formal state dinner that included enough arms and camouflaged men to initiate a war. The vice president remembered his toast:

"Mr. President," I said, "you and many other Salvadorans have demonstrated extraordinary personal courage in the struggle against tyranny and extremism." Then came the other half of the message. "But your cause is being undermined by the murderous violence of reactionary minorities. . . . These right-wing fanatics are the best friends the Soviets, the Cubans, the Sandinistas, and the Salvadoran guerrillas have. Every murderous act they commit poisons the well of friendship between our two countries and helps impose an alien dictatorship on the people of El Salvador. These cowardly death-squad terrorists are just as repugnant to me, to President Reagan, to the United States Congress, and to the American people as the terrorists of the Left."[85]

Indeed, the Bush message *had* to be delivered. A cornerstone of Reagan policy in the area was the presence of an allied anti-communist government in El Salvador. Without U.S. political and military support, the government could easily be undermined by Marxist rebels. However, because of the repulsive activities in the area carried out by government-sanctioned groups, the White House was in severe danger of having the aid cut off by a disgusted Congress. Someone high up in the administration had to make it clear to the Salvadoran leadership that its support of such activities had to cease. Bush delivered that message.

Assistant Secretary of State Tony Motley, who was present for the speech, recalled the reaction to it. "You could have heard a pin drop," said Motley. "[Bush] was strong and straightforward. You could just feel the tension in the room and how uncomfortable everyone was after that. And then he came in with a joke that made everyone laugh, and that relaxed the atmosphere a bit. It was a dynamite performance."[86]

Personally, the vice president felt the immediate response to his speech by the Salvadorans "seemed to be good." He admitted, however, that the impact was difficult to gauge.[87] Importantly, he succeeded in forcefully and unambiguously delivering a key administration message from the second-highest ranking American official, thus providing an extra level of authority to the charges made. There could be no confusion among the Salvadoran leaders about U.S. concerns. On the other hand, Motley says that there is "no doubt" in his mind that the speech "really made a difference." He states that "death-squad" activities dropped off after the speech. Motley identifies one line in particular that he believes served as a wake up call to the Salvadorans: "Bush said to them: 'I'm telling you this not because the Congress won't give you money if this continues, but because Ronald Reagan and I won't give you money if it continues.' That was the bombshell. That really woke them up."[88]

Not only did Motley feel that the vice president did "an absolute dynamite job" in reprimanding the Salvadorans,[89] but so did Secretary of State Shultz, who later fondly recalled how the vice president "came down hard" on human rights abuses during his December 1983 visit.[90]

In El Salvador, Bush conveyed the message he was supposed to deliver. Yet, according to a potentially controversial account by Constantine Menges, an area where Bush allegedly failed some basic duties was an important 1984 trip to Central America. The Menges account appears to be the only published record of Bush's performance during the trip. The author cautions that it is only one person's side of the story. The details of Menges' eyewitness account seem consistent with goals of Reagan policy in the region, confirmed through public pronouncements and NSC meetings. Still, again, it is only one perspective. As a result, the author sought confirmation of the account from a key witness, Tony Motley. Assistant Secretary of State Motley resolutely contests the credibility of Menges, whom he accuses of zealotry.[91] The next few pages employs both sides in attempting to construct the episode.

In early August 1984, the vice president began preparation for an August 10 trip to the inauguration of Leon Febres Cordero, the newly elected president of Ecuador. Menges, however, says the deeper purpose of the trip was far more meaningful and sensitive.[92] Menges, in charge of the NSC's Latin American Affairs division, and who briefed and accompanied Bush on the trip, explained:

> A lot was riding on this trip and on how Bush used it. Its formal purpose was to celebrate another positive step in the return of democracy to Latin America. All the elected leaders of Latin American countries would attend to mark the occasion of Ecuador's second consecutive democratic presidential election. But it was also an important opportunity for the vice president, on behalf of Ronald Reagan, to meet privately with the presidents of Ecuador, Venezuela, Colombia, and Bolivia and to counter the active pro-Sandinista diplomacy of the Mexican government.[93]

History remembers the climactic role of Nicaragua, the Contras, and other aspects of Central America in Reagan administration policy during the 1980s. It led to numerous clashes between the White House and Democratic Congress, among other controversies and heated debates.[94] Reagan, often accused of a hands-off organizational style, was very much hands-on when it came to this region of the world.[95] "I was very definitely involved in the decisions on the support to the [Contras]," said Reagan. "It was my idea to begin with."[96] Nicaragua and the Contras were among his pet interests.[97] Hence, it was not unusual when at two recent NSC meetings shortly before the vice president's August trip, both of which Bush attended, Reagan firmly restated his position: He wanted a *genuine* political settlement in Central America. This meant explicitly that the Nicaraguan leadership—the Sandinistas—would fulfill its 1979 pledge to the OAS to establish genuine democracy, along with an effective system to guarantee compliance. This included first and foremost free and fair elections. Only when that had occurred would aid to the Nicaraguan armed resistance—the Contras—be ended.[98]

e Contras—be ended.⁹⁸

In June 1984, however, the Mexican government drafted a treaty—the Contadora Treaty—that met neither of these conditions. On the democracy side, it made only vague references that the Sandinistas would "make progress toward pluralism." Moreover, implementation of the treaty likely meant that the Contras would have to be dismantled and military aid to the government of El Salvador—the other linchpin of administration policy in the region—would have to be discontinued. In the administration's view, it also had no effective provision for verifying that the Sandinistas would halt their support of communist guerrillas in neighboring countries. For that reason, Reagan and all four of the other Central American nations rejected it. On the other hand, it was endorsed by Colombia, Venezuela, and Panama. There was a fear within some quarters of the administration that Mexico would work with Colombia, Venezuela, and Panama to bring along the other Central American nations.⁹⁹

Thus, Menges believed, the vice president's trip could make a momentous difference. "Now, in August, the trap was set to close on our friends in Central America," stated Constantine Menges. "By speaking, Bush could head this off in Ecuador." Specifically, Menges felt, the vice president had a chance not only to pacify the Central American nations, but also to work on reversing Colombia, Venezuela, and Panama by explaining the U.S. position. At stake, believed Menges, was nothing less than the very cornerstone of administration policy in the region. A guarantee of Nicaraguan power without elections could jeopardize all White House goals in the area. Menges explained:

> It was into this invisible but churning vortex of political-diplomatic conflict that Vice President Bush was about to step. As the number-two man to a president who trusted him, he had great potential influence. If he understood the stakes and was playing his cards right, he could be the catalyst that would keep Colombia, Venezuela, and Panama out of the Sandinista diplomatic net and persuade them to support the four friendly Central American countries. Given the timing, Bush had a golden opportunity to bolster the president's policy. . . . [He] had the kind of opportunity to do good for America that seldom comes to a vice president.¹⁰⁰

This is where the accounts of Menges and Motley begin to sharply diverge. Motley suggests that Menges vastly over estimated the ability of the vice president to make a big difference in the region. As will be shown below, he charges Menges with not understanding the necessary subtleties of diplomacy that confronted Bush.

The vice president spent the next few days receiving briefings, primarily from Motley of the State Department and Menges of the NSC. The latter, in particular, stressed the urgency to reiterate the president's policy in the region and work on each of the South American presidents on the need to reject the

Contadora treaty. "Mr. Vice President, I strongly urge—in fact, I think it's critical—that you spend a few minutes with each Latin American president on the issue of Central America," said Menges to Bush. "They want to know our views, and unless we ask them to support the democratic forces and firmly oppose the procommunist forces in Central America, their tendency is to be ambiguous and simply go along with the Mexican treaty formulations which *sound* harmless." The vice president, claimed Menges, listened intently as Menges urged him to make three specific points with each of the Latin American presidents he would be meeting: (1) the Contadora treaty was fatally flawed because it did not guarantee democracy in Nicaragua and required an end to all U.S. military aid in the area, including to the Contras; (2) the administration had photos and declassified intelligence to prove that Nicaragua had been committing aggression against its neighbors through armed subversion since 1979; and (3) Nicaragua had not complied with its 1979 OAS promise to hold free elections, and evidence suggested that the coming November 1984 elections would be fraudulent. "We certainly ought to try to get this message across," Bush allegedly replied.[101]

Following the briefing, Menges provided Bush with a one-page sheet of talking points on these main issues. He brought an extra copy to the vice president shortly before his first major meeting, all the while verbally restating the significance of the opportunity Bush faced. Then the time came. Bush first spoke for twenty-five minutes with President Lusinchi of Venezuela. According to Menges, the vice president mentioned nothing about the Contadora treaty nor any of the other points. Despite a candid complaint by Menges, who was present for all the meetings, Bush allegedly made the same mistake when meeting with President Betancur of Colombia and the other leaders. "Bush had not conveyed any firm, clear message about Central America or the Contadora treaty," asserted Menges. "[B]oth Venezuela and Colombia would interpret his silence as U.S. agreement with their having gone along with Mexico." Shortly thereafter, the vice president's entourage flew away.[102]

Menges' story gives the impression that Bush blew his assignment. But Motley adamantly disagrees: "Menges seems to expect heads of sovereign states to listen to a lecture from Bush, and then in the presence of [their] own advisors say, 'You are right. I was wrong. I will do as you say.' It just doesn't happen that way." He adds: "Unless you can impose your will by force, you need to figure out how to get the other guy to follow your script. That point was lost on Menges." Motley notes that talking and negotiating are "what diplomacy is all about," and that Bush realized that more than Menges did. "I submit to you," he concludes, "that George Bush, with all his experience in foreign policy and dealing with heads of state, had a pretty good feel on how to get the mission done." The former assistant secretary of state recalls that the vice president "did his usual first class performance." Moreover, Motley goes so far as to charge that Bush and others often quickly "tuned out" Menges and avoided discussing many issues with him. "That was how it was with Menges and Bush," said Motley. "Menges would speak, Bush would listen politely and then turn to someone else."[103]

However, in defense of the NSC staffer, recall that Menges complained that Bush failed to even *mention* the Contadora issue, let alone arguing it forcefully. Additionally, a separate element of Menges' version checks out somewhat: Menges maintains that Bush fouled the mission so significantly that a letter was written from the Oval Office to try to resolve the situation. To clear up the situation, Menges recommended to Bud McFarlane that Reagan immediately send a personal letter to all four Central American presidents arguing the aforementioned three points that the vice president reportedly neglected to mention. A somewhat stern letter was in fact drafted by the NSC and then reviewed by the CIA, DoD, and State Department. McFarlane approved the letter, the president agreed and signed it, and it was immediately sent to the State Department for transmission to each of the four ambassadors. Motley confirms the letter ("presumably written by Menges") and states that it was re-done a number of times by other players before it was ultimately sent out. Menges alleges that Motley went out of his way to delay sending the letter and even pressed Shultz to try to get Menges fired. Shultz rejected the request and the letter was sent on. Only a few days later all four Central American presidents issued statements rejecting the draft treaty.[104]

So, what was the impact of the letter in light of the larger situation? "President Reagan had again rescued his Central America policy," Menges concluded. "His letter gave the four Central American presidents the courage to face the facts, reject the false draft treaty, and continue working for a genuine peace settlement."[105] Menges makes the obvious case that Bush had blown the assignment. While acknowledging the letter, Motley deduces that "the letter [was] only one of the many pebbles one drops as you stitch together a foreign-policy objective."[106] Obviously, the assistant secretary downplays the letter incident.

It is difficult to conclusively assess Bush's behavior in this case. There are two conflicting tales. However, if one momentarily assumes that Menges' account is accurate, what, then, explains Bush's actions, or lack thereof, during the trip?

Perhaps Menges, Reagan, or other staffers failed to impress upon Bush the priorities he needed to convey. Or, as Menges seems to imply, it is possible that State Department people like Assistant Secretary of State Motley, who he suggests may not have been as dedicated to the concerns of Reagan and the NSC regarding Contadora, convinced Bush not to raise the issue. It is also possible that the vice president simply continuously forgot to raise this very important matter. Once again, it is important to remember that the accounts of this episode are mixed. Consequently, unlike the Saudi example in April 1986, it cannot be said definitively that Bush failed to adequately fulfill his mission in this instance. Further, it cannot be affirmed that, once again, Reagan had to bail him out. If Menges was right on the money, then this case might provide another illustration of the problem of assigning a crucial diplomatic task to someone who was not necessarily hired to be a diplomat. At the least, it would be another illustration of the potential fallibility of using the vice president in foreign policy.

While the earlier Saudi example shows that the vice president may have been capable of an occasional insufficient performance in foreign policy—and Menges alleges likewise regarding the Contadora trip—such examples seem to be among the only negatives involving Bush abroad. The following example, in particular, reflects very positively on the vice president.

Bush's Role in Soviet Policy and 1983 Western Europe Trip

It is difficult to size up the vice president's precise role in Reagan policy toward the Soviet Union. As noted in the Saudi example, he did not seem to play a key role in the broader construction of the secret NSDDs intended to undermine the USSR.[107] Yet, he occasionally had opportunities to play prominent roles in certain aspects critical to U.S.-Soviet relations. Ironically, key among those opportunities were three funerals he attended in Moscow. Historically, vice presidents have been made fun of because of their frequent attendance at funerals of foreign dignitaries. While Bush did attend his share of funerals, his visits were typically more than just wreath-laying missions. Usually, his ceremonial trips involved some form of substantive discussion. He visited with foreign leadership and was debriefed by the president upon his return. In the case of the Soviet Union, he attended all three funerals of Russian leaders Yuri N. Andropov, Leonid Brezhnev, and Konstantin Chernenko.

Brezhnev's funeral in mid-November 1982 afforded Bush and Secretary of State Shultz an occasion to meet briefly the new Soviet leader, General Secretary Andropov. However, the event provided little opportunity for real discussion with the new leader. For Andropov's funeral in early February 1984, Bush lead a U.S. delegation to Moscow. He had a fleeting opportunity to visit with the new leader, Chernenko—although the trip was more substantive than the vice president's previous visit, involving speeches, press releases, and so forth.[108] Still, upon his return, Bush commented to Reagan that the new Soviet leader—Chernenko—seemed less hard-nosed and abrasive than Andropov. After hearing this, Reagan remarked in his diary that he had a "gut feeling" that he and Chernenko might be able to work together, "through quiet diplomacy, to reduce the psychological barriers that divided us."[109]

In the spring of 1985, Chernenko died. Reagan decided not to attend the funeral, leaving Bush and Shultz to visit with the new premier, Mikhail Gorbachev. Bush delivered an invitation to Gorbachev from Reagan to come to a summit meeting.[110] This turned out to be a consequential visit, as Reagan sensed it could be.[111] Bush and Shultz returned with highly favorable impressions of Gorbachev as a serious, confident, and capable leader. Shultz spoke to Reagan about "an opportunity for high-level dialogue." Bush opined, "If there ever was a time when we can move forward with progress in the last few years, I would say this is a good one."[112] Bush seemed engaging and dynamic during this trip, particularly in his discussions with Gorbachev, which often involved sharp exchanges. Judging from Shultz's account, this was the most assertive a vice president had been toward a Soviet leader in Moscow since Vice President Nixon's visit in 1959.[113] Bush had made the best of a ceremonial visit.

That notwithstanding, as Raymond Garthoff notes, one later meeting between Bush and Gorbachev was "particularly important." Bush and Gorbachev had met only three times, each during the funerals of the latter's predecessors. They met again in 1988 when Bush was the GOP's presidential nominee. Bush told Gorbachev that if he were elected president he would continue working toward improved U.S.-Soviet relations. This was an assurance that became especially important. The vice president told Gorbachev to disregard some of the tough campaign rhetoric he might be hearing from Bush during the coming months. Gorbachev later referred to this conversation as the "most important talk Bush and I ever had."[114]

But the most substantive role of Vice President Bush regarding Soviet policy, and arms control in general, was an extremely impressive mission he undertook in early 1983.

Bush played a major role in what some have argued was one of the Reagan administration's most important foreign-policy actions—the "Euromissile" deployment in 1983. Many have argued that this deployment sparked the Soviets to eventually sign the INF treaty.[115] The vice president made a successful whistle-stop tour of Western European capitals in February 1983 to persuade wavering governments—heavily pressured by a domineering "nuclear-freeze" crowd—to accept deployment of Pershings and cruise missiles.[116]

Before Bush began the trip, the Reagan administration's position on this issue was to favor what it called "the zero-zero solution." Under that approach, the United States would shelve plans to deploy 572 new Pershing II and cruise missiles in several European countries, starting at the end of February, if the Kremlin would agree to dismantle all of its 340 SS-20 missiles in Europe and Asia, and the 240 older SS-4s and SS-5s in Europe.[117] Deployment of forty-eight cruise missiles was scheduled to take place by late 1983 if U.S.-Soviet talks in Geneva failed to produce an arms reduction agreement. General Secretary Andropov rejected the zero-zero approach, offering instead to reduce the number of Soviet missiles in Europe to 162, equivalent to the number of French and British missiles already in place, if the United States gave up deployment of its intended new missiles. The Andropov offer was rejected by Reagan and the allied governments. Into this situation stepped the vice president.

On January 27, 1983, Bush announced he would meet with Soviet negotiators the following week at the arms talks in Geneva. The vice president's announcement came on top of Reagan's declaration nineteen days earlier that Bush would be making a special trip to Europe. This would be the first time that an official of a higher rank than the U.S. negotiators had called on the Soviet delegates to the arms talks, lending a greater deal of authority and commitment to the trip. "This is not a negotiating mission," said the vice president, but a mission of "discussion and consultations."[118] The assignment was more of the latter than the former.

A report in the *Washington Post* at the time noted that Bush's trip "has considerable political importance" because it allowed an opportunity for the administration to "demonstrate its good faith" on arms control.[119] The trip had the following central goals: It was intended to revive support among members of NATO for the planned U.S. missile deployment. White House officials said Bush's trip was also intended to counter the widening anti-nuclear movement in Western Europe and the impact on public opinion there of a recent Soviet offer to hold a summit meeting.[120] The overture had won the Kremlin some P.R. points. Finally, Bush would be involved in heavy consultation with allies and Soviet negotiators in order to gauge their positions relative to the administration's stance on missile levels. Although it was not directly acknowledged publicly, one of the vice president's purposes was to sound out alliance leaders on what kind of compromise they might regard as reasonable.[121] In the end, he would present his findings to Reagan and work with top staff to reassess the position of the White House.

The vice president arrived in Bonn on January 30 on the first stop of a twelve-day swing that included the Netherlands, Belgium, Switzerland (where the START and INF arms talks were taking place), Italy, France, and Great Britain. He would visit all the basing countries, assuring them of U.S. resolve, inviting their suggestions, and receiving confirmation of their support for the deployment schedule.[122] In his arrival statement, Bush said that the Soviet Union's "unprecedented arms buildup of the last fifteen years" had threatened to undermine the credibility of NATO's deterrent, and that the nation had a monopoly on INF forces which could strike Europe and "reach this room" in minutes. He also carefully noted that in December of 1979—before the Reagan administration entered office—all of the nations of NATO made a two-part decision: first, to deploy in Europe NATO weapons capable of deterring an attack by Soviet SS-20s and other intermediate-range nuclear forces; and second, to enter into negotiations with the Soviet Union in order to reduce the level of those weapons on both sides.[123] In particular, the December 1979 date needed to be stressed. Many were accusing the Reagan administration's advocacy of the two-part decision as a sign of the advent of a belligerent, war-mongering administration now occupying Washington. As Bush noted, however, the administration was merely supporting a decision that pre-dated its arrival.

The vice president also tackled a number of "myths" about U.S. strategy. One of the myths, said Bush, was that the INF deployments would be a step toward nuclear war-fighting and to war-fighting confined to Europe alone. The vice president explained:

> I can do no better than to quote from a European publication, *The Economist* of London, from a cover article entitled: "Can So Many Young People Be Wrong About the Bomb? Yes, They Can." The article said: "Nothing more justifiably infuriates the Americans than the allegation that they want to put cruise missiles and Pershing II missiles into Europe in order to have a purely European nuclear war. These missiles were originally proposed—by Europeans—for exactly the opposite reason." *The Economist* is right. Nothing infuriates the president and me more than the suggestion we are preparing to fight a nuclear war, because we are not preparing to fight a nuclear war. We are preparing to deter war.[124]

Bush stated that both elements of NATO's decision on INF were inseparable and mutually reinforcing. "If we are to be credible in our arms negotiations," said the vice president, "the alliance must be united in its determination to deploy the INF systems if necessary. Why? Because otherwise the Soviet Union will simply have no incentive at all to negotiate seriously. None whatsoever." He said that when Reagan entered office he reviewed the INF decision and endorsed it. Then, in November 1981, he came up with the zero-option proposal. In reply, Bush alleged, the Soviets "responded with a thundering 'nyet,' followed by a tremendous public offensive designed to drive a wedge between the United States and its European allies."[125]

The vice president would repeat these themes throughout his trip. His first day also included a surprise message from Reagan, which the vice president read at a dinner party. In the "open" letter, Reagan reiterated the zero-option proposal. "I have asked Vice President Bush," the letter read, "to propose to Soviet General Secretary Andropov that he and I meet wherever and whenever he wants in order to sign an agreement banning U.S. and Soviet intermediate-range land-based missile weapons from the face of the earth."[126] Considering the beating the administration had been taking at the hands of some peace activists in Western Europe—particularly after Andropov's perceived summit-meeting olive branch—the letter was a public-relations masterpiece: Bush, on day one of his trip, had brought with him to West Germany—where the nuclear-freeze movement was strongest—a letter from the American president offering to eliminate *all* intermediate range missiles. As Bush noted during a press conference, West Germany was a linchpin to an agreement.[127] The Reagan letter initiative—which was approved two days before Bush left, after discussion with the vice president, Shultz, Weinberger, and NSA William P. Clark[128]—now placed the onus on Andropov.

Bush also met privately with West Germany Chancellor Helmut Kohl. A Bonn government spokesman described the meeting as "unusually satisfying," and said that it had demonstrated "complete agreement" between the two sides on disarmament issues.[129]

A couple of days later, amidst a February 2 visit to Brussels, the vice president continued to meet with allied leaders and to publicly press the Reagan case:

> I think its fair to ask: What's wrong with ridding the world of a new class of missiles? If the Soviets have another plan that would seriously address this question, President Reagan has said we would give it serious consideration. So far, we have been offered a policy which allows the Soviets to keep their monopoly on intermediate-range nuclear missiles, but prevents the West from deploying any of its own.[130]

From there, the vice president headed off to Geneva to perform one of his more delicate tasks: Meet with chief Soviet arms negotiators and press them to revise Andropov's position. During two-hours of private talks, he told the negotiators that the president was "deadly serious" about achieving weapons cuts. Bush talked separately for an hour at the United States Mission with Yuli A. Kvitsinsky, head of the Soviet delegation, and for another hour with Viktor P. Karpov, chief of the Soviet delegation discussing strategic arms. Bush stated: "I asked them to take the message back to the leadership in Moscow that we are, on I.N.F., deadly serious about reaching an agreement." The discussions were very candid. Karpov relayed: "The talks were frank about the possibilities we have here, and I feel maybe it will be useful for clarifying positions." "We feel that the talks were frank," Bush agreed, "and not just in the old diplomatic sense, very frank. I think from our standpoint, I think I speak for those who attended the meeting, we feel it was extraordinarily worthwhile."[131]

After the Geneva visit, tidbits started popping up in the press about how Bush seemed to be scoring some public relations benefits for the American side. On the heels of a February 7 visit with the Pope in Rome, the *Washington Post* reported: "Bush, judging from interviews and an assessment of editorial commentary in each of the countries he has visited, has done reasonably well as a spokesman for the western position." The article added that Bush, because of his political experience and demonstrated loyalty to Reagan was serving as an "important advisor rather than just a carrier pigeon for European views."[132] In Rome, the vice president stressed the "morality" of the zero-option proposal. "I think it's fair to ask what's wrong with ridding the world of a new class of nuclear missiles," said Bush. "The only argument I've ever heard against the zero option is that the Soviet Union doesn't like it."[133]

In his final stop during his tour, the vice president went to London. He met with Prime Minister Margaret Thatcher, Foreign Secretary Pym, and other leaders. He even had a chance to exchange views with the leaders of the opposition parties. Among other things, he was confronted by a leader of Britain's antinuclear movement after a speech he gave to the Royal Institute of International Affairs. Monsignor Bruce Kent, secretary general of the Committee on Nuclear Disarmament, asked Bush why the United States had voted against a resolution of the United Nations General Assembly calling for a nuclear freeze. After eleven days of new conferences, meetings, and questions, Kent offered a rare moment of confrontation. "Do you think we don't want peace?" asked Bush, with his voice rising. "Do you think we care less than others about a nuclear war? . . . I think every clergyman, every young person should join in banning an entire generation of strategic nuclear weapons from the face of the earth." This, he told the clergyman, was genuine morality. He said that nothing had succeeded in stopping war in Europe the way NATO's deterrence policy had during the past three decades.[134]

In his departure statement from London on February 10, Bush said that the issue of Moscow's monopoly on a new class of mobile land-based nuclear missiles—"more than 300 triple-warhead SS-20 missiles while the United States and the NATO allies have none"—was the one issue that dominated both his private talks and public discussions. "Let me say that based on my consultations with European leaders," the vice president added, "there should be no misunderstanding about the resolve of the NATO alliance. We are determined to begin deployment of NATO's intermediate-range ground forces at the end of 1983 if negotiations are not successful. This is not a threat but a joint reaffirmation of the commitment to the NATO decision of December 1979." When he arrived back in Washington, said Bush, he would be giving the president a full report on what he had learned from the European leaders.[135]

What did the vice president accomplish in his mission? A number of things. From his own perspective, he felt there was now a much better perception of U.S. seriousness and willingness to achieve genuine arms cuts. "Maybe that's a little bit of an egotistical assessment," said Bush, "but I believe that the press coverage and the summations that I've seen collected from foreign press coverage would bear that out."[136] The vice president's chief of staff, Daniel J. Murphy, noted that a goal of the trip was to keep Andropov from "running away with the ballgame" in the contest for the hearts and minds of Europeans. "Andropov was on the top of the front pages there when we arrived," said Murphy. "Bush put him back on page four and five the next day."[137] In particular, Bush felt that Reagan's open letter, combined with his trip, drove home the administration's peaceful intentions. "I reminded the people in Europe that it was, indeed, President Reagan who had suggested that Brezhnev meet him informally at the United Nations," he asserted. "I reminded them—and they needed reminding, I found out—that it was our president who talked a couple of times, at least, about a summit meeting, provided it was well prepared." In reference to the contents of the Reagan letter, he said, "And this, saying I will drop everything, go anywhere, anytime to sign a agreement, puts in focus the morality and the correctness of the U.S. position."[138]

Bush conceded that when he came to Western Europe he feared he might find a "frustratingly deep division" within the alliance. He insisted he did not. The vice president felt the allies had presented "an absolute solid front" in pressing for flexibility in negotiations, favoring a more gradual approach in achieving the zero option.[139] He said, however, that he witnessed "some deeper splits" among the opposition parties, but felt that they, too, had voiced an allegiance to "common western values"—a somewhat soothing response. Bush was convinced that he had reached those people in Europe who might have thought that the United States was not serious about arms reductions. The trip, he said, "shored up the alliance in that regard."[140]

The reaction to Bush's trip was largely favorable at home also. The *Washington Post*, in particular, wrote a congratulatory editorial entitled, "George Did It." Considering the paper's tendency for liberal-Democratic partisanship, the editorial was stunningly positive, saying that Bush exhibited "steady leadership and genuine consultation." It surmised:

> There rarely arises a single event about which one can fairly say that it made the difference. Certainly it would be too early, not to say quite foolish, to conclude that as a result of Vice President George Bush's trip to Europe, the snarl of foreign-policy issues centering on the question of Euromissile negotiations and/or deployment has finally been untangled and is now on the way to a reasonable resolution.
>
> But if that cannot be said, something else can: from all accounts, the vice president did a terrific job. He arrived in a Europe gripped by a perception that the Reagan administration was not in full control of itself and was taking Europe someplace uncertain that it did not wish to go. To governments and publics in seven countries he apparently managed to convey an improved sense of administration constancy and balance. He listened carefully and he elaborated Washington's approach to the missile question in a way that allowed open-minded Europeans to consider that the administration is not missile-happy, not bent on confrontation, not wedded to one inflexible Euromissile formula, but that it is determined to assert American leadership and to deserve the confidence of the allies.[141]

The editorial said Bush returned to Washington well placed to advise the president of the best particular Euromissile formula suited to defend Europe and to strengthen the alliance.

Bush's work on the issue did not end in Europe. He continued to press the administration's proposal at home. On CBS's "Face the Nation" on February 13, he talked about the administration's willingness to undertake a two-track approach of negotiating with the Soviet Union while continuing to deploy

Pershing IIs. Regarding a timeframe, he averred that all the missiles would not be fully deployed until sometime in 1985. He also reiterated the linkage between their deployment and Soviet behavior at the negotiating table. He stated, "[A]s I said in Europe, what goes in can come out. If we are compelled to deploy because the Soviets are not as forthcoming as our allies would like to see them, we will continue to negotiate, but that deployment date is set, and we are not going to vacillate and pull away from it."[142]

Bush's appearance on "Face the Nation" was also important because it was the first forum in which he publicly disclosed that the administration might consider doing "something different in order to encourage the Soviets to do what we've asked."[143] This was among the most critical policy impacts made by Bush as a result of the trip. When he returned from gathering the thoughts of European leaders, Bush presented to Reagan recommendations about the next step in alliance negotiating strategy.[144] In that vein, White House officials said that Bush on February 10, just back from his trip, told Reagan that several allied leaders, as well as Paul H. Nitze, the American representative at the negotiations, expressed a desire for what they called an "interim solution" or compromise plan on the missile issue. According to one official, the vice president's dispatches from Europe had prepared the administration for the necessity of looking at the possibility of an interim approach. Bush reported to Reagan that by proposing an interim solution, he would help the allies to persuade their own constituents that the United States was making all possible efforts. Obviously, such a change would have constituted a key shift away from the zero-zero solution the administration advocated.[145]

In the end, the vice president was very pleased with the outcome of his work on behalf of the INF deployment. Years later, during a 1988 presidential debate, he recalled:

> I was in Europe trying to convince European public opinion that we ought to go forward with the deployment of the INF weapons, and thank God the freeze people were not heard—they were wrong—and the result is we deployed, and the Soviets kept deploying, and then we negotiated from strength, and now we have the first arms control agreement in the nuclear age to ban weapons. You just don't make unilateral cuts in the hope that the Soviets are going to behave themselves.[146]

We can debate the long-term impact of Bush's trip on the Reagan strategy for achieving INF cuts. At the least, however, it should be noted that the vice president logged a successful trip that met administration objectives. In this case, he did not betray his basic duties.

Conclusion

As the INF-Euromissile debate proves, Vice President Bush performed a number of key foreign-policy duties during his eight years in office. These included his reprimanding of the leadership of El Salvador and his crisis-management efforts during Grenada. His chairmanship of the crisis group was unprecedented in the history of the vice presidency. Regarding the INF, he influenced the administration into considering shifting its strategy toward an "interim solution," not to mention a number of other achievements. On the other hand, one of the vice president's foreign-policy missions was not performed well: the Saudi trip of 1986. There is also controversy (unresolved) regarding his Central America visit of August 1984. At least one of these two missions featured failed diplomatic duties by Bush that had the potential to be quite damaging to Reagan administration policy.

The Saudi case may indicate that there were other items (political-campaigning interests) that Bush occasionally tended to, in conflict to Reagan's needs, forcing the president to intervene and even scold the vice president. This indicates that there were limits to the president-vice president relationship that sometimes created fissures. These limits may have stemmed from different wants. Reagan wanted a loyal vice president—and got one. But when Bush strayed off course—even if it was only once—Reagan landed on him.

There are other observations that can be made from the example of Vice President Bush. For one, aside from the Saudi case, he seems to have offered nothing but absolute fealty toward Reagan throughout his eight years of foreign-policy duties. Ironically, that steadfast loyalty also appears to have led Bush to sit quietly during cabinet and NSC meetings, prompting some in the administration, such as Kirkpatrick and Pipes, to later question his abilities and leadership. Secondly, Bush's foreign-policy tasks at times led to conflict with other national-security players within the administration. For instance, his takeover of the crisis-management committee sparked an ugly reaction by Secretary of State Haig, who, not incorrectly, argued that the chairmanship historically goes to the State Department. Finally, when it comes to interests, the vice president was the leading candidate to succeed Reagan and win the GOP nomination for the presidency in 1988, unlike other national-security players in the White House. This may have limited his utility in foreign policy more than other players, since Bush was cognizant that the roles he played and policies he supported could come back to bite him in the 1988 campaign. Once again, chief among these was the Saudi-oil situation in 1986.

Some of these incidents will be reexamined in the final chapter on lessons learned and policy recommendations. They provide insights into how the vice president may be used. Yet, aside from those matters, it is also important to note that President Reagan felt comfortable enough in the vice president's abilities to give him such significant tasks in the first place. In that respect, like presidents

Truman, Eisenhower, and Carter, President Reagan should share as much of the credit for his vice president's expanded role as Bush himself. While he continued the job-enhancing duties began by Truman, Eisenhower, and Carter—from allowing the vice president to be a statutory NSC member, to preside over the NSC in the president's absence, to moving his office to the West Wing—Reagan offered his own innovation: He became the first president in history to allow his vice president to chair a major NSC committee.

George Bush himself said it best: "Given the right president, it's possible for the right vice president to have an impact on administration policy."[147] Bush said that once Reagan made his decision on the vice presidency, he viewed the Reagan-Bush ticket not simply as a convenient political alliance but as a "partnership." "[A]s president," wrote Bush, "Ronald Reagan—more than any president before him—broke down the barriers between the nation's two highest elective offices. . . . He [went] out of his way to bring his vice president inside the White House circle, and our trust and friendship had grown each passing day."

We should never forget that while the vice president is now assured somewhat of a foreign-policy role—due to certain changes by the afore-mentioned presidents—his ultimate role and influence still depends first and foremost upon the president and foreign-policy team he serves, and the unique set of circumstances they produce. In the Bush-Reagan case, the idiosyncratic variable is visible in determining how the president used his vice president in foreign policy, in addition to how other players in the administration's foreign-policy structure could or could not affect that usage. The effect of such differing idiosyncrasies among presidents, vice presidents, and their teams will become especially evident in the next two chapters. The differing foreign-policy use and influence of vice presidents Quayle and Gore are almost entirely a function of the unique president and foreign-policy team they served.

Notes

1. C. Boyden Gray, "The Coordinating Role of the Vice Presidency," in James P. Pfiffner and R. Gordon Hoxie, eds., *The Presidency in Transition* (New York: Center for the Study of the Presidency, 1989), p. 424.

2. See George Bush, with Victor Gold, *Looking Forward* (New York: Doubleday, 1987), pp. 9-11.

3. Reagan, Ronald, *Ronald Reagan: An American Life* (New York: Simon & Schuster, 1990), p. 216.

4. Bush was twice considered as a vice president before Reagan chose him—once by Richard Nixon in 1968 and again by Gerald Ford when he assumed the presidency in 1974. Bush, op. cit., pp. 5-6.

5. On Bush's role as DCI, see Duncan L. Clarke, *American Defense and Foreign Policy Institutions* (New York: Harper & Row, 1989), p. 163; and Cord Meyer, *Facing*

Reality: From World Federalism to the CIA (New York: Harper & Row, 1980), pp. 225-26.

6. Interview with Tony Motley, via telephone from Washington, D.C., December 18, 1996.

7. Paul C. Light, "The Institutional Vice Presidency," *Presidential Studies Quarterly*, Vol. XIII, No. 2, Spring 1983, p. 210.

8. Marie D. Natoli, "The Vice Presidency in the Third Century," in James P. Pfiffner and R. Gordon Hoxie, eds., *The Presidency in Transition* (New York: Center for the Study of the Presidency, 1989), pp. 421-22.

9. In a March 1981 article, Bush clearly stated that the voodoo-economics comment was "not worth discussing anymore" because of his position as vice president. *Christian Science Monitor*, March 3, 1981.

10. Ibid.

11. Natoli, "The Vice Presidency in the Third Century," p. 421.

12. Marie D. Natoli, *American Prince, American Pauper* (Westport, Conn.: Greenwood, 1985), p. 182.

13. Bush, op. cit., p. 222.

14. "Interview with Vice President George Bush: White House Leaks: 'We Have Been Undisciplined,'" *U.S. News & World Report*, December 14, 1981, Vol. 91, No. 24, p. 20.

15. Marie D. Natoli, "The Vice Presidency in the Third Century," p. 411.

16. *Christian Science Monitor*, March 3, 1981.

17. Bush, op. cit., pp. 231-22; and *U.S. News & World Report*, December 14, 1981, p. 20.

18. Constantine C. Menges, *Inside the National Security Council* (New York: Simon & Schuster, 1988), p. 73.

19. Reagan, op. cit., pp. 594-95.

20. For a detailed breakdown of this framework, including the heads of each subgroup, see Menges, op. cit., p. 167.

21. See Clarke, op. cit., pp. 7-9; Lawrence E. Walsh, *Iran-Contra: The Final Report* (New York: Times Books, Random House, 1994), p. 452; and Bush, op. cit., pp. 243-44.

22. Kenneth W. Thompson, "The Reagan Presidency: Interview with Frank Carlucci," *Miller Center Journal*, Vol. 2, Spring 1995, p. 45.

23. Martin Anderson, *Revolution* (San Diego: Harcourt Brace Jovanovich, 1988), pp. 310-13.

24. *National Journal*, June 10, 1981.

25. *Christian Science Monitor*, March 3, 1981.

26. Bush, op. cit., pp. 226-27.

27. Ibid.

28. *U.S. News & World Report*, December 14, 1981, p. 20.

29. Gerald F. Seib, "Bush's Role in Policy Is Difficult to Discern Reagan Officials Say," *The Wall Street Journal*, March 31, 1988, p. A1.

30. Carl Bernstein, "The Holy Alliance," *Time*, February 24, 1992, p. 31.

31. Randall Rothenberg, "In Search of George Bush," *The New York Times Magazine*, March 6, 1988, p. 49.

32. Anderson, op. cit., pp. 317-18.

33. Seib, op. cit., p. A1.

34. Rothenberg, op. cit., pp. 30, 44, 49, and 61.

35. For additional quotes in which Bush reaffirms this philosophy, see Seib, op. cit., pp. A1 and A13; and *Christian Science Monitor*, March 3, 1981.

36. George P. Shultz, *Turmoil and Triumph: My Years as Secretary of State* (New York: Macmillan, 1993), p. 850n.

37. Interview with Tony Motley, via letter from Washington, D.C., January 9, 1997.

38. Thompson, op. cit., p. 48.

39. Reagan, op. cit., p. 249.

40. Marie D. Natoli, "The Vice Presidency in the Third Century," p. 411.

41. Among Bush's prominent domestic assignments was a task force he headed up on government regulation. (In its goals, the task force was very similar to Vice President Quayle's Council on Competitiveness.) Reagan was very complementary regarding the achievements of the task force. He credited Bush's group with helping the president meet a key part of his administration's goals. Indeed, as noted by Reagan economic advisor Martin Anderson, regulatory reform was "one of Reagan's most important policies." Reagan, op. cit., pp. 234 and 298-99; and Anderson, op. cit., p. 260. Also, see Gray, op. cit., pp. 428-29; and Bush, op. cit., p. 233.

42. On Bush's specific role in Iran-Contra, see Barrett Seaman and Strobe Talbott, "An Interview with the Vice President (George Bush, Iran Arms Deal)," *Time*, December 8, 1986, Vol. 128, p. 42. Also, see Walsh, op. cit.; Shultz, op. cit., pp. 803, 808-09, 810, 814, 838, 849-50, and 852; Rothenberg, op. cit., p. 60; and Steven A. Holmes, "Gore Lashes Out at Bush on His Iran-Contra Role," *The New York Times*, September 4, 1992, p. A12.

43. Menges, op. cit., p. 71.

44. Bush, op. cit., p. 234.

45. For example, see Reagan, op. cit., pp. 254-55 (Japan) and 363-64 (Philippines); and Menges, op. cit., p. 347. An example of Bush strongly and angrily arguing privately against Reagan's view took place during the Manuel Noriega indictment issue. See Shultz, op. cit., pp. 1051, 1062-63, 1068, 1070-71, 1075-77.

46. There are many published examples of Bush negotiating with foreign leaders at home and abroad. Among examples not included in this chapter are the following: Menges, op. cit., pp. 117, 125-27, 219, and 300 (Latin America); 50-51 (Western Europe); and 362 (Israel). Bush, op. cit., pp. 234-35 (Pakistan and Afghanistan), 234-36 (China), and 241-42 (Israel). Seib, op. cit., p. A13 (China and Taiwan). *Christian Science Monitor*, May 4, 1982 (China and Taiwan). *Christian Science Monitor*, November 9, 1982 (Africa).

47. C. Boyden Gray remarked that "because of the enormous threat the Gephardt amendment posed to the world trading order, it may be that the vice president's contribution to its defeat may rate higher in the history books than his role in persuading Europe to deploy the cruise and Pershing missiles." Gray, op. cit., p. 429.

48. *National Journal*, June 20, 1981.

49. Reagan, op. cit., pp. 255-56.

50. "Text of White House Statement" on Bush move, *The New York Times*, March 25, 1981, p. A6.

51. Haig's specific complaints, and their potential merit, will be examined in the final chapter on lessons learned and policy recommendations, in which the feasibility of employing the vice president as chair of the administration's crisis-management team will be closely scrutinized.

52. Reagan, op. cit., pp. 255-56.

53. Raymond L. Garthoff, *The Great Transition: American-Soviet Relations and the End of the Cold War* (Washington, D.C.: The Brookings Institution, 1994), pp. 118 and 119n.

54. Ed Magnuson, "D-Day in Grenada," *Time*, Vol. 122, No. 20., November 7, 1983, p. 27; and Bush, op. cit., p. 243n.

55. Menges, op. cit., p. 70-77.

56. Reagan, op. cit., p. 449.

57. Magnuson, op. cit., p. 27; and Shultz, op. cit., p. 329.

58. Magnuson, op. cit., p. 27.

59. Bush was worried that an all-English-speaking rescue of the island would look bad. He recommended that the administration try to enlist Venezuelan help. Reagan rejected the idea, saying that a request to Venezuela would delay any action and might be leaked, thereby ruining the element of surprise and possibly sabotaging the operation. Shultz, op. cit., p 329.

60. Interview with Motley, January 9, 1997.

61. Menges, op. cit., p. 382.

62. George Bush, "Prelude to Retaliation: Building a Governmental Consensus on Terrorism," *SAIS Review*, 1987, Vol. 7, No. 1, pp. 1-9; and Menges, op. cit., pp. 268-72;

63. Menges, op. cit., p. 272

64. Ibid., pp. 381-82. For more on Menges view of the task force, see pp. 250-76.

65. For more on this policy and the task force in general, see Bush article in *SAIS Review*; "Terrorism: Special Report," *American Legion Magazine*, June 1986, Vol. 120, pp. 15-21; and Shultz, op. cit., pp. 678-80.

66. See Christopher Simpson, *National Security Directives of the Reagan and Bush Administrations: The Declassified History of U.S. Political and Military Policy, 1981-1991* (Boulder, Colo.: Westview, 1995); Peter Schweizer, *Victory: The Reagan Administration's Secret Strategy That Hastened the Collapse of the Soviet Union* (New York: The Atlantic Monthly Press, 1994); and Richard Pipes, "Misinterpreting the Cold War," *Foreign Affairs*, January/February 1995, p. 157.

67. Schweizer, op. cit., p. xvi and xix. In his memoirs, George Shultz affirms that he was not made aware of many of these issues, including the announcement of SDI, until the last minute (if at all). Shultz, op. cit.

68. For more on this plan, see Bernstein, op. cit., pp. 28-35; Keith Schneider, "Reagan-Pope Plan to Topple Warsaw Is Reported," *The New York Times*, February 18, 1992; and Michael Ledeen, "This Political Pope," *The American Enterprise*, July 1993, Vol. 4, No. 4, pp. 40-43; Schweizer, op. cit., pp. xviii and 68-69; and Garthoff, op. cit., pp. 31-23.

69. Schweizer, op. cit., pp. 25-26.

70. Paul Taylor, "Furor over Remarks Fails to Dismay Bush," *Washington Post*, April 14, 1986; Schweizer, op. cit., pp. 242-43; and Richard Alm, "Alarm bells over cheaper oil; while consumers cheer plummeting prices, Vice President Bush and others are warning enough is enough," *U.S. News & World Report*, April 14, 1986, Vol. 100, p. 24. A read of the *U.S. News & World Report* article demonstrates the extent to which the media was unaware of the true reason for the increase in Saudi oil production and low prices.

71. Schweizer, op. cit., pp. 242-43.

72. Ibid., pp. 255-56 and 261.

73. Ibid., p. 256.

74. Maureen Santini, "Knee-Deep in Troubled Waters," *U.S. News & World Report*, Vol. 100, No. 15, April 21, 1986, pp. 33-34.

75. Rowland Evans and Robert Novak, "Oil Blooper," *Washington Post*, April 9, 1986; and Taylor, op. cit.

76. Alm, op. cit., p. 24.

77. Ibid., p. 24.

78. "Vice President Bush Visits Persian Gulf," *U.S. Department of State Bulletin*, June 1986, Vol. 86, No. 2111, p. 28; and Schweizer, op. cit., pp. 260-61.

79. Schweizer, op. cit., p. 261.

80. Evans and Novak were not even fully aware of how far "off the reservation" Bush had gone. They knew nothing about the overall strategic plan; instead, they were cognizant only of Bush not towing the administration's line on allowing market forces to determine oil prices. Evans and Novak, op. cit., p. A23.

81. Taylor, op. cit.

82. Evans and Novak, op. cit., p. A23.

83. Bush, op. cit., p. 234.

84. See "Vice President Bush Visits Latin America," *U.S. Department of State Bulletin*, February 1984, Vol. 84, No. 2083, p. 9.

85. Bush, op. cit., pp. 236-38.

86. Interview with Motley.

87. Bush, op. cit., p. 238.

88. Interview with Motley.

89. For similar such remarks by Motley, see Seib, op. cit., p. A13.

90. Shultz, op. cit., p. 404.

91. Interview with Motley, January 9, 1997.

92. Surprisingly, there is no record in the *U.S. Department of State Bulletin* on Bush's August 10 trip—a highly conspicuous omission that likely reflects on its sensitivity. In a lengthy article, the October 1984 issue remarks on the August 10 inauguration, as well as the entire Contadora process, without mentioning Bush's visit. See Langhorne A. (Tony) Motley, "Democracy in Latin America and the Caribbean," *U.S. Department of State Bulletin*, October 1984, Vol. 84, No. 2091, pp. 1-17. Moreover, there was no coverage of the trip in the major newspapers, including the *New York Times*, *Los Angeles Times*, and the *Washington Post*. (Of course, it was an election year and these papers were busily making an issue of how Bush's financial records made him out to be far more "rich" than the Democratic vice-presidential candidate, Geraldine Ferraro.) The only press reference the author was able to locate was a brief two-sentence blurb by Reuters on August 11.

93. Menges, op. cit., p. 131.

94. See John D. Martz, ed., *United States Policy in Latin America: A Decade of Crisis and Challenge* (Lincoln: University of Nebraska Press, 1995); and Howard J. Wiarda, *American Foreign Policy toward Latin America in the 80s and 90s: Issues and Controversies from Reagan and Bush* (New York: New York University Press, 1992). For an excellent account of the fight between the administration and Democratic Congress on this issue, see Gordon S. Jones and John A. Marini, eds., *The Imperial Congress: Crisis in the Separation of Powers* (New York: Pharos Books, 1988).

95. Fred I. Greenstein refers to Reagan derisively as a consistently "*no-hands* president"—in contrast, of course, to Greenstein's famous "hidden-hand" Eisenhower. Fred I. Greenstein, "Ronald Reagan—Another Hidden Hand Ike?" *PS: Political Science &*

Politics, Vol. XXIII, No. 1, March 1990, pp. 7-13.

96. "Reagan, Remarks and a Question-and-Answer Session with Southeast Regional Editors and Broadcasters," May 15, 1987, *Public Papers of the Presidents*, 1987, Vol. I, p. 514.

97. In essence, how Reagan performed as a thinker or strategist seemed to depend on the issue, perhaps reflecting his preference for larger, Cold War matters. Statements by people from Frank Carlucci to Lou Cannon chronicle how Reagan's policy involvement and strategic capabilities were often dependent upon his level of interest in the subject matter at hand. See, for example: Thompson, op. cit., p. 47; Lou Cannon, *Reagan* (New York: G. P. Putnam's Sons, 1982), p. 375; and Paul Kengor, "Comparing Presidents Reagan and Eisenhower," *Presidential Studies Quarterly*, Vol. XXVIII, No. 2, Spring 1998, pp. 366-93.

98. Secretary of State George Shultz, "Nicaragua: Will Democracy Prevail?" Statement before the Senate Foreign Relations Committee on February 27, 1986, *U.S. Department of State Bulletin*, April 1986, Vol. 86, No. 2109, pp. 32-39; Elliott Abrams, "Development of U.S.-Nicaragua Policy," U.S. Department of State, Bureau of Public Affairs, Editorial Division, 1987; and Menges, op. cit., pp. 131-32.

99. Elliott Abrams, "Permanent Dictatorship in Nicaragua?" U.S. Department of State, Bureau of Public Affairs, Editorial Division, 1986; and Menges, op. cit., pp. 131-33.

100. Menges, op. cit., pp. 131-33.

101. Ibid., pp. 133-34. A few months after completing this mission, Bush demonstrated that he understood these goals and their implications in a February 28, 1985 speech before the Austin Council on Foreign Affairs, in which he clearly articulated the "genuine peace" notion. See Vice President George Bush, "Nicaragua: A Threat to Democracy," Address before the Austin Council on Foreign Affairs on February 28, 1985, *U.S. Department of State Bulletin*, May 1985, Vol. 85, No. 2098, p. 24.

102. Menges, op. cit., pp. 134-39.

103. Interview with Motley, January 9, 1997.

104. Menges, op. cit., pp. 139-45; and Interview with Motley, January 9, 1997.

105. Menges, op. cit., pp. 139-45.

106. Interview with Motley, January 9, 1997.

107. Bush did, of course, have strong opinions. In essence, he seemed more dovish than Reagan during the first term, often being uncomfortable with some of the harsh anti-Soviet policies and pronouncements. Yet, in the latter part of the second Reagan term he appears to have been more hawkish and skeptical than the president, fearing Reagan had gone too far in conciliation. Bush was privately appalled at the high stakes bargaining at Reykjavik in 1986. Later, in mid-1988, while Reagan was basking in the glow of world acclaim with Gorbachev in the Kremlin and Red Square, the vice president was notably unenthusiastic as he watched on television from his summer home in Kennebunkport, Maine. When asked by reporters about his reaction to the Moscow summit, Bush muttered, "The Cold War isn't over." Don Oberdorfer, *The Turn: From the Cold War to a New Era* (New York: Poseidon Press, 1991), p. 329.

108. Garthoff, op. cit., pp. 52 and 169-70; and Bush, op. cit., pp. 234-35.

109. Reagan, op. cit., pp. 559 and 592.

110. Ibid., pp. 378, 572, and 611-12; and Schweizer, op. cit., p. 236.

111. On Reagan's optimistic attitude *before* the trip, see "Magazine Publishers Association," March 14, 1985, *Presidential Documents*, March 18, 1985, Vol. 21, p. 301.

112. Shultz, op. cit., pp. 528-33; Garthoff, op. cit., p. 207; Oberdorfer, op. cit., pp. 109-11; and "Vice President's Visit to Moscow: News Conference," remarks in Moscow on March 13, 1985, *U.S. Department of State Bulletin* May 1985. Vol. 85, p. 18.

113. For a detailed account of the exchanges, see Shultz, op. cit., pp. 529-31.

114. Garthoff, op. cit., pp. 333-34; and Michael R. Beschloss and Strobe Talbott, *At the Highest Levels: The Inside Story of the End of the Cold War* (Boston: Little, Brown, 1993), pp. 3-4.

115. Among those supporting derivations of this 'peace through strength' perspective are: John Lewis Gaddis, "Hanging Tough Paid Off," *Bulletin of Atomic Scientists*, 45, January 1989, pp. 11-14; Robert Einhorn, *Negotiating from Strength: Leverage in U.S.-Soviet Arms Control* (New York: Praeger, 1985); Anthony Dolan, *Undoing the Evil Empire: How Reagan Won the Cold War* (Washington, D.C.: American Enterprise Institute, 1992); Richard Pipes, "Can the Soviet Union Reform?" *Foreign Affairs*, Vol. 63, No. 1 (1984), pp. 47-61; and Valery Giscard d'Estaing, Yasuhiro Nakasono, and Henry Kissinger, "East-West Relations," *Foreign Affairs*, Vol. 68, No. 3, Summer 1989, pp. 1-21. In the latter citation, the authors argue: "What made the start of [arms] reductions possible was the willingness of the democracies to maintain an adequate deterrence posture. What will sustain the process of reductions is the willingness to ensure that at every level of reductions, deterrence is maintained and preferably strengthened."

116. For a focus on the strength of the nuclear-freeze movement in allegedly ending the Cold War, see Thomas Risse-Kappen, "Did 'Peace through Strength' End the Cold War: Lessons from INF," *International Security*, Vol. 16, No. 1, Summer 1991.

117. The U.S. weapons were all intermediate-range, land-based nuclear missiles.

118. "Vice President Bush Visits Europe," *U.S. Department of State Bulletin*, Vol. 83, No. 2072, March 1983, p. 1; and Michael Getler, "Bush Will Confer In Geneva With Soviet Negotiators," *Washington Post*, January 28, 1983, p. A1.

119. Getler, op. cit., p. A1.

120. Juan Williams, "Bush to Go to Europe for Talks," *Washington Post*, January 9, 1983, p. A1.

121. A *New York Times* reporter perceptively picked up on this at the time. See John Vinocur, "Bush Says Reagan Arms Offer Stands," *The New York Times*, February 3, 1983.

122. Shultz, op. cit., p. 350.

123. *U.S. State Department Bulletin*, March 1983, pp. 3-4.

124. Ibid.

125. Ibid., p. 4.

126. John Vinocur, "President Urges Soviet to Agree to Missile Curb," *The New York Times*, February 1, 1983, p. A1.

127. *U.S. State Department Bulletin*, March 1983, p. 12.

128. Vinocur, "President Urges Soviet to Agree to Missile Curb," p. A1.

129. Ibid.

130. Vinocur, "Bush Says Reagan Arms Offer Stands," p. A1.

131. *U.S. State Department Bulletin*, March 1983, pp. 17-18; and John Vinocur, "Bush Says the U.S. Is 'Deadly Serious' on Weapons Curbs," *The New York Times*, February 5, 1983, p. A1.

132. Michael Getler, "Bush Emphasizes 'Moral Position' of Reagan Arms Control Plan," *Washington Post*, February 8, 1983, p. A11.

133. "Bush Urges 'Zero Option' in Tour of Western Europe," *Editorials on File*

1983, p. 151.

134. John Vinocur, "Bush, in London, Challenged by Nuclear Foe," *The New York Times*, February 10, 1983.

135. *U.S. State Department Bulletin*, March 1983, p. 25.

136. Ibid., p. 27.

137. Francis X. Clines, "The Vice President: No Comment on the Future," *The New York Times*, February 25, 1983.

138. *U.S. State Department Bulletin*, March 1983, p. 27.

139. *Editorials on File 1983*, p. 151.

140. John Vinocur, "Bush Finds Allies Open on Arms Pact," *The New York Times*, February 11, 1983.

141. Editorial, "George Did It," *Washington Post*, February 13, 1983, p. C6.

142. "Vice President Interviewed on 'Face the Nation' (excerpts)," *U.S. Department of State Bulletin*, Vol. 83, No. 2072, March 1983, pp. 37-38.

143. Ibid., p. 38.

144. Michael Getler, "U.S. Is 'Deadly Serious' on Arms Reduction, Bush Tells Soviets," *Washington Post*, February 5, 1983, pp. A1 and A22.

145. Bernard Gwertzman, "U.S. Called Ready to Consider Shift on Missiles Plan," *The New York Times*, February 14, 1983, p. A1.

146. Transcript of the second presidential debate, *The New York Times*, October 15, 1988, p. A11.

147. Bush, op. cit., p. 7.

Chapter 6

A "War-Time" Vice President: J. Danforth Quayle (1989-93)

"You know what it's a question of? Judgment. The Democratic leadership made an erroneous judgment about a very important national security issue. Are they to be held accountable for their judgment? I would certainly hope so."
Vice President Quayle, in a postwar interview with Business Week, addressing the question of whether it was fair to attack Democrats for their vote against the use of force in the Persian Gulf conflict

Introduction

Few vice presidents suffered the ridicule and torment received by Vice President Dan Quayle during his four years in office. While Quayle sometimes earned the abuse because of various malaprops and *faux pas*, the truth is that other vice presidents, such as Vice President Al Gore, have made similar slip ups that did not receive publicity.[1] Quayle defenders were often justified in pointing to unfair treatment. Occasionally, influential media figures that helped construct the poor image of Quayle let their guard down and fessed up to their biases. Take, for instance, the following remark by *Baltimore Sun* reporter Jules Witcover, whose duty as a member of the press corps on one of the vice president's trips abroad was to report on the substance of Quayle's trip: "On his first notable fact-finding trip abroad, a twelve-day swing through four Far Eastern countries . . . Quayle traveled with an unusually large American press corps along, essentially on a gaffe watch." Witcover aimed to report not on Quayle's mission but on trivial remarks he made that seemed humorous or might embarrass the vice president.[2]

It is too bad that Witcover and others reported on the vice president as they did. They missed a few good stories, particularly when it came to his role in foreign policy. There are a number of examples of Quayle's role in global affairs. Most of his missions and tasks were performed quite well. He did not seem to make any big mistakes. He occasionally made statements and took positions that outraged the State Department, such as a speech he made to the American-Israel Public Affairs Committee and comments he made about Soviet leader Mikhail Gorbachev. The latter reportedly earned him a reprimand from President George Bush. Both incidents were deliberate, rather than slip ups.

This chapter focuses on these and other matters. Primarily, however, it focuses on Quayle's role in the Persian Gulf episode.³ In that sense, it is the only chapter of this study that concentrates solely on one specific foreign-policy case in examining a particular vice president.⁴ During the Gulf crisis, Quayle was highly active and played an impressive role that did not receive much publicity at the time. In particular, he assumed strong roles as an administration spokesman and as a liaison to the U.S. Congress—expressing the views of both himself and the administration in a number of speeches, interviews, and public statements. The vice president also took part in some very sensitive negotiating and fact-finding missions abroad during the crisis, including in Latin America and the Middle East. The lessons learned from his experiences will be considered in the final chapter on policy recommendations.

Quayle's Selection and Role Definition

To some in the media, George Bush's selection of Dan Quayle as his running mate was a shock. In fact, however, it made a lot of sense. Bush, as noted in the last chapter, always had difficulty appealing to the formidable conservative wing of the Republican party. Conservatives always viewed Bush suspiciously, dating back to the 1980 campaign days in which he ridiculed Reagan's supply-side economics policies as "voodoo economics." Quayle himself notes how "even after eight years as [Reagan's] loyal vice president, [Bush] had to contend with the suspicions of some right-wing elements in the party."⁵ As a result, Bush needed to pick a running mate who could mollify that segment of the party, especially since he was receiving a decent challenge from the supply-side/traditional-values conservative, Jack Kemp. Thus, Quayle was a perfect fit. Not only was he conservative on cultural, economics, and defense issues—earning him high ratings by the American Conservative Union—but was also young and energetic. Conservatives would have an advocate in Quayle. He was also hugely popular in the state of Indiana and had won reelection by substantial margins against popular Democrats. Additionally, Quayle was a baby boomer and, among him, Bush, Michael Dukakis, and Lloyd Bentsen, would be the only midwesterner. Moreover, Quayle was well recommended outside of conservative circles. Early on, academic Richard Fenno featured him as a rising star among a number of senators from both sides of the aisle.⁶ Quayle's work in the Senate also led him to receive high compliments from the likes of traditional Democrats like Ted Kennedy, who worked closely with Quayle in co-sponsoring the Job Training Partnership Act. This all served to make Quayle an attractive choice for Bush. Bush was rightly alarmed when the media backlash to his choice immediately began with a vengeance. In fact, Quayle and the Bush campaign had been discussing such a ticket for at least a month before the convention.⁷

In considering different assignments and roles during the transition period, Quayle met with a number of past vice presidents, including Richard Nixon and Walter Mondale. Nixon stressed the need for loyalty to the president and, not surprisingly, recommended that Quayle do a great deal of international travel, as Nixon had done for Ike in the 1950s. Mondale, certainly recalling the conflicts he faced with Vance and Brzezinski over the Middle East and other issues, warned how the vice president can find himself "blocked" by cabinet members and "competing power centers" within the administration. But perhaps the most help from former vice presidents came from Quayle's own boss, President Bush. "President Bush," Quayle recalled, "from the moment he took office, made it clear to everyone in the West Wing that I was to have all the access that I wanted. He hoped that would make me conversant with all aspects of the presidency, the only way I could be properly prepared in the event of suddenly having to assume the office."[8] It is not clear if Bush and Quayle formally agreed to a well-laid out plan of activities for the vice president, as Mondale and Carter did. Instead, his specific duties seemed to develop over time. However, the vice president's broader role definition was pretty much set early in the administration. Most importantly, as will be seen in the next section, throughout his tenure Quayle would be the beneficiary of a considerable amount of empathy from Bush.

The President-Vice President Relationship

Henry Kissinger wrote that the "relationship between the president and any vice president is never easy; it is, after all, disconcerting to have at one's side a man whose life's ambition will be achieved by one's death."[9] As noted earlier, LBJ recalled, "every time I came into John Kennedy's presence, I felt like a goddamn raven hovering over his shoulder."[10] In the case of Quayle, however, the vice president seemed very comfortable around the president. The two men enjoyed an exceptionally good rapport. David Broder and Bob Woodward, in an in-depth series on the vice president in the *Washington Post*, agreed that Quayle enjoyed a good relationship with the president.[11] Fortunately for Quayle, he had a president in Bush who also served as a vice president. Consequently, as vice president, Quayle was the beneficiary of a certain amount of empathy from Bush. Bush aides said the president was especially sympathetic to the abuse Quayle received.[12] Quayle shared some of Bush's advice:

> He has said a number of times, "I've got a whole drawer full of press clippings from when I was vice president. If you ever feel down, help yourself." And I say, "No, Mr. President, that's OK. I read them, too." There are a lot of rewarding moments. It's an awkward job. It's awkward con-

stitutionally—president of the Senate, member of the executive branch. But I've learned lessons from [Bush]: Just plow ahead, don't pay attention to the critics. Do the job and things will turn out.[13]

Senator Alan K. Simpson (R-Wyo.), a close friend of Bush and Quayle, recalled that during the early months of the administration, when Quayle was the butt of jokes, the "greatest thing [Bush] told him—I don't know when it was—but he said, 'What do you think of all those cartoons and editorials and attacks?' and Dan said, 'Wow!' and just shook his head. And [Bush] said, 'Well, why don't you take [out] the word "Quayle" and insert the word "Bush" wherever it appears, and that's the crap I took for eight years. Wimp. Sycophant. Lap dog. Poop. Lightweight. Boob. Squirrel. [Pejorative]. George Bush.'. . . That meant more to Dan, I think, than anything," Simpson said. (Quayle commented that Simpson's language sounded more like Simpson than Bush, but that the statement was accurate.)[14]

In a striking resemblance to Bush as vice president, Quayle tried to provide input to the president mainly in private. "I like to give him my ideas in privacy," said Quayle. "When we're in a large group where it's probably going to get out, I try to be somewhat circumspect. . . . I try not to take time at large cabinet meetings. I try to be somewhat judicious so people can't read it that the president feels this way, but the vice president feels that way."[15] Also very much like Vice President Bush, Quayle's quiet manner in offering advice to the president made it difficult for outsiders to measure his impact. In defense of the same sort of charges that Vice President Bush received during his tenure, Jon Glassman, Quayle's deputy NSA, states of his vice president: "He viewed his role as serving the president. Period."[16]

Helping to solidify the Quayle-Bush relationship was a generous degree of access by the president. The vice president later said that Bush urged him "to attend absolutely any Oval Office meeting, on domestic or foreign policy, that I wanted to. In fact, he was offering an astonishing amount of access—unprecedented." He said that while his vice presidency presented many challenges, having access to the president was not one of them.[17]

Quayle had a regular Thursday lunch with Bush, which he termed the "centerpiece of my contact" with the president. The lunches were informal. The two would talk about their foreign travels or whatever was going on in a given week. Sometimes, when there was a key event involving one of Quayle's domestic domains—such as his Space[18] or Competitiveness councils—the vice president would go in with a slightly more formal agenda that featured a sheet with a list of points he wanted to go over. "The lunches became such an institution that other members of the administration learned to get in touch with me on Thursday mornings to request that I pass something on to the president," said Quayle. Citing a number of examples, the vice president said he was often approached with the request: "Could you tell the boss. . .?"[19] Carnes Lord, the vice president's NSA, said that Quayle's foreign-policy staff viewed these lunches as opportunities to "raise real issues" with the president.[20]

Administration officials believed that Quayle's proximity to the president, on a daily basis and in crisis meetings, had a cumulative effect on their relationship. "You can't underestimate the slow, water-faucet-dripping impact of the [private] Thursday lunches" Bush and Quayle had each week, a close Bush advisor said in 1992. "Quayle's influence cannot be measured by a single event, but in my judgment [during the three years] . . . there has been a very definite favorable accumulation" of influence with the president.[21]

According to reports, Bush seemed satisfied with Quayle's performance, even though he was at times a clear political liability. (This is a close parallel to Eisenhower and Vice President Nixon. Although both Quayle and Nixon had dedicated allies in the GOP, they often served as general liabilities to their presidents.) "From time to time I'd be told by mutual friends that Bush had gone out of his way to mention my name and let it be known that he was pleased with me," stated Quayle.[22]

Judging from accounts, it seems that the only time Bush became displeased with Quayle's actions was when the vice president blasted Soviet leader Mikhail Gorbachev in a speech, especially outraging the Baker State Department, which was decidedly more pro-Gorbachev than Quayle, who leaned toward Yeltsin.[23] Quayle stepped out of line by publicly disclosing a controversial opinion regarding what he perceived as the expansionary tendencies of the Soviet Union and Gorbachev. That was at the time of Bush's summit meeting with the Soviet general secretary in Malta. Quayle zinged Gorbachev in a speech. It was reported that Bush landed on him and told him to stop it, and Quayle obeyed.[24] The vice president recalled that he was "sure" that Bush was irritated with him because of his comments. "When I sensed that I had gone too far on the Soviet question, I brought it up myself, volunteering to be taken to the woodshed," Quayle later wrote. "He just dismissed it. I suppose he figured that if I was bothered enough to mention it, then his message, however indirectly it had been sent, had gotten through. When the president got angry, he didn't get loud; he got quiet."[25]

Quayle's Place within the Bush Administration's Foreign- and Security-Policy Structure

As noted earlier, Truman's statutory changes provide the vice president somewhat of a guaranteed place within any White House foreign- and security-policy structure. He is, for instance, now a statutory member of the NSC. Quayle, continuing that practice, also served in such capacity. Unlike Vice President Bush, he did not head up any major interagency foreign-policy groups or NSC committees.[26] Like many second-office holders, this lack of a particular domain in foreign policy at times frustrated him. "The job is awkward, an awkward job," he said. He was "much more free and independent" during his eight years as a senator. The vice presidency, said Quayle after three years on the job, was a "much more confining job. You don't have your own agenda. Your agenda is the president's agenda. . . . Wherever I might go, somebody has primary jurisdiction, and that's one of the problems with being vice president. . . . Anything you do, you're going to be getting into somebody else's domain." "It's an uncomfortable position to be in," agreed Secretary of Defense Dick Cheney. "The vice president is there sort of as an overall generalist. . . . He's here as the president's understudy, in a sense."[27]

The informal core of the administration's defense and foreign-policy structure was the "Big Eight" foreign-policy team—of which Quayle was a member. The big eight players were Bush, Quayle, Secretary of State James Baker, Scowcroft, Cheney, Chief of Staff John Sununu, Chairman of the Joint Chiefs of Staff Colin Powell, and Deputy National Security Advisor Robert Gates.[28] Broder and Woodward reported that on security matters Quayle was a "second-team player" among this team. A former aide called Quayle the "odd man out" among the "big eight" national security advisors because he alone had no clearly defined foreign-policy role.[29] Yet, another former aide maintains that Quayle was very much in the "inner-inner circle" in foreign policy, made up of four people—Quayle, Bush, Baker, and Scowcroft.[30] In reality, it is difficult to place Quayle in this regard. In general, however, most accounts situate him in the Big Eight rather than the "inner-inner circle." As Cheney intimated, the lack of jurisdiction for the vice president likely played a constraining influence.

In addition, Quayle himself believed that his contribution in foreign policy was downsized by the president's own (and his team's) expertise and penchant for foreign-policy issues. "I can bring certain facts and things to the table that are important to [Bush]," he said, "but he has so many resources on foreign policy and he is so steeped in foreign policy himself."[31] Bill Kristol concedes that with "heavy hitters" in foreign policy like Bush, Baker, Scowcroft, and Cheney, there was not much leeway for Quayle to spread his wings in foreign policy, whether he wanted to or not: "Between Bush, Baker, and Scowcroft there wasn't that much room for him to maneuver. They didn't need a lot of expertise."[32] Joe DeSutter, a foreign-policy and national-security advisor to Quayle, colorfully states that President Bush could have had George Marshall or Henry Kissinger as vice president and it would not have mattered, "Bush would still have been his own man on foreign policy. He was a national expert on foreign policy. That was his thing." Bush, notes DeSutter, did not really need the help of his vice president in foreign policy, regardless of who he was. (As will be noted in the next chapter, Vice President Gore faces the complete opposite in the Clinton administration: a lack of foreign-policy experience by the president he serves and a somewhat weak foreign-policy team, allowing him more opportunity to move around in foreign affairs. DeSutter, who worked for both Quayle and Gore confirms this, especially in regard to the foreign-policy stature and experience of the two presidents.)[33]

The vice president had his own defense and foreign-policy team that helped keep him abreast of developments inside and outside of the White House structure. His foreign and security policy staff included a national security advisor and a deputy NSA—continuing the practice begun by vice presidents Mondale and Bush. He had two NSAs during his four years, Carnes Lord and Karl Jackson. Jon Glassman, a Latin America specialist from the State Department, was his deputy NSA. There was also a small staff underneath the two chief NSA positions, including three military personnel—one each from the Army, Navy, and Air Force. The military people dealt primarily with arms control, SDI issues, and science and technology. They also deal directly with what DeSutter calls the "security aspects of presidential succession," referring to control during a nuclear exchange and retaliatory orders.[34] In addition, the vice president had a staffer who served as a liaison to the intelligence community. In total, including the support staff, Quayle's foreign and defense team ranged from seven to nine people, about five of which were medium- to top-level professionals.[35]

While Quayle played the role of loyal servant to the president, the advice he offered within NSC and cabinet settings led to occasional clashes of opinion with others in the structure. Bill Kristol, the vice president's chief of staff, elaborates on the differing world views of Quayle and Secretary of State Baker, noting that there were "ideological tensions" between the two men. "We were just generally more Reaganite and more hawkish than Baker," he remarks. "We were more pro-Yeltsin. He was more pro-Gorbachev. [The vice president] was more suspicious of Gorbachev. . . . Quayle did go to dinner with Yeltsin before Yeltsin became president, that must have been early 1991, and said some nice things about Yeltsin that got a few noses at 'State' out of joint because they were still pretty much backing Gorbachev. You know, there were lots of instances where we would sort of pull at the margins of policy and I think Baker didn't like that much. . . . There was a certain amount of tension; they didn't quite regard us as trustworthy from their point of view at the State Department."[36]

Furthermore, in regard to Quayle and Baker, off-the-record sources confirmed a fact well known within GOP circles: The two men, both with presidential aspirations, saw each other as political competitors.[37] "Quayle had a following among conservatives that made him formidable," said one source who asked not to be identified. "Baker had political ambitions and viewed Quayle as a political rival due to his conservative base." Joe DeSutter, an advisor to Quayle, adds: "I don't think there's any secret about the bad blood between the two, going all the way back to New Orleans and the campaign in 1988."[38] One source feels that the conspicuously absent lack of a trip by Quayle to Moscow stemmed from obstruction by Baker. "During my tenure Dan Quayle never went to Moscow, and it wasn't because he didn't want to," said the source. Carnes Lord, Quayle's NSA, adds that the vice president also never went to Eastern Europe and that Baker may have been a key reason.[39] Joe DeSutter adds that Quayle, aside from his Desert Storm duties, never went to the Middle East either (another of Baker's pet interests), and that, "He loved the Middle East and Israel. He was an expert on it and would've liked to have gone there." When I asked if he felt Baker had actually obstructed Quayle from traveling to Moscow or the Middle East, DeSutter was cautiously vague, but conceded that I was "probably on the right wavelength there."[40]

This says a lot about the limits of Quayle within the foreign-policy structure, in part imposed by other players, such as the secretary of state. It appears that Baker did play an obstructionist role regarding some of Quayle's activities in foreign policy. (Moreover, as will be noted in the final chapter, this does not bode well for suggestions that the vice president play a coordinating role in helping the State Department—at least not in the Bush administration.)

Still, whatever Baker's role regarding Quayle's activities, the vice president did manage to be active in the foreign and defense-policy realm. As for Quayle's impact within the White House foreign and defense structure, interpretations have varied. Burt Solomon of the *National Journal* quoted an administration official as saying that although the vice president did not rival Baker, Cheney, Scowcroft or Powell in influencing policy, he was "more than a potted palm."[41] Barone and Walsh of *U.S. News & World Report* reported that Quayle had "made his mark on some policies. He has been given at least as much responsibility as his two predecessors, Bush and Walter Mondale."[42] Fred Barnes reported that "Quayle is a very effective inside player in White House policymaking."[43] Broder and Woodward wrote that there appeared no evidence that the vice president had a strong role in shaping the administration's foreign policy. They did claim, however, that Quayle was hardly left in the dark on national security matters.[44] Michael Duffy reported that the vice president did "not sit quietly at Cabinet meetings. . . . Instead, he injects his opinion frequently, often disagreeing with administration heavyweights such as [Baker] and [Sununu]. His speeches, particularly on foreign policy, are often well ahead of White House guidance, and not always by design."[45] A White House official quoted in *Newsweek* stated: "He has not had a particularly significant role in the policymaking, nor has he been absent from the table—he's been doing what vice presidents do."[46]

What the mixed reviews may prove best is what the vice president himself once stated, that he preferred to offer the president his advice in private. As noted earlier, Quayle said that he liked to be "somewhat circumspect . . . when we're in a large group where it's probably going to get out." The vice president said he tried "to be somewhat judicious so people can't read it that the vice president feels this way, but the president feels that way." (Once again, it is worth remembering the similarities here with Vice President Bush.) Broder and

Woodward quote former Vice President Mondale, who agrees that for a vice president, "the dumbest thing to do is to go around and brag" about his influence on the president.[47] In light of the differing reports, the main section of this chapter—focusing on Quayle's role during the 1990-91 Gulf crisis—may provide some clarification.

Quayle's Foreign-Policy Role

Before going into the Persian Gulf crisis, the following should be considered regarding Quayle's general foreign-policy activities. Bill Kristol agrees that because of the lesson of FDR and Truman—not to mention common sense—President Bush worked to keep Quayle informed in foreign policy. "I think generally Bush, for that reason, kept Quayle fully apprised," says the former chief of staff to Quayle. "And, as has become custom in the modern presidency, we had access to everything. Quayle personally had access to everything. The staff had access to most everything. We were included in meetings and all that so Quayle would have been ready."[48] Continuing a practice begun with vice presidents Mondale and Bush, Quayle each morning participated with the president in the Presidential Daily Brief. He also was tied to the president's paper flow. "Every piece of paper that went to the president went past him," says Jon Glassman.[49]

The most important part of the vice president's day was the time he spent with the president. Every morning at 7:45 he met with Bush and CIA briefers for a thirty-minute national security briefing. At 8:15, he and Bush stayed on for a meeting on national security with NSA Brent Scowcroft, Deputy NSA Gates, and Chief of Staff Sununu. Following the national security briefing, Quayle remained for another half-hour meeting between Bush and the chief of staff, where they would talk about whatever issue was on the "front burner."[50]

The regular briefings, meetings and lunches, exceptional access, and sound relationship with the president kept Quayle, in the words of Jon Glassman, "totally informed."[51]

According to Quayle, he and Bush agreed on six "constituencies," domestic and foreign, that he served as vice president. Three of these involved foreign-policy activities:

- Quayle was to serve the president as both policy advisor and public spokesman, as well as an emissary when necessary.
- Quayle was a liaison to Congress for the administration.
- Quayle represented the administration in his trips to foreign countries.[52]

One area where Quayle seemed to have a more defined role centered around the mileage he logged on behalf of the administration at home and abroad. He stumped from city to city representing the administration's domestic agenda. On the international front, he made a number of trips abroad. In June 1991, the vice president spent five days in Eastern Europe, speaking to the heads of state of Bulgaria, Czechoslovakia, Hungary, and Poland. Upon his return, he urged the president, in a two-page memo on June 11, to relax trade barriers on the importation of Eastern European cheese, steel, and textiles. Also, Quayle visited Australia, Thailand, and Japan. He made eight relatively well-publicized trips to Latin America.[53]

Aides to the vice president said that Quayle was determined that his trips have concrete results. They complained, however, that he often became tied up by State Department "ceremonialists" who filled his trips with a tedious schedule of wreath-layings and routine appointments.[54] Nonetheless, as the next section will show, whenever possible he exploited ceremonial trips as a chance to engage in substantive discussions.

Quayle's Role in the Persian Gulf Crisis of 1990-1991

Before profiling the day-to-day and general activities of Quayle during the Persian Gulf crisis of 1990-91, it is necessary to be informed of two separate "contexts" (background information) that are fundamental to understanding and appreciating his activities and influence during the crisis. These two contexts—referred to as Context I and Context II—cover his senatorial and vice-presidential years, looking specifically at Quayle's views on defense strategies and the Middle East, respectively. As the reader proceeds through the chapter, he or she will come to understand the importance of these two contexts.

Context I: Quayle's Views on Defense Strategies as a Senator and Vice President

It is important to step back to Quayle's pre-Gulf crisis years, especially those in the Congress. Much of his understanding of defense and foreign-policy issues can be traced to his days as a freshman senator on the Armed Services Committee. Quayle's experiences on Armed Services would lay the foundation for his interest in strategic defenses—aspects of which would play a key role during the Gulf crisis.

In a November 1987 Senate debate on the ABM Treaty, Senator Quayle stated, "I believe that sometime, someday, despite what this Congress may or may not do this year, we will see the deployment of a strategic defense system in the world."[55] At the core of strategic defenses is the Strategic Defense Initiative, of which Quayle was always a major supporter. He would later be lauded by conservatives for his senate work as a defender of Patriot air-defense missiles, which operated effectively during the Gulf War in shooting down incoming missiles.[56] In Congress, he was the Reagan administration's point man in 1985-86 in saving the Patriot.[57]

On the offensive side, he would also be hailed for his Senate work as a proponent of the Tomahawk cruise missile—another celebrity of the Gulf War. In an August 1987 article for the *Armed Forces Journal International*, Quayle encouraged a "serious effort" to improve upon cruise-missile development and production. In the article he created a fictional scenario in which a radical faction within an oil-rich Persian Gulf state teams up with the Soviet Union to cause a shake up in the Middle East. He used the example to demonstrate the unreadiness of the U.S. cruise-missiles system. He offered three recommendations for improvements:

> First . . . our cruise missiles . . . accuracy will have to be improved. Our experiences with attacking . . . bridges in North Vietnam proved that without delivery accuracies of a few feet, bridge spans or tunnels are virtually impossible to hit and permanently destroy. But cruise missile accuracies are currently measured in many meters, not feet, and they won't do. Second . . . our cruise missiles must fly lower than they do now. In fact, their terrain-following capabilities were frozen with early 1970s technology. Because of this, they fly relatively high above the ground—high enough to be seen and hit by Soviet SAMs and new Soviet aircraft equipped with look-down/shoot-down radar. Improved terrain-following performance for our cruise missiles is critical if they are to evade such detection.
> Finally, the mission planning to target these bridges and tunnels must be available within days, not weeks—something we cannot provide today.[58]

Quayle warned that without a few upgrades, American cruise missiles would be "too vulnerable, too short-legged, too inaccurate, too inflexible in their mission planning, and too few in number to get the job done . . . for many of the highest priority missions in the [1990s]."[59] He recommended pursuing the U.S. Navy's Long Range Master Plan for the Tomahawk cruise missile to address some of the shortcomings. He suggested near-zero Circular Error Probable (CEP) accuracy to improve missile performance:

> one program that showed great promise in satisfying the zero-CEP accuracy requirement back in 1984 was the Autonomous Terminal Homing (ATH) program, now renamed the Cruise Missile Advanced Guidance (CMAG) program. CMAG is a forward-looking CO_2 laser/imaging infrared seeker that would fit in the nose of a cruise missile. It has a near-zero CEP accuracy and could operate day/night in adverse weather. But just as

important, it can reduce the mission planning time to a matter of hours, improve survivability by allowing the missile to fly much lower, increase range by flying in a more direct path to the target, and improve overall missile performance by being able to look forward in anticipation of terrain variations.[60]

To achieve these recommendations, Quayle introduced legislation into the 1988/89 Department of Defense (DoD) Authorization Bill that would ensure that DoD pursued a program to demonstrate a near-zero CEP seeker for future and existing cruise missiles. The bill also required out-year planning and funding for the program. He intended to press the armed services on developing a comprehensive program to address the requirements listed in the Navy's Long Range Master Plan. "The Tomahawk cruise missile R&D program has suffered major reductions in the House 1988/89 DoD reauthorization process," he concluded. "These reductions need to be carefully reviewed before final action is taken on this year's DoD bill."[61]

An interesting aspect of Quayle's support for a system with the advanced capability of the Tomahawk cruise missile was not only its offensive potential but rather the opportunities it afforded to improving strategic defenses. To be sure, Quayle's strategic defenses were comprised mainly of anti-tactical missile defenses. However, he viewed cruise missiles as a way to check countries developing ballistic missiles—and, in that sense, provide a form of defense. The logic here is that the United States could employ highly accurate cruise missiles as a means of holding a country in check. This could serve as form of deterrence that might be termed "deterrence by denial."

In a 1987 op-ed piece for *The Washington Post*, Quayle, then a member of the Armed Services subcommittee on strategic forces and nuclear deterrence, wrote of the dangers of missile proliferation in the Third World. Among the nations of the Middle East, he singled out Syria, Egypt, Israel, and Iraq. He recommended three steps to halt the spread of missile technology. First, the United States should renew its security assurances to its Third World allies, making them "recognize that they have more to gain from maintaining their security ties with the United States than from developing offensive ballistic missiles of their own." His second suggestion reflects the cruise missile part of the equation: "We need to make it expensive for fledgling nations to have missile forces. We should make it very clear that their emerging missile forces will remain extremely vulnerable to highly precise, stealthy, conventional long-range cruise missiles unless they spend heavily for air defenses, missile hardening and mobile bases to protect them." Quayle's final point was prescient in light of the success of the Patriot and actions of Saddam Hussein during the Gulf War:

> Finally, we need to develop anti-tactical missile defenses to protect our forces and allies abroad. The better these defenses are, the stronger we can

make our alliances and the further we can reduce other nations' attraction to cruise or ballistic missiles as a quick, cheap way to increase their regional influence.

This last point is critical. So long as nations think they can make a quantum jump in military power easily by acquiring missiles, many will try. What we've got to do is make sure that missile technology is difficult, expensive and militarily counterproductive for them. If we don't, this technology will spread faster than we can cope with it—so fast that it will make our current crisis in the Persian Gulf [the 1987 cruise missile attack against the U.S.S. Stark] the least of our missile woes."[62]

Ideas such as improving the range and accuracy of conventional cruise missiles are part of what Quayle called "competitive strategies." He brought up the concept of competitive strategies in the 1987 journal article and elaborated on it occasionally in speeches as vice president. Quayle said that competitive strategies "emphasizes some of the newer technologies that will be very advantageous to the West—it accentuates our positive capabilities and exploits our potential opponents' vulnerabilities." He said that the concept was a serious one that merited increased attention as defense resources decline. "I find that not only does the president continue to support the concept, but they are working on it in DoD," Quayle stated. "Competitive strategies is something that I think will be implemented in the months ahead."[63]

Quayle liked to emphasize the importance of strategy and the need for policymakers to think "strategically." "Now, in a time of peace and in a time when things are going our way, it is vital that we remind ourselves of the importance of strategy," Quayle, then vice president, told a National Defense University symposium on November 17, 1989. "As we move into the 1990s," he said, "the hard challenge ahead will be to renew U.S. strategy and strategic thinking in the context of the new international realities."[64] As a senator he cosponsored a law that required the president to annually submit a National Security Strategy.[65]

Most integral to Quayle's concept of strategic defense was SDI. In a 1989 article the vice president authored for *Policy Review*, Quayle wrote:

> For most of our history, America was protected by the blessings of geography.... Our virtual invulnerability came to an end after World War II. Technology reduced dramatically the time it took to traverse the oceans, and the destructiveness of deliverable weapons posed an unprecedented threat, with no realistic prospects for defense of the horizon.... In the absence of technologically viable options for strategic defense, our doctrines of offensive deterrence came to be regarded not only as inevitable, but eventually as *preferable*.... The principles of assured destruction—"defending" ourselves by threats of offensive retaliation—acquired the status of a strategy, and were enshrined in treaties, alliance commitments, and

weapon acquisition policies . . . the Strategic Defense Initiative in 1983 reopened discussion of defense as a realistic element of strategic deterrence. . . . [It] gave official "permission" to think once again about the prospect of defending ourselves.[66]

In the article he again raised the prospect of "accidental launch" and "madman" scenarios in which an irrational leader "acquires ballistic launchers and marries them with primitive nuclear, chemical, or biological weapons of mass destruction." These concerns are not hypothetical, he wrote in 1989, "Iran and Iraq have already engaged in a ballistic missile conflict; Iraq made active and extensive use of chemical weapons in its war with Iran."[67]

Quayle believed that the proliferation of ballistic missiles gave weight to arguments favoring the deployment of an SDI system.[68] However, he stated in a February 1990 interview, "Not only do you have the potential of a nuclear warhead [on a ballistic missile] but, in the shorter term, there's the chemical capability. So you look at a chemical warhead that goes on one of these missiles and realize that if it were to be launched, whether against Israel or another country, there would be tremendous devastation."[69] This precise scenario became reality exactly one year later, as Saddam's Iraq fired Scud missiles at Israel and the allies during the Persian Gulf conflict. It was believed that in some cases Saddam tried to marry the Scuds with chemical weapons. At the least, such a threat was imminent. One need only remember the sight of Jews in Tel Aviv fastening on gas masks as Iraqi Scuds whistled through the air and exploded on the ground. Moreover, the Patriot missile was Israel's only answer to the Scuds, since the nation was exercising restraint (i.e., not retaliating) in order to avoid being drawn into the conflict and thus possibly splintering the fragile allied coalition—which, of course, Saddam Hussein hoped to provoke.

This leads to the subject of the vice president and Israel. Quayle was always a strong advocate of Israel, as well as its ground-based strategic-defense interceptor. "I think one of the most serious candidates, right now, for deployment of a ground-based SDI-type program is Israel's Arrow project," he commented. Quayle continued:

> The Israelis are threatened by ballistic missiles on all sides. You've got the Syrians, the Saudis, you have Iran and Iraq—and they all have these missiles capable of hitting Tel Aviv or Jerusalem. And, you know, the Israelis don't like the only options being one, to absorb a hit and retaliate; two, to just be vulnerable; or three, going in and having a preemptive strike against these targets. None of these options is very attractive.
>
> A fourth option that would be much more attractive would be to be able to defend against these missiles if they were ever to be launched against Israel. Once you see that the capability is there, then I think other nations

will catch on [to strategic defense]—including our own.[70]

Context II: Quayle's Views on the Middle East as a Senator and Vice President

The preceding and current sections are critical to understanding Quayle's actions during the Gulf crisis. The preceding section and its discussion of the vice president's concepts of competitive strategies, long-range convention cruise missiles, and strategic defenses underscores his basic strategic thinking. They form the foundation of how he would address such problems as Third World instability and missile proliferation. This section, however, is integral to understanding how those perceptions fit into the context of the Middle East—and subsequently, the war in the Gulf.

Quayle never seemed to elaborate on regional conflicts in the Middle East as deeply as he did on strategic defense or cruise missiles. But he made many comments on the Arab-Israeli conflict and openly expressed his ardent support for Israel. Moreover, his penchant for issues concerning weapons proliferation in the Third World often led him directly into the Middle East.

It is difficult to locate personal references by Quayle regarding Palestinians and Arabs. Comments in his speeches relating to these two groups often reiterated the administration's position on Arab-Israeli issues. But the manner in which he displayed a strikingly strong identification with the Israelis may in itself illustrate his stance towards Israel's neighbors. "I think it's fair to say that not only Israelis, but the entire Jewish people, were seized by a justifiable exhilaration on June 11, 1967. Even non-Jews like myself rejoiced," Quayle told the American Israel Public Affairs Committee on June 11, 1990. "And why not? After all, the attempt to destroy the state of Israel had failed. Jerusalem was united, its Holy Places open to all, and Jews prayed before the Western Wall for the first time in 19 years."[71] He concluded the AIPAC speech by boldly referring to the occupied West Bank and Gaza Strip as Judea and Samaria, thereby ignoring long-standing U.S. policy. While Quayle's comment pleased the Israeli lobby it incensed the White House, State Department, and Arab allies.[72]

Quayle was always a strong supporter of the nation of Israel, going back to his early days in the Senate. "When several [senators] criticize Israel for its [1982] bombing of Lebanon," Senator Quayle told author Richard F. Fenno, Jr., "I have not changed my position of absolute support for Israel one iota. My support is ironclad."[73]

That support did not waver once he joined the Bush administration. In December 1989 the vice president, with strong support from American Jewish organizations, committed the administration to the repeal of the much maligned 1975 U.N. resolution describing Zionism as a form of racism. Quayle argued that a repeal would increase the United Nations' "moral authority" and allow it to play a constructive role in the Middle East.[74] "There is yet another item on the agenda of the American-Israeli alliance—our campaign to restore the moral integrity of the United Nations," he later said in June 1990. "In November 1975, the United Nations' integrity was severely comprised when the General Assembly adopted Resolution 3379, equating Zionism with racism." Quayle demanded: "Last December, I publicly called on the Soviet Union to work with us to repeal it. . . . I want to renew my call: this infamous resolution should—and will be—repealed. And we will work to make this happen."[75]

In the AIPAC speech, Quayle lamented that Israel's "great victory in 1967 did not bring peace. Instead of the approaches to discuss peace that Israel confidently expected, Israel got the 'three no's' of Khartoum: no peace, no recognition, no negotiations."[76] While many of these are personal remarks, the speech also illustrates Quayle's role as a spokesman on behalf of the Bush administration. For instance, the vice president also spelled out the importance of the strategic relationship between the United States and Israeli:

> make no mistake about it: The alliance between the U.S. and Israel is strong and needs to remain strong. . . . The benefits of our alliance with Israel have been significant. Israel has been, and remains, a bulwark against the forces of radicalism, instability and terror. . . . What is the future agenda of the U.S.-Israeli relationship? . . . We need to continue our cooperation on strategic issues. Let me assure you that President Bush fully appreciates the strategic importance of our close ties with Israel. . . . When I was in the Senate, I sponsored legislation designed to advance strategic defenses with our allies. I was impressed then, as I am now, with how quickly Israel seized this opportunity, and I am pleased by the progress we have made in U.S.-Israeli cooperation in SDI.[77]

In a memorable April 1990 speech before the Washington Institute for Near East Policy, Quayle (again well before the Gulf War) warned of the dangers posed to Israel by Saddam Hussein and his Scud missiles—both on their way to eventual infamy some nine months later:

> Iraq, and subsequently Iran, have helped bring the issue of chemical weapons proliferation to the forefront of the U.S. Middle East agenda.
> As everyone here knows, concerns about the proliferation of chemical weapons became especially acute earlier this month.
> President Saddam Hussein of Iraq, boasting that he had acquired advanced chemical weapons, threatened Israel directly. "We will make the fire eat up half of Israel," he warned, "if it tries to do anything against Iraq." Iraq has also moved launchers for its Scud-B missiles to western Iraq, closer to Israel's borders.[78]

In the April speech, Quayle elaborated on the changing dimension of the Arab-Israeli conflict, presaging the multinational allied-coalition effort that would take place within a year. "In the past, the Arab-Israeli conflict took place within a bipolar strategic context," he noted. "While this bipolar context sometimes exacerbated regional tensions—as in 1967—it also provided a certain degree of stability, predictability and rationality to the Arab-Israeli conflict." Quayle stated that the world is now witnessing a shift from a bipolar to a multipolar context, "a context in which both Israel and some Arab states, such as Iraq, Syria, and Libya, are capable of producing weapons of mass destruction on their own. . . . I am afraid the Middle East could well become a much more dangerous place over the next few years."[79]

Never missing a chance to plug his pet interests, Quayle seized the opportunity presented by Saddam's incendiary threats to sound the alarm in support of deterrence and defense against the use of chemical or nuclear weapons by Third World countries. He reiterated his 1989 calls for controls on both the "demand side and supply side" of nuclear weapons and the need for strategic defenses. Quayle commented:

> [Perhaps] we are beginning to hear some new sentiments from long time critics of strategic defense in our own country . . . in response to the threat of missile attacks by Third World nations on the U.S. and its allies. And I predict that you will hear more appreciation of the case for *defense* against missiles, both at home and abroad, as the ballistic missile threat grows, and as our means to deal with it defensively mature. . . . Indeed, I sponsored legislation four years ago designed to share the workload and the benefits of advanced strategic defenses with our allies. . . . I was impressed then, as I am now, with how quickly Israel seized this opportunity.
> Israel's Arrow program is a direct product of these policies.[80]

Quayle concluded by emphasizing how strategic defense should comprise a central part of the "deterrence equation" for both the United States and Israel, and urged the Israelis to move beyond viewing the Arrow program as a big defense contract and to instead "integrate such thinking into their plans and doctrines for the near future."[81]

Ironically, Quayle's preoccupations with strategic defense would be seemingly vindicated in Israel during the Gulf War. The vindicator would be the U.S. ground-based Patriot missile rather than Israel's Arrow program, which—as Quayle had mentioned in his April 1990 speech—was just entering the actual experimentation stage.[82]

The Vice President's Role during the Persian Gulf Crisis

Gulf-Crisis Schedule

The vice president spent much of his time during the Gulf crisis in close proximity to the president. This was evident publicly. He stood behind Bush in the Rose Garden on February 22 as the president issued an ultimatum to Hussein to leave Kuwait. He was situated likewise on February 26 as Bush demanded the surrender of the Iraqi dictator. On February 23, as Bush and Baker returned from Camp David after ground combat had begun, Quayle walked between them as they crossed the South lawn from the helicopter to the White House entrance. The following morning, Quayle attended church with Bush before another afternoon White House discussion about the situation in the Gulf.[83]

Quayle was a regular participant in the Oval Office meetings, where he sometimes spent up to four hours a day. His schedule included an hour or longer national security briefing each morning by Scowcroft and often an additional two hours with some or all of the "big eight" Persian Gulf policymakers—Bush, Quayle, Baker, Scowcroft, Cheney, Sununu, Powell, and Gates.[84] In these crisis discussions, said an administration official, Quayle did not rival Baker, Cheney, Scowcroft or Powell in influencing policy, but he was "more than a potted palm."[85] In addition to seeking his occasional counsel, the president aimed to keep Quayle completely informed in the event the 'unthinkable' happened. Continuing with regular practice, the vice president had his own daily CIA briefings and received all paper that was routed toward the president. He had an open invitation to all executive meetings. Quayle was present at all of the president's war councils.[86] This allowed Quayle "a seat around the table [but] no direct operational responsibility," according to former White House political director Frank J. Donatelli.[87]

Indeed, it is difficult to measure the vice president's influence—as he himself claimed, he preferred to offer his advice to the president in private. In this respect, only Quayle and Bush know his true impact. Having said that, the vice president—beyond his basic constitutional and statutory duties—filled basically three roles during the crisis. First, he was a spokesman for the administration. This role allowed him to express the views of both himself and the administration in a number of speeches, as well as to serve as an emissary to foreign governments and visit U.S. troops on trips abroad. Second, he was a liaison to the Congress. Third, he assumed the integral but nasty role of what might be called the administration's 'point man,' attacking liberal Democrats and war protesters, as well as other critics of the administration's Gulf policy. The following examines each of these roles.

Quayle the Gulf-Crisis Spokesman

As noted earlier, the vice president made many trips abroad delivering speeches and meeting with foreign leaders. While many of these trips were publicity-filled events on behalf of the administration, they did present occasional opportunities for Quayle to make public foreign-policy statements reflecting both his own views and those of the administration. The crisis in the Gulf afforded just such opportunities, which the vice president seized by delivering seven speeches relating to the crisis between August 29, 1990 and March 13, 1991. He would publicly outline the administration's Gulf policy objectives in each speech. The vice president personally referred to this as his "salesman's role," in which he regularly hit the road "explaining the rationale for our involvement in the Arabian peninsula."[88] Justifiably it appears, Carnes Lord feels that through his speeches the vice president was "very successful" in articulating the rationale for the war: "I felt he helped put together the complete case for why we should care about the Gulf and what the strategic interests were."[89]

In a key speech he rightly considers "the most important speech" of his vice presidency, Quayle addressed a crowd at Seton Hall University on November 29, 1990, where he meticulously explained U.S. objectives in the Gulf. The speech is cited as an example in which he assumed a larger foreign-policy role.[90] Broder and Woodward stated that the speech—which was crafted by Quayle and his staff and cleared by Scowcroft's office—was "cited by Quayle aides as an instance in which he helped shape policy, and in fact its themes became the basis of some of Bush's own later statements on the crisis."[91]

In the speech, the vice president attempted to explain U.S. interests in the Gulf. He provided a brief historical treatment of American involvement in the region during the Cold War, speaking on the Truman and Carter doctrines. Quayle asked:

> Why is the [Middle East] so important? What have the strategic goals of U.S. Middle East policy been over the last forty years? And how do these goals apply in the current crisis?
> The Middle East, as everyone knows, is the source of much of the oil on which the industrialized world and developing nations depend. It is a region of striking contrasts: Vast wealth and grinding poverty; secular radicalism and religious fundamentalism; hatred of the West and emulation of the West. Most importantly, perhaps, the Middle East is caught up in a vast process of change, as ancient societies and cultures strive to adapt to the modern world. This process of adaptation, which entails much turmoil and instability, is what makes the Middle East such an interesting place. Unfortunately, it also makes the Middle East a dangerous place.
> Since the onset of the Cold War, the United States has had . . . strategic

objectives in the region. . . . But the Cold War is over. And because it is over, because *one* of America's strategic objectives has been realized, some commentators have assumed that *all* of our objectives have been realized. They could not be more mistaken. For in addition to containing the Soviets, American foreign policy has traditionally pursued two other strategic objectives in the Middle East. It has sought to prevent any local Middle East power from achieving hegemony over its neighbors, and it has sought to secure the uninterrupted supply of oil at a reasonable price.[92]

In the aforementioned, Quayle is apparently citing balance-of-power considerations as a continued U.S. interest in the region. This observation is particularly poignant in hindsight, considering the administration's decision to 'leave' Saddam in power. A key reason why the administration decided against trying to eliminate Saddam was in order to maintain the balance of power in the Middle East.

The vice president also turned up the heat on the Iraqi leader by telling the crowd that he posed a "major threat" to all of the states of the Middle East. "Saddam's ambitions are not confined to Kuwait. Rather, his goal is to dominate the Persian Gulf region and use its vast wealth to become the greatest Arab hero of modern times, the leader of a new Arab super power." Quayle noted that Saddam had spent some $50 billion on arms imports during the 1980s and had launched wars against Iran and Kuwait, at a cost of a million lives. He pointed out that Saddam had built the world's sixth largest military force and had used chemical weapons against the Iraqi Kurds. He also noted Hussein's desire to acquire nuclear weapons and his stockpiles of chemical and biological weapons. "The United States opposes Saddam Hussein's bid for regional hegemony for the same reasons that we have opposed other bids," Quayle explained. "We do not think any government has the right to impose its political will on other countries through subversion or conquest." Moreover, the United States does "not think Israel's existence, or the existence of other friendly regional states, should be threatened. And, of course, the prospect of Saddam Hussein strutting across the world stage at the head of a malevolent global power, armed to the teeth with weapons of mass destruction, and controlling a large portion of the world's energy supplies, is something no person would welcome." The vice president also named the uninterrupted flow of oil as a key strategic goal of U.S. policy in the Middle East. "This does not mean, as some cynics have suggested, that we are risking war to prevent the price of oil from going up a few cents a gallon," he stated. "During the Arab oil-embargo of 1973-74, and during the 1979 oil price shock that came in the wake of the Iranian revolution, the price of oil went up much more than that."[93]

Importantly, the vice president, as an administration spokesman, also hit on a theme in the speech that was essential to explaining overall U.S. strategic objectives in the Gulf: the president's concept of a new world order. Quayle explained:

> So far, I have talked about traditional U.S. strategic objectives in the Middle East. But there is another strategic American objective in the current crisis that is not traditional—that has only emerged, in fact, as a result of the end of the Cold War. This objective might be described as strengthening the foundations of world order. Let me explain what I mean. . . . Iraq's invasion of Kuwait is the first crisis of the post-Cold War world. One way or another, it is bound to set a precedent—either on behalf of greater world order or on behalf of greater chaos. If Saddam Hussein succeeds in his aggression, it is likely that his success will embolden other dictators to emulate his example. But if he fails . . . others will draw the lesson that might does not make right and that aggression will not be allowed to succeed.
> This is why President Bush has sought to rally the international community against Iraq's aggression. . . . Everyone recognizes that this is a test case.[94]

Quayle, however, took a different tack in his Seton Hall speech, adding (on his own initiative) a new reason to the administration's list for pursuing quick military action: delaying U.S. military action might increase American casualties. In preceding weeks, the administration had provided a host of reasons for forcing a resolution of the crisis, but Quayle's suggestion of heightened U.S. casualties was a new step to win public support for its policy.[95] The point about casualties was also part of a new, personal theme that Quayle would repeat often during the crisis: the concept of a "moral course of action." He explained:

> As we exercise patience and restraint, we must also be alert to the moral costs of such a course. Consider, for example, the fate of the people of Kuwait. With everyday that passes, their plight grows more desperate. Being patient with Iraq allows Saddam Hussein to prolong their agony. Is this a moral course of action?
> Or consider the fate of American military personnel in Saudi Arabia. The longer we refrain from action against Iraq, the more time Saddam Hussein has to tighten his grip on Kuwait, and the harder it may be to breaken that grip, if and when war comes. Does patience today risk greater American casualties tomorrow? And if so, is this a moral course of action?[96]

Quayle later said his Seton Hall remarks "were intended to be not just an outline of the administration's aims in the Gulf but also a moral justification for pursuing them." He said the speech was made at his initiative because he thought there had been a gap in the administration's "otherwise forceful" explanation of why force should be used to expel Iraq from Kuwait. The vice president felt that if war came to the Gulf "the moral case for force had to be made."[97]

Many of the above speech citations reflect the vice president's personal thoughts and feelings about the crisis. But to further underscore the point that a primary role of Quayle during the crisis was to be a spokesman for the administration, one can look at the timing of this important address. The speech came as the president prepared to meet that weekend at Camp David with the Joint Chiefs of Staff on the Gulf situation. Moreover, he spoke as the Senate Armed Services Committee continued hearings on the Gulf, receiving conflicting recommendations from two former Pentagon officials, a military expert and three specialists on Iraq.[98] "I wanted these points to be heard by the Senate Armed Services Committee," said Quayle, "which I was afraid might not support any action beyond economic sanctions."[99] Most importantly, the speech came on the day that the U.N. Security Council was expected to adopt a resolution endorsing the use of force against Iraq if Saddam refused to withdraw his forces from Kuwait. Obviously aware of this, Quayle drew an analogy between the administration and the U.N. and Winston Churchill calling on the League of Nations on March 13, 1936, to take tough action against Hitler's moving of German troops into the Rhineland. Despite Churchill's warnings, the League of Nations fatefully acquiesced to Hitler's aggression. "Today, the U.N. Security Council stands poised at [a] historic juncture not unlike that faced by the League of Nations in 1936," Quayle exclaimed. "We are hopeful . . . that it will not fail the test. Saddam has shown that he understands no language other than the language of force."[100]

The Security Council would vote twelve to two with one abstention to authorize the United States and its allies to expel Iraq from Kuwait by force if Saddam did not withdraw his forces by January 15, 1991. Quayle would continue his role as a spokesman by reiterating U.S. objectives in the Persian Gulf. U.S. objectives called for the:

- Immediate implementation of all relevant U.N. Security Council resolutions;
- Immediate, complete, and unconditional withdrawal of all Iraqi forces from Kuwait;
- Restoration of Kuwait's legitimate government;
- Security and stability of Saudi Arabia and the Persian Gulf;
- Protection of American citizens held hostage by Iraq, both in Iraq and Kuwait.[101]

In a December 18, 1990 speech, responding to public criticism over American forces shouldering too much of the burden in the Gulf, Quayle focused on the multinational makeup of the forces in the Gulf. He noted that over one-third of the half million troops stationed in the Gulf at the time were provided by U.S. allies. Twenty-eight nations had committed military support to the allied effort, Quayle stated, with some countries contributing a proportionately greater percentage of forces than the United States. Contributing military forces to the crisis were eleven Muslim nations, members of the Warsaw Pact, Egypt, Saudi Arabia, Syria, Turkey, France, and Britain. The vice president pointed out that Germany and Japan had pledged "considerable sums of money." He noted that a majority of the American public supported the president's decision to send troops to the Gulf.[102] Moreover, he attempted to quell critics of the administration who questioned the morality of U.S. troops coming to the defense of a Kuwaiti regime viewed by some as "feudal," "reactionary," and "repressive." Quayle stated:

> Quite frankly, I am always astonished whenever I hear these charges made. First of all, the accusations against Kuwait are false. Second—since when has it become acceptable to loot and rape and torture people because they happen to live in a society whose customs differ from our own? . . .
> The government of Kuwait is not the result of conspiracy and *coup d' etat*, and its rule is not enforced by terror and repression. The United States and the world therefore have no reason to apologize for demanding that the legitimate government of Kuwait be restored.[103]

Quayle as a Gulf-Crisis Emissary and Negotiator

Part of Quayle's role as a spokesman was to travel to the Gulf and elsewhere to represent the administration as an emissary during the crisis. This often involved the vice president's participation in delicate negotiating tasks.

In a very important trip that involved not merely *representing* the administration but *negotiating* on behalf of it, Quayle paid a visit to Bogota, Colombia in August 1990, less than a week after Saddam had invaded Kuwait. Initially, the vice president had not been keen about making the trip, reported Michael Duffy of *Time* magazine. Taking off to South America to represent the United States at the inauguration of the new Colombian president while war was stirring in the Gulf was not the kind of assignment that would show Quayle 'in the center of things' at the White House. But Bush insisted that the vice president go.[104]

Quayle's real mission required a considerable degree of diplomatic acumen. He lobbied Venezuelan President Carlos Andres Perez to increase his country's oil production to make up for any shortfall resulting from the turmoil in the Gulf. Additionally, in two separate meetings, he pressed the leaders of Brazil and Argentina to halt transfers of ballistic-missile technology to Iraq. Within days, all three nations had complied with the vice president's requests.[105]

Exactly how instrumental of a role Quayle played in swaying the Latin American leaders is difficult to ascertain without full information. Jon Glassman, however, suggests the vice president made a difference. He points to Quayle working with Carlos Andres Peres in pushing Venezuela to raise oil production. Asked if the vice president alone made the difference, Glassman responded: "[It's] not always a question of swaying or arm twisting but reasoning with a person. But Peres' mind was not set on the issue before Quayle got there."[106]

The achievements made during the vice president's trip cannot be dismissed. As for the first goal, Venezuela, Mexico, and Colombia all boosted oil production and exports to make up for the Gulf production shortfall, which, according to Assistant Secretary of State for Inter-American Affairs Bernard W. Aronson, "was not noted at the time but made a crucial difference in stabilizing prices." As for the latter, under the military dictatorship that ruled Argentina the military was developing a medium-range ballistic missile called the Condor Missile Project, financed by the Iraqis and Egyptians. Aronson stated that "had that missile gone into full production and had it been deployed, the conflict in the Gulf would have been very different and not to our benefit." The government of Carlos Menem definitively ended the program. Brazil and Argentina reversed the policies of the previous military regimes and agreed to negotiate a bilateral agreement which will allow them to call for full-scope safeguards over their nuclear programs to ensure that they did not develop a nuclear-weapons capability.[107]

To understand how Quayle was able to effect such a change, one must be briefly informed of his role in the Bush administration's Latin America policy. Quayle was not exaggerating when he asserted that he developed into "the administration's most active man for Latin America affairs"—a claim backed by his NSA, Carnes Lord, and by his deputy NSA, Jon Glassman (who later became U.S. ambassador to Paraguay). In assuming this role, Quayle was a good fit because he was young and aggressive, like the new generation of Latin American leaders themselves. Those leaders respected the fact that the administration sent the second highest person in the U.S. government down to represent them. "He was young, like the Latin American leaders, and had a lot in common with them," says Glassman. "Dan Quayle got along very well with these guys. He was viewed as the U.S. leader down there."[108] As a result, Quayle, and his word, had clout with Latin American leaders. Additionally, notes Carnes Lord, Quayle was very familiar and knowledgeable with the region. Lord recalls five trips he made to the region with Quayle and says that the vice president, in general, "made some real 'money' diplomatically" in Latin America.[109]

A few months later, in November, the vice president made a trip to Tokyo that on the surface was conducted to represent the White House at the enthronement of Crown Prince Akihito as emperor. However, Quayle also went to talk to the Japanese government and the array of leaders who were gathered there, including President Corazon Aquino and Prime Minster Ozal of Turkey, whose support in Desert Storm was essential because of his country's common border with Iraq. The vice president met with Japan's Prime Minister Kaifu after the ceremonies and urged him not only to support the growing allied coalition with money but also to send some military equipment and some of Japan's special forces to the Gulf.[110] Ultimately, Japan would contribute nine billion dollars to the allied effort. While it is unclear how much credit Quayle can take for the total pledge, he was careful to point out its significance in public statements, such as during the December 18 speech and in a *Business Week* interview.[111]

Similarly, shortly before the war itself was underway, Quayle made a trip to the Persian Gulf region that also involved lobbying for financial assistance. On December 30, 1990, he spent the first part of a three-day tour of the Gulf region in Riyadh where he met with King Fahd of Saudi Arabia. He reassured Fahd of U.S. resolve on the Gulf.[112] Even more important, Quayle persuaded the king to approve of any potential land phase that would take place in the event that war would ensue in the region. This was a key achievement. "Prince Salman was saying that Saddam is not all that bad and that they could deal with him," says Jon Glassman. "It wasn't looking too good. But Quayle argued the opposite." Glassman states that the vice president was "very influential" in pressing the administration's case and "in making it happen."[113]

Later that day he visited the aircraft carrier USS John F. Kennedy and held talks with exiled Kuwaiti leader Emir Sheik Jabir Ahmed Sabah. On December 31, the vice president paid a New Year's Eve visit to the troops in Saudi Arabia. He traveled by helicopter to the frontlines and played basketball and volleyball with the troops and delivered two speeches during an eight-hour visit to eastern Saudi Arabia.[114] Part of the purpose of the trip was to drum up support and increase troop morale. To that end, Quayle was well-received. He told the troops that U.S. force would be "quick, massive and decisive," and assured them that "this will not be another Vietnam."[115] A ten-minute speech to thousands of marines was greeted enthusiastically by a standing ovation and loud cheers.[116] Quayle said he was in the region to reassure U.S. allies of America's commitment to oust Iraq from Kuwait and to pass on the president's thanks to the troops. He would deliver his speech four times in two days.[117]

Quayle completed his three-day tour of the Gulf region on January 1, 1991. He met with the Kuwait Emir at the exiled government's headquarters in a Taif (Saudi Arabia) hotel to discuss the increased need for Kuwaiti financial support for Operation Desert Shield. As he did with King Fahd two days earlier, Quayle told Kuwaiti leaders that all nations involved against Iraq would have to pay more as the crisis continued. The emir agreed, according to a senior administration official traveling with the vice president (and other reports), but the official said no figures were discussed.[118] "We do expect collective responsibility to be exhibited," said Quayle. He thanked the Saudis and Kuwaitis "for the contributions they have made thus far," but pointed out that they "will have to be making more contributions."[119]

Quayle was expected to meet with the president upon his return to sum up his trip to the Persian Gulf and give his assessment of the readiness of the international force and the willingness of Gulf War allies to grant further financial aid to the coalition effort.[120]

Quayle as a Gulf-Crisis Liaison to Congress

Aside from his spokesman and emissary roles, the vice president served the administration as a liaison to the Congress. By official accounts, wrote one reporter, throughout his vice presidency Quayle seemed to weigh in less on policy than on congressional and political strategy.[121] He had a very good understanding of the goings on in Congress. Although his preference was foreign policy, the administration felt his more natural home was Congress. As a former member of both the House and Senate, he maintained close ties with a broad range of Republicans and Democrats. The close ties were aided by Quayle having two offices on Capitol Hill, one just off the Senate floor and another in the Dirksen Senate Office Building.[122] Bush aides described him as a kind of "legislative counselor" to the president.[123]

According to three dozen congressmen from both parties interviewed by Broder and Woodward, the vice president gave them the impression that they had a direct channel to the White House through him. By most accounts, he was more influential and active in this area than Bush was as vice president.[124] The *Los Angeles Times* called him "a persuasive advocate on Capitol Hill."[125] Quayle was the only member of Bush's inner circle who had congressional experience from both chambers. He was intimate with all the congressional players and was extensively involved in issues requiring congressional support.[126] He lobbied each side of the aisle on nearly every major issue. Chief of Staff Sununu commented that Quayle's "social contacts" on Capitol Hill were "invaluable. . . . When we lay out a legislative strategy, almost automatically, he's a key part of the discussions." Cheney added that Quayle "probably has better ties at any given moment, or a better read on . . . the mood of the Senate Republicans—and the Senate generally—than just about anybody else."[127]

On the domestic front, realizing the importance of enlisting the support of key senators in pushing through the confirmation of Judge Clarence Thomas to the Supreme Court, Quayle was the first White House official to call senators John Danforth (R-Mo.) and Sam Nunn (D-Ga.) to ask for their endorsement of Thomas. On a defense issue, The vice president also gathered conservative support for the president's veto of technology restrictions on the FSX fighter plane, which was to be developed in conjunction with Japan. "Quayle was the one that persuaded a very reluctant Steering Committee to go along," said Malcolm Wallop (R-Wyo.), chairman of the caucus of about twenty conservative Republicans.[128] Finally, the administration faced stiff congressional opposition to securing funding for the Cambodian resistance to the Khmer Rouge. "The State Department said it was impossible to turn around due to congressional opposition," said Jon Glassman, the vice president's deputy NSA. However, Quayle began calling Christopher Dodd (D-Conn.) and other key senators and was uniquely instrumental in gaining the necessary support. States Glassman: "Quayle called Chris Dodd and others and worked the phone, and was able to turn that around by himself."[129]

The vice president continued his liaison role during the crisis in the Gulf. Bill Kristol affirms that "Quayle did firm up our Hill [congressional] relations during the Gulf War, especially since he was the only ex-senator in the senior reaches of the administration."[130]

The administration had a difficult time with Congress during the Gulf crisis. (Recall that at the time the Congress was controlled by Democrats.) It feared the possibility that too much noise by the congress might be interpreted globally as a lack of resolve by the United States. The administration's apprehensions grew as the prospects of Congress voting against the authorization of force increased. These fears were justified. The final Senate vote on the joint resolution authorizing the president to go to war was very close.

Quayle believed that the longer the administration decided to prolong the seeking of congressional approval the more support would dwindle. The vice president was especially cognizant of the dangers in prolonging a vote. "There [were] many times and many moments where you could see the political support slipping away," said Quayle, "and you could see people beginning to question the president. He had *terrible* problems with the Congress, and this was not as easy, as people, being Monday morning quarterbacks, think that it was."[131]

Robert Gates spoke of the lobbying done by administration players to try to persuade members of Congress to come to the president's side: "We all manned the telephones. I'm not sure we changed very many votes, frankly. But there were a lot of phone calls made." Special Assistant to the President, Richard Haass, seconded the notion by saying that "an awful lot of time was spent on individual members. You had the president, but you also had, quite honestly, all of his chief aides and lieutenants involved with phone calls and meetings."[132] Quayle stepped up his personal lobbying efforts during the Gulf crisis. "I did everything I could to help the president get the votes he needed," the vice president later stated.[133]

It was this sense of urgency that incited Quayle to encourage Bush to seek Congress' support. He was the first administration member to urge the president to acquiesce to Congress on a war vote, and subsequently led the charge in pushing the president. Joe DeSutter does not recall anyone "who pushed it like [Quayle] did." The vice president predicted the president would win and could thereby begin building a consensus for war.[134] "I was one that was encouraging the president to go in December [1990] to ask for the support of Congress," said Quayle. "I felt the earlier the better."[135]

Indeed, during internal administration debates, Quayle had pushed the president to seek the resolution before Christmas of 1990—but lost. The president was not willing to risk a vote without the guarantee of a nearly unanimous endorsement, but Quayle argued that even a simple majority would help.[136] "I thought that it would be politically much more feasible—and much better for the country—if the president went to war with the authorization of Congress," the vice president later recalled. "I also thought we could get a resolution through, though I knew it would be difficult. I argued for an early vote: hold Congress' feet to the fire before the Christmas vacation."[137] Bush eventually made the request of Congress a few weeks later in early January.[138] The resolution passed just days before the initiation of the war, with Quayle present to cast the deciding vote should the Senate have been deadlocked.

The vice president partook in some personal lobbying with members of Congress. Reflecting on his efforts, Quayle remarked:

> The arguments that I made to members of Congress were these: (1) Saddam Hussein was *not* going to get out, (2) Give the President the benefit of the doubt on a foreign-policy matter, (3) *Don't* let history record you being on the side of Saddam Hussein and against the American president. You may think that that's unfair, but that's the way history is going to record it. Please be on the right side. Let the president do what is right. Give him the flexibility; this is a sensitive foreign-policy matter.[139]

The congressional aspects of Quayle's role during the crisis took him a step beyond the role of mere liaison. During the latter stages of the Gulf crisis, and into the war itself, he became the point man for the administration in attacking members of Congress—as well as many others—who were reluctant to support the administration's Gulf policy.

Quayle as the Administration's Gulf-Crisis "Point Man"

During election campaigns presidential candidates spend some of their time blasting opponents but typically try to curtail the bitterness of their remarks for the purpose of appearing statesmanlike. As a result, someone else must assume major responsibility for attacking critics. The vice president is often chosen for the role. "The most common form of propaganda in which vice-presidential candidates engage in is not praise of their partner but abuses of their opponents," wrote Joel Goldstein.[140] A vice president can take on a similar role during a time of war, as was evidenced by Spiro Agnew during the Vietnam war.

As the Gulf crisis began to pick up momentum as the weeks approached toward the conflict's initiation, critics of the administration continued to surface. The administration needed a 'point man,' a sort of 'attack dog,' to fend off the criticisms. The vice president appears to have been chosen for that role. Quayle's principle targets were liberal Democrats who were perceived to be weak on using military force in the Gulf, but he also focused on critics of the administration in general, including war protesters.

Attacking Congressional Critics

Quayle had made tough, partisan remarks toward congressional Democrats earlier in the fall of 1990 during the tax debate between the administration and Democratic critics. But his comments would turn more rancorous as the crisis in the Gulf loomed. Testament to the contentiousness of his criticisms was a speech he presented in New York before the Republican Governors' Association on December 10, 1990.

The vice president charged that some Democrats holding hearings on the deployment of American troops were "playing politics" and undermining the U.S. position in the crisis. He chastised the Senate Armed Services and Foreign Relations Committees for their choice of witnesses critical of the administration's actions. He commented that while the hearings had heard "clear, candid and convincing" testimony from shapers of the administration's policy, the overall content of the hearings was useful for Saddam's "political war against the United States." "Saddam Hussein has even gone so far as to heap praise on the Congress," said Quayle. "Saddam's purpose in all of this is perfectly clear. He hopes to encourage Congress to deprive the Bush administration of its option to use force." He added, "Unfortunately, by portraying themselves as the party of peace, and the administration as the party of war, some Congressional Democrats—but by no means all Congressional Democrats—seem to have placed partisanship above statesmanship." He claimed that a Congress solidly united behind the president "would strengthen our chances for peace." "Despite the efforts of some in Congress, the fact of the matter is that the American people support the president," Quayle concluded. "Once again, the American people are ahead of their Congress."[141]

The vice president turned up the heat on Congress as the January 15 deadline drew near. On January 8 he made the following comments to the Los Angeles World Affairs Council:

> Unfortunately, Saddam may still not believe that force is a credible option. He may have a difficult time understanding our political system. Democracy is by far the best political system ever created, but it is complex and, at times, messy.

> When a Senator or Congressman criticizes the President's policy the media deem it newsworthy. . . . Thus, when he sees our Congressional critics getting world media coverage the message to Saddam may be that the President cannot and will not use force because the Congress will not let him.
>
> Let me set the record straight: Unless Congress denies funds for Operation Desert Shield, as suggested by Democratic Majority leader [Richard] Gephardt, Saddam Hussein should understand that his aggression will not stand. Saddam Hussein should understand that we will use force, if necessary, to expel him from Kuwait.
>
> Congress could help Saddam Hussein understand this. It could pass a favorable resolution in support of the United Nations resolutions. . . . This would be helpful.
>
> On the other hand, Congress could choose to pass resolutions that would be harmful. Any resolution that suggested to Saddam Hussein that the threat of force is not credible would, in fact, undermine the chances for a peaceful resolution. Simply put, it would take the pressure of Saddam Hussein to pull out now. . . .
>
> Thus, Congress has the following choices: To support the President, to dispute the President, or not to act at all. . . . What Congress must know is that the world watches and interprets every move it makes. This is our political system.
>
> If Congress supports the President, we may at this eleventh hour be able to convince Saddam Hussein that the threat of force is not an idle one.[142]

As the war began to subside—and take on the appearance of a route by allied forces—congressmen critical of the administration began to run for cover. Quayle did not let them off the hook. In a postwar interview with *Business Week*, the vice president addressed the question of whether it was fair to attack Democrats for their vote against the use of force in the Gulf. "You know what it's a question of?" he asked. "Judgment. The Democratic leadership made an erroneous judgment about a very important national security issue. Are they to be held accountable for their judgment? I would certainly hope so."[143]

Attacking Critics in General

Among the public critics of the administration were war protesters. It seems the administration perceived the protesters as an annoying but harmless group organized against U.S. policy. Prior to the actual war, the White House made a point to ignore the antiwar demonstrations across the country.[144] The apparent intent of the administration was to downplay the demonstrations in order to diminish their impact on public opinion. But as the U.S. military presence in the

Gulf turned to armed confrontation with Iraqi troops, the vice president began to offer some public criticisms of the protesters.

Judging from available information, Quayle did not devote significant amounts of time or space to the protesters in policy speeches, but he did offer some snide remarks. As Maureen Dowd of *The New York Times* pointed out, the vice president provided no catchy epithets to the magnitude of former Vice President Spiro Agnew's comments during the Vietnam War. (Agnew referred to the press as "pusillanimous pussyfooters" and Vietnam War protesters as an "effete corps of impudent snobs who characterize themselves as intellectuals.") But Quayle did tell members of the armed forces and their families at three different military bases on January 23, 1991, that the protests against the Gulf War were among the "less inspiring sights at this time of conflict" and had been exaggerated by the news media. When asked later, in an interview with Dowd on Air Force Two, if his remarks were a departure from the more benign approach the administration had been taking toward the protesters, Quayle stated: "Go ahead and do it. You can cover it any way you want. But . . . when you go out and say there are these massive demonstrations and when you see how massive they [actually] are, I would think that perhaps the coverage ought to be somewhat of the percentage involved."[145] In response, *Newsweek*—which published some remarkably biased, superficial, and childish articles on Quayle during the crisis—conceded that in his Fort Bragg speech, "Quayle was right about one thing: opponents of the war are a small minority of the American people." A *Newsweek* poll at the time showed that 86 percent of the public supported the president's policy.[146]

In a speech to military families at Fort Bliss, Texas, on February 6, the vice president took a sharper shot at the protesters, as well as noting where the majority stood. "Saddam hopes the ideas of the protesters and demonstrators will prevail," he commented. "Saddam should not misinterpret what he sees. The protesters are a tiny vocal minority. The American people have shown overwhelming support for President George Bush's Persian Gulf policy."[147]

Quayle would say he believed the protesters were not much different than those of Vietnam. He said he was convinced that the war in the Gulf would not be another Vietnam, and it would therefore "be very difficult for the protesters to get too much a head of steam."[148] The Vietnam analogy, however, was important for another point: It was one of the most cited examples by administration critics of what might happen in the Gulf. The Vietnam analogy fueled the arguments of many White House opponents. As the administration's attacker of such critics, Quayle tackled what had come to be known as the "Vietnam Syndrome." Twisting the Vietnam argument against the critics themselves, Quayle argued that a policy of pursing economic sanctions to drive Iraq from Kuwait could be a recipe for a potential repeat of the Vietnam debacle. He referred to the sanctions option as a policy of "patience." Quayle stated:

advocates of endless patience should talk to our troops in the Gulf. . . . They feel they have been patient. . . . They don't look forward to spending the next couple of years waiting around in the Saudi desert while Congress debates what to do next. As the President has said, "This will not be another Vietnam."

I am convinced that if force is necessary it will be quick, massive and decisive. President Bush knows the lessons of Vietnam. He knows that the policy of "gradual escalation" that we pursued in Southeast Asia turned out to be a recipe for stalemate. . . . He knows that war is a terrible thing—but if we must use force, there can be no half-measures. . . . The real question is: Have the President's critics learned the lessons of Vietnam? . . . Aren't their calls for endless patience a sure-fire formula for getting us bogged down in the Gulf indefinitely?[149]

Quayle reaffirmed that Operation Desert Storm would not be another Vietnam. The troops "will not be asked to fight with one hand tied behind their backs," he said. "We will win the conflict; then, as soon as possible, our troops will come home."[150] Later reflecting on the success of the U.S. military operation in the Gulf in a postwar speech to the Mid-America Committee, Quayle took an opportunity to allude to the Vietnam syndrome when stating that the reason for the "superb performance of our armed forces in Desert Storm was that they were allowed to do their job. Washington didn't try to 'micro-manage' this war." He added: "The President set the war's broad objectives. He carefully defined the military's mission. And having done all that, he let the military itself carry out that mission. He treated our servicemen and women like professionals—not like puppets of the Federal bureaucracy."[151]

Quayle's Personal Views and Actions during the Gulf Crisis

The information cited in the previous section contains many statements made by the vice president on behalf of the administration, as well as his own views. Its main intention was to spell out the vice president's role and tasks during the crisis. Additionally, many of the comments contained within Quayle's speeches reflect a consistency with his basic foreign-policy beliefs and strategic thinking, set out through his years as a public official. In that vein, the final section of this case pieces together information reflecting the vice president's personal opinions and actions during the crisis beyond his formal tasks and roles.

Quayle and Israel

Throughout the administration, the vice president helped smooth relations with Israeli officials, with whom he had friendlier ties than Bush and Baker.[152] A top Israeli lobbyist said that Quayle was "a friend and a factor."[153] Bill Kristol agrees that Quayle "generally was much friendlier to the Likud government than anyone else in the Bush administration."[154] Israelis never forgot his past Senate support and remarks throughout his vice presidency, such as the Judea and Samaria comments. In the early months of the Gulf conflict, Quayle, against widespread opposition, won approval for a $700 million weapons shipment for Israel.[155] In general, Kristol feels that Quayle did help push the administration "toward a more pro-Israeli Middle East policy." He remarks: "Quayle was more pro-Israel than Bush and Baker. . . . Quayle did try to make the administration a little more pro-Israel than it tended to be at some key points. Quayle got in trouble for being a little bit too pro-Israel at times, with Richard Haass and some of the other people in the administration."[156] Among the Big Eight involved in the tightly controlled sessions on the Gulf crisis, Cheney and Eagleburger typically joined Quayle in his pro-Israel sympathies, usually opposed by Baker and State.[157]

Columnist Fred Barnes reported that Quayle's influence with the president increased during the Gulf crisis. This influence was reflected in his ability to synthesize his friendly relationships with both the president and Israeli leadership in a manner that was extremely productive in key aspects of administration actions in the Gulf. For instance, notes Fred Barnes, "Unswervingly pro-Israeli, Quayle persuaded Bush that Israeli Prime Minister Yitzhak Shamir was a guy Bush could deal with. Were Israel attacked, Shamir wouldn't necessarily draw Israel into the Gulf War. Quayle was right."[158] Bill Kristol confirms that both he and Quayle, because of their strong pro-Israel stance, "had independent contacts with members of the Israeli government" that served the administration well during the Gulf conflict. He bolsters the point that Quayle pushed Bush on the Shamir factor. Yet, Kristol also speaks of how Quayle angled his relationship with the Israelis to help persuade *them* to use restraint in the event of an attack on their home soil. "During the war there was some back channel communications where . . . Quayle used his friendship with [Israeli Defense Minster Moshe] Arens and others to sort of try to keep the Israelis from going off on their own and to be sure the Israelis did the right thing." Hence, on the issue of restraint, Quayle prodded both the U.S. and Israeli leadership. The importance of this cannot be underestimated. If the Israelis had responded with force to Saddam's Scud missile attacks, the Iraqi leader would have succeeded in drawing Israel into the conflict and thus might have been able to split up the tenuous allied coalition.

Bill Kristol also adds (somewhat cryptically): "In December to January

[1991] there was some tension before we went to war as to whether we were going to follow through and sharing of codes with the Israelis. There were some secrets and sensitive stuff. Quayle was somewhat involved and I was involved, too, in working with the ambassador on some of these matters." He says that "we had independent sources of information in Israel . . . on some of these issues."[159] In essence, Kristol acknowledges that Quayle did some work behind the scenes in facilitating communications between Israel and the United States during the conflict. Ironically, the pro-Israel overtures he made earlier—which so infuriated the State Department—paid off during the Gulf crisis. Israel trusted Quayle as a loyal and friendly liaison.

Quayle on Saddam and the Use of Military Force

"The President from the very outset never ruled any options out. He told us that privately. He conveyed that publicly. But we were not at that point looking at intervention as the best option. It was way too premature."[160] That is the vice president's summation of the early days of the administration's decision-making process on how to deal with Saddam's invasion of Kuwait. As noted earlier, Quayle got an early jump on Saddam's Gulf actions, denouncing him in the April 1990 speech, where he warned of the dangers posed by Saddam's moving Scud missiles into western Iraq, closer to Israeli's borders. His April warnings would continue through statements, interviews and speeches over the next fourteen months, using tough language to impugn Saddam's actions.

The vice president's personal feelings about Saddam's psyche were unambiguous, as evidenced in this February 18, 1991 interview with *U.S. News & World Report*:

> From the mores that we believe in, [Saddam] is totally irrational. He has a different background, he's got a different culture, he has total control of the country. He's brutal, doesn't hesitate to kill; human life means very little to him. Throughout this ordeal, Saddam has been consistent. He has been consistent in refusing to get out of Kuwait. He has been consistent in refusing to look for a political resolution. He has been consistent in saying he and Iraq will be victorious. He is wrong on all those counts.[161]

Quayle warned against "changing the meaning" of U.N. resolutions, saying that such actions could create political problems. He wanted the resolve of the multinational force to be very clear. "If Saddam . . . is going to stay in power," he demanded, "first he's got to get all of his troops and people out of Kuwait."[162] In a book published a year after the crisis, it was reported that Quayle, from the beginning and consistently, argued that the administration's ultimate objective should be to defang Saddam's military machine, and especially to destroy his weapons of mass destruction. He had been supported by Secretary of Defense Cheney, Under Secretary of Defense Paul Wolfowitz, and Deputy NSA Gates. Both goals went well beyond the publicly stated objective of simply driving Hussein out of Kuwait. Quayle, Cheney, and Gates repeatedly raised concerns about Bush's limited objectives in the Gulf. While the president respectfully listened to their concerns, he eventually decided against them.[163]

In the February 1991 interview, Quayle was asked about his position on the makeup of postwar Iraq. "We would simply not want to see [Iraq's] military force rebuilt to where it was before, and therefore certain sanctions would possibly have to be extended," he remarked. Quayle also raised a minor point that seemed somewhat irrelevant at the time but may hold some significance in retrospect, saying, "We don't know who would succeed Saddam Hussein, but whoever his successor may be would be hard pressed to have the total control over the country that Saddam Hussein has in the short term." While the comment is stated rather disingenuously (and was not picked up by the interviewer), it appears to be the first public remark suggesting that Quayle might have favored removing Saddam himself. When asked—in a separate interview on the same day by *U.S. News & World Report*—about the prospects of Saddam remaining in power after the U.S. intervention, Quayle stated, "I make no bones about it, it will certainly complicate the situation."[164] In a May 10, 1991, op-ed piece in *The Washington Post*, columnist Charles Krauthammer states that Quayle favored U.S. troops going into Baghdad to 'get' Saddam. "And after the war, Quayle's was one of the few voices within the administration that favored finishing the job," writes Krauthammer, reporting that the vice president had taken the "minority view" within the administration.[165]

To this day, Quayle has never confirmed the perception that he favored deposing Saddam, not even in his memoirs. Yet, giving credence to the notion that he may have favored such an action were May 1994 comments he made during an interview on ABC's "PrimeTime Live." In the interview with Dianne Sawyer, the vice president stated the following:

> **Dianne Sawyer:** And what about Saddam—the man who outlasted his enemy George Bush? You say that you believe the executive order prohibiting assassination of foreign leaders should be rescinded.
> **Dan Quayle:** Yes. I think that the president ought to have the option to consider covert actions.
> **Dianne Sawyer:** But it is deliberate, specific murder.
> **Dan Quayle:** It is.
> **Dianne Sawyer:** State-sponsored murder.
> **Dan Quayle:** I would like to be able to consider covert operations.
> **Dianne Sawyer:** And you might have done it with Saddam?
> **Dan Quayle:** I'd like to have considered it and we couldn't.[166]

Clearly, it seems that Vice President Quayle considered, if not favored, eliminating Saddam. Carnes Lord, who, as Quayle's NSA during the crisis was very aware of his boss's views, recalled: "I don't remember him talking seriously at the time about the assassination ban. But he did favor a more serious effort than others regarding bringing down the regime."[167]

At the very least, it is fair to say that Quayle was one of the most hawkish members of the administration. A book on the Gulf War by *U.S. News & World Report* goes a step further, asserting that, "Among the president's men, Quayle was the *most* hawkish" (italics added).[168] Bill Kristol, while not willing to rank the president's team according to dovish-hawkish tendencies, concedes that Quayle took aggressive positions: "I think his instincts were less to defer to the U.N. and to reject the notion that some of our allies [may have] wanted us to stop. I'm not sure he was ready to march to Baghdad so concretely. . . . I'm not sure how much of a different end game he would have pushed for. But he was always on the hawkish side."[169]

Nonetheless, Quayle—fulfilling the loyal vice president role—refrained from any dissension in public statements concerning the conflict's termination, even voicing approval of the president's decision to end the war when he did: "And I was there with the president, and I can assure you that up and down the chain of command there was total unanimity and consensus that all military objectives had been achieved."[170] Even in his memoirs, he continued the supportive tone: "We had fought the war to get Saddam Hussein out of Kuwait, and we had done that. We had *not* fought it to dislodge Saddam from power."[171]

Quayle and the Gulf's Vindication of Strategic Defense

The dates to remember, noted Fred Barnes of *The New Republic*, were January 3 and 18 of 1991. On January 3 the president headed for the Situation Room in the White House basement for his first full briefing on the Pentagon's scaled back version of SDI. The new SDI had a post-Cold War mission to protect against limited missile attacks by countries like Iraq, rather than deter a massive strike on the United States from the Soviet Union. The new program was known as GPALS, or Global Protection Against Limited Strikes.[172] Quayle was a proponent of GPALS.

The president quickly approved GPALS, though its chances of gaining congressional approval were weak. Then, as Barnes notes, on January 18, a Scud missile launched from Iraq was intercepted by a U.S.-made Patriot missile. According to a Pentagon official, it was the first destruction of an enemy ballistic missile in a combat situation. The apparent success of the Patriot gave a huge political boost to missile defense programs and presented an opportunity for the administration to gain explicit congressional approval of a space-based antimissile system.[173] Early in the conflict, Quayle remarked in his diary: "Patriots down eight missiles out of nine. . . . A big boost for SDI." He later noted that the Patriot "proved a lifesaver for the Israelis."[174]

The timing of the Patriot's success coincided with the president's State of the Union address. Taking advantage of its war-time fame and Bush's endorsement of GPALS, Quayle made sure Bush plugged GPALS in his January 29 address. At Quayle's urging, the president said, "with remarkable technological advances like the Patriot missile, we can defend against ballistic missile attacks aimed at innocent civilians." As a result, SDI was being "refocused on providing protection from limited ballistic missile strikes, whatever their source."[175]

The success of anti-missile defense during the Gulf War provided a vindication of what Quayle had advocated, in terms of strategic defense, throughout his years as a public official. Perhaps in no other policy area was Quayle as adamant as in this one. "The Patriot would have died if it weren't for Quayle," argues DeSutter, who advised Quayle on SDI issues. "No one should forget that. But, of course, they have. It really did vindicate his entire work in the Senate. This is not trivial."[176]

In upcoming public statements and speeches, the vice president would seize the opportunity presented by the Patriot's success to push for further research in missile defense. Additionally, he would note the considerable success of the Tomahawk cruise missile as an example of the importance of upgrading cruise missiles—a subject of which he had written as a senator. In an interview with *U.S. News & World Report*, Quayle commented:

> During the Reagan build-up, there were many critics [who claimed] we were simply spending money on $700 toilet seats. The fact is that we were spending money on important weapons systems like the Patriot and the Tomahawk cruise missile, and they have been critical to success in the Persian Gulf. . . .
> The war not only vindicates the Strategic Defense Initiative but it makes SDI more of a reality. People are amazed at the capability of the Patriot. But they will be amazed at the capability of SDI when its deployed. . . .
> The fact of the matter is that you *can* have a bullet hit a bullet. As we get into more sophisticated ballistic missiles and Scuds, as other countries acquire ballistic-missile capability, it is going to make eminent sense, to protect American lives, to be able to knock those missiles down over the country which launches them.[177]

In a March 13, 1991 speech the vice president returned to a theme he had articulated in the 1989 *Policy Review* article: relying on offensive weapons alone as a means of deterrence was unwise; the United states needed defensive weapons. Quayle stated:

In the past . . . some had urged us to rely for our defense on theories of deterrence rather than on technologies of defense. They argued that security can be achieved by relying on offensive weapons alone. Well, as President Bush put it [in a speech on February 15, 1991], "Thank God that when the Scuds came in, the people of Israel and Saudi Arabia and the brave forces of our coalition had more to protect them than some abstract theory of deterrence." They had defensive weapons. Thank God for the American creativity and technology, which saved thousands of priceless human lives.[178]

The vice president would continue to attack past critics of the Patriot. "I wonder how many Americans are aware of what an uphill battle it was to get Theater Ballistic Missile Defenses funded over the years," he asked. "Critics of the Patriot came up with all kinds of excuses. . . . The naysayers were simply wrong. The Patriot is doing its job, and *it works*."[179]

Quayle drew a parallel between critics of the Patriot and those of SDI, saying that the same arguments used against the former were now being used against the latter. "We're already proving every day, with technologies well beyond those we've used in the Patriot, that strategic defense is both doable and affordable," he concluded. "It's time to get moving: to build even better antimissile systems, and to renew our commitment to SDI."[180]

Summary of Quayle's Role during the Persian Gulf Crisis

The role of the vice president during the Gulf crisis was basically threefold. He served as a spokesman for the administration—citing its objectives in the Gulf in a number of speeches and statements—as well as an emissary and negotiator on trips abroad. He served as a liaison to Congress, monitoring the mood of congressmen key to White House support. Finally, he assumed the role of a 'point man' of sorts, blasting critics of the president's Gulf strategy. When it came to influencing administration policy, it appears the vice president did have some impact. To rehash a few examples: Quayle persuaded Bush that they could work with Israeli Prime Minister Shamir in dissuading the Israelis from being drawn into the Gulf conflict in the event it was attacked by Iraqi missiles; he prodded key U.S. allies, such as Kuwait and Japan, into providing extra financial help; Quayle seems to have felt the administration should go into Baghdad to 'finish the job' with Saddam; he reportedly served a strong diplomatic role in Latin America in successfully lobbying Venezuela to increase oil production during the Gulf crisis and pushing Brazil and Argentina to stop transfers of missile technology to Iraq; and Quayle was the first member of the administration to urge the president to acquiesce to Congress on a war vote. Additionally, the crisis provided a golden opportunity for his basic foreign-policy beliefs on such issues as strategic defenses and competitive strategies to be field tested in the context of the Gulf War—a war which took place in Quayle's choice scenario using his choice offensive and defensive weapons, cruise missiles and interceptor-missiles. The war would provide a chance for the senator's and vice president's favorite technologies to prove their mettle.

Conclusion

According to Hubert H. Humphrey, who served as vice president in the Johnson administration, what the vice president is permitted to do is determined by what the president assigns to him and the power and authority that he is willing to share with him. "The president can bestow assignments and authority and can remove that authority and power at will," stated Humphrey. "I used to call this Humphrey's law—'He who giveth can taketh away and often does.'"[181] The activities of the vice president often depend upon presidential generosity. Adds Joel K. Goldstein, the "extent and significance of functions presidents give their vice presidents depend on the relationship between the two individuals."[182] While statutory changes in the post-World War II era have guaranteed the vice president a certain degree of involvement in foreign policy, the level to which he is active depends upon him and the president he serves.

Fortunately for Dan Quayle, he had a president in Bush who also served as a vice president. Consequently, as vice president, Quayle was the beneficiary of a certain amount of empathy from Bush. He had a sympathetic president who was once in Quayle's shoes. As noted in the previous section, this translated into some meaningful roles for Quayle in foreign policy, despite the fact that the degree of his involvement was constrained by the steeped foreign-policy experience of the senior staff around him, including the president himself. (As we shall see in the next chapter, Vice President Al Gore faces a complete opposite situation.) In particular, his duties during the Gulf crisis would hardly be considered unimportant.

Kristol sums up his view on the vice president's influence in the administration:

> He was pretty active [in foreign policy]. He was personally very interested in it. Obviously he had experience in it from his time in the Senate on the Committee on Armed Services. We certainly did lots of foreign trips where we had substantive discussions. On the other hand, I couldn't in all honesty say, with the exception of one or two cases, that we influenced foreign policy much. . . . Quayle was part of the inner group; they met in the Oval Office during the Gulf War and other times. . . . I would think Quayle had some influence at that level. I think at the staff level we had influence on a few issues. We carried out a lot of foreign policy. When we

were on trips obviously we had 'State' and 'Defense' people with us and we'd carry out whatever administration foreign policy was—some of it was fairly interesting and, of course, some of it was pretty routine.[183]

While Kristol applauds the many admirable tasks performed by Quayle—pointing to his Gulf-conflict duties, Philippines crisis management, and Latin America assignments—he admits: "At the end of the day would Bush's foreign policy have been different if someone else were vice president? Probably not. . . . There's not too many areas where he made much of a *decisive* difference. But that would be true for most vice presidents."[184] Kristol seems to be making a bit of an understatement. In actuality, the Bush administration's foreign policy may have been a little bit different in some aspects had it not been for Quayle. This applies to Israeli relations and his role in Latin America during the Gulf crisis. Almost certainly, strategic defense would have been treated differently had it not been for Quayle. In that sense, Kristol agrees that Quayle made a difference on a number of individual matters, but whether or not he made a decisive difference on the larger picture is another question. This is not an indictment of Quayle as much as it may be a statement of reality on the general impact of a vice president. The deeper policy implications of this and other statements and examples in this chapter will be assessed in the final chapter on lessons learned and policy recommendations.

Notes

1. Quayle himself notes a number of highly unreported Gore gaffes that took place in the first few months of 1993 alone. There is no question that many of them were editorial-cartoon material. See Dan Quayle, *Standing Firm: A Vice-Presidential Memoir* (New York: HarperCollins, 1994), pp. 49-50. While the case of media bias against Quayle is an intriguing issue, it is not being examined in this study.

2. See Jules Witcover, *Crapshoot: Rolling the Dice on the Vice Presidency* (New York: Crown Publishers, 1992), pp. 383-84.

3. A shorter examination of Quayle's role during the Gulf crisis was published by the author in the Fall 1994 issue of *Presidential Studies Quarterly*. This chapter's analysis of that episode has been updated in key areas to include valuable sources not available to the author at the time he wrote the previous piece. The new sources include interviews with key players and Quayle's memoirs, among other items. For a copy of the earlier version, see Paul Kengor, "The Role of the Vice President during the Crisis in the Persian Gulf," *Presidential Studies Quarterly*, Fall 1994, Vol. XXIV, No. 4, pp. 783-807.

4. Among the extremely impressive cases that are not examined in this chapter are Quayle's crisis-management role during a coup attempt in the Philippines and his role in Latin America policy. Regarding the latter, Quayle was probably not exaggerating when he asserted that he developed into "the administration's most active man for Latin

J. Danforth Quayle (1989-93)   205

America affairs"—a claim backed by his deputy NSA, Jon Glassman. I chose not to focus on these because of space constraints, largely caused by the wealth of information collected on Quayle's role in the Persian Gulf crisis. Sources on Latin America remark: Quayle, *Standing Firm*, p. 146; and Interview with Jon Glassman, former Deputy NSA to Vice President Quayle, in Washington, D.C., at State Department, May 24, 1996. Sources on the Philippines (among others): Interview with Glassman; Bob Woodward, *The Commanders* (New York: Simon & Schuster, 1991), pp. 147-53; and Interview with Kenneth T. Walsh and Michael Barone, "The Vice President's View: 'It's an Awkward Job,'" *U.S. News & World Report*, Vol. 110, No. 19, p. 21.

   5. Quayle, *Standing Firm*, p. 18.
   6. The updated book by Fenno is entitled *The Making of a Senator: Dan Quayle* (Washington, D.C.: Congressional Quarterly, 1989), p. 140.
   7. Quayle, *Standing Firm*, p. 26.
   8. Ibid., pp. 75-76.
   9. Henry Kissinger, *White House Years* (Boston: 1979), p. 713.
   10. Quoted in Dorothy Kearns, *Lyndon Johnson and the American Dream* (New York: Harper & Row, 1976), p. 164.
   11. David S. Broder and Bob Woodward, "Facing Limitations in an 'Awkward Job,'" *Washington Post*, January 8, 1992, p. A14.
   12. Michael Barone and Kenneth T. Walsh, "His Place at the Table," *U.S. News & World Report*, Vol. 110, No. 19, pp. 20-21.
   13. Interview with Walsh and Barone, op. cit., pp. 20-21.
   14. David S. Broder, Bob Woodward, and David Greenberg, "Quayles and Bushes, Almost Like Family," *Washington Post*, January 8, 1992, p. A14.
   15. Broder and Woodward, op. cit., p. A14.
   16. Interview with Glassman.
   17. Quayle, *Standing Firm*, pp. 92 and 102.
   18. Quayle's chairmanship of the Space Council often allowed him to play a part in Soviet policy initiatives, thus somewhat reaching into the area of "foreign policy." In fact, in interviews with former Quayle staffers, staff members volunteer information on Quayle's success in this area and how it sometimes involved "diplomatic dealings" with Russia. Quayle allegedly played a key role in launching a Mars mission. Interview with Carnes Lord, former NSA to Vice President Quayle, via telephone from Medford, Massachusetts, December 11, 1996; Interview with Joe DeSutter, former foreign-policy and national security advisor to both vice presidents Quayle and Gore, via telephone from Washington, D.C., December 18, 1996; and Interview with Jon Glassman.
   19. Ibid., pp. 103-04.
   20. Interview with Carnes Lord.
   21. Broder and Woodward, op. cit., p. A14.
   22. Quayle, *Standing Firm*, p. 92.
   23. Ibid., p. 92.
   24. Fred Barnes, "White House Watch: Quayle Alert," *The New Republic*, May 27, 1991, Vol. 24, No. 21, p. 12.
   25. Quayle, *Standing Firm*, pp. 92-93.
   26. Once again, the Space Council that Quayle chaired was a major interagency group that sometimes crossed into the international realm (see note 18).
   27. Broder and Woodward, op. cit., p. A14.

28. Burt Solomon, "War Bolsters Quayle's Visibility . . . But Hasn't Increased His Stature," *National Journal*, March 2, 1991, Vol. 23, No. 9, p. 522.; Quayle, *Standing Firm*, p. 242; and U.S. News & World Report, *Triumph without Victory: The Unreported History of the Persian Gulf War* (New York: Random House, Times Books, 1992), p. 32.

29. Broder and Woodward, op. cit., p. A14.

30. Interview with Joe DeSutter.

31. Broder and Woodward, op. cit., p. A14.

32. Interview with Bill Kristol, former chief of staff to Vice President Quayle, via telephone, May 28, 1996.

33. Interview with Joe DeSutter. For an analysis of the differing relationships between the vice president and secretary of state in the Bush and Clinton administrations, see Paul Kengor, "Vice-Presidential Involvement in Foreign Policy: A Tale of Two Vice Presidents and Their Secretaries of State," *Political Science Quarterly*, forthcoming in 2000.

34. Ibid. Among differing advisors and aides, DeSutter focused on SDI, arms control, and the Middle East.

35. Interview with Kristol; Interview with Glassman; and Quayle, *Standing Firm*, pp. 88-89.

36. Interview with Kristol.

37. For examples of clashes between Quayle and Baker, see Quayle, *Standing Firm*, pp. 37, 69, 97, 183-84.

38. Interview with Joe DeSutter.

39. Interview with Carnes Lord, former NSA to Vice President Quayle, December 11, 1996.

40. Interview with DeSutter.

41. Solomon, op. cit., p. 522.

42. Barone and Walsh (article), op. cit., p. 20.

43. Barnes, "Quayle Alert," May 27, 1991, p. 12.

44. Broder and Woodward, op. cit., p. A14.

45. Michael Duffy, "Is He Really That Bad?" *Time*, May 20, 1991, pp. 21-22.

46. Tom Mathews, "Dan Quayle's Crisis Duty," *Newsweek*, September 24, 1990, Vol. 116, No. 13, p. 28.

47. Broder and Woodward, op. cit., p. A14.

48. Interview with Kristol.

49. Interview with Glassman.

50. Broder and Woodward, op. cit., p. A14; and Quayle, *Standing Firm*, pp. 88 and 104.

51. Interview with Glassman.

52. Broder and Woodward, op. cit., p. A14.

53. Ibid.

54. Ibid.

55. U.S. Senator Dan Quayle, from an address delivered on the floor of the U.S. Senate, May 13, 1987, during consideration of S. 1174, the National Defense Authorization Act for Fiscal Years 1988 and 1989, "Should Congress Approve the ABM Treaty Controversy? Con:" The Congressional Digest, November 1987, Vol. 66, No. 11, p. 275.

56. Fred Barnes, "White House Watch: Brilliant Pebble," *The New Republic*, April 1, 1991, p. 13.

57. See Solomon, op. cit., p. 522; and "Washington Outlook: Now the Right Is Taking Potshots at Star Wars," *Business Week*, October 20, 1986, p. 39.

58. Senator Dan Quayle, "Upgrading Our Cruise Missiles: Imperative for the 1990s," *Armed Forces Journal International*, August 1987, Vol. 125, No. 1, pp. 76-77.

59. Ibid., p. 76.

60. Ibid., p. 80.

61. Ibid.

62. Dan Quayle, "Missile Woes," *Washington Post*, July 14, 1987, p. A15.

63. Interview with John G. Roos and Benjamin F. Schemmer, "An Exclusive AFJI Interview with Vice President Dan Quayle," *Armed Forces Journal International*, February 1, 1990, Vol. 127, No. 7, pp. 70-72.

64. Vice President Dan Quayle, Office of the Vice President, "Text of Remarks by the Vice President, National Defense University Symposium, Department of Defense," L'Enfant Plaza—Monet Room, Washington, D.C., November 17, 1989, pp. 2-4.

65. Roos and Schemmer, op. cit., p. 72.

66. Vice President Dan Quayle, "SDI and Its Enemies," *Policy Review*, Fall 1989, No. 50, p. 2.

67. Ibid., p. 4.

68. Significantly, Quayle military aide Joe DeSutter credits the vice president with introducing "Brilliant Pebbles" to the public, and then saving the program. He did this in two speeches in 1989. The first introduced Brilliant Pebbles. The second speech gave control of Brilliant Pebbles to SDIO (Strategic Defense Initiative Organization) rather than to the Air Force. Quayle and his staff feared that if the Air Force had control of Brilliant Pebbles it would "price the program out of existence." Interview with DeSutter.

69. Roos and Schemmer, op. cit., p. 74.

70. Ibid.

71. "Text of Remarks by the Vice President to the American Israel Public Affairs Committee on June 11, 1990," *American-Arab Affairs*, Summer 1990, No. 33, p. 167.

72. Ibid., p. 171; and Duffy, op. cit., p. 22.

73. Fenno, op. cit., p. 140.

74. Paul Lewis, "U.S. to Postpone Debate on Zionism," *The New York Times*, September 16, 1990, p. A17.

75. "Text of Remarks by the Vice President to the American Israel Public Affairs Committee on June 11, 1990," *American-Arab Affairs*, Summer 1990, No. 33, p. 170.

76. Ibid., p. 167.

77. Ibid., p. 168.

78. Vice President Dan Quayle, Office of the Vice President, "Prepared Text of Remarks by the Vice President, The Washington Institute for Near East Policy," April 30, 1990, p. 3.

79. Ibid., pp. 3-4.

80. Ibid., pp. 7-9.

81. Ibid., p. 10. There was a view that the Israelis often saw the U.S.-funded Arrow program as somewhat of a "free" defense contract that had mainly engineering and scientific implications. Quayle argued that the Israelis had to move beyond such thinking and instead view the Arrow program as something that could be used for real defense and hence ought to be integrated into the nation's plans and doctrines. Interview with DeSutter.

208 Chapter 6

82. Ibid., p. 9.
83. Solomon, op. cit., p. 522.
84. Solomon, op. cit., p. 522; Quayle, *Standing Firm*, p. 242; and U.S. News & World Report, *Triumph without Victory*, p. 32.
85. Solomon, op. cit., p. 522.
86. Maureen Dowd, "Quayle Aims at Protests, A la Agnew," *The New York Times*, January 24, 1991, p. A13.
87. Solomon, op. cit., p. 522.
88. Quayle, *Standing Firm*, p. 207.
89. Interview with Carnes Lord.
90. Ibid., p. 214.
91. Ibid.; Duffy, op. cit., p. 22. It seems that only with the oft ridiculed Quayle would one find the following tidbit: "Bill Kristol, the vice president's chief of staff, said Quayle wrote the speech himself. 'I've been asked [who wrote the speech] a hundred times, and my answer is the same,' he said, 'The vice president did.'" Ann Devroy, "Quayle Cites 'Moral Costs' of Waiting," *The Washington Post*, November 30, 1990, p. A21. Carnes Lord states that all of the vice presidents' Gulf War speeches were written by he and his staff. Interview with Carnes Lord.
92. Vice President Dan Quayle, Office of the Vice President, "Prepared Text of Remarks by the Vice President, Seton Hall University," South Orange, New Jersey, November 29, 1990, pp. 2-3.
93. Ibid., pp. 3-5.
94. Ibid., pp. 6-7. The emphasis on the "first crisis of the post-Cold War world" was made by Quayle many times, including in a late August 1990 speech to the annual American Legion convention in Indianapolis, only three weeks after Saddam invaded Kuwait. See Quayle, *Standing Firm*, pp. 207-08 and 215.
95. Michael R. Gordon, "Quayle Says Delaying War Would Increase Risks," *The New York Times*, November 30, 1990, p. A11.
96. Quayle, Seton Hall University speech, p. 8.
97. Quayle, *Standing Firm*, p. 214. Also, see Devroy, op. cit., p. A21.
98. Gordon, op. cit., p. A11.
99. Quayle, *Standing Firm*, p. 214.
100. Quayle, Seton Hall University speech, pp. 9-10; and Quayle, *Standing Firm*, pp. 213-15. Interestingly, Quayle would later say that his "most changed view" during his tenure as vice president involved the effectiveness of the U.N. "I was exceedingly skeptical of the [U.N.]," he said. "But after seeing how President Bush worked the U.N., I have altered my viewpoint. Before, my tendency was to dismiss it as a soapbox. I don't view it that way anymore." Interview with Walsh and Barone, op. cit., p. 21. Also, see Quayle, *Standing Firm*, p. 210.
101. Overview of U.S. objectives in the Persian Gulf crisis based on statements by President Bush and Secretary Baker and actions of the U.N. Security Council, "Gulf Crisis Update," *U.S. Department of State Dispatch*, January 7, 1991, p. 5.
102. Vice President Dan Quayle, Office of the Vice President, "Prepared Text of Remarks by the Vice President, Foreign Policy Research Institute Conference," Washington, D.C., December 18, 1990, pp. 5-6. In an April 1991 interview Quayle was asked about Japan's "reluctance" to join the allied war effort. "Do we think Japan should do more in the area of international responsibility? Certainly," said Quayle. "There is a per-

ception that because Japan did not send military forces, there was a lack of commitment to the coalition. I would point out that their $9 billion contribution was quite significant, and it did not come without a political price in Japan." Interview with Lee Walczak and Douglas Harbrecht, "A Talk with Dan Quayle: 'Washington Loves a Free Lunch,'" *Business Week*, April 1, 1991, p. 27.

103. Quayle, Foreign Policy Research Institute Conference speech, pp. 4-5.

104. Duffy, op. cit., p. 21.

105. Ibid., p. 21; and Mathews, op. cit., p. 28. Brazil and Argentina referred to such technology as "space-launch technology," but were quite aware of what Hussein was doing with it. Interview with DeSutter.

106. Interview with Glassman.

107. Statement of Bernard W. Aronson, Assistant Secretary of State for Inter-American Affairs, "Fiscal Year 1992 Foreign Assistance Request for the Western Hemisphere," Hearings before the Subcommittee on western Hemisphere and Peace Corps Affairs of the Committee on Foreign Relations, United States Senate, First Session, 102nd Congress, April 18, 1991, pp. 4 and 9.

108. Interview with Glassman.

109. Interview with Carnes Lord.

110. Quayle, *Standing Firm*, pp. 211-12.

111. Quayle, December 18, 1990 speech, pp. 5-6; and Interview with Walczak and Harbrecht, op. cit., p. 27.

112. Guy Gugliotta, "Quayle Vows Swift Stroke in Gulf War," *The Washington Post*, January 1, 1991, p. A17.

113. Interview with Glassman. Glassman correctly notes that there has been no published account of this move by Quayle, including not only the popular press but also the various memoirs of Bush players.

114. Gugliotta, op. cit., p. A17.

115. Vice President Dan Quayle, Office of the Vice President, "Prepared Text of Remarks by the Vice President, 48th Tactical Fighter Wing, U.S. Air Force," Deployed, Saudi Arabia, January 1, 1991, p. 3.

116. Philip Shenon, "Quayle Draws Ovation on Visit to the Troops," *The New York Times*, January 1, 1991, p. A6; Quayle, *Standing Firm*, pp. 219-20; and U.S. News & World Report, *Triumph without Victory*, p. 197.

117. "Quayle Sees Kuwait Emir on Funding," *The Washington Post*, January 2, 1991, p. A22.

118. Ibid.; Quayle, *Standing Firm*, pp. 218-19; and U.S. News & World Report, *Triumph without Victory*, p. 197.

119. "Quayle Meets with Saudi Royalty and Seeks More Aid for Military," *The New York Times*, December 31, 1990, p. A6.

120. Clifford Kauss, "Top Bush Advisors Called In to Meet on Iraq Strategy," *The New York Times*, January 2, 1991, p. A6; and U.S. News & World Report, *Triumph without Victory*, p. 197.

121. Solomon, op. cit., p. 522.

122. Quayle, *Standing Firm*, p. 87.

123. Broder and Woodward, op. cit., p. A15; and Interview with Carnes Lord.

124. Ibid.

125. *The Los Angeles Times*, May 9, 1991, p. A1.

126. Interview with Kristol; and Interview with Glassman. Note: Defense Secretary Dick Cheney also had congressional experience, although he never served as a senator. Quayle was the only ex-senator.
127. Broder and Woodward, op. cit., p. A15.
128. Ibid., p. A14.
129. Interview with Glassman.
130. Interview with Kristol.
131. Video tape, "The Gulf Crisis: The Road to War," American Enterprise Institute, Washington, D.C., Brian Lapping Associates for Discovery Communications, Inc., 1992.
132. Ibid.
133. Quayle, *Standing Firm*, p. 223. For more details on Quayle's congressional role, see pp. 223-27.
134. Fred Barnes, "White House Watch: Quayle Alert," *The New Republic*, May 27, 1991, p. 12; Interview with Carnes Lord; and Interview with Joe DeSutter.
135. Video tape.
136. Broder and Woodward, op. cit., p. A14; and Duffy, op. cit., p. 22.
137. Quayle, *Standing Firm*, p. 217.
138. Broder and Woodward, op. cit., p. A14.
139. Video tape.
140. Joel K. Goldstein, *The Modern American Vice Presidency* (Princeton, N.J.: Princeton University Press, 1982), p. 104.
141. Ronald Smothers, "Quayle, in Sharp Attack, Accuses Some Democrats of 'Playing Politics' on the Gulf," *The New York Times,* December 11, 1990, p. A16.
142. Vice President Dan Quayle, Office of the Vice President, "Prepared Text of Remarks by the Vice President, Los Angeles World Affairs Council," Los Angeles, California, January 8, 1991, pp. 6-7.
143. Interview with Walsh and Barone, p. 21.
144. Dowd, op. cit., p. A13.
145. Ibid.
146. Jerry Adler, "The War Within," *Newsweek*, February 4, 1991, Vol. 117, No. 5, p. 58.
147. Vice President Dan Quayle, Office of the Vice President, "Prepared Text of Remarks by the Vice President to Military Families," Fort Bliss, Texas, February 6, 1991, p. 6.
148. Interview with Kenneth T. Walsh, "Quayle of Hussein: 'He Is Totally Irrational,'" *U.S. News & World Report*, February 18, 1991, p. 27.
149. Vice President Dan Quayle, Office of the Vice President, "Prepared Text of Remarks by the Vice President, Los Angeles World Affairs Council," Los Angeles, California, January 8, 1991, pp. 5-6.
150. Quayle, Fort Bliss speech, p. 4.
151. Vice President Dan Quayle, Office of the Vice President, "Prepared Text of Remarks by the Vice President, The Mid-America Committee," Chicago, Illinois, March 13, 1991, p. 6. For more on how a policy of "patience" or sanctions could hurt U.S. troops, allies, the fledgling nations of Eastern Europe (due to the economic impact of increased oil prices), U.S. hostages in Iraq, Kuwaiti citizens, etc., see Quayle, Seton Hall University speech, p. 8; Quayle, Los Angeles World Affairs Council speech, pp. 3-5; and

Maureen Dowd, "U.S. Rebuffs Iraq on the Palestinians," *The New York Times*, December 2, 1990, p. A18.

152. Solomon, op. cit., p. 522.

153. Duffy, op. cit., p. 22.

154. The view that the Israelis knew Quayle would be more friendly to them than Bush or Baker was confirmed by others the author interviewed. Interview with Kristol; Interview with Glassman; Interview with Lord; and Interview with DeSutter.

155. Duffy, op. cit., p. 22.

156. Interview with Kristol.

157. Quayle, *Standing Firm*, p. 229-30.

158. Barnes also reported that in the postwar period Quayle alone was adamant in telling Bush that the United States had a "moral obligation" to the Iraqi Kurds. "The president came around belatedly," wrote Barnes. This unique concern for the Kurds by the vice president in the postwar period was confirmed by Carnes Lord. Barnes, "Quayle Alert," May 27, 1991, p. 12; and Interview with Carnes Lord.

159. Interview with Kristol.

160. Video tape.

161. Walsh interview, February 18, 1991, p. 27.

162. Ibid.

163. U.S. News & World Report, *Triumph without Victory*, pp. 140-42.

164. Interview with Stephen Budiansky, "The Gulf War: The Real Target?" *U.S. News & World Report*, February 18, 1991, p. 20.

165. Charles Krauthammer, "Dan Quayle's Bum Rap," *The Washington Post*, May 10, 1991, p. A23.

166. *ABC News PrimeTime Live*, "Standing Firm," Interview Transcript, May 5, 1994, p. 8. Quayle made the same point on assassination in his memoirs. See Quayle, *Standing Firm*, p. 216.

167. Interview with Carnes Lord.

168. U.S. News & World Report, *Triumph without Victory*, p. 140.

169. Interview with Kristol.

170. Video tape.

171. Dan Quayle, *Standing Firm*, pp. 239-40.

172. Barnes, "Brilliant Pebble," April 1, 1991, p. 10.

173. Ibid.

174. Quayle, *Standing Firm*, p. 230-31.

175. Scowcroft and the NSC were not as enthusiastic about strategic defense as was Quayle and his staff. The State of the Union situation is just one example of how the vice president was able to insert pitches for strategic defense into various Bush speeches. Barnes, "Brilliant Pebble," April 1, 1991, p. 11; and Interview with Carnes Lord.

176. Interview with Joe DeSutter, former foreign-policy and national security advisor to both vice presidents Quayle and Gore, via telephone from Washington, D.C., January 23, 1997.

177. Walsh interview, February 18, 1991, p. 27. Also, see Quayle, *Standing Firm*, p. 231.

178. Vice President Dan Quayle, Office of the Vice President, "Prepared Text of Remarks by the Vice President, The Mid-America Committee," Chicago, Illinois, March 13, 1991, p. 3.

179. Quayle, Fort Bliss speech, p. 3.
180. Ibid.
181. Hubert H. Humphrey, "Changes in the Vice Presidency," *Current History*, 1974, Vol. 67, pp. 58-59; Goldstein, op. cit., p. 146.
182. Goldstein, op. cit., p. 146.
183. Interview with Kristol.
184. Ibid.

Chapter 7
A "Presidential" Vice President? Al Gore (1993-)

"To some, [Gore] seems more presidential than the president."
The Economist, *September 10, 1994*

We must make the rescue of the environment the central organizing principle for civilization. . . . It is not merely in the service of analogy that I have referred so often to the struggles against Nazi and communist totalitarianism, because I believe the emerging effort to save the environment is a continuation of these struggles.
Al Gore, Earth in the Balance

"Al Gore's grim vision (of the earth) is . . . nonsense. . . . The only serious question is whether the vice president is just another scare monger or a man whose zealotry has deprived him of balanced and rational thought."
George Melloan, Wall Street Journal, *July 12, 1993*

Introduction

Nowhere in this study is the idiosyncratic variable more apparent than in the case of Vice President Al Gore. He has been very active and influential in foreign policy, due in large part to the unique circumstances in which he finds himself. Chief among these are a president who came to office with less experience in foreign policy than his own vice president, not to mention a weak reputation in that area early in office. It was at that point—in the administration's first two years—that quotes such as the above from *The Economist* began popping up. The view of Gore as a "presidential vice president" was primarily derived from a low view of President Bill Clinton. Clinton was very unpopular at the time and suffered one of history's most stunning rebukes of a president during the 1994 mid-term elections. During that election, not a single Republican incumbent lost a reelection bid at the congressional or gubernatorial level across the United States, and the GOP claimed both chambers of Congress for the first time in nearly five decades.

Moreover, Gore's initial thrust into foreign affairs was provided by a very willing and passive secretary of state, Warren Christopher. That beneficence granted by the secretary of state has not reversed course under Secretary of State Madeleine Albright. On December 6, 1996, this became immediately apparent as Albright, during the very press conference in which Clinton announced her nomination, took the highly unusual gesture of thanking not just the president but also his vice president. With Albright's support, in December 1997, during a weeklong visit to Asia, the vice president became the highest ranking U.S. official to visit China in eight years.

Like his immediate predecessors—vice presidents Mondale, Bush, and Quayle—Vice President Gore has traveled abroad to engage in substantive issue-oriented meetings with foreign officials, often involving bargaining for the Clinton administration or announcing key U.S. objectives, which, as we shall see, he has done at major U.N. conferences and other venues. Gore has continued the trend whereby modern vice presidents' "foreign-policy" roles are no longer confined to "wreath-laying missions" at funerals of foreign dignitaries. In some respects, it is fitting that the profiles of the five vice presidents in this study ends with Vice President Gore. Not only is he at the end chronologically, but he has performed most of, and added to, the tasks of the others, with the exception of chairing a major interagency crisis committee, *a la* Vice President Bush. He has added a couple of features that none of the other four were fortunate enough to undertake: he co-chairs three foreign-policy groups outside of the White House: the Gore-Chernomyrdin Commission, the Gore-Mubarak Commission, named for Egyptian President Hosni Mubarak, and the Gore-Mbeki Commission, named for South African Deputy President Thabo Mbeki.

Of these three commissions, the most notable is the Gore-Chernomyrdin Commission. In his role as the administration's "main spokesman on Russia," Gore established a critical link with Prime Minister Viktor Chernomyrdin. Their ongoing relationship was called the main channel between the White House and Moscow. His relationship has continued with the revolving door of multiple Russian prime ministers since Chernomyrdin. Throughout most of the Clinton years, it was correctly reported that Gore has signed numerous consequential agreements with Russia and Kazakhstan. As this book goes to press, however, the work of the Gore-Chernomyrdin commission is beginning to come under fierce attack by mainstream media sources such as the *Washington Post*. Under attack is not merely the commission generally, but the specific role of Gore himself. This chapter lays out the points of contention.

Many initial assessments of Gore's role were hyperbolic. "Gore is playing a more important role in this administration than any previous vice president has played," said Thomas Mann, director of governmental studies at the Brookings Institution. "It's really quite extraordinary." Mann's remarks came barely a year into the Clinton administration—long before Gore received substantive duties, particularly in foreign policy. Likewise, Richard Berke of *The New York Times* agreed that in just one year, Gore had given the office of vice president its most consequential place in history.[1] Carter Eskew, who was Gore's media advisor during his 1988 presidential run, asserted, "If you have one defining event in your entire vice presidency, you're lucky. What was Bush's? Iran-Contra. What was Quayle's? Was it 'potatoe' or just getting chosen? But Al has had this series of huge successes."[2] Secretary of State Christopher called Gore "the most influential vice president in history."[3] President Bill Clinton himself has stated: "I believe with all my heart that Al Gore will go down in American history as the most influential and productive vice president in our country's history."[4] Larry Sabato, University of Virginia political science professor, added, "Compared with other vice presidents, he's clearly in a different league. In the public's eye, he may turn out to be the most active and most substantive vice president ever."[5]

While many such assessments were exaggerated at the time, Sabato's makes an important distinction by noting that Gore is especially active "in the public's eye." Gore has not received the negative publicity that hounded his predecessor, with the exception of that offered by conservative publications, columnists, and the nation's few right-wing editorial boards. Nonetheless, despite numerous stretches about Vice President Gore's role being unprecedented in the history of the American vice presidency, there is no doubt that it has been substantial—and that clearly includes his involvement in the nation's foreign policy. In the realm of international affairs, Gore has at least extended the post-World War II trend toward greater vice-presidential involvement. In this sense, Paul Light is wise to assert that Gore has succeeded in "extending the model that was there to its ultimate degree."[6] Moreover, while Gore's list of duties may not be unprecedented, his influence with the president likely is. The only vice president who seemed to rival him in that area was Mondale. This chapter underscores Gore's foreign-policy role within the Clinton administration and the reasons for it. In so doing, it also provides crucial policy insights that will be re-examined in the final (next) chapter.[7]

Last, a warning: This chapter aims to illuminate Gore's role in foreign policy, not to assess or comment on his beliefs. One small exception is the section on Gore's environmentalism. Any responsible examination of Gore is forced to acknowledge and grapple with his views on the environment, which are very much part of his foreign-policy beliefs. The vice president's environmental views are, to put it mildly, alarming. As will be noted later, some of his statements about the environment—made publicly and written in his book—are shocking and even outrageous. In all seriousness, Gore's *Earth in the Balance* is possibly the single most radical manifesto ever penned by an American vice president before, during, or after his vice presidency. Importantly, Gore himself says the book is his "heart and soul" and repeatedly and unhesitantly stands by it to this day.[8]

Gore's Background and Selection

Before reaching the Clinton administration, Gore spent sixteen years as a member of the House and Senate. He has run for the presidency and maintains solid supporters that have always desired him to be president. This is an ambition he and his family have always professed. "I would like to be president one day," Gore stated candidly years before his 2000 candidacy.[9] His 1988 run for the presidency was largely uneventful, as he garnered limited support. Ironically, one of the only memorable moments of the campaign has been ignored by political liberals and most of the media but is at times brought up by political conservatives: The infamous Willie Horton ad used by President Bush against Governor Michael Dukakis in the 1988 presidential campaign was actually first began by Senator Gore, who used it in the Democratic primaries.[10]

He was a member of the Senate Armed Services Committee and often found himself on the opposite side of his committee colleague, Senator Dan Quayle, on the issue of missile defense and the Strategic Defense Initiative; the latter of which Gore opposed out of concern for how it might conflict with the ABM treaty.[11] Moreover, his optimism about the abilities of science and technology does not extend to SDI. On other issues, Gore has always been an unabashed supporter of Israel. In the Senate, he assailed President Bush for failing to stop the genocide in Bosnia. An issue that has particular importance—for both its modern relevance and Gore's dedication to it—concerns the senator's position on the U.S.-Iraq conflict.

One of the things that has made Gore stand out among Democrats has been his political independence and proclivity to take moderate stances on foreign-policy issues within a party whose majority of members have become increasingly liberal. A notable example was his support—rare among Senate Democrats—for President Bush's 1991 use of military force in the Persian Gulf. In his January 12 Senate statement announcing his backing of authorization for the Bush administration's use of force in the Persian Gulf, Gore expressed ambivalence about his position, noting that he had alternated back and forth in recent months over whether he felt the administration should pursue a course of continued sanctions or military action:

> My decision today is the product of an intense, may I say excruciating, effort to find my way to a place as close to a sense of the ultimate truth in this matter as I am capable of getting. I've struggled to confront this issue in its bare essence—to separate what I think is fact, or at least highly probable, from what I think is false, or at least highly improbable—to strike a balance and to take my stand. . . .
>
> I felt, up until recently, especially after the hearings in which I played an active role, questioning, probing, searching for the truth, I felt that I

would support a move to continue the sanctions and hold open the option of force at a later time. As I searched my heart on this issue over the last few days with special intensity after we all heard the Secretary of State enunciate the word regrettably in Geneva, I found myself feeling that if I voted for the Mitchell nonresolution I would do so hoping that it did not prevail. I found myself feeling even late last night that since it now appears that there is a majority in favor of the other point of view that it would pass and will pass regardless of how I vote. I found myself pulled once again to support the Mitchell nonresolution, speaking only of the process I've gone through.

And, Mr. President, I feel that I owe it to those who are there [in the Persian Gulf] prepared to make the ultimate sacrifice, to give the best judgment of my head and my heart on what this nation should now do. I cannot reconcile myself to a point of view and a vote that says in effect, we will let this deadline come and go and try the sanctions perhaps until the next window, next August when military operations would again become feasible.[12]

The statement, ironically, was a rather cryptic and weak endorsement along the lines of that made at the time by Governor Bill Clinton[13]—of which President Bush took advantage during the campaign as a case instance in the art of waffling on a key foreign-policy issue.[14] Later, however, Gore would become more focused, even becoming an outspoken critic of President Bush for not following up more strongly in Iraq, especially in regard to Saddam's lingering position of power and the status of the Kurdish refugees.

Senator Gore wrote an op-ed for *The New York Times* stating that while he supported the president's moves to force Saddam to comply with the terms of the Gulf cease-fire, he disagreed with the administration's "view of Saddam Hussein as an acceptable part of the landscape." In essence, Gore believed the Bush policy of allowing Hussein to remain in power was wrong. In the op-ed, he did not focus on the difficult issue of what happens if Saddam is forced from power, particularly in the sense of the ominous leadership vacuum that would take place; instead, he suggested policies aimed at toppling Hussein and his Baathist regime—both of which he felt were possible. "In general, the formula for deposing him involves [three] elements," he averred: "blocking his access to international support, building up his opponents and cutting off resources for rebuilding his military machine." Within these headings, he suggested a number of moves. He wanted to begin diminishing Saddam's support through overt and covert methods designed to inform Iraqis and the Arab world of the long list of war crimes committed against Kuwait. He also suggested that the United States "isolate Saddam Hussein by improving our relations with Iran as rapidly as conditions permit. Meanwhile, the central U.S. role in Mideast peace talks, from which Iraq is completely excluded, has the benefit of destroying his usefulness to the Palestinians." At the same time, Gore favored helping Iraqi opposition forces—most in exile—unify and better organize.[15] This echoed calls he made in the past for the Bush administration to support the Iraqi Kurdish opposition in northern Iraq and anti-Saddam Arab groups fighting for their existence in the south.[16]

Additionally, in the op-ed, Gore advocated tightening the "economic tourniquet," stating that "the message to the Iraqi people has to be that Saddam Hussein is not only powerless to end their misery but is its cause." Displaying his belief in supply-side measures to halt nuclear proliferation, Gore also emphasized blocking Iraqi access to knowledge and technology: "That means doing everything to halt Iraqi work in space science and nuclear physics to the extent they depend on equipment, services or training—including university training—from countries with advanced capabilities." Finally, the senator demanded that the United States do a better job exposing the foreign suppliers that Iraq used to acquire nuclear, chemical, and biological materials. "If this means deeply embarrassing certain friendly governments, so be it," Gore asserted. "Otherwise, nothing will change." In a somewhat bold move, he specifically cited Switzerland as "a well-known haven for arms dealers and proliferators," stating that it was "time for the Swiss to live up to their image of clean rectitude." Gore concluded by writing:

> We can no more look forward to a constructive long-term relationship with Saddam Hussein than we could hope to housebreak a cobra. . . . Sooner or later, he will go. Sooner is better. And with him, the entire Ba-athist rule by terror has to go as well, or we may simply exchange one brutal character for the next.[17]

Gore made some harsh statements about the president's Persian Gulf decisions, stating quite dramatically that Bush's handling of the postwar insurrection in Iraq, "revives the most bitter memories of humankind's worst moments."[18] He also blasted the administration for basing its policy on a fear of the consequences of undermining Saddam, calling it a "cruel irony and mistake in judgment."[19] He felt that Bush should have done more to back the Kurds, stating that the United States should warn Iraq that it is "prepared to seek ways" to help Kurdish forces if Iraq continues to pursue them."[20] On earlier prewar criticism of Bush, Gore rejected the president's warnings that Iraq was on the verge of developing a nuclear bomb, contending that Iraq was nowhere near having that capacity and that the president was exploiting the rationale to gain support for his Persian Gulf prewar policy. Bush replied: "If he [Gore] wants to gamble on the future about the construction of atomic weapons by Saddam Hussein, I don't."[21] It is now universally known that Saddam was within one to two years of having a workable nuclear device at the time of his invasion of Kuwait.

Gore's tendency for independence among liberal Democrats appealed to Clinton. The senator was known for sometimes taking moderate stances on foreign-policy issues. Clinton was also initially attracted to Gore because of his credentials as a so-called New Democrat—a belief in a smaller, more efficient, entrepreneurial government that breaks with much of the hard liberalism of the modern Democratic party. The group responsible for articulating and popularizing the New Democrat philosophy was Al From's Democratic Leadership Council, of which Gore was a founding member and Clinton its chairman before resigning to run for president. DLC ideas became the core of the Clinton-Gore ticket. Policy off-shoots of its philosophy include administration initiatives aimed at reinventing government, welfare reform, national service, etc. (At this point, most observers seem to believe that Gore reflects the New Democrat philosophy more than Clinton. In part this may be due to the president's early support of a health-care reform plan that was decidedly a big-government initiative.)

The two men always viewed one another equally. Peter Boyer maintains that when Clinton approached Gore about the vice presidency in July 1992, it was more of a "negotiation between equals than a tryout" for Gore. Although Clinton had the nomination locked up, he was still plagued by questions about infidelity and avoiding the Vietnam War. Gore made up for questions about Clinton's marriage through his own solid family background; countered the draft problem by his own military service in Vietnam;[22] and shored up Clinton's foreign-policy inexperience via his Senate work on issues of arms control and other areas. He would also be savvy to the ways of Washington—helpful to an outsider like Clinton. (Since both men were Southerners, region was not a key factor in Clinton's choice.) Gore may have provided a boost to Clinton's chances. After the choice of Gore was announced, and Perot temporarily left the race, Clinton surged to a ten-point lead in the polls that propelled him to victory.[23]

The President-Vice President Relationship

The relationship between Vice President Gore and President Clinton surely was not hurt during the 1992 campaign. In general, the two men have appeared to get along quite well from the outset. The only perceptible public strains appeared when Gore tried to distance himself from President Clinton's character problems during his 2000 presidential bid. Breaking his long silence on the scandal, in 1999 Gore angered Clinton when referring to the president's conduct with Monica Lewinsky as "inexcusable" and "terribly wrong."[24]

The two men also seem to have an unusual relationship whereby the vice president's input is extremely influential. Their kinship and Gore's style and personality have made him a force in the administration, resulting in what is likely an unprecedented influence by a vice president. Gore describes himself as playing a "general-advisor role" to the president, counseling him on virtually every major issue.[25] Numerous reports buttress the assertion that Gore, along with or behind First Lady Hillary Rodham Clinton, is the president's closest day-to-day advisor.[26] William Safire rates Gore—whom he calls "grimly obsequious to the president in public, candid in private"—second highest in the administration in terms of clout, behind only Hillary Rodham.[27] "In this case, the conventional wisdom is right," said former senior advisor George Stephanopoulos.[28]

Aside from his foreign-policy experience, White House advisors maintain that Gore brings several critical traits the president lacks, such as self-discipline. In an odd twist in the standard president-vice presidential relationship, Gore reportedly convinced the president to pace himself, get his schedule under control, and put aside more private time to collect his thoughts.[29] *The Economist* states: "Associates have become generous in their praise of [Gore's] fine mind, his pleasant presence and (in contrast to the public Gore-the-bore) his private wit. One senior official calls him 'the strongest and steadiest advisor that the president has.' In a sometimes tempestuous administration he can be a calming influence, including on the president himself."[30] In nearly all reports on Gore, his personal qualities are deliberately featured in a positive light when compared to Clinton's. Praise of Gore from many Democrats, including within the administration, is often a veiled criticism of Clinton's shortcomings.

When Gore's aides describe how he works, they often end up praising the qualities of discipline and focus that Clinton allegedly lacks. "He will set aside large blocks of time and will sit down and think these things through," said Gore's chief of staff, Jack Quinn. "He doesn't do anything off the cuff. He never shoots from the hip. He is thoughtful, he is prepared, he is careful."[31] "Gore is disciplined, focused, very oriented to decision-making and to avoiding having problems fester," said one administration official, echoing a very common theme. "To him, governing is a series of decisions, many of them uncomfortable, you have to make and move on."[32] According to many reports, while Gore agonizes over decisions, he eventually decides.[33] (This was evident in the aforementioned statement he made as a senator concerning the dispatch of U.S. troops to the Persian Gulf.) "Clinton is a natural in a way that Gore will never be," said an advisor who is close to both men. "On the other hand, Gore has all the will and determination and discipline that would serve him very well as president."[34]

In another peculiar twist on the typical president-vice president relationship, Gore finds himself frustrated and dismayed by the chaos ensuing within the White House as a result of Clinton's decision-making difficulties.[35] Clinton's tendency to avoid firm decisions has raised the ire of the vice president himself. A dramatic illustration of this comes from Bob Woodward's book on the inner workings of the Clinton administration. Gore reportedly once got so frustrated with Clinton's indecisiveness that, after an incident marked by inconclusive rambling on a particular domestic issue, Clinton turned to Gore and asked, "What can I do?" In reply, Gore answered tersely: "You can get with the goddamn program!"[36] According to Peter Boyer, the unnerving lack of discipline in the White House—numerous voices urging varying directions—led Gore to persuade Clinton to replace his friend Mack McLarty, the chief of staff, with Leon Panetta, in hopes of imposing a measure of order in the White House.[37]

Early on in the administration, when mismanagement had much of the White House in a shambles, Clinton reportedly turned to the vice president for advice. Gore released his own chief of staff, Roy Neel, to help Mack McLarty straighten out the mess. In part to help moderate the views of the administration, Gore urged Clinton to bring in longtime GOP strategist David Gergen as a senior counselor and communications czar.[38] When a key official is being considered for the White House, he or she routinely passes Gore's scrutiny. Among other examples, the vice president reportedly blocked the appointment of the Pentagon's Marguerite Sullivan to a cabinet secretary post in order to put his own choice in place.[39]

White House aides say the president has become so dependent on Gore that he does not make any decision of significance without him. "I cannot imagine the president making a major decision before talking it through with the vice president," Stephanopoulos said. Sometimes, Clinton has held up big decisions just to await Gore's say. In December 1994, when Gore was in Moscow and the president's advisors were reviewing their first round of budget cuts in the wake of the brutal midterm elections and pondering whether to propose tax breaks for the middle class, Clinton held off until Gore returned. All the players had to come back for a second meeting so Gore could hear the proposals firsthand. When Clinton was unsure whether to eliminate the Department of Energy as part of the streamlining of the government, Gore pushed him into a decision to keep the agency.[40]

Clinton clearly respects Gore's opinions.

"At the end of the day, there is no one who can buck up the president more, who can engage him more on a subject area, who can represent him better," said presidential assistant Mark Gearan. "You can search but you won't find one major policy decision in this administration that President Clinton made without discussing it with the vice president. Just doesn't happen."[41] "In meetings, when a lot of people talk, you'll see the president looking around the room," said Mike McCurry, the White House spokesman. "When Gore talks, the president is absolutely riveted." Gore has emerged stronger than ever as the president's public sidekick now that Hillary Rodham Clinton, in free-fall since the disastrous release of the administration's health-care plan, wields her influence mostly in private.[42]

Evidence provides a picture in which Gore and Clinton act as equal partners, where Gore feels secure enough to openly state his own views even if they are contrary to Clinton's.[43] Democratic Representative Mike Synar of Oklahoma says that Gore's stature with the president means he is "not just a partner [to Clinton] but an equal partner."[44] Clinton reportedly encourages Gore to speak up and disagree with him and the going line, which he often does.[45]

Over the first four years, the vice president emerged as President Clinton's most trusted official advisor and his ultimate troubleshooter, the one most likely to seize opportunities and enforce decisions. Gore's partisans said he had finally come into his own. But, in fact, the reality may be that in an administration that was plagued by disorganization and indecision, inexperienced aides in some top jobs and power vacuums in key agencies, Gore became markedly appealing. Disillusioned by Clinton early on, Democrats who once doubted Gore's ability to shine in a national campaign began to quietly whisper about his presidential prospects.[46] "To some," *The Economist* contended, Gore "seems more presidential than the president."[47]

Early on, Gore was such a strong presence that during the 1994-95 period he had to quell speculation about him challenging his own president's 1996 reelection bid.[48] His approval ratings were regularly higher than the president's. Playing the role of faithful vice president, he asserted: "President Clinton is going to be renominated and is going to run a very strong campaign. I predict that he will be re-elected to a second term."[49] He is playing the proper loyal supporter role a vice president plays. "Everything I do is according to one simple game plan: how can I best help President Clinton be the best President he can possibly be," says Gore.[50] "And so my own record as vice president is necessarily obscured to a significant measure because so much of my energy goes into trying to help him."[51]

Gore's Foreign-Policy Role within the Administration

Not surprisingly, Gore's sizable influence and positive relationship with the president has paid off in the area of foreign policy. This section examines his foreign-policy role, including the origins of his involvement, as well as his role as the president's 'attack dog' during campaign fights, and as an administration spokesman. Unlike other chapters in this study—which focused on one to three specific case studies for each vice president in foreign policy—this one gives a larger number of examples with more brief descriptions.[52] In so doing, it also illuminates Gore's place among the Clinton administration's defense and foreign-policy team.

Among the Clinton administration's major foreign-policy concerns are: pushing reform in Russia, modernizing NATO, concentrating on Asia, promoting peace in the Middle East, and focusing on issues such as non-proliferation and human rights. Also at the top of the priority list is what the White House terms "economic security," which includes an emphasis on driving trade issues like NAFTA and GATT. Even the environment, population growth, and women's issues have become "foreign-policy issues" in the Clinton administration, in large part due to the influence of members like Gore and Hillary Rodham Clinton. Nearly all of these issues has witnessed a role by Vice President Gore. In part, Gore's emergence can be explained by the general foreign-policy leadership vacuum that was so prominent during the first four years of the administration.

In mid-October 1993, to address the problem of the leadership vacuum and the president's uneven policy management, Secretary of State Christopher asked President Clinton to commit himself to a weekly meeting with his top foreign-policy advisors. "While the president has agreed, the schedule has yet to be regularized," reported a December 1993 article in the *Wall Street Journal*. "The daily intelligence briefings aren't daily and usually are rushed. And aides say that they are still looking for a way to carve out more 'quality time' between the president and NSA Lake."[53]

Clearly, a vacuum existed in the White House.

Weeks before the Gore-Perot November 1993 NAFTA debate, Clinton decided to try to shore up his foreign-policy team as a result of unceasing attacks on his leadership, policy management, and other matters. But the president did not want to fire any of his principals. Hence, he approached Gore in October and asked him to speak out more on foreign affairs. Gore's two biggest boosters in the White House, Gergen and McLarty, strongly encouraged it. There were no formal discussions on the move, nor any consultations with Congress. There was no announcement.[54] Additional reports say Clinton's move was inspired by Secretary of State Christopher, to whom the charge of missing leadership in international affairs was also ascribed. Christopher's early stumbles abroad resulted in calls for his resignation by a number of sources, such as the influential *Economist*. Taking a cue from Secretary of State Dean Acheson, Christopher soon learned the fine art of delegation. A beneficiary of that delegation was the vice president, who received an enhanced foreign-policy role in large part due to the behest of Christopher, who urged Clinton after a series of foreign-policy setbacks in the fall of 1993 to give Gore a more active role.[55] "I can only be in one place at a time," Christopher explained. "No Secretary of State can do it all. It would be foolish if he thought he could. One reason I'm so confident is that the vice president is thoroughly reliable."[56]

Gore then went on to perform tasks that in other administrations were reserved strictly for the secretary of state, national security advisor, and even the president.[57] "Foreign policy is Clinton's weak area, so this makes sense," Larry Sabato commented. "It's a wise move for [Gore], it's a wise move for Clinton, and it helps all of them in various ways."[58] Behind the scenes, Gore began telling Clinton that he had to pay more attention to foreign policy, act decisively, and accept the consequences.[59] He has since helped fill the vacuum. Clinton's lack of passion for foreign policy, combined with Christopher's willingness to cede vast amounts of his authority to other agencies, have given Gore the chance to do diplomacy.[60]

Regardless of who was responsible for Gore's increased role, his influence is unmistakable—as recognized by the then-secretary of state. Due to continuing difficulties in scheduling and securing regular meetings with Clinton, Christopher instead arranged to meet with Gore every Friday. "I know he'll be a very influential figure if we talk something through," said Christopher. Gore "is relied on more heavily than any vice president has ever been in the past. Not just in foreign policy, but as far as I can tell, across the board."[61] Of course, while this reflects positively on Gore, it may raise questions about the stature and leadership of the then-secretary of state, president, and rest of the Clinton foreign-policy team.

According to Fred Barnes, Gore's emergence in foreign policy became a sensitive issue at the White House. Ironically, his job as a major spokesman on foreign policy threatened to diminish the role of Secretary of State Christopher, who, of course, helped boost Gore's role in the first place. To ease Christopher's fears, White House aides insisted that Gore was not displacing him, just supplementing him. They also worried about the vice president's success coming at the expense of the president.[62] (The latter seemed to be unfolding.) Nonetheless, Christopher himself suggested the role for Gore and Clinton happily leaned on him for advice.

Gore's decisiveness, combined with Clinton's indecisiveness, worked in the foreign-policy realm to create a leadership role for the vice president. "I think [Gore] helps the president to arrive at a conclusion that the president knows he has to make, and to do it a lot quicker," said a former White House aide. Peter J. Boyer quotes a White House foreign-policy advisor who has observed Clinton and Gore in "countless" meetings:

> [Gore is] very good at forcing decisions, at bringing issues to closure. His stock-in-trade, in part, is that he does not like to let things linger. He likes to get things done and move on, for better or worse. He may make mistakes, but he does like to get it done. In meeting after meeting where I've been with him, his role is wrapping things up at the end and saying [to President Clinton], "We need to get this done here. You've got to make this decision. It's time for a decision." I think there is a tendency in a lot of meetings with him, when others are in the room, to look to him to sort of do the benediction and bring it to conclusion. He has that relationship with Clinton to make it happen.[63]

Like his predecessor, Gore begins his daily foreign-policy activities by joining the president, along with the NSA and deputy NSA, and (occasionally) the White House chief of staff, for a briefing from a representative of the CIA on developments overnight in world affairs.[64] Gore is a statutory member of the NSC. He also attends all of Clinton's White House meetings with foreign leaders.[65] Clinton and Gore have lunch together once per week.[66] At the beginning of the administration, Gore made his "foreign-policy" priorities clear to the staff: technology, the environment, and nonproliferation.[67]

On foreign policy, he selectively chose areas of interest to him. He also benefits from a rare situation for a vice president: his national security advisor, Leon Fuerth—a former foreign service officer and arms-control expert[68]—sits in on meetings with administration foreign-policy advisors as well as Oval Office meetings, allowing Gore to monitor decisions and better influence policy.[69] Specifically, Fuerth sits at the table in the all-important deliberations of the Deputies Committee, first run by Sandy Berger. It consists of the number two or three officials from each of the national security departments. Four or more times weekly, the group meets in the Situation Room in the White House basement. In two- to three-hour sessions, members hammer out policy options for their bosses.[70] It is an interagency group that manages foreign-policy issues and crises.[71] The committee has in the past been criticized for dropping the ball on Somalia and Haiti.[72]

There is more proof of the level of Fuerth's influence. Joe DeSutter, the only advisor from Quayle's staff who stayed on with Gore, says that Leon Fuerth had a "determinate voice" in every decision that went before the NSC. He had a vote on NSC decisions, whereas Quayle's NSAs did not. In fact, says DeSutter, if the president's NSA, Anthony Lake, advised something to Clinton that Fuerth disagreed with, "it would be a significant event. It would not be inconsequential." He added that it "wouldn't be obvious" who the president would side with in such a disagreement, particularly since Clinton understands that Fuerth speaks for Gore, who, to the president, truly is the second-highest person in the U.S. government.[73]

There are examples of how Gore has benefited from Fuerth's presence. In Bosnia, for instance, Fuerth—as part of his duties on the Deputies Committee—was given the task of overseeing sanctions against the Serbs. As events would dictate, such a task became a primary pillar of U.S. policy in trying to settle the war in the Balkans.[74] A memo written by Fuerth at the request of Gore taking issue with a proposal to lift sanctions against Serbia became a list of the essential U.S. conditions with allies and Russia when it came to easing sanctions on Serbia.[75]

In an administration not known for adventurism abroad, Gore has emerged as one of the White House's leading hawks.[76] According to *U.S. News & World Report*, before ordering a military strike against Saddam Hussein in June 1993 in retaliation for a foiled assassination attempt on President Bush, Clinton consulted extensively with Gore, who steered him firmly toward retaliation well before the formal FBI and CIA reports on the Iraqi attempt on Bush's life were complete. Gore undertook his own formal inquiry into the assassination plot, working through his national security advisor, Fuerth. The vice president concluded that retaliation was absolutely necessary. Doing nothing, Gore told Clinton, would make the president seem weak and rekindle old fears that Democrats are too squeamish about using military force. The highly positive public reaction to the strike confirmed Clinton's respect for Gore's judgment on such matters.[77] Gore's action here is laudable for another reason: Up to that point, the retaliatory strike on Iraq was one of the few examples of Clinton toughness cited by critics of the administration's foreign policy. And, it turns out, the move took place primarily at the behest of Gore.

In other displays of sternness, it was Gore who acted as former President Carter's conduit to the White House during his forays in North Korea and Haiti.[78] In that regard, it was also Gore who kept Carter at bay when he was looking to negotiate a deal with Fidel Castro during the August-September 1994 Cuban-refugee situation.[79] Gore took on the task of firmly telling Carter to stay in Atlanta. While others in the administration have been timid about the use of force, Gore, according to longtime friend and *New Republic* owner Martin Peretz, "thinks that arms and armies are there to be used."[80]

Sometimes, however, Gore gets carried away in his role. He once said that the World Bank had imposed intolerably harsh conditions on Russia.[81] Acting on that belief during a visit to Moscow in December 1993, he demanded that the World Bank and International Monetary Fund lend more money to Russia, saying that he did not care if his statements provoked a "diplomatic incident." As it turned out, they did. The protests that followed caused Gore to soften his criticism. In late 1993, Gore decided to spice up a speech in Mexico City that he thought "lacked a center," one of his aides said, by calling for a hemispheric summit meeting. Although he had consulted with NSA Tony Lake, who got the go-ahead from the president, the announcement stunned the Latins and blindsided most of the State Department.[82]

The following offers specific examples of Gore's various foreign-policy tasks and roles. Unlike other chapters in this study, this one briefly looks at ten different areas of Gore's foreign-policy involvement, from his spokesman role to his activities in Russia and the Ukraine.

Gore as a Foreign-Policy Spokesman

Vice President Gore's foreign-policy duties include that of a spokesman at home and abroad on global issues. This role started early. For various reasons, from pitching his own projects to stumping for Democrats to speaking on behalf of the administration, Gore has traveled throughout the country, visiting forty-five of fifty states as of the end of June 1995.[83] These duties at times allow him to be involved in or speak out on foreign-policy issues. He has given many speeches on foreign policy, appeared often on television to discuss and promote the administration's agenda, and has even hosted "town meetings" in the former Soviet Union. These roles began early. Witness his January 17, 1993 appearance on NBC's "Meet the Press," where the vice president-elect was interviewed by Tim Russert, Tom Brokaw, and Andrea Mitchell on the incoming administration and problems in Somalia, Serbia, and Iraq.[84] Most everyone remembers his debate with Ross Perot on CNN. Gore held press conferences in Jordan with King Hussein. There are many more examples, some of which will be referred to as they present themselves in this chapter.

To be sure, Gore has not escaped ceremonial visits, such as the 50th anniversary of the Allies' victory over Nazi Germany, where he and Western European leaders met in Germany to observe the occasion. But he has also made such trips with the added intention of making key foreign-policy announcements. For example, his first major speech abroad was in Poland on April 20, 1993, where he marked the 50th anniversary of the Warsaw ghetto uprising. While in Poland, he seized the opportunity to offer the administration's position on the principles and future of U.S.-Polish relations.[85] He also took advantage of the situation by meeting with Lech Walesa and Israeli Prime Minister Yitzhak Rabin, who was on hand for the commemoration.[86]

Gore asserted that since taking office, both he and the president had met with almost all of the leaders of every central and Eastern European nation and many of the leaders of the Soviet republics.[87] He meets with foreign leaders when they come to Washington. In February 1994, to cite one example, he and NSA Lake met with South Korea's foreign minister, Han Sung Joo, who was in Washington to discuss the North Korea nuclear issue.[88]

Finally, Gore's spokesman role was facilitated by the initial aforementioned bumbling in foreign policy by chief members of the administration. Occasionally he gets called upon or volunteers to clean-up a problem. In one example early in the administration, President Clinton told *The New York Times* that he wanted to "depersonalize" the American conflict with Saddam Hussein. The comment was reported as a dramatic change from Bush's policy, which had been to insist on the dictator's removal before U.S. relations with Iraq could be resumed. Clinton reacted with anger and confusion, insisting that no policy change had been made. Christopher, testifying to Congress that day, coolly backed away from the gaffe and decided not to act—as did NSA Lake. Gore stepped in and somberly stated that he would go on a talk show the next day to place the policy back in line.[89]

Gore as a Campaign "Attack Dog" on Foreign Policy

As an offshoot of Gore's spokesman activities, the vice president has assumed a Spiro Agnew-like "pit bull" or "attack dog" role, particularly during political campaigns and on some foreign-policy issues. During campaigns presidential candidates spend some of their time blasting opponents but typically try to curtail the bitterness of their remarks for the purpose of appearing statesmanlike. Consequently, someone else must assume responsibility for attacking critics. The vice president is often chosen for the role.

Gore concedes such a mission. "As the campaign season begins," he noted, "clearly part of my role will be how can I best insure that Bill Clinton is reelected."[90] He hit the campaign trail with candidates and made television appearances promoting the Democratic party in general. Interestingly, since assuming the vice presidency, Gore's role on the campaign stump has become especially salient due to the fact that congressional candidates preferred to have *his* public support rather than that of the president, who, for example, was extremely unpopular at the time of the 1994 mid-term elections. A *Business Week* article shortly before the 1994 mid-term elections claimed that Gore was being booked for twice as many campaign stops as Clinton, as his popularity rose while the president's dropped precipitously.[91] Clinton's name was so poisonous in Gore's home state of Tennessee that when the vice president traveled there to campaign for his old friend Jim Sasser, he and Sasser managed to give eight speeches in four Tennessee cities without once mentioning Bill Clinton's name.[92]

The attack-dog role began for Gore during the 1992 presidential campaign and only gotten nastier, beginning with his attacks on President Bush and hitting a crescendo via some nasty personal statements he made about Virginia Senatorial candidate Ollie North. Both instances also allowed him to speak out on foreign-policy matters.

On Bush, the Clinton staff had a 1992 campaign plan that called for the vice-presidential nominee—rather than Clinton himself—to attack President Bush on Iran Contra.[93] In a sharp and personal attack on Bush, Senator Gore on a September 1992 campaign stop questioned the president's explanation of his role in the Iran-contra affair, stopping short of calling him a liar. In remarks inserted into his basic campaign speech, Gore repeatedly referred to Bush's "credibility canyon." "George Bush is still saying he didn't know anything about one of the most controversial policies of the Reagan administration," said Gore. "Now we have some reasons to wonder about the story George Bush has told." In a strategic sense, Gore was raising questions about Bush's veracity and character at a time when new questions were raised about explanations by Governor Clinton on his avoidance of the Vietnam draft—although Gore claimed his remarks were not an attempt to deflect the character issue from Clinton.[94]

But the campaign remarks about Bush were nothing compared to those Gore prepared for former Iran-Contra figure Ollie North—on whom Gore had no problem applying the word liar. The remarks on North should be placed in context. As time progressed to the 1994 mid-term elections, President Clinton was facing one of history's most stunning rebukes of a sitting president. Incredibly, after all the votes were tallied, not a single Republican incumbent in the entire country lost a race for the Senate, House, or a governorship. Rising Democratic stars like Oklahoma Rep. Dave McCurdy were tossed from office in large part because of their affiliation with Clinton. The GOP would take both chambers of Congress for the first time in nearly half a century. Foreseeing much of the carnage, to the Clinton administration an even greater rebuke would be a Senate victory in nearby Virginia by Oliver North. The administration worked feverishly to prevent a North victory, and the vice president led the charge.

North had suggested that military cutbacks and a lack of White House preparation was leaving U.S. forces vulnerable to the point where the administration would be unable to repel an Iraqi attack on Kuwait. About a month before election day, Vice President Gore lashed out at North's remarks as irresponsible, dangerous and wrong, asserting that U.S. forces were fully prepared in the Persian Gulf while others were engaged in Haiti. Gore accused North of placing politics above national security. "It is despicable, it is unpatriotic, and, as is often the case with statements from Oliver North, it is also patently untrue," Gore said, adding that North should apologize and "for once in his life admit he has stated a falsehood."[95]

Pay back time would come for North a few weeks later when—ironically seizing on the type of political correctness that liberals have come to use with artful precision—accused Gore in the intervening weeks of insulting people with Down's syndrome by referring to North's supporters as "the extreme right wing, the extra-chromosome right wing." 'The Vice President's insensitive, cheap shot insulted every American by poking fun at those who have mental and physical disabilities," North told a crowd of about 300 people. "My friends, it is a moral outrage that they do these things." The vice president apologized for using "a poor choice of words."[96]

Additional salvos were fired in Alexandria, VA, on the final day of the campaign, where Gore joined North's Democratic challenger, Senator Chuck Robb, who kept up the angry personal attacks. Robb sent the crowd of more than 1,000 supporters into a frenzy by referring to the former Marine as a "document-shredding, Constitution-trashing, Commander in Chief-bashing, Congress-thrashing, uniform-shaming, Ayatollah-loving, arms-dealing, criminal-protecting, resume-enhancing, Noriega-coddling, Social Security-threatening, public school-denigrating, Swiss-banking-law-breaking, letter-faking, self-serving, election-losing, snake-oil salesman who can't tell the difference between the truth and a lie." In an encore to Robb, Gore flatly called

North a "pathological liar." Additionally, in a statement that seemed peculiar considering his and Robb's contentious words, he accused Republicans of trying "to create as much anger and hostility and discord and hatefulness as they possibly can and follow a scorched-earth political strategy, burn down the house in hopes that you'll inherit the ashes."[97]

While this book's focus is the vice president's foreign-policy role, it is useful to briefly mention here that Gore's attack-dog role in general has displayed what seems to be a mean-spiritedness by the vice president—particularly when he blasts opponents on domestic issues. Journalist Donald Lambro has deemed this trait "the dark side of Al Gore."[98]

The vice president often portrays Republicans as (at the least) extremists and (at the worst) fire-breathing demons literally afflicted with mental retardation. In 1995, he declared: "The Republican leadership is conducting a jihad against the environment in the most right-wing, extremist agenda we have seen in America in this century."[99] Worse, as will be seen later, he is very fond of Nazi metaphors when characterizing his opposition on environmental issues—language that seems to trivialize the actual Holocaust and likely ought to anger Jewish groups. Finally, some of his attack-dog statements are so packed with exaggeration that he later is forced to contradict himself. For instance, during the 1992 campaign he continually misrepresented the state of the economy as the "worst economy since the Great Depression"—a breathtakingly inaccurate distortion. In July 1999, Gore acknowledged that the economic boom transpiring during the Clinton years had in fact began midway through the Bush administration.[100]

While the preceding two sections noted general foreign-policy tasks of the vice president, the following are examples of Gore's duties in foreign-policy issue areas.

The Balkans / Kosovo 1999

From the outset, Gore has taken part in White House meetings on the Balkans. In the first couple years of the administration, he was a player within a group that included the secretary of defense, the Chairman of the Joint Chiefs of Staff, U.S. delegate to the United Nations Madeleine Albright, Anthony Lake, Samuel Berger, and the chief of staff. In those meetings, the vice president continually argued for aggressive use of U.S. force in Bosnia.[101] He was a potent voice early within the administration lobbying for the airlift to Bosnia. "He felt that it was the right approach, that it would help de-logjam some of the blockades on the ground," said Chief of Staff McLarty.[102] He long advocated lifting the arms embargo on Bosnia—an action that required a two-thirds congressional majority in July 1995 to override President Clinton's veto.[103] Throughout the first year and a half of the administration, Gore argued passionately for punitive air strikes against the Serbs. When Clinton wavered at crucial moments, Gore stiffened Clinton's spine by delivering lengthy soliloquies about morality and the right of the Bosnians to defend themselves.[104]

In the first term, Clinton described Gore as pressing him almost daily on the Bosnia question.[105] Gore's tenacity reportedly led former Secretary of State Christopher to grumble to his advisors that the vice president seemed determined to get the United States caught in a war in Bosnia.[106] The vice president's tough stance on the conflict should come as no surprise. Senator Gore had been quite vocal on U.S. policy in the Balkans, often being critical of the Bush administration. His interest in the issue has not flagged since becoming vice president.[107]

Gore feels that the world community had "an interest" in trying to prevent the genocide taking place in Bosnia. On "This Week with David Brinkley," he was asked by Cokie Roberts if the failure of the United Nations in Bosnia provided a lesson that it should not be involved in the business of peacekeeping. "There's a lot of lessons to be learned from this, but I would not draw the wrong lesson," said Gore. "Here on the 50th anniversary of the United Nations, let's also remember that in places like Cambodia, and Namibia, and El Salvador, the United Nations has been responsible for transforming civil wars into peaceful democracies." Roberts replied that the situations cited by Gore involved U.N. intervention after a peace settlement was already reached. "But they also involved the limited use of U.N. forces to try to separate the sides and to try to enhance the odds to move toward peace," the vice president retorted.[108]

Gore's role in the Balkans conflict has not been resigned to debate within the White House. In an intriguing foreign-policy assignment that involved a substantive role, the vice president—only a few weeks after the inauguration—was chosen to meet in February 1993 with Bosnian President Alija Izetbegovic. His task was quite sensitive: inform the Muslim leader that, despite Clinton's tough campaign talk, the United States would not intervene militarily to rescue the Bosnians. The official explanation for the meeting was that Gore had a "preexisting relationship" with the Bosnian leader. White House officials said that they wanted the meeting to receive less publicity than if Izetbegovic had met with President Clinton; at the same time, having Gore deliver the message would allow the authority of it to be affirmed.[109]

Later, on March 12, 1995, Gore met in Copenhagen with Croatian President Franjo Tudjman. After the meeting, Tudjman agreed to allow U.N. peacekeepers to remain in Croatia, but under a new mandate that would move troops to Croatia's borders with Bosnia and Serbia.[110] The agreement was announced in Copenhagen by the vice president, who was in the region to speak at a U.N. conference on poverty. The accord also required two new Security Council resolutions creating separate U.N. forces for Bosnia and Croatia.

While it is unclear how much of a persuasive role was personally played by the vice president, it seems he made a difference. Talking to reporters at a news conference with Tudjman, Gore said the Croatian leader had agreed to allow the peacekeepers already there to remain in place even if the two Security Council resolutions were not in effect by March 31, when the current mandate for their deployment there expired. Gore described his meeting with Tudjman as "excellent," and added that the Croatian president would be going to Washington that week and would meet with President Clinton. "I assured him of full U.S. support for restoring Croatian sovereignty to all parts of Croatia," Gore said.[111] National Public Radio credited Gore for scoring an "international success by getting" Tudjman to agree to allow UN peacekeeping troops to remain in his country longer than originally mandated.[112]

Given his hawkishness in the Balkans from the start, it is not surprising that Gore became an outspoken proponent of the massive NATO air campaign launched against Slobodan Milosevic's Serbian forces from March to April 1999. This was evident in a series of carefully staged public appearances as well as closed-door military sessions. During the war, Gore openly pursued a high-profile role. He did many on-the-record interviews and statements enunciating the administration's policy. The Gore team saw the crisis as an opportunity to display the vice president's knowledge of complex foreign-policy matters and general toughness.[113]

As usual, Gore received very substantive duties during the crisis. Behind the scenes, Clinton tapped him in late March (1999) to brief three former presidents on the looming crisis and to alert Russian Prime Minister Yevgeny Primakov of the likelihood of airstrikes. NSC spokesman P.J. Crowley commented on Gore's impact: "He's been very involved in the decision-making process and a very strong advocate for an aggressive response to President Milosevic's offensive in Kosovo. . . . He plays an integral role in the development of policy."[114]

Russia

Gore's involvement in Russia yields some sticky and unclear findings. On the positive side, Russia is another example of how Gore's trips abroad have given him valuable experience working with foreign leaders. The vice president visited Russia in December 1993 and conferred with President Boris Yeltsin, a precursor to Clinton's January trip.[115] In part, the aim of the trip was to assess Yeltsin's standing after the election.[116] Gore reportedly tried to calm Yeltsin's opposition to NATO expansion by assuring him that there were no plans to extend membership to former East Bloc countries either that year or the next.[117] (As it turned out, the administration did extend that invitation shortly after Gore's assurance to Yeltsin.)

Gore has been perhaps the administration's main spokesman on Russia, particularly since key events shaping Russia's future have taken place while Gore was in Moscow working on a special commission with Prime Minister

Viktor Chernomyrdin, among other things (more on this later). Even at home, however, Gore has been called upon to juggle the shaky task of trying to support Yeltsin's political control while bloodshed continued in Chechnya—an issue on which Yeltsin has sternly warned the United States to let him handle. (In a harsh speech in Budapest, Yeltsin, in the presence of Clinton, warned the United States not to try to manage the "destinies of the world community," and said, "Europe is in danger of plunging into a cold peace.")[118] In 1995, Gore had to continue this balancing act while GOP presidential candidate Bob Dole questioned Yeltsin's control and U.S. support for the Russian leader as he ordered more fighting in Chechnya. For instance, on the CBS News program "Face the Nation," Gore expressed concern over the fighting, but said of Yeltsin, "We believe that he is in control."[119]

Gore's early Moscow visit coincided with the December 15, 1993 Russian elections that resulted in an unexpectedly strong showing by anti-reformers, including ultranationalist Vladimir V. Zhirinovsky. The elections provided Gore with an opportunity to shine as an administration spokesman on a key foreign-policy issue, offering perhaps the most damning indictment of a Russian politician or policy by a visiting American vice president since Richard Nixon's "Kitchen Debate" with Soviet Premier Nikita Khrushchev. It also gave Gore a chance to personally affirm the U.S. position in support of Yeltsin and his reforms, thus taking away early momentum gained by Zhirinovsky. In comments coordinated with the White House, Gore delivered the administration's most scathing criticism of Zhirinovsky, telling reporters, "The views expressed by Zhirinovsky on issues such as the use of nuclear weapons, the expansion of borders, the treatment of ethnic minorities, are reprehensible and anathema to all freedom-loving people in Russia, in the United States and everywhere in the world." Raising the specter that the rise of ultranationalism could lead to terrible violence, Gore said, "If you want a laboratory test of those views, then look at Bosnia." The two officials briefing reporters on the elections at the White House stated that Gore would not meet Zhirinovsky in Moscow.[120]

Just as important—but increasingly controversial—is the critical link Gore established with Russia outside normal diplomatic channels, developing a close relationship with Prime Minister Viktor Chernomyrdin. Their relationship was called the main channel between the administration and Moscow.[121] On September 1-2, 1993, Gore and Chernomyrdin initiated a joint commission designed to facilitate U.S.-Russian cooperation on a variety of issues, including: space cooperation, trade and business development, defense conversion, science and technology, energy, nuclear safety, and the environment.[122] The Gore-Chernomyrdin Commission, which involved six cabinet members, had become a way to get the administration's views through to Moscow and establish a relationship with the man who some thought could be president of Russia.[123] (The likelihood of a Chernomyrdin presidency in 2000 is now quite remote.)

There appears to be good news and possibly bad news concerning Gore's role on the commission. First, the good news.

The commission seemed to produce quick and impressive results—although it must be stressed that it is unclear how much of a *personal* role Gore played in the below-listed achievements. On December 16, 1993, Gore and Chernomyrdin signed pacts in Moscow that formally joined the United States and Russia as partners on an international space station and announced that the first Russian astronaut would fly in the space shuttle Discovery. According to the *Current Digest of the Post-Soviet Press*, it will allow the United States to save on the order of $2 billion and to put the station into space two years earlier than would otherwise be the case. At the same time, Russia will receive $400 million over four years. Agreements were signed on such issues as economic development, high-technology ventures, the environment, and oil and gas exploration. Some pacts were for small but possibly fruitful projects, like plans to build as many as twenty-five privately financed gas stations in Russia. Seventeen accords and agreements, five joint statements, and a communiqué were signed in Moscow. Chernomyrdin hailed the projects envisioned in the documents as "projects worth billions. This is exactly what we need right now."[124]

Gore and Chernomyrdin later signed another major accord during their June 21-23, 1994 meeting in Washington. The accord will begin the phase-out of Russian nuclear reactors that have produced plutonium for weapons purposes. Because the United States has not produced plutonium since 1988, the agreement applies mainly to Russian facilities. The details were hammered out by U.S. and Russian technical working groups during May 23-26 meetings in Moscow. The pact will have five main provisions:

- Russia will shut down its dual-use reactors at Tomsk-7 and Krasnoyarsk-26 "no later than the year 2000"—each produce both energy for electricity and weapons-grade plutonium.
- Each side will "take all practical steps" to enable Russia to shut down reactors "as soon as possible prior to the year 2000" and create alternative energies, such as natural gas turbines at Tomsk and a coal-fired facility at Krasnoyarsk.
- Russia agreed not to use for weapons purposes any plutonium produced in these reactors before they cease to operate.
- Verification regimes were to be worked out within six months of the signing that will include on-site inspections not only at Tomsk-7 and Krasnoyarsk-26, but also at Russian and U.S. reactors that used to produce weapons-grade plutonium.
- The United States and Russia will seek a broader agreement "as early as possible" that would prohibit the use of any plutonium produced after the agreement is signed for nuclear weapons.[125]

Reports contended that the relationship between Yeltsin and President Clinton is not a healthy one. This left much critical diplomatic work between the two countries to take place between the vice president and Chernomyrdin within their commission. To further illustrate what a force the Gore-Chernomyrdin had become, when Secretary of State Christopher met with Foreign Minister Andrei Kozyrev in Geneva in January 1995, they barely discussed the contentious issue of Yeltsin's unfulfilled pledge to disclose Russia's arms deals with Iran. That was the responsibility of Gore-Chernomyrdin, Christopher's aides said.[126]

That's the good news about the commission. As this book goes to press, however, questions are being raised about the group, especially Gore's personal role and judgment.[127] The questions stem from a common criticism of the Clinton administration's Russia policy: Was the administration too willing to turn a blind eye to the organized crime, racketeering, money laundering, graft and general corruption and lawlessness of the Russian government? Was the administration too supportive of the government? Was it tolerant to a fault? Did it acquiesce in Russia's decay and decline?

And, if those charges hold, what can be said about Gore's role?

In a *Washington Post* article titled, "Who Robbed Russia? Did Al Gore know about the massive lootings," David Ignatius asks: "What did the vice president know about the looting of Russia by organized crime, and why didn't he do more to stop it?" Among the issues is whether the bank of New York—which the *New York Times* revealed was the victim of $10 billion of laundered money by the Russian mob[128]—served as one of the conduits for over $200 million in diverted IMF loans to Russia. Vice President Gore, as noted earlier, has been a loud advocate of continued IMF lending to Russia, even as evidence mounted that some of it was being misused by Russia's business "oligarchs" and their corrupt cronies. Ignatius writes:

> Pinning down the details of that assertion—what did Gore know about the involvement of top Russian politicians in corrupt activities and what did he do about it?—will be a crucial reporting challenge for the U.S. and Russian press as we head into this campaign season. Gore may live to regret his decision to take a leading role in Russia policy, through what was known as the "Gore-Chernomyrdin Commission."[129]

Reports claim that Chernomyrdin was involved in the mountain of corruption, and that Gore knew of the prime minister's activities as early as 1995. Ignatius quotes a former government official as saying: "It was all laid out for Gore . . . and he didn't want to hear it. Our government knew damn well what was happening." Another official blasted the commission as a "Soviet-style bureaucracy in which success was mandatory, and any information that would contradict success was simply filed forever."[130]

Why does this matter? This latest Russian scandal is not just a story about corrupt politicians and businessmen. It is a story about the bleeding to death of the struggling Russian state. Ignatius explains:

> What makes the Russian case so sad is that the Clinton administration may have squandered one of the most precious assets imaginable—which is the idealism and goodwill of the Russian people as they emerged from 70 years of Communist rule. The Russian debacle may haunt us for generations. Gore played a key role in that messy process, and he has a lot of explaining to do.[131]

It is not yet clear whether the Gore-Chernomyrdin Commission, or Gore himself, should be held accountable for any of this. At this point, it seems that (at the worst) the vice president may be guilty of bad judgment, poor policy, and naivete, rather than crimes or unethical behavior. Time will tell.

Interestingly, as noted by the *Washington Post*'s Ceci Connolly in a front-page article, after years of boasting about Gore's role on the commission, his grasp of modern Russia, and his overseeing relations with Russia, "Gore's advisors now fiind themselves shifting to the defensive about foreign policy credentials they hoped would be a campaign asset." The vice president's advisors now are being forced to dubiously argue that Gore was both intimately involved with the good things but "out of the loop" on the bad things.[132]

Either way, questions are being raised and will likely persist. As journalist Arnaud de Borchgrave asserts: "The 'Who Lost Russia?' question now looms large as a presidential campaign issue. And Mr. Gore will be on the firing line."[133]

Chernomyrdin has since been fired by the erratic Yeltsin. Incredibly, Yeltsin fired six prime ministers during an eighteen-month period prior to August 1999. Consequently, the commission changed as well. Nonetheless, the Gore-Chernomyrdin lasted through a majority of the Clinton years.

Importantly, Gore's work in Russia has continued despite big changes in personnel around him. While Chernomyrdin and Warren Christopher have moved on, Gore has piled on more achievements—seemingly positive. Here are just two examples. First, in July 1998, he made a one-day visit to Moscow, where he met with Russian Prime Minister Sergei Kiriyenko. The two men produced agreements to retrain nuclear scientists to use their skills in civilian industries and to cooperate in controlling plutonium removed from dismantled nuclear weapons. While there, Gore urged the communist-dominated Duma to ratify the languishing START II treaty so talks could begin on a third pact to reduce strategic nuclear arms. He also spoke over the phone that week with a vacationing Yeltsin.[134] Second, during the December 1998 U.S. strike against Iraq, which (intentionally or not) took place the day that an impeachment vote was scheduled by the House against President Clinton, Gore discussed the crisis over the telephone with Russian Prime Minister Yevgevy Primakov.[135] Again, each of the two examples in this paragraph—both taking place as recently as 1998—demonstrate that Gore continues to be substantively involved in U.S.-Russia policy even as the major players are replaced by others.

Kazakhstan and Ukraine

The vice president's busy work within the former Soviet Union has not been resigned merely to Russia. Kazakhstan endorsed an international treaty on December 13, 1993 to halt the spread of arms and signed an agreement with the United States to dismantle its nuclear arsenal. The actions, which came during a visit by Gore, were important because Kazakhstan had the third-largest nuclear arsenal of the former Soviet republics, behind Russia and Ukraine. The moves were intended to put additional pressure on Ukraine, where leaders were adamant in not relinquishing their missiles.[136]

There was reportedly no doubt before Gore's arrival that Kazakhstan's President Nursultan Nazarbayev would sign the arms pact, under which Kazakhstan was to begin dismantling its nuclear weapons in return for more than $84 million in aid from the United States. But it was never certain that Kazakhstan would endorse the NPT. Administration officials claimed that Gore prodded Nazarbayev to act on the NPT issue.[137] On a separate note, in an article short on specifics, *The New York Times* stated that Gore also "used his contacts to negotiate an ultra-secret deal with Russia and Kazakhstan to bring more than half a ton of bomb-grade uranium from Kazakhstan to the United States last year [1994]."[138]

Gore has done impressive work in Kazakhstan with Prime Minister Kazhegeldin, inking numerous agreements. On March 27, 1995, the two leaders signed the U.S.-Kazakhstan Declaration on Trade, Investment and Economic Cooperation, outlining steps for the two countries to develop an expanded, long-term relationship. On trade, they agreed to reduce trade barriers and facilitate market access consistent with trade laws. On economic cooperation, the United States agreed to continue substantial technical assistance to Kazakhstan's program for de-monopolization and privatization. Reflecting Gore's own pet interests, the leaders signed two major environmental pacts—an Agreement on Global Learning and Observations to Benefit the Environment (GLOBE), and an Agreement on Cooperation in the Fields of Protection of the Environment and Natural Resources. The latter results in the creation of a joint U.S.-Kazakhstan Environment, Science, and Technology Committee. On the military security front, the two leaders signed a Joint Statement on Peace, Security, and Nonproliferation, and, importantly, a Joint Statement on Cooperation in Promoting the Rule of Law and Combating Crime, which takes steps to curb nuclear materials smuggling.[139]

Finally, another former Soviet republic of interest to the vice president has been the Ukraine. According to Peter Boyer, Gore led the secret negotiations with the Ukrainian President Leonid Kravchuk that resulted in Ukraine's surrender of nuclear weapons.[140] A number of reports contend that the vice president "persuaded" the Ukraine to give up its nuclear arsenal.[141] Most of these reports, however, have lacked details.

NAFTA/Western Hemisphere

While Gore made some big achievements in the former Soviet Union, he has also done a lot within his own hemisphere, particularly on international economic policy, which the Clinton administration defines as a "security issue."

On the semi-ceremonial side, Gore was in Mexico City on December 1, 1993 for the inauguration of Mexico's new president Ernesto Zedillo, where he gave a speech on foreign policy and discussed the implementation of NAFTA with Mexican officials.[142] NAFTA is an issue Gore will be associated with for a long time. In what falls under the administration's category of "economic security," on November 9, 1993, the vice president debated NAFTA with 1992 presidential candidate Ross Perot on CNN's "Larry King show" before an audience of millions. Roughly 46 percent of Americans saw all or part of the debate.[143] The debate set a television record; it was seen in 11.2 million homes, the largest audience for any regularly scheduled program in the history of cable television.[144] The highly effective debate propelled a then sagging Gore into domestic and international credibility and played a key role into pushing him into more of a foreign-policy role within the Clinton administration.

Before the debate, a Gore advisor conceded, "We were convinced Perot was hurting NAFTA." Thus there was a desire to confront him directly and try to sway public opinion on a critical trade issue. The administration chose "Larry King" because the show had always been Perot's forum of choice, and advisors felt that Perot would not say "no" to an invite. During the debate, Gore's barrage of timely facts and cool demeanor, contrasted with Perot's struggle with statistics and combativeness, earned the vice president a "victory" as judged by public-opinion polls, commentators, and even conservative critics. In one of the more memorable and entertaining moments during the debate, Gore presented Perot with a framed photograph of Senator Reed Smoot and Representative Willis Hawley (i.e., "Smoot-Hawley") in order to underscore the dangerous depths of Perot's protectionism. Mack McLarty maintains that Gore's debate triumph "changed the political landscape." The numbers show that he is likely correct.[145] The overnight Gallup numbers showed that support for NAFTA grew to 57 percent from 34 percent, while Perot's unfavorable rating rose to 51 percent from a pre-debate 39 percent.[146] Most importantly, in the process Gore served up perhaps the White House's best public defense in support of NAFTA, which would eventually win approval.

Clinton, who was enthusiastic about the vice president's performance, said that two days after the speech he was approached repeatedly as he toured a veterans hospital by people who said they saw the debate and had changed their minds in favor of the trade accord. McLarty theorizes that Gore made it possible for NAFTA supporters to come out of the closet, including those on Capitol Hill, who received positive responses from their constituents similar to what Clinton heard at the veterans hospital. Reporter Fred Barnes relays some noteworthy information on how Gore prepared for and performed in the debate:

> Gore succeeded beyond his wildest dreams in the debate. No matter what happened, Gore figured he would win on facts. His fear was that Perot would toss off a half-dozen one-liners and, as one aide put it, "Dominate in a theatrical sense." But Gore, unusually succinct, won on style. In a videotaped practice, he had been long-winded, giving a five-minute answer to the first question (Why are you for NAFTA?). His trainers halted the session and told him to be less verbose, like Perot. . . .
> What surprised Gore and his aides [during the debate] was how thin-skinned Perot is. Perot unraveled when Gore countered his standard charges. This was no accident. The White House has developed an extensive file on Perot. Democratic Representative Mike Synar of Oklahoma, who played Perot in practice sessions with Gore, says it includes "practically everything Perot has written or said over a lifetime." Gore spent two full days studying the Perot material. He was ready when Perot said government estimates are unreliable. He reminded Perot that he had predicted 40,000 American soldiers would be killed in Desert Storm and 100 banks would fail after last year's election. Perot looked stricken. And when Perot blamed NAFTA on foreign-paid lobbyists in Washington, Gore said Perot had hired a platoon of lobbyists to press the House Ways and Means Committee for tax breaks. Perot sputtered an unpersuasive denial. For days afterward, Gore's office got calls from lobbyists who said they had worked for Perot.[147]

William Safire called Clinton's decision to have the vice president take on Perot a "media masterstroke" and says that Gore forced Perot to reveal himself as a "bossy old billionaire bully." Safire says that the vice president proved that "a politician armed with courage and civility could beat a bully every time."[148] *The Wall Street Journal* called the debate "Al Gore's big knockout," commenting favorably: "We don't know what the future holds for Al Gore, but he may have earned himself a corner of history Tuesday night. He surely won what the two men showed up to do—hold a debate on NAFTA."[149] President Clinton now commonly refers to it as "that magic moment on Larry King."[150]

As noted earlier, Clinton had approached the vice president about playing a greater role in White House international relations a few weeks before the NAFTA debate. Nonetheless, it is likely no coincidence that Gore's foreign-policy stock shot up after November 9, 1993. After that period, he would begin to play more of a role in global affairs.

Haiti

A separate issue within the Western Hemisphere seemed to give the vice president some experience in the area of crisis duty. Iin the case of Haiti, Gore continued a recent trend whereby vice presidents play a more active role within the administration during key international situations. While his role in crises in general does not seem to rival the unprecedented involvement of Vice President Bush—who chaired a White House crisis committee—Gore seemed extensively involved in White House decision making and at least played a role as a key administration spokesman during the Haiti situation, similar to that done by Vice President Quayle during the Bush administration's crisis in the Persian Gulf.

On the policy influence and formulation side, Peter Boyer writes that Gore was a "key force in pushing Clinton to change policy and eventually to intervene" in Haiti.[151] He aggressively advocated military action in Haiti to restore its government.[152] When Clinton began to waver on Haiti, Gore braced him by saying that the United States must be willing to use force at the right moment. The vice president pushed to keep up the pressure on the junta.[153] He was involved in White House decision making during the crisis, often meeting with a tight inner core in the Oval Office that included Clinton, NSA Lake, and Chief of Staff Panetta.[154] With a likely date for an invasion approaching, Clinton and Gore telephoned[155] a dozen world leaders—nine by Clinton and three by Gore—on September 9 and 10 mainly to recruit international monitors to supervise an interim Haitian police force.[156] Stephanopoulos contends that Gore "played a critical role in Haiti. He was on the phone with [Jean-Bertrand] Aristede a lot."[157]

On the spokesman front, in April 1994, Gore presented the administration's latest plan on Haiti to exiled president, Aristede. It called for Lieutenant General Raoul Cedras to resign his army command, for Aristede to name a new prime minister, and for Haiti's parliament to pass an amnesty bill. During the meeting where he presented the plan, Gore told Aristede that the United States would push to tighten the trade embargo on Haiti and would no longer press him to make widespread concessions before Haiti's military committed itself to surrender power.[158]

In other examples of Gore acting as a spokesman on the Haiti issue, the vice president appeared on the television program CNN's "Late Edition" on September 18, 1994 to discuss, under the limitations of the ongoing talks in Haiti, the nature of those talks and what the American delegation dispatched there hoped to accomplish. In part making up for President Clinton's difficulties in addressing military crowds, Gore visited troops at Fort Bragg, NC, on September 20, 1994, which two days earlier were recalled in mid-flight while on their way to invade Haiti. Gore told a gathering of soldiers that once the planes were in the air, "dictators down there said, 'We choose peace instead of war.'"[159] Likely in part to underscore Gore's participation in the talks, Gore made a statement at a September 16, 1994 press conference with President Clinton and Aristede announcing the administration line on Haiti.[160]

The Environment

While the Haiti crisis was a big foreign-policy issue for the administration, many outside the White House would justifiably question whether the environment is a foreign-policy issue. While such is certainly a matter of debate, what is important is that to Al Gore, the environment is unquestionably a foreign-policy issue. In that vein, he has succeeded in *making* it a foreign-policy issue within this particular administration. Whether that is a positive or negative development depends on one's view of Gore's unique brand of environmentalism.

Gore's pet interest in the environment dates back to his pre-vice-presidential period when he wrote a popular but controversial book called *Earth in the Balance*, in which he professed a global need to reverse "cataclysmic" changes in the environment.[161] The book has been derided by critics as extreme, even turning off some New Democrats. One account asserts that Gore's own staff believes the book to be damning, and is fearful about how it may hurt their guy in his 2000 presidential run.[162]

As noted earlier, Gore's rhetoric regularly relies on Nazi metaphors. Nowhere is this more obvious than his environmental writings. He has a college-freshman-like obsession with such metaphors. He certainly over-applies the analogies in an almost juvenile and demeaning fashion. In *Earth in the Balance*, he employs terms like "environmental holocaust" and "ecological Kristallnacht." Regarding the latter, says Gore, "Today the evidence of an ecological *Kristallnacht* is as clear as the sound of glass shattering in Berlin."[163] Because of the nation's purported damage to the environment, he has called it a "dysfunctional civilization" and has stated that America's desire to "consume the earth and its resources" is reminiscent of what forced Germany into fascism. Gore characterizes the environmental insensitivity of free markets as "philosophically . . . similar in some ways to the moral blindness implicit in racism and anti-semitism."[164]

To ensure that he's not being misunderstood, Gore makes it abundantly clear that he understands the weight of his Nazi analogies:

> It is not merely in the service of analogy that I have referred so often to the struggles against Nazi and communist totalitarianism, because I believe that the emerging effort to save the environment is a continuation of these struggles, a crucial new phase of the long battle for true freedom and human dignity.[165]

Gore is saying that his crusade to save the environment is another historic moral struggle—a literal, direct continuation of the war against Nazi genocide against the Jews and Bolshevik totalitarian communism. Frankly, it is surprising that Jewish groups have not expressed outrage over Gore's blithe application of Nazi imagery to a situation not remotely comparable to the real Holocaust. The book is chock-full of Nazi analogies.

Often speaking of the environment as a sort of religion, Gore has said that the "environmental crisis" demands "a new faith in the future of life on earth." In some of *Earth in the Balance*'s rather silly moments, Gore employs a lot of sappy New Age spiritualism. This is salient in chapter 13 of the book, titled "Environmentalism of the Spirit" (pp. 238-65). It is also very evident in chapter 12, titled "Dysfunctional Civilization" (pp. 216-37). To cite just one quote from chapter 12, Gore remarks: "The froth and frenzy of industrial civilization mask our deep loneliness for that communion with the world that can lift our spirits and fill our senses with the richness and immediacy of life itself."[166]

The vice president feels that the only appropriate long-term solution to our ecological "crisis" (he uses that particular word incessantly) requires that we "dramatically change our civilization and our way of thinking about the relationship between humankind and the earth."[167] Again, it is fundamentally important to understand that Gore wants to be taken literally. This is not merely an embellished statement made for point of emphasis.

It has been said that Gore believes the automobile is the single greatest threat to civilization, and that modern cars ought to be eliminated. This is largely true. On page 325 of *Earth in the Balance*, where he makes reference to the planet's "hundreds of millions of automobiles," he writes: "We now know that their cumulative impact on the global environment is posing a mortal threat to the security of every nation that is more deadly than that of any military enemy we are ever again likely to confront."

Gore states unequivocally that he views cars as the ultimate mortal enemy. Worse, he sees no other likely military threat as severe as cars.

Such a threat, obviously, must be killed at the source. That is precisely what Gore proposes on pages 325-26. He writes: "[I]t ought to be possible to establish a coordinated global program to accomplish the strategic goal of completely eliminating the internal combustion engine over, say, a twenty-five-year period."

That's quite a foreign-policy goal: a global effort to completely eliminate the international combustion engine within twenty-five years.

At times, it is literally difficult to distinguish between some of Gore's statements and those of the Unabomber.

Hence, it is also critical to understand that, by nearly all accounts, Gore wrote *Earth in the Balance* by himself, without assistance from a ghostwriter—a feat almost unheard of among politicians today.

Adam Wolfson is one of the few writers who fully grasps the gravity of Gore's thoughts as expressed in *Earth in the Balance*. Wolfson asserts:

> Yes, the book is full of wild speculation about the environment, and, yes, Gore offers some silly ideas about how to address the problem. But it is the book's political and moral content that is remarkable, even frightening.[168]

Wolfson avers that Gore feels we need not merely reinvent government but also human nature itself—a textbook totalitarian notion.[169] A careful read of *Earth in the Balance* reveals that Wolfson is not exaggerating. To cite just one of countless examples, on page 274 Gore insists that "sacrifice, struggle, and a wrenching transformation of society will be necessary" to "rescue" the environment from the flames he sees engulfing it.

Wolfson carefully elaborates on one of the book's more terrifying elements. The vice president hails ecological activists as "resistance fighters" and "people of conscience" who must ready themselves for a "just war" akin to the WWII resistance that took on the Nazis. Indeed, Gore is quite serious about the "war" idea. Absent the "wrenching" changes that are necessary for our "civilization," the vice president foresees the outbreak "of a kind of global civil war between those who refuse to consider the consequences of civilization's relentless advance and those who refuse to be silent partners in the destruction."[170] Wolfson cautions that Gore's irresponsible and juvenile invocation of such rhetoric might understandably lead to injuries and even deaths.[171]

Considering these ideas, is it unreasonable to suspect that a President Gore would be eagerly willing to engage American troops in wars of ecological liberation? Someone should ask him this question.

In chapter 15—by far the book's longest chapter—Gore calls for a "Global Marshall Plan" to rescue the environment. As president, would Gore attempt such a plan? If so, what would be its financial cost?

The cost issue is worth pondering. This is especially apparent in chapter 14 of *Earth in the Balance*, which is titled "A New Common Purpose," where Gore persistently asserts that "we must make the rescue of the environment the central organizing principle for civilization."[172] Those are probably the book's three most important words—central organizing principle. I encourage the use of the acronym "c.o.p." as a mnemonic device to remember this critical notion. Those three words certainly comprise the book's overarching theme. What do they mean?

Gore says that a c.o.p. is a unifying concept under which a nation's government and society rallies behind in order to defeat an ultimate evil. He cites the American and western efforts to defeat the Nazis in WWII and to roll back the communists after WWII—via policies like the Marshall Plan and Truman Doctrine. These programs, says Gore, "gained sufficient support from society as a whole because they served the central organizing principle to which we were wholeheartedly committed." He warns the "Chamberlains" of today that these same 1940s efforts now need directed toward the environment.[173] What does this mean practically? Gore writes:

> Adopting a central organizing principle—one agreed to voluntarily—means embarking on an all-out effort to use every policy and program, every law and institution, every treaty and alliance, every tactic and strategy, every plan and course of action—to use, in short, every means to halt the destruction of the environment and to preserve and nurture our ecological system. Minor shifts in policy, marginal adjustments in ongoing programs, moderate improvements in laws and regulations, rhetoric offered in lieu of genuine change—these are all forms of appeasement, designed to satisfy the public's desire to believe that sacrifice, struggle, and a wrenching transformation of society will be necessary.[174]

This is no small task. What would be the financial cost? He doesn't say.

Could there be yet more behind the c.o.p.? For most peoples and societies throughout history, the "central organizing principle" has ranged from not just unifying battles and ideologies but also God or gods. Gore's notion of a central organizing principle refers to battles or ideologies—and thus his crusade to "save" the environment. It is not clear if he regards religion as a c.o.p. Indeed, some may question whether Gore's exalted view of the environment approaches the position of a deity in his personal outlook. It has been said that he treats the environment as a sort of "religion." He is not clear on this, and (given his reverence for the environment) we certainly shouldn't assume we know without an unambiguous answer. The answer, of course, is known only to Gore. Gore is a Baptist who professes a belief in God.[175] In a 1999 statement on the campaign stump—surely partly motivated to appeal to Christian and religious voters—the vice president asserted: "The purpose of life is to glorify God."[176]

Either way, a reporter should ask Gore to juxtapose his religious and environmental beliefs and candidly assess the priority he grants to each.

Understandably, the vice president's rhetoric has created a backlash, especially among the business-minded, who see Gore's environmentalism as leading to unnecessary regulations, among other issues. For instance, while the *Wall Street Journal* has complemented Gore's pro-trade stance and reinventing government initiative, it routinely frets over (and makes fun of) his strident environmentalism. In juxtaposing one of Gore's more apocalyptic statements to a passage from the Biblical Book of Revelation, *Wall Street Journal* columnist George Melloan opined:

> Theologians have for centuries puzzled over the Book of Revelation's dramatic "seven seals" prophecies. Al Gore's grim vision (of the earth) is easier to interpret. It's nonsense. . . . The only serious question is whether the vice president is just another scare monger or a man whose zealotry has deprived him of balanced and rational thought.[177]

All of this notwithstanding, Gore has lots of clout in the administration when it comes to environmental policy. He blocked the appointment of World Bank economist Lawrence Summers to the chairman of the president's Council of Economic Advisors because he was disturbed by a 1991 Summers' internal memo that had been targeted by Greenpeace as hostile to the environment, particularly within Third World countries.[178] He regularly coordinates with Secretary of the Interior Bruce Babbitt on protecting public lands. He talks on the telephone several times a week with EPA Administrator Carol Browner, a former Gore aide who was appointed by Clinton at the request of the vice president.[179]

Yet, most importantly for the purposes of this work, the vice president has managed to turn his environmentalism into a sort of "foreign-policy" issue—though, mercifully, not to the radical extent suggested by *Earth in the Balance*. His adamant stance on the matter has worked for him abroad—becoming a key subject of discussion with leaders of Poland and China and even the basis for agreements with Russia and Kazakhstan. When a German government delegation visited David Gergen a few days after the NAFTA debate, they talked about Gore as a big time player not only because of his vanquishing of Perot but also because *Earth in the Balance* was a best-seller in "green-crazy" Germany.[180] Environmental issues were high on Gore's agenda during two weeks of talks by the vice president in Asia in March 1997. He spoke at length about environmental problems while in Japan and China.[181]

Gore's ability to transform his environmentalism into a global issue is no light matter. White House officials said that he has suggested earmarking a large amount of U.S. aid (hundreds of millions of dollars) to improve the safety of Russian nuclear reactors and for environmental clean-up programs.[182] Depending on one's view, Gore could be seen as a hero or pariah in this regard. Either way, he has successfully transformed the environment into a foreign-policy matter that has earned him both respect (deserved or not) and trips abroad, as well as resulted in international agreements with key foreign officials.[183]

Nuclear Weapons, Nonproliferation, and Missile Defense

As opposed to the environment, there is little doubt that nuclear nonproliferation remains a traditional foreign-policy matter. Gore has been deeply involved in nonproliferation issues since his days in Congress. This includes the debate over whether a missile-defense system could or should be built and deployed as a means to protect the nation from missile strikes.

Gore has been consistent on missile defense since his earliest days in Congress: he is against missile defense because be believes such a U.S. system would violate the 1972 Anti-Ballistic Missile (ABM) Treaty signed with the former Soviet Union. In the 1980s, this put Gore at odds with Senate conservatives Like Dan Quayle. In 1999, this may or may not put him slightly at odds within his own administration, as Clinton has announced that it is time for the United States to modify the ABM Treaty and build a missile-defense system. The administration's shift in support of a missile defense was backed by a ninety-seven to three vote in the Senate that included all but three Democrats. The sentiment against the ABM Treaty is embodied in statements by the man instrumental in forging the 1972 agreement—Henry Kissinger. Kissinger called the treaty "outdated," and added, "This treaty may have worked in a two-power nuclear world, although even that is questionable, but in the multi-nuclear world, it is reckless."[184]

It would seem that Gore should support such a shift in policy, since it involves modifying the agreement that forms the source of his opposition. (This assumes the Russians will tolerate a modification of the treaty, which they likely will not. The Duma is opposed.) Yet, there is still the issue of whether Gore believes a system can actually be built. In the 1980s, he argued that missile defense, at least as it was then discussed, was not technically feasible.[185] It is unclear whether he now believes that some sort of system is doable.

Gore has substantial influence on this issue within the Clinton White House. Journalist Bill Gertz goes so far as to claim that after the 1992 election, "Mr. Clinton for the most part passed arms-control policy over to Vice President Al Gore." If accurate, this reflects quite a prominent role for Gore on missile defense. In turn, Gertz maintains, Gore tapped Robert Bell, the former top arms-control aide to Senator Sam Nunn, to lead arms control in the administration. Bell, too, is a big believer in the ABM Treaty.[186]

Rather than exploiting missile defense, Gore prefers to contain the danger of nuclear weapons by halting their spread among nations. His policy preference is to vigorously pursue nonproliferation agreements. In this area, too, Gore has been active as a vice president.

In April 1995, the vice president appeared to have played a pivotal U.S. role in trying to extend the Nuclear Nonproliferation Treaty (NPT) at a major U.N. conference—a move he feels is critical to curbing the proliferation of nuclear weapons. His duties in this regard also demonstrate his role as an administration representative and bargainer abroad. As noted earlier, nonproliferation is one of the three foreign-policy areas that he chose to focus on from the initial days of the administration.

In an April 19 speech on behalf of the United States, Gore sought to assure delegates that the United States and other nuclear powers were not using the treaty in ways unfair to nations without nuclear weapons. The speech may also provide telling information on Gore's personal view on the efficacy of the NPT. "The case for indefinite extension can be stated succinctly and convincingly," said Gore. "First and foremost, the treaty creates a more secure world for all its members, nuclear-weapons states and nonnuclear-weapons states alike. By providing an internationally recognized, verifiable means for states to forswear weapons forever, the treaty helps prevent regional rivalries from evolving into regional arms races. Without the treaty, many more nations would have already decided, however reluctantly, that they needed nuclear arms to deter a neighbor or hedge against future uncertainty." He listed what he perceived as five major arguments against indefinite extension and summarized accomplishments of the NPT.[187]

It was noted at the time of the conference that international support for indefinite renewal of the treaty hinged in part of the influence of South Africa. Arms-control experts claimed that South Africa could produce a far wider margin of consensus for an indefinite extension of the NPT than the United States could achieve alone. "The South Africans have offered us a bridge to the nonaligned, one that the United States should walk over," said Joseph Cirincione, executive director of the Campaign for the Nonproliferation Treaty, a Washington-based coalition of independent arms-control groups. "With their help, we could get an overwhelming vote for extension." In a speech to the conference on April 19, South Africa's Foreign Minister, Alfred Nzo, outlined a plan for indefinite renewal with two new elements. Tom Zamora Collina, director of policy and research at the Institute for Science and International Security, an independent organization in Washington, said the South Africans outlined their proposal in a letter the previous week to Vice President Gore and discussed it there with Secretary of State Christopher on April 18.[188] Just before Gore's speech, Nzo informed the United States of South Africa's backing of an indefinite extension of the treaty.[189]

It was not, however, clear from published reports if Gore, along with Christopher, personally worked with the South Africans in hammering out the final version of their proposal, nor how much they personally influenced the move. Yet, the very positive relationship between Gore and South Africa—in part stemming from his work on the Gore-Mbeki Commission, named for South African Deputy President Thabo Mbeki—likely did not hurt.

Gore has done other things in South Africa, such as giving an October 1994 speech on the flourishing of democracy there since the end of apartheid and the

U.S. commitment to promoting democratic ideals in South Africa, stating that the United States wants to form a political and economic partnership with South Africa.[190] In a casual conversation with friends following the October 1994 visit to Washington by the South African President Nelson Mandela, Gore remarked that Mandela was the world leader that he most admired.[191] Gore headed up a May 1994 delegation to attend Mandela's inauguration.

Population Control and Abortion

Not unlike the environment, the issues of population control and abortion are notable here because they seem to fall under both the vice president's and administration's definition of "foreign policy." To Al Gore, population control is a pet interest and a crucial global-security issue. He has given more than one speech on the security threats he perceives from population growth.

At a September 1994 international conference on population, he argued that such conferences were becoming a reality because many countries recognize that the "rapid and unsustainable" growth of the human population is an urgent issue countries must address.[192] Gore feels the end of the Cold War has brought nations closer together and opened the way for cooperation on population growth.[193] A controversial example of his stridency on this issue took place at the Cairo conference in August 1994, where he spoke on the challenges of preparing for the twenty-first century in the areas of population and sustainable development. Sounding like Thomas Robert Malthus centuries before him—who predicted that population growth would outpace the food supply—Gore averred that integration of population, the environment, and development is an imperative for peace and global security, and that the United States is determined and committed to following policies that achieve that goal.[194]

The following example—which hits on population and birth control—also reflects the obvious fact that, for a vice president, being an administration spokesman on controversial global issues is not always as glamorous as it seems. At a September 1994 U.N. conference, Gore spoke out in support of a woman's right to an abortion, angering the Vatican in the process. He took a vicious hit on the subject from Rome. The vice president asserted that although the United States felt that every nation should decide for itself whether to permit abortions, the United States would never assert that a woman's right to choose an abortion should be internationally guaranteed.[195]

The Vatican, however, was suspicious of Gore's remarks, employing some of the strongest words it has ever used against a U.S. official, not to mention taking the highly uncharacteristic step (the first time ever) of referring to an American politician—in this case, Gore—by name. The Pope's representative impugned the sincerity of Gore's assertion that the U.S. did not seek an international right to abortion. The papal spokesman seemed to suggest that Gore was a hypocrite.[196] The accusations were a setback for the administration's effort to lower the level of rancor with the Vatican over the conference. They also signaled the Vatican's readiness to confront the United States over moral issues. Since preparations for the conference began in April 1994, Pope John Paul II and his aides had taken the lead in condemning it as likely to legitimize abortion as a means of birth and population control—under the tutelage of the United States—in direct contradiction of Roman Catholic doctrine on the sanctity of life from the moment of conception. "Mr. Al Gore, Vice President of the U.S.A. and member of the American delegation, recently stated that 'the United States has not sought, does not seek and will not seek to establish an international right to abortion,'" said Joaquin Navarro-Valls, the Pope's chief spokesman. "The draft population document, which has the United States as its principal sponsor, contradicts, in reality, Mr. Gore's statement."[197]

Conclusion

One big advantage Gore enjoys over previous post-World War II vice presidents is that he initially brought to the White House greater expertise in foreign policy than the president he serves. Gore's situation is a strong case of the idiosyncratic variable manifesting itself in explaining how *this* particular vice president has been so involved and influential in foreign policy. In this case, the idiosyncrasies stemmed from Clinton's early lack of foreign-policy experience and perceived weakness in international affairs; likewise with his national security team. While these weaknesses may or may not have changed, they were undeniable initially, thus creating an opportunity seized upon by Gore. For instance, regarding the foreign-policy team, few secretaries of state would concede to their vice president the amount of foreign policy that Christopher did to Gore—certainly not Jim Baker or Al Haig, and, to a lesser degree, Cyrus Vance. In most administrations, the secretary of state is a domineering force in foreign policy. But Gore faced the opposite with Secretary of State Christopher.

While recent vice presidents have been allowed to spread their wings somewhat in foreign policy, few faced a leadership vacuum like that of the early Clinton administration. As a result, there was a gap to be filled by Gore. Quayle and Agnew, for instance, both served under presidents and foreign-policy teams renowned for their abilities in foreign affairs before and during office. Vice President Quayle was hindered in foreign affairs within the Bush administration because of the strength of the president and his team. "I can bring certain facts and things to the table that are important to [Bush], but he has so many resources on foreign policy and he is so steeped in foreign policy himself," said Quayle, in a point made by Bill Kristol and others.[198] Joe DeSutter, the only advisor who served both Quayle and Gore, confirms this view. DeSutter notes that Bush's expertise in foreign policy meant he was his "own brief" on the subject—opposite of Clinton. As noted earlier, DeSutter said Bush could have had "George Marshall or Henry Kissinger" as his vice president but still would have been his own brief on foreign policy. Clinton, on the other hand, could have a vice president with little experience in foreign policy and still need to consult with him because he is not his own brief in foreign policy.[199]

In part, then, Gore's heavy influence in Clinton administration foreign policy is somewhat due to default: the administration lacked an assertive voice in international affairs. Yet, while such was a contributing factor, it would be unfair to not acknowledge the vice president's ability to carry on an inordinate amount of tasks at home and abroad. Moreover, the fact that he has gained the president's ear in foreign policy more than other vice presidents stems in part from his own ability to impress Clinton.

In the Clinton administration's foreign policy, Vice President Gore is clearly a player. His list of duties are long, important, impressive, unique, and even imaginative. They should be remembered for what they say about the continuing development of vice-presidential activity in foreign affairs, not to mention Gore himself. In that sense, unlike the other chapters in this study, this one may be most helpful in an added prospective sense: Of all the vice presidents profiled herein, Vice President Gore understandably has the best chance of becoming a president. To cite just one piece of evidence, a January 1999 *Wall Street Journal* / NBC News poll of Democratic voters saw Gore with 49 percent, followed in a distant second by Bill Bradley's 12 percent, Jesse Jackson's 11 percent, and Dick Gephardt's 7 percent.[200] While Bradley has narrowed that gap, I have little doubt that Gore will be the top Democrat in 2000.

Thus, due to the 2000 presidential factor, there a number of findings in this chapter that are worth rehashing. These factors tell us much about how a President Gore might act on certain issues:

Gore, as a member of Congress and vice president, has a history of independence. As a senator, he was one of few Democrats who supported President Bush's use of force in the Persian Gulf. He later favored deposing Saddam. A President Gore would likely have invaded Haiti if necessary.[201]

Gore has been hawkish on the Balkans from the outset. He long advocated lifting the arms embargo on Bosnia as well as pushing for airstrikes to punish Serb atrocities. Gore's toughness in the Balkans reportedly led Secretary of State Christopher to grumble to his advisors that Gore seemed determined to get the United States caught in a war in Bosnia. By 1999, Gore had become an outspoken proponent of the massive NATO air campaign launched against Slobodan Milosevic's Serbian forces from March to April 1999. The vice president had impressive duties during the crisis, including briefing three former presidents on the crisis and alerting Russian Prime Minister Yevgeny Primakov of the likelihood of airstrikes.

Would a President Gore have acted on these matters? Evidence herein shows him to be independent and a strong decision maker who prefers to make a choice, live with it, and move on.²⁰² As a result, one can be fairly certain that where Gore stands on an issue is likely indicative of how a President Gore might act under specific scenarios.

On other issues and ideology, Gore is a big free trader who desires a hemispheric trading bloc. If asked, he would likely define "foreign policy" quite broadly, including unconventional threats that go even beyond "economic security," such as the environment and population growth. In March 1995, the vice president outlined a new "national security role" for science, saying that it must contend with social collapse in less-developed countries (LDCs) and global environmental degradation.²⁰³ Gore's passionate views on population growth earn him the scorn of many as being hysterical—with views that, whether correct or not, are at least out of the mainstream in many cases.

In the area of missile defense, Gore is unwavering is his belief that a misisle defense system would violate the 1972 ABM Treaty, and thus would not pursue a total or limited system. Significantly, journalist Bill Gertz goes so far as to claim that after the 1992 election, "Mr. Clinton for the most part passed arms-control policy over to Vice President Al Gore." If accurate, this reflects quite a prominent role for Gore on missile defense. Institutionally, it is an impressive role for the vice presidency.

The most alarming of Gore's views stem from his radical environmentalism. Any American casting a vote for Gore for president has a civic and moral responsibility to first rectify his or her vote with the ideas expressed in the vice president's personal manifesto, *Earth in the Balance*. I'm unaware of any previous book by a vice president that is more extreme and alarming. Considering the ideas in Gore's book, it is reasonable to suspect that a President Gore might engage American troops in wars of ecological liberation. Someone should ask him precisely that question. That aside, he has loudly and proudly called for a "Global Marshall Plan."

Within the administration, Gore has been involved in policy formulation on numerous international situations and issues. In the first term, he met with Christopher every Friday to discuss foreign policy. On Haiti, he seemed to have played a significant day-to-day role in White House policy formulation; likewise with Bosnia. His personal NSA, Leon Fuerth, sits in on meetings of key administration foreign-policy advisors, allowing Gore to monitor national security decisions and directly influence policy, including a major role in a retaliatory U.S. military strike against Iraq.

The vice president has been perhaps the administration's main spokesman on Russia. He established a critical link with Prime Minister Chernomyrdin; their ongoing relationship was called the main channel between the administration and Moscow. To illustrate what a force the Gore-Chernomyrdin had become, when Secretary of State Christopher met with Foreign Minister Kozyrev in Geneva in January 1995, they barely discussed the contentious issue of Yeltsin's unfulfilled pledge to disclose Russia's arms deals with Iran. That was the responsibility of Gore-Chernomyrdin, Christopher's aides said.

Yet, it must be noted that the Gore-Chernomyrdin is now coming under fierce attack. David Ignatius writes: "Gore may live to regret his decision to take a leading role in Russia policy, through what was known as the 'Gore-Chernomyrdin Commission.'" One U.S. official blasted the commission as a "Soviet-style bureaucracy in which success was mandatory, and any information that would contradict success was simply filed forever."

These tough remarks come just as this book goes to press. Time will tell whether they bear fruit. If they hold water, then any good done by the commission will certainly be weighed against what could be quite bad.

Although Chernomyrdin no longer holds the prime-minister post,[204] the vice president has continued to produce agreements with Russia. These, to be sure, appear positive. They include agreements such as those announced by Gore and Russian Prime Minister Kiriyenko in July 1998. Overall, Gore has signed numerous impressive agreements with Russia as well as Kazakhstan and other former Soviet republics. Whether 1994 or 1998, whether his partner's name is Chernomyrdin, Kiriyenko, Primakov, etc., and whether the task involves signing a bilateral agreement on weapons or briefing the prime minister on U.S. airstrikes against Iraq, Gore has continuously been substantively involved in U.S.-Russia policy.

Across the board, Gore has been a key player in administration foreign policy. Moreover, few other vice presidents have had such influence with a president. Gore is influential, being perhaps the president's closest day-to-day advisor, rivaling only Hillary Rodham Clinton. A typical assessment of Gore's remarkable influence with Clinton was provided by Mark Gearan, presidential assistant: "At the end of the day, there is no one who can buck up the president more, who can engage him more on a subject area, who can represent him better. You can search but you won't find one major policy decision in this administration that President Clinton made without discussing it with the vice president. Just doesn't happen." Clearly, *that's* influence. (Evidence suggests Gearan is not exaggerating.) Yet, despite this influence, Gore has also been a model vice president in that he is careful not to overshadow the president, praising Clinton in public and consistently offering self-deprecating comments about himself, stating that his job is "to stand behind the president motionless and keep my mouth shut." Asked how a basketball injury that left him on crutches would effect his duties, Gore jokingly replied, "It takes me twice as long to walk Socks [the first family's cat]."[205] He has wisely followed the advice of his predecessors in this regard. As Walter Mondale once noted, for a vice president "the dumbest thing to do is to go around and brag" about his influence on the president.[206]

Finally, regarding past and potential policy recommendations, there are some lessons to be learned from this chapter, especially concerning the use of the vice president in foreign-policy groups/commissions outside of the White

House and the benefits of a vice president having an active defense and foreign-policy aide like Gore's NSA, Fuerth. These and other issues concerning all the vice presidents in this study will be taken up in the next, concluding chapter.

Notes

1. Richard L. Berke, *New York Times Magazine*, February 20, 1994, p. 30.
2. Peter J. Boyer, "Gore's Dilemma," *The New Yorker*, November 28, 1994, Vol. 70, No. 39, p. 110.
3. Elaine Sciolino and Todd S. Purdum, "Al Gore, One Vice President Who Is Eluding the Shadows," *The New York Times*, February 19, 1995, p. A1.
4. Excerpt from June 22, 1995 speech. *This Week with David Brinkley*, ABC-TV, June 25, 1995.
5. Pat Griffith, "Gore Has Revolutionized the Role of the Vice President," *Pittsburgh Post-Gazette*, December 26, 1993, p. A8.
6. "Lexington: Reinventing the Vice Presidency," *The Economist*, September 10, 1994, p. 30.
7. This chapter does not tackle the highly troubling matters surrounding Gore's foreign fundraising activities, alleged Chinese "money" connections, visits to Buddhist temples, and so on. These controversies certainly fall outside the range of traditional foreign policy. It is not the purpose of this work to root out answers to those issues. Among numerous references, see Michael Grunwald, "Justice Dept. Looks Again At Gore Fund-Raising Role," *Washington Post*, August 21, 1998, p. A1; "Gore Solicited from White House Phone," *Associated Press*, August 6, 1997; "Fund-Raising Scandal Imperils Gore's Image," *Associated Press*, September 15, 1997; and "Panel Backs Immunity for Nuns' Testimony," *Investor's Business Daily*, July 24, 1997, p. A1.
8. In March 1992, Gore confided to *Roll Call*: "I put my whole heart and soul into this [book]." For one such recent reference, see *Time*, April 26, 1999.
9. Boyer, op. cit., pp. 100-03 and 110. In a similar assessment, former National Security Advisor Robert McFarlane said that President Ronald Reagan possessed a "self-confidence that he was an historic figure. . . . He had enormous self-confidence in the ability of a single heroic figure to change history." Don Oberdorfer, *The Turn* (New York: Poseidon Press, 1991).
10. "No Willie Horton," Editorial, *Wall Street Journal*, April 14, 1992.
11. George Melloan, "Global View: Congress Is Scuppering Missile Defense," op-ed, *Wall Street Journal*, December 16, 1993.
12. "Remarks in Congress during the Last Hours of Debate," *The New York Times*, January 13, 1991, p. A10.
13. See Michael Kelly, "Where Clinton Stood on War with Iraq," *The New York Times*, July 31, 1992, p. A13.
14. Gore's predecessor, who was present in the event of a tie vote, was unimpressed by the speech. "As I listened carefully to the speech he made before announcing his vote," recalled Quayle, "he offered so many arguments *against* the administration's position that I thought he had changed his mind. . . . In fact, he was trying to have it both

ways." Dan Quayle, *Standing Firm: A Vice-Presidential Memoir* (New York: HarperCollins, 1994), pp. 225-26.

15. Albert Gore, Jr., "Defeating Hussein, Once and for All," op-ed, *The New York Times*, September 26, 1991, p. A27.

16. A. M. Rosenthal, "Saddam and Gore," op-ed, *The New York Times*, July 28, 1992, p. A19.

17. Gore, "Defeating Hussein, Once and for All," p. A27.

18. *The New York Times*, April 13, 1991.

19. *The New York Times*, April 5, 1991.

20. *Wall Street Journal*, April 4, 1991.

21. Ann Devroy, "Bush Prepares Mission to Iraq as Final Bid to Preserve Peace," *Washington Post*, December 1, 1990, p. A1.

22. It is likely no coincidence that it would be Gore—not Clinton—who would call for an end to cynicism over Vietnam, likely in part to deflect attacks on the president by veterans groups. "The Vatican vs. the VP," Editorial, *Washington Post*, June 10, 1994.

23. Boyer, op. cit., p. 103.

24. See Katharine Q. Seelye, "Gore Terms Clinton Affair 'Inexcusable,'" *The New York Times*, June 16, 1999; John F. Harris and Ceci Connolly, "Clinton and Gore Camps on Edge," *Washington Post*, June 27, 1999, p. A2; and Andrew Cain, "Clinton Says Gore Rebuke Didn't Make Him Angry," *The Washington Times*, July 2, 1999, p. A1.

25. Kenneth T. Walsh and Matthew Cooper, "A Vice President Who Counts," *U.S. News & World Report*, Vol. 115, No. 3, July 19, 1993, p. 29.

26. See Owen Ullmann, "Who Has Clinton's Ear Now?" *Washingtonian*, Vol. 29, No. 4, January 1994, pp. 42-45; *The Economist*, September 10, 1994, p. 30; William Safire, "Who's Got Clout," *The New York Times*, Sunday Magazine, June 20, 1993; and Boyer, op. cit., p. 105.

27. Safire, "Who's Got Clout," June 20, 1993.

28. Ann Devroy and Stephen Barr, "Gore Bucks Tradition in Vice President's Role," *Washington Post*, February 18, 1995, p. A8.

29. Walsh and Cooper, op. cit., p. 29.

30. *The Economist*, September 10, 1994, p. 30.

31. Sciolino and Purdum, op. cit., p. A1.

32. Devroy and Barr, "Gore Bucks Tradition in Vice President's Role," p. A8.

33. Among others, see Boyer, op. cit., p. 105.

34. Sciolino and Purdum, op. cit., p. A1.

35. Boyer, op. cit., p. 105; and Devroy and Barr, "Gore Bucks Tradition in Vice President's Role," p. A8.

36. Bob Woodward, *The Agenda: Inside the Clinton White House* (New York: Simon & Schuster, 1994), pp. 280-81.

37. Boyer, op. cit., p. 105; and Devroy and Barr, "Gore Bucks Tradition in Vice President's Role," p. A8.

38. Walsh and Cooper, op. cit., p. 29; and Ann Devroy and Stephen Barr, "Gore Bucks Tradition in Vice President's Role," *Washington Post*, February 18, 1995, p. A8.

39. Devroy and Barr, "Gore Bucks Tradition in Vice President's Role," p. A8.

40. Ibid.

41. Ibid.

42. Sciolino and Purdum, op. cit., p. A1.

43. Devroy and Barr, "Gore Bucks Tradition in Vice President's Role," p. A8.
44. Fred Barnes, "More Gore," *The New Republic*, Vol. 209, No. 23, December 6, 1993.
45. Leslie H. Gelb, "Foreign Affairs; Where's Bill?" op-ed, *The New York Times*, March 11, 1993.
46. Sciolino and Purdum, op. cit., p. A1.
47. *The Economist*, September 10, 1994, p. 30.
48. See, among others, Jonathan Adler, "Imagine Dumping Bill," *Newsweek*, Vol. 24, No. 23, December 5, 1994, p. 30.
49. *The New York Times*, January 7, 1995.
50. Sciolino and Purdum, op. cit., p. A1.
51. Boyer, op. cit., p. 110.
52. In large part, this approach was taken because of the lack of rich information on the vice president. This should not be a surprise for a sitting vice president who has not yet completed a full term. Obviously, there is a dearth of memoirs by foreign-policy players, presidential papers, etc., that usually arise later.
53. Carla Anne Robbins, "Gore's Success in Foreign Policy Role Depends on Committment from Clinton," *Wall Street Journal*, December 13, 1993, p. A11.
54. Barnes, "More Gore," p. 14.
55. "Lexington: The Tortoise of Foggy Bottom," *The Economist*, January 8, 1994, p. 34; Sciolino and Purdum, op. cit., p. A1; and *The New York Times*, January 2, 1994.
56. Sciolino and Purdum, op. cit., p. A1.
57. Sciolino and Purdum, op. cit., p. A1.
58. Griffith, op. cit., p. A8.
59. Karen Breslau and Bob Cohn, "Al Gore: Talk a Lot, and Carry a Big Stick," *Newsweek*, October 31, 1994, p. 30.
60. Sciolino and Purdum, op. cit., p. A1.
61. Breslau and Cohn, op. cit., p. 30.
62. Barnes, "More Gore," p. 15.
63. Boyer, op. cit., p. 105.
64. *The New York Times*, February 8, 1993.
65. Michael K. Frisby and Barbara Rosewicz, "Gore, Adding Efficiency Study to His Portfolio," *Wall Street Journal*, March 4, 1993, p. A16.
66. Robbins, op. cit., p. A11.
67. Frisby and Rosewicz, op. cit., p. A16.
68. Breslau and Cohn, op. cit., p. 30.
69. Devroy and Barr, op. cit., p. A8; and Interview with Joe DeSutter, former foreign-policy and national security advisor to both vice presidents Quayle and Gore, via telephone from Washington, D.C., December 18, 1996.
70. Gelb, "Foreign Affairs; Where's Bill?" March 11, 1993.
71. Frisby and Rosewicz, op. cit., p. A16.
72. Robbins, op. cit., p. A11.
73. DeSutter talks about the elevated status of the vice president's staff under Gore compared to Quayle. Under Quayle, said DeSutter, he had to be persistent in getting information from the NSC. Under Gore, however, "The people in the NSC now came to me." He notes that the change had nothing to do with him personally or his position—neither of which changed—but instead with the level of foreign-policy stature granted to

ther of which changed—but instead with the level of foreign-policy stature granted to and secured by Gore. Interview with Joe DeSutter.

74. Devroy and Barr, op. cit., p. A8; and Frisby and Rosewicz, op. cit., p. A16.

75. Devroy and Barr, op. cit., p. A8.

76. In a markedly nonconservative display, Gore was the only one of fifteen aides who in the early administration urged Clinton not to compromise with Congress on allowing gays in the military. His stance did not align him with Pentagon hawks, who were confounded that a veteran such as Gore could be so adamant. Of course, this example also further illustrates Gore's history of political independence. "Military People Split over Ban on Homosexuals," *The New York Times*, January 28, 1993, p. A16.

77. Walsh and Cooper, op. cit., p. 29.

78. In a very interesting parallel made in an article for *The New Yorker*, Peter J. Boyer maintains that the 1994 mid-term election massacre of Clinton and his party horrified Gore partisans of another possible Carter disaster, whereby a Clinton failure could mean that Gore, rather than fulfilling their long-time dream of becoming president, may become the 'Walter Mondale of the nineties.' Boyer, op. cit., pp. 100-10.

79. Ibid., p. 106; and Breslau and Cohn, op. cit., p. 30.

80. Breslau and Cohn, op. cit., p. 30.

81. *The Wall Street Journal*, December 12, 1993.

82. Sciolino and Purdum, op. cit., p. A1.

83. *This Week with David Brinkley*, ABC-TV, June 25, 1995.

84. "Vice President-Elect Al Gore," Television Program: *Meet the Press with Tim Russert*, NBC-TV, January 17, 1993, pp. 1-18.

85. Al Gore, "The Principles and Future of U.S.-Polish Relations," *U.S. Department of State Dispatch*, Vol. 4, No. 18, May 3, 1993, pp. 313-17.

86. Jane Perlez, "Gore Congratulates Poland on Its Democracy," *The New York Times*, April 21, 1993, p. A5.

87. Al Gore, "Forging a Partnership for Peace and Prosperity," *U.S. Department of State Dispatch*, Vol. 5, No. 2, January 10, 1994, p. 13.

88. *The New York Times*, February 12, 1994.

89. Safire, "Who's Got Clout," June 20, 1993.

90. Sciolino and Purdum, op. cit., p. A1.

91. Susan B. Garland, "The Teflon Vice President," *Business Week*, No. 3395, October 24, 1994, p. 36.

92. Boyer, op. cit., p. 100.

93. *The New York Times*, September 8, 1992.

94. Steven A. Holmes, "Gore Lashes Out at Bush on His Iran-Contra Role," *The New York Times*, September 4, 1992, p. A12.

95. Michael Janofsky, "Gore Criticizes North's Remarks on U.S. Military Preparedness," *The New York Times*, October 12, 1994, p. A21.

96. Michael Janofsky, "A Senate Race Plunges Further into Nastiness," *The New York Times*, October 30, 1994, p. A24.

97. Michael Janofsky, "Harsh Words in Final Day of Campaign for the Senate," *The New York Times*, November 8, 1994, p. A21.

98. Donald Lambro, "The Dark Side of Al Gore," *The Washington Times*, National Weekly Edition, March 29-April 4, 1999, p. 30.

99. Jay Nordlinger, "Terrible Tony," *National Review*, June 14, 1999, p. 26.

100. Bill Sammon, "Gore Admits Boom Began with Bush," *The Washington Times*, July 12, 1999.
101. Walsh and Cooper, op. cit., p. 29.
102. Frisby and Rosewicz, op. cit., p. A16.
103. Breslau and Cohn, op. cit., p. 30.
104. Sciolino and Purdum, op. cit., p. A1; and Boyer, op. cit., p. 105.
105. *Wall Street Journal*, April 28, 1993.
106. Breslau and Cohn, op. cit., p. 30.
107. *This Week with David Brinkley*, ABC-TV, June 25, 1995.
108. Ibid.
109. Frisby and Rosewicz, op. cit., p. A16.
110. Barbara Crossette, "New U.N. Force in Croatia to Be Given Limited Power," *The New York Times*, March 20, 1995, p. A2.
111. Barbara Crossette, "Croatian Leader Agrees to Continuation of U.N. Force," *The New York Times*, March 13, 1995, p. A9.
112. "U.N. Troops to Remain in Croatia Longer than Mandated," Radio Program: *Morning Edition*, National Public Radio, March 13, 1995, Program n1561.
113. Ceci Connolly, "Gore Increases Role in Kosovo Crisis," *Washington Post*, March 31, 1999, p. A4.
114. Ibid.
115. Barnes, op. cit., p. 14. Fulfilling a key spokesman role, Gore appeared on ABC's *This Week with David Brinkley* in March 1993 to discuss what at the time appeared to be a rapidly escalating confrontation between Russian President Boris Yeltsin and the Russian Congress. "Turmoil in Russia," Television Program: *This Week with David Brinkley*, NBC-TV, March 28, 1993, Program n596.
116. Griffith, op. cit., p. A8.
117. Devroy and Barr, op. cit., p. A8.
118. Steven Erlanger, "Gore Upbeat after Talks with Top Russian Leaders," *The New York Times*, December 17, 1994, p. A7.
119. "Dole and Gore Differ," *Associated Press*, January 8, 1995.
120. Elaine Sciolino, "Clinton Reaffirms Policy on Yeltsin," *The New York Times*, December 16, 1993, p. A11.
121. Boyer, op. cit., p. 105.
122. "Fact Sheet: Gore-Chernomyrdin Commission," *U.S. Department of State Dispatch*, Vol. 5, No. 1, January 3, 1994, pp. 2-3.
123. As of July 1996, Gore had completed seven visits with Chernomyrdin. See Jonas Bernstein, "Russia Watch: Not Yet the Worst," *The American Spectator*, Vol. 29, No. 9, September 1996, p. 64.
124. Aleksandr Shalnev, "United States," *Current Digest of the Post-Soviet Press*, Vol. 45, No. 50, January 12, 1994, pp. 27-28.
125. Dunbar Lockwood, "U.S., Russia Agree to Phase-Out of Nuclear Weapons Reactors," *Arms Control Today*, Vol. 24, No. 6, July/August 1994, p. 24.
126. Sciolino and Purdum, op. cit., p. A1.
127. The *Washington Post* has an interest in the story, as evidenced by a number of reports and an August 29, 1999 editorial titled, "Mr. Gore's Russia Problem," p. B6.
128. Raymond Bonner and Timothy L. O'Brien, "Activity at Bank Raises Suspicions of Russia Mob Tie," *The New York Times*, August 19, 1999, p. A1.

129. David Ignatius, "Who Robbed Russia? Did Al Gore Know About the Massive Lootings?" *Washington Post*, August 25, 1999, p. A17.
130. Ibid.
131. Ibid.
132. Ceci Connolly, "Gore Faces Ticklish Issue on Russian Corruption," *Washington Post*, August 27, 1999, p. A1.
133. Arnaud de Borchgrave, "Who Wasn't Minding the Bear?" *The Washington Times*, August 30, 1999.
134. Carol J. Williams, "Gore's Moscow Visit Breaks New Ground," *Los Angeles Times*, July 25, 1998, p. A1.
135. Martin Sieff, "'Domineering' U.S. and Its Iraq Strike Infuriates Russia," *Washington Times*, National Weekly Edition, December 28-January 3, 1999, p. 18.
136. Richard L. Berke, "Prodded by Gore, Kazakhstan Signs Arms Accord," *The New York Times*, December 14, 1993, p. A15.
137. Ibid.
138. Sciolino and Purdum, op. cit., p. A1.
139. "U.S.-Kazakhstan Agreements," The White House, Office of the Vice President, March 27, 1995.
140. Boyer, op. cit., p. 105.
141. See also Breslau and Cohn, op. cit., p. 30.
142. "Vice President Al Gore Travels to Mexico City," Radio Program: *Morning Edition*, National Public Radio, December 1, 1993, Program n1228.
143. Barnes, "More Gore," p. 15.
144. "Al Gore's Big Knockout," Editorial, *Wall Street Journal*, November 9, 1993.
145. Barnes, "More Gore," p. 15.
146. "Al Gore's Big Knockout," November 9, 1993.
147. Barnes, "More Gore," pp. 15-16.
148. William Safire, "Gore Flattens Perot," op-ed, *The New York Times*, November 11, 1993, p. A27.
149. "Al Gore's Big Knockout," November 9, 1993.
150. Griffith, op. cit., p. A8.
151. Boyer, op. cit., p. 105.
152. Devroy and Barr, "Gore Bucks Tradition in Vice President's Role," p. A8.
153. Breslau and Cohn, op. cit., p. 30.
154. *The New York Times*, September 19, 1994.
155. This is one of a number of examples of Gore working the phones during a crisis. In November 1998 he joined Secretary of State Albright in calling Crown Prince Abdallah and King Fahd in trying to marshal Saudi support against Iraq. Barry Schweld, "Saudi Help Sought against Iraq," *Associated Press*, November 4, 1998.
156. *The New York Times*, September 11, 1994.
157. Barnes, "More Gore," p. 15.
158. *The New York Times*, March 30, 1994.
159. *The New York Times*, September 21, 1994.
160. "The Crisis in Haiti," *U.S. Department of State Dispatch*, Vol. 5, No. 38, September 19, 1994.
161. Albert Gore, *Earth in the Balance: Ecology and the Human Spirit* (Boston: Houghton Mifflin, 1992). For a scholarly critique of Gore's book, see John A. Baden,

ed., *Environmental Gore: A Constructive Response to Earth in the Balance* (San Francisco, Calif.: Pacific Research Institute for Public Policy, 1994).

162. Adam Wolfson, "Apocalypse Gore," *National Review*, March 8, 1999, p. 37.

163. Gore, *Earth in the Balance*, p. 177.

164. Al Gore, "Ecology: The New Sacred Agenda," *New Perspectives Quarterly*, Vol. 10, No. 1, Winter 1993, pp. 44-45; Devroy and Barr, op. cit., p. A8; Henry I. Miller, "The Vice President in the Balance: He's Delusional," *The Washington Times*, National Weekly Edition, April 12-18, 1999, p. 32; and Boyer, op. cit., p. 105.

165. Gore, *Earth in the Balance*, p. 275.

166. He makes similar statements on pp. 12 and 367, among others.

167. Gore, *Earth in the Balance*, p. 163.

168. Wolfson, op. cit., p. 37.

169. Ibid, p. 39.

170. Gore, *Earth in the Balance*, pp. 269, 282-83, and 293-94.

171. Wolfson, p. 40.

172. Gore, *Earth in the Balance*, p. 270.

173. Ibid., pp. 270-74.

174. Ibid., p. 274.

175. Ibid., pp. 244 and 265.

176. Nat Hentoff, "God in School," *Washington Post*, August 7, 1999, p. A19.

177. George Melloan, "Al Gore's Seven Seals and What They Cost," op-ed, *Wall Street Journal*, July 12, 1993, p. A13.

178. "Dump this Nominee," Editorial, *The Nation*, Vol. 256, No. 7, February 22, 1993, p. 217.

179. Walsh and Cooper, op. cit., p. 29.

180. Barnes, op. cit., p. 14; and Patrick E. Tyler, "Visit by Gore to China Is under Study," *The New York Times*, December 20, 1994, p. A3.

181. "Gore Stresses Environment while Asia," *Associated Press*, March 24, 1997.

182. *Wall Street Journal*, March 29, 1993.

183. In an example of how this has also worked for him regarding China policy, see Patrick E. Tyler, "Visit by Gore to China Is under Study," p. A3; and Patrick E. Tyler, "The U.S.-China Slide," *The New York Times*, May 23, 1995, p. A10.

184. Jasminka Skrlec, "Kissinger: ABM Pact Is Outdated," *Washington Times*, National Weekly Edition, May 31-June 6, 1999.

185. Lou Cannon notes that Gore argued in the 1980s that a defensive shield was not possible, while also arguing that pursuing such a shield would prove so destabilizing that it might prompt a first strike from the Soviets. Lou Cannon's son, Carl Cannon, pointed out to Gore that his stance seemed contradictory: Why would the Soviets fear a weapon system that could not possibly work? "Which is it, Al?" he asked. Reportedly, Gore chuckled and did not answer the question. Lou Cannon, "Reagan's Big Idea," *National Review*, February 22, 1999, p. 42.

186. Bill Gertz, "On Missile Defense, Clinton Is Consistent: He's against It," *The Washington Times*, National Weekly Edition, June 7-13, 1999, p. 20.

187. Barbara Crossette, "Gore, at U.N., Says Nuclear Powers Are Fair on Weapons Treaty," *The New York Times*, April 20, 1995, p. A14.

188. Barbara Crossette, "South Africa Emerges as a Force for Extending Nuclear Arms," *The New York Times*, April 23, 1995, p. A16.

189. Crossette, "Gore Says Nuclear Powers Are Fair on Weapons Treaty," p. A14.

190. Al Gore, "Partnership with South Africa," *U.S. Department of State Dispatch*, Vol. 5, No. 44, October 31, 1994, pp. 723-24.

191. Boyer, op. cit., p. 104.

192. Al Gore, "International Conference on Population Development," *U.S. Department of State Dispatch*, Vol. 5, No. 38, September 19, 1994, pp. 618-20.

193. Al Gore, "The Rapid Growth of the Human Population: Sustainable Economic Growth," *Vital Speeches of the Day*, Vol. 60, No. 24, October 1, 1994, pp. 741-45.

194. Al Gore, "The Cairo Conference: Defining Agenda of Hope, Opportunity," *U.S. Department of State Dispatch*, Vol. 5, No. 35, August 29, 1994, pp. 569-73.

195. John H. Cushman, Jr., "Gore Wants U.N. to Leave Abortion up to Each Nation," *The New York Times*, August 26, 1994, p. A2.

196. William Safire, "The Vatican vs. the VP: Papal Population Politics," op-ed, *The New York Times*, September 5, 1994, p. A17.

197. Alan Cowell, "Vatican Says Gore Is Misrepresenting Population Talks," *The New York Times*, September 1, 1994, p. A1.

198. David S. Broder and Bob Woodward, "Facing Limitations in an 'Awkward Job,'" *The Washington Post*, January 8, 1992, pp. A1 and A14.

199. Interview with DeSutter.

200. The remaining percent was split among many candidates, none higher than 3 percent. John Harwood, "Gore Is Seen as Daunting Front-Runner for 2000 Race," *Wall Street Journal*, January 4, 1999, p. A40.

201. As noted in an earlier footnote, a President Gore also would have lifted the ban on gays in the military. This further illustrates his political independence as well as liberal position on some issues.

202. An example of how Gore can talk tough in negotiations: When Clinton politely asked Yeltsin for his views on a Caspian Sea gas deal proposed by Chevron Oil, Gore interjected, "You guys will get a 10 percent cut. That's not such a bad deal. And it's a way to get Azerbaijan off the Russian dole." Breslau and Cohn, op. cit., p. 30.

203. Colin Macilwain, "New 'Security Role Urged for Science,'" *Nature*, Vol. 374, No. 6522, April 6, 1995, p. 485.

204. The Gore-Chernomyrdin relationship became so close that in December 1997, when the United States protested spying charges brought by Moscow against American businessman Richard Bliss, it did so via a phone call from Gore to Chernomyrdin. "American Charged in Spy Case," *Reuters*, December 6, 1997.

205. Breslau and Cohn, op. cit., p. 31.

206. Broder and Woodward, op. cit., p. A14.

Chapter 8
Conclusion: Lessons Learned and Policy Recommendations

"The experience of the modern vice presidency has demonstrated that this office can indeed serve more of a function than merely its constitutional one of presiding over the Senate or breaking a tie. The recent history of the office has demonstrated that it can encompass significant functions."
Marie D. Natoli, *American Prince, American Pauper*, 1985

"[There is an] opportunity to make more out of the office than merely a waiting room for the expiration of two terms, resignation, impeachment or death."
C. Boyden Gray, 1989

The wisdom of the above statements requires further evaluation. In that sense, this chapter is the heart of the study. The previous pages illuminated the foreign-policy roles and activities of five active vice presidents. As noted, there are many examples of the five vice presidents performing well in certain foreign-policy tasks and missions. Yet, there are also some negative examples. These appear to include Nixon's advocacy of deposing Castro, as well as his Indochina remarks in 1954; Mondale's South Africa assignment; Bush's misrepresentation of the administration during talks with King Fahd in Saudi Arabia, as well as possibly some of his Central America duties; and, potentially, some of Gore's activities concerning the Gore-Chernomyrdin Commission. Within the literature, these examples are featured in an almost exclusively positive light, with a neglect of the deleterious aspects. This chapter draws lessons from those experiences in light of various policy recommendations intended to best use the vice president in an administration's foreign policy. If anything, I hope that a closer look at these examples will guard future reformers from being overly aggressive.

The vice president has two basic constitutional duties: succeed the president in cases of emergency and preside over the Senate. Experience, however, has led to a much more ambitious job description—foreign policy included. "The experience of the modern vice presidency has demonstrated that this office can indeed serve more of a function than merely its constitutional one of presiding over the Senate or breaking a tie," writes Marie D. Natoli. "The recent history of the office has demonstrated that it can encompass significant functions."[1] The following table lists past recommendations—some significant—made in regard to the vice president's foreign-policy role. Some have been implemented without opposition, some have not, while others are newly conceived by myself. The reader should not be deceived by the fact that the majority of them are assessed as a "must" or having "potential" that varies by administration. Many of these are no-brainers that were created by Truman and have been continued because of obvious necessity. Typically, they have the goal of keeping the vice president informed in case succession is necessary. The more difficult recommendations, requiring deeper analysis, are found toward the end of the table. In fact, those are the recommendations that this study first and foremost aimed to examine. In those recommendations we find the major lessons learned in this book. The proceeding pages will examine each of them. The following table is a summary.

Table 8.1: Policy Recommendations for the Vice President vis-à-vis Foreign Policy

Policy Recommendation	Feasibility (author's assesment)
1. VP serves as statutory member of the NSC	Must
2. VP attends all NSC and Cabinet meetings	Must
3. VP presides over NSC and Cabinet meetings in absence of president	Must
4. VP receives copies of all presidential papers	Must
5. VP takes part in president's daily intelligence briefing	Must
6. VP has weekly one-on-one lunch or breakfast with the president	Must
7. VP has weekly one-on-one foreign-policy meeting with the president, in addition to regular meeting	Reject
8. VP has office in West Wing of the White House	Must
9. VP has own office in the Senate	Must
10. VP serves as a "congressional liaison"	Potential (varies by administration)
11. VP serves as a general "troubleshooter" or "general advisor" to the president	Potential (varies by administration)
12. VP acts as an emissary to foreign nations and as a negotiator with foreign leaders	Potential
13. VP serves as a foreign-policy spokesman	Potential
14. VP chair a short-term executive-level task force or group inside or outside of the White House	Potential
15. VP has his own defense and foreign-policy advisors	Must
16. VP defense or foreign-policy aide be a member of a senior-level foreign-policy group	Potential (if applicable)
17. VP head an executive-level department	Reject
18. VP play a coordinating role in assisting the State Department	Reject
19. VP chair a major interagency group, executive-level committee, or NSC subgroup	Reject
20. VP chair a crisis-management group	Reject

Many of these policy recommendations are statutory and already in place, such as having the vice president serve as a statutory member of the NSC and receive copies of all paper work that goes to the president. In such cases, my recommendation merely affirms that current practices be continued. Consequently, such suggestions are largely noncontroversial. For instance, I know of no one who has argued that the vice president's practice of serving as a statutory member of the National Security Council be abolished.

In a number of cases, I have made my own recommendations based on the experiences of the vice presidents in this study—i.e., the vice president should have a West Wing office, or should have his own defense and foreign-policy advisors. It is also important to note that the aforementioned recommendations are interrelated. For example, I believe the vice president should continue to have his own office in the Senate. Of course, this is somewhat of a prerequisite to having the second-office holder serve as a congressional liaison to the White House—without the seat on Capitol Hill, he might not be an effective congressional liaison.

Finally, the most important aspects of this chapter—and the primary focus of the study as a whole—are policy recommendations made by scholars and policy makers like Kevin Mulcahy, C. Boyden Gray, and others. Such observers have argued, among other things, that the vice president chair a major interagency or executive-level committee, or assist the State Department in coordinating foreign policy. These are ambitious recommendations which are debatable. Hence, they will be explored over the following pages in a detailed fashion.

Policy Recommendations 1 through 5

The first five policy suggestions listed above assert that the vice president should continue to: (1) serve as a statutory member of the NSC; (2) attend all NSC and Cabinet meetings; (3) preside over NSC and Cabinet meetings in the president's absence; (4) receive copies of all presidential papers; and (5) take part in the president's daily intelligence briefing. These five recommendations grew out of the experiences of Truman and FDR. Just about every president and vice president in this study is quoted as referring to the "lesson of Truman and FDR." Recall the quote from George Bush that leads off chapter 1 of the study, or the December 1976 (a few weeks after the election) meeting between Mondale and the president-elect at Blair House, the transition residency of Carter, to discuss their plans for the vice presidency. He and Carter recalled the Truman-FDR lesson. Remember, also, that immediately after Ike was nominated for the presidency in 1952 he summoned Nixon to his hotel suite. He recalled how FDR had failed to inform Truman on many basic, critical decisions and the serious situation this created when Truman was elevated to the presidency in 1945. It was vitally important, said Ike, that this never happen again. As a result, he would make sure that Nixon participated in all policymaking meetings. Nixon was deliberately given assignments to prepare him for the possibility that he might suddenly become president.[2] This included foreign policy in particular. Finally, a military aide who served both vice presidents Quayle and Gore finds the FDR-Truman situation unfathomable and refers to it as "one of the most amazing things in American history." He asks: "Can you imagine anything as irresponsible? What on earth was [FDR] thinking?"[3]

Though it took place many years ago, none of the presidents or vice presidents (as well as many of their aides) in this study have forgotten about the Truman episode. They all seem to view the implementation of policy recommendations one through five as a safeguard against a repeat of the debacle.

Indeed, Vice President Truman did not have any of these duties. As noted earlier, he had met with his president only eight times in the one-and-a-half years he served him as vice president. He found himself totally uninformed when he assumed the presidency under the most critical circumstances imaginable. He scrambled to find out basic information on crucial matters like the atomic bomb and private talks between FDR, Churchill, and Stalin. Potsdam was only a few weeks away. Hence, Truman took steps, both statutory and informal, to allow the vice president to be more informed in foreign policy. Four of these five recommendations were made directly by Truman. The third of the five—the vice president should preside over NSC and Cabinet meetings in the president's absence—was started by Eisenhower. He made the change for reasons that grew from the Truman-FDR experience: It would not only keep the vice president more informed of crucial foreign-policy developments but would also give him valuable training in policy management in the event he had to succeed the president.

Wisely, no president has ever seen a reason to change any of the five actions begun by Truman and Eisenhower. This study recommends unequivocally that they all be continued.

Policy Recommendations 6 and 7

The first of these two policy recommendations stresses the vice president's need to have a weekly one-on-one meeting with the president, in which anything can be discussed—including, of course, foreign policy. The second considers an additional one-on-one meeting focused exclusively on foreign policy.

Typically, the regular, general meeting between the two men has taken the form of a breakfast or lunch in which the president and vice president talk about a number of issues key to the administration—foreign and domestic. For instance, Vice President Mondale and President Carter lunched together on Mondays to discuss any matter of interest to Mondale. Hamilton Jordan says this was known colloquially as the "Vice President's time." These were valuable meetings between the president and vice president. Likewise, Reagan and Bush and Bush and Quayle had such sessions. These meetings helped keep the vice president informed on foreign policy for both his own personal enhancement as well as the nation's.

In addition to such meetings, some might suggest that the vice president have his own one-on-one weekly foreign-policy meeting with the president, in addition to their regular weekly sit down on general issues. Such a meeting seems unnecessary. The regular meeting between the president and vice president would allow for candid one-on-one discussion between the two men on issues of foreign policy. In addition, the vice president has opportunities to discuss foreign policy with the president during NSC and Cabinet meetings and during the morning intelligence brief. We can use Mondale again as an example. Each day, Carter had his Presidential Daily Briefing, which brought to the president a highly secret document that was distributed to only five people: the president, vice president, secretaries of state and defense, and the NSA. Mondale had an open invitation to all Oval Office meetings, even those that the president was holding with foreign chiefs of state. He attended the president's weekly breakfasts with foreign-policy advisors. Carter gave instructions that Mondale receive the full paper flow sent to the president's desk. He participated in the weekly, Friday foreign-policy breakfasts, along with the president, secretary of state, secretary of defense, and the national security advisor. (Mondale was not involved in the other foreign-policy meeting—the foreign-policy lunch held between the president, Vance, Brown, and Brzezinski, a.k.a., the "VBB luncheon".) In most of these areas, Mondale's routine was matched almost identically by vice presidents Bush and Quayle.

Considering all of this, an extra meeting added to the mix would seem to be a waste of time (unless, of course, the president disagrees and finds it necessary). If a special circumstance arose in foreign policy, the vice president could always use his West Wing office to drop in on the commander in chief, or employ some other method for communicating his thoughts.

Policy Recommendation 8

Like recommendations 1 through 7, this one has the goal of keeping the vice president more informed of policy, rather than any sort of personal aggrandizement. It was not until Mondale that vice presidents had their own office in the West Wing. Not until President John F. Kennedy was a vice president given space even in the Executive Office Building.[4] The vice president's office once had five or six different locations. The vice president's staff is now consolidated on the second floor of the Old Executive Office Building, with outposts on Capitol Hill and in the West Wing.[5]

A number of informed observers believe the office should be permanently moved to the West Wing—and for good reason. Vice President Bush noted how the West Wing office added to his ability to interact with the president on issues, saying it allowed him "ample opportunity to just walk down the hall and go in to see him alone."[6] Advocates of the West Wing move include, not surprisingly, Carter, Mondale, and Bush.[7] Vice President Bush, in crediting Carter for "upgrading the prestige of the vice presidency," specifically points to the benefit of giving the vice president office space in the White House.[8]

Quayle's deputy NSA, Jon Glassman, stresses the benefit of the West Wing location. Sketching out on his desk a crude diagram of the White House office arrangement, he shows how the vice president can profit by having an office two doors down from the president and in between the president's NSA and chief of staff. The order in the Bush White House featured Scowcroft's office, (moving rightward) followed by Quayle's, followed by Sununu's, and ending with the Oval Office. Hence, NSA Scowcroft had to walk by the vice president's office every time he headed over to see Bush in the Oval Office. As also shown in the below remark by NSA Brzezinski in the Carter administration, this allowed for easy, quick foreign-policy chats between him and the vice president. "This seems funny," concedes Glassman, "but I'm telling you: it makes a difference." He says that this subtle difference helped Quayle in foreign policy.[9]

This issue does seem trivial on the surface, but it is quite the contrary in practice. Mondale desired to be "in the loop" with an office in the West Wing, as opposed to a spot in the Executive Office Building. Carter located Mondale's office adjacent to his own. Carter noted that the West Wing move was a first in the history of the vice presidency.[10] Reflecting on this innovation, Mike Berman commented: "The White House operates not by structure but by osmosis. Most of the business is done by floating in and out of each other's offices, bumping into people in the hall, dealing in the White House restaurant. If you are out of the loop, it is very hard to be part of the process."[11] Brzezinski alludes to how the West Wing location of his and Mondale's offices allowed the vice president to be kept more abreast of foreign-affairs issues:

> Our offices in the West Wing of the White House were adjoining, and that made for easy and informal contact. When there was something to talk about, Fritz . . . would simply pop into my office, or I would stick my head into his. . . . Ten days or so after assuming office, I jotted in my journal: "It is quite striking how often Mondale now drops by to chat. . . . For example, today he came in to talk about our relations with Europe."[12]

Continuing the West Wing location practice should only help keep the vice president better informed on foreign-policy issues, and certainly should not hurt.

Policy Recommendations 9 and 10

These two recommendations are tightly interrelated.[13] The second is entirely contingent upon accepting the first. The first asserts that the vice president should have his own office in the Senate. This has been an accepted practice due to the vice president's constitutional duty of presiding over the Senate. The second suggests the vice president be used as a congressional liaison. The first is required to perform the second effectively. Also, prior congressional experience by a vice president significantly boosts his ability to be an effective congressional liaison.

Typically, most vice presidents have had legislative experience in the U.S. Congress. All of the vice presidents profiled in this study had prior experience on Capitol Hill. And, not surprisingly, they all performed key roles as congressional liaisons. Their success as liaisons included helping the administration with foreign-policy initiatives. Examples cited herein include Mondale during the debates over SALT and the Panama Canal treaties, as well as Quayle monitoring the moods of congressmen, tallying their votes, and pressuring them when it came to seeking authorization for the administration's use of force in the Persian Gulf. Quayle accurately told President Bush that the administration had the votes and should seek the political support that would be secured by a congressional vote on the use of force. "Quayle did firm up our Hill [congressional] relations during the Gulf War especially since he was the only ex-senator in the senior reaches of the administration," said Bill Kristol, Quayle's chief of staff, echoing near-identical comments made by John Sununu and Dick Cheney.[14]

There is no constitutional problem with having the vice president continue the liaison role. Since he already has an office on Capitol Hill, is constitutionally assigned with the duty of breaking a tie during certain votes, and often has previous congressional experience, he seems to be a natural fit for such a role. Equally important, he is not infringing upon the turf of any other administration official, unlike elsewhere (as we shall see). Perhaps most importantly, I have found no examples which show that the vice president's tendency to be used in this capacity has been a detriment to the president's foreign policy.

Having said this, I do not consider the role a "must" in the same sense as the vice president needing to be a statutory member of the NSC and participating in foreign-policy briefings. After all, the vice president can be exempted from the congressional-liaison role and still be kept adequately informed of foreign policy. Moreover, a president-elect may in the future choose a governor as his running mate rather than an ex-congressman, suggesting that his vice president may not be as suitable for that role as another administration member—although, again, his office and continued presence on Capitol Hill would eventually make him a good fit anyway. In sum, I have assessed the congressional-liaison role as holding "potential" simply because it is not an absolute necessity. At the same time, he views such a role as an asset that each new administration should consider and should probably pursue.

Policy Recommendation 11

This recommendation suggests the vice president serve as an all-around "troubleshooter" or "general advisor" to the president. Of all the recommendations made hereafter, this one probably has the least potential of stepping on the bureaucratic toes of other members of the administration, since it does not suggest that the vice president concentrate on, usurp, or share duties with a particular agency or department.

This type of role has been referred to as the "Mondale model." Mondale himself advocated that the vice president's role should be that of a general advisor. In the area of foreign policy, Mondale appeared to have been given free reign to troubleshoot whichever issues he chose. It does not appear that Carter kept Mondale away from certain foreign-policy matters and prohibited the vice president from "trouble shooting" them.

Ben W. Heineman Jr., pointing to Mondale's successes and general happiness with this model, says all vice presidents should be elevated to this type of assignment. He refers to the vice president as someone who can serve as a "senior advisor without [a] portfolio." The vice president "should ask questions, use his political antennae, and give the president his best judgment on important issues based on the work flowing from the others to the president," writes Heineman. "In so using the vice president, the president is not only getting something very important—the seasoned, inside view of a senior person who has no bureaucratic ax to grind—but he is giving the vice president the best possible training in the event that he must assume the highest office after presidential death or disability."[15] For these reasons, Heineman—and Mondale—believe that the vice president is uniquely suited, more than other administration members, for the general-advisor role.

Heineman is not alone in perceiving Mondale's role as worthy of emulation. Steve Gillon writes: "It seems likely that the new role that Mondale pioneered will become a model for all future vice presidents." As evidence, Gillon points to remarks by Bush expressing a willingness to continue the Mondale archetype. "My conclusion is that the Mondale model is a very good model," Bush told reports in January 1981.[16] Shortly after, he added:

Lessons Learned and Policy Recommendations 269

Mondale had the best relationship with the president of any vice president in history.... Mondale set a pattern—a mold—that I think is very good. It helped us start off—President Reagan and me—on what I hope will be for him a constructive way to go. Clearly it is constructive for me. Mondale persevered. The general feeling is that he was a useful vice president.[17]

Bush would not have gotten an argument from President Carter. Shortly after losing the 1980 election, Cutler asked Carter if he thought president-elect Reagan would "involve George Bush as you did Fritz." Carter replied: "They would be smart to."[18] Thus, Heineman, Gillon, Mondale, Bush, and Carter all endorse the notion of implementing the Mondale format. The primary reason is that Mondale's role was usually fairly successful and received good publicity, not to mention the fact that modern vice presidents take tips from other (living) modern vice presidents regarding ideas on what roles they should have. In this latter respect, Mondale has recommended the general-advisor role to vice presidents Bush, Quayle, and Gore—all of his succeeding vice presidents. Likewise, Nixon had served effectively as an advisor years earlier. Such success stories among recent vice presidents sometimes seem to get passed down like legends, often with exaggerations of the positives and neglect of the negatives.

In reality, is this role a good idea? In part, experience would suggest it is. The fact that Mondale and Bush adopted similar approaches with a considerable degree of influence and success is noteworthy. Likewise with Vice President Gore, who describes himself as playing a similar "general-advisor role" to President Clinton, counseling him on virtually every major issue. Over the past four years, the vice president has emerged as Clinton's most trusted official advisor (rivaled only by Hillary Rodham Clinton) and his ultimate trouble-shooter.

As noted, Heineman has put some flesh on the Mondale model. However, although Heineman's argument has merit, there are at least three key problems with it.

First, while the vice president does typically have useful political antennae and no "bureaucratic ax" to grind, he does have his own selfish-political interests that can sometimes cloud his judgment. This reality, proven by Bush in Saudi Arabia and Mondale's abandonment of South Africa duties, will be further detailed below; although, to be fair, Heineman is correct in noting that he has no bureaucratic interest in the classical sense. Second, if the intention is to give the vice president "the best possible training" in case he must assume the top office, there are other ways of gaining such instruction, as shown above. While the senior-advisor role might add to the training, there are other ways of providing the necessary experience.

Third, Heineman himself concedes that such a move may necessarily imply an expanded vice-presidential staff. He asserts: "The last thing that the invariably overblown [Executive Office of the President] needs is yet another large staff."[19] This is especially noteworthy in budget-conscious times and in an era in which the second-office holder's staff size increased dramatically under Vice President Mondale and once again under Vice President Gore.[20] The vice president's staff size grew markedly in the 1970s, particularly under Mondale. Mondale had a staff of between fifty-five and sixty people, compared an office size of less than twenty staff members in 1960.[21] By the early 1980s, the vice president's office had reached seventy permanent positions. The number would decline under Quayle and would rise again under Gore. The office, which once had no executive budget, by the early 1980s had its own line with an annual budget of two million dollars. The vice president's office is now a replica of the president's office, with a national security advisor, chief of staff, press secretary, domestic issues staff, scheduling team, advance, appointment, administration, and counsel's office.[22]

Moreover, one should consider that while vice presidents Mondale and Gore both took on such a senior-advisor role, seemingly to the benefit of their administrations, Vice President Quayle was not granted similar status. And many would argue that the Bush administration's foreign policy still managed to be quite successful. Quayle's own chief of staff avers: "At the end of the day would Bush's foreign policy have been different if someone else had been vice president? Probably not."[23] At the same time, however, Quayle was able to play a very effective foreign-policy role in the Bush administration, as proven by his duties during the 1990-91 Persian Gulf crisis and in Latin America, not to mention his SDI work. So, why not leave well enough alone? Why elevate a Vice President Quayle or any other vice president to a senior-advisor role if he can perform effectively in other capacities?

Finally, I concede that—using the rationale of Heineman and Mondale—the vice president, more than other administration members, *seems* uniquely suited in many ways for the general-advisor role. Yet, one must ask: Is this not a duty that can be adequately fulfilled by another administration member, such as a regular presidential advisor with no bureaucratic-parochial interest? Of course it is. Recall, however, that a key added benefit of giving such a role to the vice president, rather than a standard presidential advisor, is that it provides the second-office holder with some valuable training in case he must someday assume the Oval Office. (This same line of argument will come up again concerning the use of the vice president as an emissary abroad, that is, policy recommendation 13.) Indeed, there are pros and cons.

In sum, as these questions indicate, Heineman's suggestion merits close investigation.

While such a role is not a "must," it should not be immediately rejected as a notion that invites a lot of unforeseen trouble. It has "potential" that likely varies by administration. Mondale played a troubleshooter role that seemed to work fairly well. While he did encounter bumps of opposition from Vance and Brzezinski, one should expect such conflicts. Quayle did not play such a role, and the administration's foreign policy did not appear to suffer as a result. In short, the notion seems innocuous. Most importantly, *not* playing such a role would not lead to another Truman-FDR incident. Other elements (see policy recommendations 1 through 5) would ensure the needed knowledge in the event that a succession would take place.

Policy Recommendations 12 and 13

The first of these recommendations refers to using the vice president as an emissary to foreign nations and as a negotiator with leaders abroad. The second relates to employing him as a foreign-policy spokesman, which often entails giving speeches at home and overseas on the president's foreign policy, appearing on media outlets, sometimes even hammering political opponents on foreign-policy issues *a la* Quayle and Gore, or blasting critics of the administration's war polices as Quayle did during the conflict in the Persian Gulf and Spiro Agnew did during the Vietnam War.

As opposed to being "musts," both of the recommendations have "potential." Their results, in practice, are often mixed. Both have witnessed gaffes as well as successes.

First, consider the spokesman role—policy recommendation 13. Recall the usefulness of Vice President Bush in reprimanding the Salvadoran leadership in December 1983, aptly described by Tony Motley as a "dynamite performance" that may have made a difference in how the leaders did business. In another example, as a spokesman Quayle was a big asset during the Gulf War. On the other hand, as a 'pre-Gulf' spokesman, he angered Bush and the State Department twice by speaking out of line during speeches: In one case he zinged Gorbachev; in another he broke long-held protocol by boldly referring to the West Bank and Gaza Strip as Judea and Samaria. In other mixed examples, Nixon caused a serious rift with his "off-the-record" Indochina remarks in 1954, despite performing brilliantly during a press conference in Moscow in 1960. Gore made a brash statement on Russia that caused a minor "diplomatic incident."

Perhaps it might be wise to turn over some sensitive foreign-policy-spokesman activities to trained, skilled diplomats—the "Robert Murphys" and "Harold Saunders" of the world—rather than to vice presidents not quite as nuanced in the subtleties of diplomacy. After all, vice presidents, as noted by Gerald Pomper and other scholars, are traditionally picked for political reasons, rather than their ability to operate as cool-tempered spokesmen abroad. On the other hand, State Department staff who typically handle such duties—Lawrence Eagleburger, Warren Christopher, etc.—typically are brought up through the ranks and have past experience in handling such issues. (Obviously, however, some secretaries of state, under secretaries, and so on, are chosen because of ideology or politics, such as Al Haig or Jim Baker or Strobe Talbott, and may not have the standard FSO-type training.) Moreover, many of the State Department hands are not politicians who are running for elected office, particularly the presidency—unlike the vice president. Hence, most are not as likely to speak out of line or behave ostentatiously for the sake of getting some good "P.R." or impressing voters back home.

Consider, for instance, Mondale's role and influence in South Africa policy. His general role was especially impressive for a vice president and was historically unique as far as the institution itself is concerned. However, his lack of diplomatic experience may have hurt the administration in terms of South Africa policy. Hence, the case may provide an example of why some foreign policy should be left to diplomats as opposed to vice presidents.

The Carter administration favored a "one-man, one-vote" policy in which each black in South Africa was permitted to vote along with each white, a stance totally at odds with the South African leadership. Realizing the sensitivity of this matter, the administration decided to bite its tongue in pushing the issue at the current time, out of fear of sabotaging the early discussions it had been having. However, when asked by a reporter at a press conference following his meeting with South African leader John Vorster, Mondale asserted that "every citizen [in South Africa] should have the right to vote and every vote should be equally weighted," thus endorsing the one-man, one-vote policy. Not only did Vorster respond angrily to Mondale's suggestion, but he also used the comment to rally white support and hinder reform. Mondale transgressed the fine line between discussion and telling a nation what to do. Although the president himself, only two to three months before the Mondale-Vorster meeting, had told the United Nations in a major human-rights speech that none of its members "can claim that mistreatment of its citizens is solely its own business," the White House did understand the sensitivity of dictating to a nation like South Africa about its own internal affairs.

The vice president's remark may seem like an unfortunate slip of the tongue that anyone could make. But it is also possible that Mondale—a traditional civil-rights liberal who was attracted to the South Africa issue because of its obvious political pay offs—was doing a little posturing in order to appeal to certain segments of the Democratic party back home. Whatever the impetus, it was a serious diplomatic mistake that may in large part have explained why the Carter administration, and the vice president himself, were unable to make much headway in future efforts with the country. This case may provide an example of the limits of using the vice president as a foreign-policy spokesman. While any U.S. official can make a casual but critical misstatement, the chances of such occurring might be higher when the person—in this case a vice president thrust into a sensitive situation—is inexperienced in global diplomacy and is partly driven by politics. On the other hand, an unelected, trained diplomat or State Department official might be more skilled in the delicacies of such matters. Mondale faded from view on South Africa policy after the Vorster meeting, despite originally helping Carter lay out the grand design for the administration's Africa policy. Not surprisingly, it is instructive that the detailed, day-to-day execution was handed over to professional diplomats and area specialists.

Nonetheless, as we shall see, the least damaging of these two recommendations for using the vice president is the spokesman role—although the potential for trouble is hardly nonexistent. Any speeches he gives at home or abroad pitching the administration's strategy are usually cleared by the president's office, the NSA, etc. Because of this process, what the vice president says is usually closely monitored and gaffes are typically prevented—but not always. In general, however, the vice president often travels abroad for a number of reasons. Delivering a key or even minor speech for the administration is not an overwhelmingly problematic task. While continuing the practice is not essential, discontinuing it makes little sense. Moreover, the Mondale gaffe involved sort of an *advanced* spokesmen role that almost qualified as an emissary/negotiator-type duty. He went well beyond just showing up and giving a speech. Hence, the president must be especially careful when it comes to assigning duties to a vice president that come close to traversing into the emissary/negotiator area.

In that vein, having the vice president serve as a negotiator or emissary abroad (policy recommendation 12) is an issue that must be considered quite judiciously. Such a role takes the vice president a significant step beyond the spokesman role. Once again, there are highly positive and highly negative examples of how the vice president has been used in this capacity.

For example, on the plus side, there is Quayle's use during the Gulf crisis, particularly via trips to Brazil, Argentina, and Venezuela. In a very important trip that involved negotiating on behalf of the administration, the vice president visited Bogota, Colombia in August 1990, less than a week after Saddam Hussein had invaded Kuwait, where he lobbied Venezuelan President Carlos Andres Perez to increase his country's oil production to make up for any shortfall resulting from the turmoil in the Gulf. Additionally, in two separate meetings, Quayle pressed the leaders of Brazil and Argentina to halt transfers of ballistic-missile technology to Iraq. Within days, all three nations had complied with the vice president's requests.

There are similar success stories involving Vice President Gore in Russia, Kazakhstan, and the Ukraine. His busy work within the former Soviet Union has not been resigned merely to the Gore-Chernomyrdin Commission (although some of that work is just now coming under fire). For instance, Kazakhstan endorsed an international treaty on December 13, 1993 to halt the spread of arms and signed an agreement with the United States to dismantle its nuclear arsenal. The actions, which came during a visit by Gore, were important because Kazakhstan had the third-largest nuclear arsenal of the former Soviet republics, behind Russia and Ukraine. The moves were intended to put additional pressure on Ukraine, where leaders were adamant in not relinquishing their missiles.

There was reportedly no doubt before Gore's arrival that Kazakhstan's President Nursultan Nazarbayev would sign the arms pact, under which Kazakhstan was to begin dismantling its nuclear weapons in return for more than $84 million in aid from the United States. But it was never certain that it would endorse the NPT. Reports and administration officials claimed that Gore prodded Nazarbayev to act. On a separate note, in an article short on specifics, *The New York Times* stated that Gore also "used his contacts to negotiate an ultra-secret deal with Russia and Kazakhstan to bring more than half a ton of bomb-grade uranium from Kazakhstan to the United States last year [1994]." He has done impressive work in Kazakhstan with Prime Minister Kazhegeldin, inking numerous agreements. Finally, another former Soviet republic of interest to Gore has been the Ukraine. According to Peter J. Boyer, Gore led the secret negotiations with the Ukrainian President Leonid Kravchuk that resulted in Ukraine's surrender of nuclear weapons. A number of reports contend that Gore "persuaded" the Ukraine to give up its nuclear arsenal.

Importantly, a possible key explanation for the success of the vice president as an emissary and negotiator abroad has to do with the authority he brings to the table. In particular, this issue will be discussed in analysis of the next policy recommendation (14). In short, while the vice president is not the president, he is next in the line of succession and hence the second highest person in the U.S. government. As a result, by sending a vice president on a negotiating mission abroad, the administration is sending a signal that it means business. Moreover, it brings a certain level of authority that someone other than the vice president or president simply might not be able to deliver, even including the secretary of state. Regarding Quayle's trips to Latin America, James Glassman noted: "In Latin America . . . they want the face-to-face contact and the voice of the president. The vice president coming down from the White House has a special weight to it, rather than someone coming from the bureaucracy or State Department."[24] In a similar conclusion from a separate example, C. Boyden Gray underscores Vice President Bush's "major contributing role in what many see as President Reagan's most important foreign-policy achievement," namely the Euromissile deployment and the subsequent INF treaty. "It is doubtful in today's circumstances that a secretary of state or defense could have achieved the results that Vice President Bush did," Gray contends. He doubts "that any Cabinet officer, or any congressional official for that matter, can achieve the dominant stature necessary to command the ultimate result."[25]

So, it may be true that while other administration members can handle negotiating roles, few may be able to convey the authority required in certain situations—such as the substantial issues Quayle negotiated in Latin America during the Gulf conflict, or Bush's role in the Euromissile deployment. Of course, much depends on the case at hand. Sometimes the vice president may or may not be better situated than a lower-level negotiator.

Yet, there are also negatives associated with using the vice president in this capacity abroad. Consider the case of Vice President Bush. While his 1983 trip to Western Europe—centered on the INF-Euromissile deployment—was a major success, the same cannot be said for his work in Saudi Arabia in 1986. This was a case (not uncommon) in which a vice president's foreign-policy activities appeared to be motivated by personal political aspirations. It demonstrates a clear hindrance plaguing the negotiator/emissary role.

As noted in chapter 5, the Reagan administration had a major covert action plan with the Saudi leadership to increase oil production as a means of crippling the Soviet Union economically. The strategy seemed to be working and the Kremlin (along with Libya and Iran), already suspicious, was getting quite angry with the Saudis. King Fahd and other apprehensive members of the royal family kept seeking, and receiving, reassurances from administration members that they were doing the right thing and that the United States would stand beside them. Vice President Bush, however, sensing danger in the plummeting prices, took another view. He repeatedly (and publicly) expressed concern about the low prices and called for stability in the market. He pressed these views during private talks with the highest echelons of Saudi leadership during his April 1986 visit. The vice president was supposed to argue the exact opposite. Instead, rather than reassuring the Saudis, he merely confused and further worried them. In the end, Reagan had to personally step in and resolve a very delicate situation.

It was speculated by the media and members of the administration that Bush's damaging actions were motivated more by political considerations than ignorance or any other factor. The vice president was only two years away from a presidential campaign, in which he needed the support of the oil-sensitive southwest. The fact that Reagan angrily reproached Bush suggests the vice president's behavior was dictated primarily by politics.

In as much as Bush's actions were motivated by future political aspirations, this episode suggests that a vice president does have selfish-political interests that can effect his ability to be leveraged in foreign policy. This factor, missed by numerous scholars who assert the vice president lacks selfish or parochial interests, is crucial in considering how the second-office holder may or may not be used in foreign policy. In fact, modern vice presidents seem as tied to selfish-political interests as much if not more than any cabinet member dedicated to his or her department, or service chief to his military branch. As stated earlier, Vice President Bush during the Saudi oil crisis may have been as concerned about his southern-oil constituency as would be any congressman from Texas. He may have been as willing to go to bat for the oil industry as the top chief of the Air Force might for a fighter plane that had become obsolete and cost prohibitive. Bush very well may have been so motivated by personal political concerns that he was willing to go against the president's policy.

While the vice president may at times be a valuable asset in foreign policy, it is foolish to argue that such is the case because he is uncorrupted by selfish interests. Five of the last twelve vice presidents have assumed the presidency and most make quite clear their desire to run for the presidency in the future—which nearly all of them do. While a second-term president has essentially quit running for re-election, his vice president has just begun. Hence, the vice president does have a constituency beyond the president he serves; we can call it the vice president's "succession constituency." Not surprisingly, campaign-type politics often appear to drive the actions of many vice presidents in foreign-policy situations. Again, this reality flies in the face of the premise by many scholars that the vice president can be a valuable asset in foreign affairs because he allegedly lacks selfish-parochial interests.

The Bush case demonstrates how intently the vice president's actions can be dictated by politics. But it is not the only example. Recall examples from Nixon and Mondale.

Regarding Castro and Cuba, the Nixon experience is instructive. Overall, his early duties in this assignment—in terms of assessing Castro—were carried out in an exemplary fashion. Yet, his later actions regarding how the administration should react to Castro may have been motivated by his own personal political fortunes, as opposed to the paramount factor of whether or not deposing the Cuban leader at the time was good policy for the United States.

Mondale faded from view on South Africa policy after the Vorster meeting, despite originally helping Carter lay out the grand design for the administration's Africa policy. Again, not coincidentally, the detailed, day-to-day execution was handed over to professional diplomats and area specialists. However, there was another reason why Mondale abandoned the issue: The deepening turmoil on the continent, including the ugly situation in Rhodesia, was turning Africa into a political "tarbaby" (Mondale's words), and hence a no-win issue. According to Finlay Lewis, the astute politician "felt he had no more to contribute and a great deal to lose by a continuing political association with an inherently intractable problem."[26] Not wanting to hurt his future political standing, the vice president bailed out.

This should clearly prove a reality: While using the vice president as a negotiator/emissary abroad sounds great, it is not as neat as it may seem on the surface. To be sure, it has advantages, particularly in the aforementioned authority it brings to the table. And, as many examples show, it has been successful in the past. Yet, vice presidents are political beasts, and many are obsessed with the top prize: someday becoming president. As a result, that constraint can sometimes cloud their ability to properly fulfill a negotiating/emissary mission. I recommend that presidents keep this option open, realizing the benefits it can bring. At the same time, they must not plunge into it without careful consideration. At the least, the president must evaluate each case gingerly before inserting his understudy into it.[27]

Policy Recommendation 14

This recommendation considers having the vice president chair a *short-term*, executive-level task force or group inside or outside the White House. I believe it has "potential" that varies by administration. It is certainly not a "must" that is critical to a stable transition in the event the second steward is forced into running the nation's foreign policy—although chairing such a group can surely add to his knowledge, management, and coordinating skills. There are successes to point to in this area, often stemming from the vice president's authority abroad. Also, the task force or group that the vice president undertakes can be chosen selectively, thus implying the discovery of a need or temporary gap the vice president might fill without stepping on the toes of other cabinet members. Certain vice presidents have certain strengths that are worthy of being exploited. For instance, Quayle had considerable Senate experience in arms-control issues that could have been tapped in some type of task-force capacity (but were not). Also, such roles are transient, meaning that poor performance by the vice president does not place the president in a long-term bind that involves hand-wringing over how to discharge his understudy of his duties, without any political fallout from the vice president's supporters. Overall, because of these reasons, assigning the vice president to such a duty is not a poor idea. Once again, however, assigning him in this fashion is clearly not a *crucial* recommendation.

First consider the vice president chairing a short-term, executive-level group within the White House. Vice President Bush headed up Reagan's task force on terrorism. The group had a real impact. Among the useful outcomes of the task force was the formulation of a policy on terrorism that led to the 1986 U.S. bombing of Libya in reprisal for Kaddafi-sponsored terrorist activities against Americans. The vice president's unique level of authority in this situation helped the task force accomplish its objectives. For instance, Constantine Menges noted that Bush, "was seen by the government agencies as a possible future president, and this added to both his authority and his ability to provide real leadership on a complex political-legal-security issue such as terrorism. After all, he was the *vice president*."[28]

This same point about the benefits of the vice president on the authority front was made by Martin Anderson, one of Reagan's top economic advisors. In a argument similar to that of Menges, Anderson stated the following about the vice president being placed as chairman of the president's task force on regulatory reform: "Putting the vice president in charge of regulatory reform emphasized to everyone, especially his new cabinet members, how important it was to Reagan." To Anderson, this was also a positive harbinger that things might get done.[29]

As an example of the success of a short-term foreign-policy group *outside* the White House, there is only one vice president to point to as an example: Al

Gore. Gore co-chairs three foreign-policy groups outside of the White House: the Gore-Chernomyrdin Commission, the Gore-Mubarak Commission, named for Egyptian President Hosni Mubarak, and the Gore-Mbeki Commission, named for South African Deputy President Thabo Mbeki.

The first of these three groups was especially notable. As this book goes to print, Gore's role on the commission, as well as the commission itself, are being questioned, especially by reporters and editorial writers on the *Washington Post* staff. Whether these criticisms hold water remains to be seen.

Yet, the Gore-Chernomyrdin Commission also generated some laudable successes. Here is a brief rehash: On December 16, 1993, Gore and Chernomyrdin signed pacts in Moscow that formally joined the United States and Russia as partners on an international space station and announced that the first Russian astronaut would fly in the space shuttle Discovery. According to the *Current Digest of the Post-Soviet Press*, it will allow the United States to save on the order of $2 billion and to put the station into space two years earlier than would otherwise be the case. At the same time, Russia will receive $400 million over four years. Agreements were signed on such issues as economic development, high-technology ventures, the environment, and oil and gas exploration. Some pacts were for small but possibly fruitful projects, like plans to build as many as twenty-five privately financed gas stations in Russia. Seventeen accords and agreements, five joint statements and a communiqué were signed in Moscow. Chernomyrdin hailed the projects envisioned in the documents as "projects worth billions. This is exactly what we need right now." The two men later signed another major accord during their June 21-23, 1994 meeting in Washington. It will begin the phase-out of Russia's nuclear reactors that have produced plutonium for weapons purposes. Because the United States has not produced plutonium since 1988, the agreement applies mainly to Russian facilities. The details were hammered out by U.S. and Russian technical working groups during May 23-26 meetings in Moscow.

Likewise, vice-presidential authority—seemingly an oxymoron to many American scholars—has worked for Gore in his negotiations on the task force and elsewhere. Recalling a case from the Balkans, the vice president—only a few weeks after the inauguration—was chosen to meet in February 1993 with Bosnian President Alija Izetbegovic in order to perform a quite sensitive duty: inform the Muslim leader that, despite Clinton's tough campaign talk, the United States would not intervene militarily to rescue the Bosnians. The official explanation for the meeting was that Gore had a "pre-existing relationship" with the Bosnian leader. White House officials said that they wanted the meeting to receive less publicity than if Izetbegovic had met with President Clinton. Yet, at the same time, officials correctly estimated that having the vice president deliver the message would allow the authority of it to be affirmed.

Policy Recommendations 15 and 16

These two recommendations suggest that the vice president: (1) have his own defense and foreign-policy advisors; and (2) have a defense or foreign-policy aide sit in on regular meetings of a senior-level foreign-policy group. The first of these, recommendation 15, I consider a "must." The other, recommendation 16, I feel can be helpful but is not crucial; its applicability would seem to vary depending upon the president and administration.

Heretofore, I have reserved the "must" assessment for recommendations that seek to ensure primarily what Truman intended: the vice president being kept informed of crucial foreign-policy developments in the event the unthinkable happens to the commander in chief. Regarding policy recommendation 15, I concede that Truman's goals can be accomplished without the vice president having his own defense and foreign-policy advisors—assuming, of course, that he continue to be a statutory NSC member, sit in on all NSC and cabinet meetings, meet weekly with the president, receive all copies of the presidents paperwork, and receive the same daily intelligence briefing as the president. Nonetheless, while having his own defense and foreign-policy advisors is not essential to those goals, it does help the vice president to fully achieve them. This is especially true in an age in which the duties of the federal government have become so vast, suggesting the vice president could use some help from staffers in staying informed—not to mention securing other unexpected benefits helpful to the vice president personally and to the nation's foreign policy as a whole. "I think it is an important function," agrees Quayle's NSA, Carnes Lord. "It is important to have a senior level person on his staff in foreign and security policy. It keeps him more informed."[30] Finally, as long as the vice president's foreign-policy team continues to comprise only a handful of personnel, including an NSA and deputy NSA, the staff size should not be a cost problem, especially since some of the members come from different payrolls.[31]

Consider the following issues concerning policy recommendation 15.[32]

Paul C. Light notes that the vice president's increased role in recent years stems from the increased institutional support the office has gotten due to the addition of staff:

> The vice president's policy role starts with the institutional support needed to give advice.... Unlike [Vice President Lyndon] Johnson, who relied on State Department or NSC experts, Mondale had his own team of foreign advisors. Mondale was never forced to depend on Carter's staff for basic political support. That provided a level of independence not previously found in the vice presidency.[33]

While the addition of defense and foreign-policy advisors was begun by

Mondale, vice presidents who followed him have been rewarded by the change. Consider the case of Quayle. His own defense and foreign-policy team helped keep him abreast of developments. His foreign- and security-policy staff included a national security advisor and a deputy NSA—continuing the practice begun by vice presidents Mondale and Bush. He had two NSAs during his four years, Carnes Lord and Karl Jackson. Jon Glassman, a Latin America specialist from the State Department, was his deputy NSA. There was also a small staff underneath the two chief NSA positions, including three military personnel—one each from the Army, Navy, and Air Force. The military people dealt primarily with arms control, SDI issues, and science and technology. In addition, the vice president had a staffer who served as a liaison to the intelligence community. In total, including the support staff, Quayle's foreign and defense team ranged from seven to nine people, about five of which were medium- to top-level professionals.[34]

An example of how these aides helped enhance Quayle's foreign-policy activities was the influence of Jon Glassman. Quayle was probably not exaggerating when he asserted that he developed into "the administration's most active man for Latin America affairs"—a claim backed by Glassman, to whom he rightly gives a large degree of credit for this development. Glassman urged Quayle to seek such a role and to turn Latin America into his special area of interest. The deputy NSA, who was a Latin America specialist from the State Department, recognized a vacuum in Latin America for someone among the Big Eight in the Bush administration defense and foreign-policy team. "I identified a niche for him," Glassman acknowledges.[35] Helping to create a vacuum was Jim Baker's understandable preoccupation with Russia, post-Cold War Europe, and the Middle East. As Carnes Lord notes, it was a "portfolio relatively attended," and Quayle picked it up.[36] Glassman also recognized that Latin America was witnessing an era of fast economic growth, coming out of the depression of the 1980s, and that it could be a "very hot area." He also felt Quayle would be a nice fit because he was young and aggressive, like the new generation of Latin American leaders themselves. Additionally, those leaders would respect the fact that the administration sent the second highest person in the U.S. government down to represent them. "He was young, like the Latin American leaders, and had a lot in common with them," says Glassman. "Dan Quayle got along very well with these guys. He was viewed as the U.S. leader down there."[37]

To again recall just one example of how Quayle's Latin America relationship benefited not just himself but also the administration: In a very important trip that involved negotiating on behalf of the administration, the vice president visited Bogota, Colombia in August 1990, less than a week after Saddam had invaded Kuwait, where he lobbied Venezuelan President Carlos Andres Perez to increase his country's oil production to make up for any shortfall resulting from the turmoil in the Gulf. Additionally, in two separate meetings, Quayle pressed the leaders of Brazil and Argentina to halt transfers of ballistic-missile technology to Iraq. As noted earlier, within days, all three nations had complied with the vice president's requests. As to the effect of Quayle's actions, Assistant Secretary of State Bernard Aronson later noted that the oil boost "was not noted at the time but made a crucial difference in stabilizing prices." He added that had Argentina's Condor Missile Project "gone into full production and had it been deployed, the conflict in the Gulf would have been much different and not to our benefit."

It is probably fair to say that without Glassman (or some other Quayle aide) identifying and urging the vice president to assume the Latin America role, the vice president would probably not have taken it. Glassman, other Quayle staffers, and even Quayle himself all seem to agree with this assertion.

Likewise, the Clinton administration has benefited from such aides for Vice President Gore. For instance, according to *U.S. News & World Report*, before ordering a military strike against Saddam Hussein in June 1993 in retaliation for a foiled assassination attempt on President Bush, Clinton consulted extensively with Gore, who steered him firmly toward retaliation well before the formal FBI and CIA reports on the Iraqi attempt on Bush's life were complete. Gore undertook his own formal inquiry into the assassination plot, working through his NSA, Leon Fuerth. He concluded that retaliation was absolutely necessary. Doing nothing, Gore told Clinton, would make the president seem weak and rekindle old fears that Democrats are too squeamish about using military force. The highly positive public reaction to the strike confirmed Clinton's respect for Gore's judgment on such matters. Gore's action here is laudable for another reason. To this day, the retaliatory strike on Iraq is one of the few examples of Clinton toughness cited by critics of the administration's foreign policy. And, it turns out, the move took place primarily at the behest of his vice president, who was helped by his NSA.

Last, Joe DeSutter, an advisor to vice presidents Quayle and Gore, states that because the vice president is a statutory member of the NSC and second in command during a nuclear-exchange situation, he needs his own support staff. He says that the vice president, like the president, has a military aide with him wherever he goes. This aide, like that of the president, carries with him the proverbial nuclear "football." At the very least, then, the vice president needs a military aide on his staff to fulfill this function.[38]

For these reasons, I believe that policy recommendation 15—the vice president should have his own defense and foreign-policy advisors—should be continued. Yet, I feel that recommendation 16, which is somewhat of an extension of 15, is not as important.

Recommendation 16 suggests that the vice president's top defense or foreign-policy aide be a member of a senior-level foreign-policy group. The only precedent for this suggestion is Vice President Gore. His NSA, Fuerth—a former foreign service officer and an arms-control expert—actually sits in on and actively participates in meetings of key administration foreign-policy advisors, allowing Gore to monitor foreign-policy decisions and influence foreign policy probably better than past vice presidents with such aides.[39] Specifically, Fuerth sits at the table in the all-important deliberations of the Deputies Committee, headed by Samuel Berger. It consists of the number two or three officials from each of the national security departments. Four or more times weekly, the group meets in the Situation Room in the White House basement. In two- to three-hour sessions, committee members hammer out policy options for their bosses. The interagency group manages foreign-policy issues and crises.

There are examples of how this has enabled Gore to influence policy. In Bosnia, Fuerth—as part of his duties within the Deputies Committee—was given the task of overseeing sanctions against the Serbs. As events would dictate, such a task became a primary pillar of U.S. policy in trying to settle the war in the Balkans. A memo written by Fuerth at the request of Gore taking issue with a proposal to lift sanctions against Serbia allegedly became a list of the essential U.S. conditions with allies and Russia when it came to easing sanctions on Serbia.

As noted above, I recommend that the practice of a vice president having his own small team of defense and foreign-policy advisors (recommendation 15) should be continued. But what about policy recommendation 16? Should a member of the vice president's staff be as involved as Fuerth? It is one thing for a vice president to have his own defense and foreign-policy advisors. But it is another matter entirely for those advisors to be a part of the *president's* top team.

Certainly, such a situation probably does not hurt. It may have the added plus of getting the vice president more tightly involved in foreign policy than otherwise—as Fuerth-Gore seem to have proven in Balkans policy and elsewhere. Yet, this is not a critically important action. A vice president's NSA or defense and foreign-policy advisors could still maintain the important task of keeping him abreast of foreign policy—in addition to what he learns in his NSC and cabinet meetings, daily briefings, and weekly meetings with the president—even if he is not involved to the degree that Fuerth is. Certainly, this type of action is not as important as the vice president being a statutory NSC member or receiving daily foreign and security briefings. I would suggest that the practice be continued in future administrations only if all the participants feel it wise and are comfortable with the situation. If it becomes problematic, with the vice president's representative becoming a nuisance, disruption, or whatever, his participation should be terminated. It is hardly crucial and should not develop an institutionalized life of its own.

Policy Recommendations 17 and 18

These two recommendations have common threads. Recommendation 18 suggests the vice president play a coordinating role in assisting the primary executive-level department that runs foreign policy—the Department of State. The suggestion was made by C. Boyden Gray, an assistant to Vice President Bush.

Suggestion 17 goes further. It was broached during the 1988 vice-presidential-nominee considerations, when it was believed that Sam Nunn, Democratic senator from Georgia and chair of the Senate Foreign Relations Committee, might be the nominee. It was suggested that Nunn, if he became vice president, could also serve as the Secretary of State or Secretary of Defense.[40] This recommendation was floated by a number of Democrats at the time. It was, and is, an absurd notion. It would be purely self-serving in terms of inflating the job description of the vice presidency. It would not be beneficial to the State Department, DoD, nor the administration's foreign policy in general. Most important, it simply isn't necessary. Despite problems, these departments have been run fairly effectively without inserting the vice president. Including the vice president may add a host of entirely new problems to their operation.

Additionally, though I have criticized scholars who maintain that the vice president lacks certain interests, it is true that they are correct in noting that he does not have a literal *bureaucratic*-parochial interest—i.e., a department or agency. He has only one direct interest he must serve: the president. However, in implementing the Nunn suggestion, reformers would, ironically, be giving the vice president a huge bureaucratic-parochial interest that might come between his loyalties/duties to the president. This is unnecessary and ill-advised.[41]

A less dramatic notion would be to give the vice president a coordinating role in assisting the State Department, as noted in policy recommendation 18 and as suggested by Gray.[42] The basis for Gray's argument is similar to Mulcahy's in policy recommendation 19. Gray notes that one of the biggest problems in modern government is the increasing difficulty of coordinating the overlapping and sometimes competing policy roles of great bureaucracies, both foreign and domestic, and the greater difficulty of coordinating between domestic and foreign policy. This difficulty in coordination has been augmented by the politicization of the NSA. As a result, says Gray, there are few people available to "coordinate the coordinators" who are themselves supposed to work out conflicts between senior-level bureaucrats. Given all of these competing bureaucracies, asks Gray, who among them can call a meeting that everyone can comfortably attend without a loss of face? The answer, he says, is very few. "And since the president does not have time," he argues, "the system does, by the process of elimination, put considerable pressure on the vice president to resolve disputes (subject always, of course, to final decision by the president)." In particular, Gray points to the NSC and State Department.[43]

Mainly, Gray singles out the State Department. In many cases today, he argues, the State Department has simply become overburdened with duties and could benefit from a senior administration official like the vice president, in addition to the top secretaries. He says the department can no longer satisfy the lobbying and protocol demands of foreign visitors. Gray, speaking from experience as a top aide to Vice President Bush, maintains that foreign visitors often look to the vice president—whom they often establish a relationship with during a visit by him to their country—to help them resolve conflicts during their protocol visits to Washington.

Gray's suggestion, however, is motivated by more than visits. He points to coordinating roles Bush played in effecting a change in policy toward sub-Saharan Africa in February 1983. The vice president brought together AID, the State Department, and World Bank. Gray maintains that Bush "was able to coordinate" the efforts of these three groups to effect a positive policy outcome that was previously stymied by a lack of a strong, authoritative, bureaucratically neutral, coordinating presence. The vice president offered that presence. Gray believes that the coordinating aspects of the vice presidency have the potential to play "the most critical role" in the development of the office in the next century. He also points to Bush's role in 1983 on the issue of the Euromissile deployment as evidence of how the vice president can use his authority to help State in some foreign policy. "It is doubtful in today's circumstances that a secretary of state or defense could have achieved the results that Vice President Bush did," Gray contends. "This is because, given the fragmentation of power, it is unlikely that any Cabinet officer, or any congressional official for that matter, can achieve the dominant stature necessary to command the ultimate result."

Gray's argument merits consideration. It contains three elements in arguing why the vice president should play a coordinating role in assisting the State Department and the foreign-policy bureaucracy in general. First, like Mulcahy, Gray believes the competing parochial interests of various bureaucracies leaves an opening that a bureaucratically neutral vice president could fill. Second, he feels the duties of the State Department have become so overwhelming that the vice president could lend a hand of assistance. Third, Gray argues that the vice president can help in foreign policy because of the "dominant stature" he provides.

Each of these three elements has validity, particularly the third. As demonstrated earlier, Bush deserves tremendous credit for his skill in this area. Almost certainly, his position as the second most important person in the U.S. government lent significant credibility to his mission in persuading stubborn Western European constituencies to accept the Euromissile in 1983. Could the secretary of state had made the same impact? Perhaps his position—unlike that of the president or vice president—did not have sufficient authority or credibility. Is Gray correct: the dominant stature provided by the vice president's authoritative title may have made the difference in persuasion in a way that the secretary of state's title could not? We will never know, but it might be true. At the least, if it is true, Gray is reaffirming the point that the vice president can *at times* serve as an effective negotiator/emissary abroad (see policy recommendation 12), aside from the more ambitious agenda Gray is here advocating.

There are problems with Gray's suggestion. As pointed out in the analysis of earlier recommendations, most vice presidents have their eyes on a run for the presidency. The vice president is an elected official interested in getting good press coverage. Like any politician, he may shirk from tough assignments that could damage his political standing. This could become an issue when he is called upon to intervene in politically unsavory matters when assisting the State Department. Moreover, once again, it is difficult to fire a vice president if he performs poorly in such a capacity. The reason stems from how the vice president is chosen by the president as his running mate in the first place: for the purpose of winning a presidential election. This may involve appeals to a disgruntled party faction, age, geography, religion, ethnicity, and so on. The chief of staff to Vice President Quayle notes that because of these factors the vice president is less accountable than other presidential staff:

> In principal, in my view, you want staff people to the president to be in control of those departments and agencies. You know, vice presidents also have their own agenda. . . . They have electoral futures. If I were the president, or the chief of staff to the president, I would want someone working for the president who is "fireable" by the president, and accountable to the president in the way a staff person is, not the way the vice president is.[44]

The importance of this point cannot be overlooked. The vice president is less accountable than other presidential staff, primarily because he is difficult to fire[45] due to the uniquely political reasons why he was chosen in the first place: to satisfy some constituency critical to the president's electability. To cite two examples, Mondale was chosen by Carter to satisfy the liberal wing of the Democratic party and to convince skeptics therein that Mondale would keep the Carter administration from drifting too far away from the left. Similarly, George Bush was always viewed by conservative Republicans as not being one of them. As a result, his choosing of Quayle—a staunch, dynamic conservative—was an overture that helped mollify them. If either Carter or Bush was forced to remove these vice presidents either totally out of the White House or from a high-profile staff position—such as assisting the State Department, or, as noted in the next recommendation, running the NSC or a top NSC group—it could anger the liberal or conservative factions he initially sought to pacify. The president *might* pay for this at the ballot box. As a result, the well-intended reform could prove to be counterproductive.

Finally, Bill Kristol has a telling insight into Gray's suggestion that the vice president be given an increased foreign-policy role in assisting the State Department:

> The Secretary of State is first among equals. You could try to sort of rope the State Department in under the National Security Council, as Nixon did. But "State" is institutionally very powerful. That's one of the first things you really learn when you're in an administration. They have all those ambassadors and embassies and all that bureaucracy, which is in touch with all those foreign governments. . . . The vice president's staff would get involved. Then the vice president's press secretary wants to get good press for the VP. And suddenly it just gets too complicated.

Indeed, the State Department has its own staff and resources, as does the White House. Adding the vice president to the mix may not be as tidy as it sounds. And such an inclusion of an allegedly "neutral" vice president would certainly not be as pure, in the sense of lacking bureaucratic infighting and parochial interests, as some imagine. There are many examples of bureaucratic infighting that has taken place between the vice president and State Department. Recall some examples, such as the following from Mondale and Quayle.

In late June 1977, Mondale planned a major speech at the Northern California World Affairs Club, in which he hoped to quell Jewish concerns about Carter policy in the Middle East. In his briefing notes, Mondale noted that the address would offer "a good occasion for a public statement on our Middle East policy that can be helpful domestically." As always, he was heavily motivated by the domestic-political implications of such a speech for both himself and the administration. What Mondale hoped to say, however, was toned down during weeks of haggling with the State Department over the speech's language. Additionally, although Mondale wanted to announce new administration objectives that might placate Israel, Carter demanded that it merely clarify existing policy. In vain, the vice president strongly objected to Carter. In the end, Mondale gave a speech that simply towed the administration line, sparking the *New York Times* to aptly call it "a reaffirmation of the basic American policy that had aroused Jewish and Israeli concerns." The speech sparked a point-by-point rebuttal by New York Senator Jacob Javits, who called the speech "unrealistic." According to Steve Gillon, Javits' rebuttal included many of the points that Mondale had hoped to make. Needless to say, the speech was a bust from Mondale's perspective.

Later on in the peace process, after which Mondale believed his efforts had resurrected stalled negotiations, he began to make a number of policy proposals, all of which were rejected by either the State Department, or Carter, or both. Mondale was rightly concerned that the State Department might undermine his efforts. The vice president said that a negotiating paper prepared by Secretary of State Vance for the Leeds Conference contained, in Mondale's words, "every buzz word," including a canned statement about "legitimate Palestinian rights." The vice president complained that the draft was a product of "Arabists in the State Department" and pushed to get it changed. He told the president that such continued public statements were creating hostility among the Israelis. Mondale tried to convince Carter of the need to avoid making such public statements and to instead shift the debate to private forums. "We've got to get it off the public dialogue," said Mondale. "If there's a public debate over this stuff, if we're exchanging papers that get into the press, we'll never get this thing settled." Understanding that it would be impossible to keep the issue out of the papers, the vice president made a bold proposal: He suggested Carter appoint former Secretary of State Henry Kissinger as a special negotiator in the region. This, he hoped, would not only increase bipartisan support but would also make use of Kissinger's negotiating skills, which Mondale admired. Further, said Mondale, appointing a special negotiator would remove responsibility from the State Department, which was mistrusted by both Mondale and the Israelis. Although the president was reportedly receptive to the idea, he refused. Vance stated: "I felt the Middle East was something that the Secretary of State had to be involved in every day."

Much of this is expected bickering. No big deal. But imagine if Mondale was operating under Gray's suggestion that he be given the authority needed to assist the State Department in numerous ways. In such a scenario, the aforementioned examples would likely not have been resolved as easily as they were. Consider how the press may have reacted to the incident. Might one of the vice president's staffers, in the interest of giving their guy some P.R., leaked it? Who would have higher authority—the vice president or secretary of state? Who does the president side with? Again, the potential for trouble is very much present.

As one last, brief example, note how Vice President Quayle's actions in foreign policy often angered the State Department. His chief of staff elaborates on the differing world views of Quayle and Secretary of State Baker, noting that there were "ideological tensions" between the two men. "We were just generally more Reaganite and more hawkish than Baker," he remarks. "We were more pro-Yeltsin. He was more pro-Gorbachev. [The vice president] was more suspicious of Gorbachev. . . . Quayle did go to dinner with Yeltsin before Yeltsin became president, that must have been early 1991, and said some nice things about Yeltsin, and that got a few noses at 'State' out of joint because they were still pretty much backing Gorbachev." He adds: "You know, there were lots of instances where we would sort of pull at the margins of policy and I think Baker didn't like that much. . . . There was a certain amount of tension; they didn't quite regard us as trustworthy from their point of view at the State Department."[46] Recalling earlier cited examples: There was the speech Quayle made to the AIPAC, where he referred to the West Bank and Gaza Strip as Judea and Samaria—violating long-held U.S. protocol—and highly negative comments he made about Soviet leader Mikhail Gorbachev.

Moreover, in the case of Quayle and Baker, off-the-record sources confirmed to me a fact known within Republican party circles: The two men, both with their eyes on the presidency, viewed one another as political competitors angling for differing bases within the GOP.[47] "Quayle had a following among conservatives that made him formidable," said one source who asked not to be indentified. "Baker had political ambitions and viewed Quayle as a political rival due to his conservative base." Joe DeSutter, an advisor to Quayle, adds: "I don't think there's any secret about the bad blood between the two, going all the way back to New Orleans and the campaign in 1988."[48]

Also, some of their top staffers simply did not like one another. Kristol and Baker were not fond of one another. In fact, when I floated this policy recommendation by Kristol, the former chief of staff to Quayle snickered, knowing it would not work in the Bush administration because of the tension between the office of the vice president and the secretary of state. One source even told me that the glaring lack of a trip by Quayle to Moscow stemmed from obstruction by Baker. "During my tenure Dan Quayle never went to Moscow, and it wasn't because he didn't want to," said the source. Carnes Lord, Quayle's NSA, adds that the vice president also never went to Eastern Europe and that Baker was probably a key reason ("The exact reason, I'm not sure.")[49] Joe DeSutter adds that Quayle, aside from his Desert Storm duties, never went to the Middle East either (another of Baker's pet interests), and that, "He loved the Middle East and Israel. He was an expert on it and would've liked to have gone there." When asked if he felt Baker had actually obstructed Quayle from traveling to Moscow or the Middle East, DeSutter was cautiously vague, but conceded that I was "probably on the right wavelength there."[50] Clearly, this does not bode well for a coordinating role by the vice president in helping the State Department, or at least not in the case of the Bush administration.

The Quayle-Baker example demonstrates another deficiency in Gray's suggestion.[51] If a president decides to allow his vice president a coordinating role in assisting the State Department, he better ensure that his vice president and secretary of state—as well as their staffs—are politically, ideologically, and personally compatible. Such a match may be impossible from the outset, depending upon why each man is chosen.

In sum, Gray's suggestion is not as simple and solid as it sounds. While it clearly appears to possess positives, it is too troublesome and should be rejected. First and foremost, having the vice president *not* fulfill such a role would hardly take away from the chief objective of Truman and others: keeping him informed in foreign policy.

Policy Recommendations 19 and 20

Respectively, these two final policy recommendations suggest that, (1) the vice president chair a major interagency group, executive-level committee, or an NSC subgroup; and (2) the vice president chair a crisis-management committee. The two suggestions are only slightly different, and should be rejected for similar reasons.

The rationale for both recommendations stems from common lines of logic. Kevin Mulcahy details the parochialism and incoherence that can plague White House foreign policy due to the number and variety of departments and interests within the foreign policy-making apparatus. He contends that there is a need for a presiding official who transcends both existing loyalties and organizational interests. He suggests this duty be delegated to the vice president. The vice president, he maintains, could chair major NSC committees, such as the Senior Review Group or SALT verification panel during the Reagan administration. He suggests an executive order to accomplish this recommendation.[52]

Mulcahy argues that the vice president has no bureaucratic-parochial interest—unlike other cabinet-level foreign-policy players—and can thus offer a neutral foreign-policy voice, particularly in administrations with activist NSCs. A key component of his argument is that even those in foreign policy who are supposed to be neutral, such as the NSA, often are not. He correctly cautions that even the sometimes politicized NSA may have an agenda. The NSA is supposed to concentrate on broader foreign-policy interests, but often represents the interests of an increasingly independent National Security Council. As Robert E. Hunter and others have noted, the NSC system was created in 1947 to transcend the trappings of departmentalism.[53] In reality, however, the opposite has at times prevailed, as demonstrated by infighting among various NSAs and secretaries of state—such as Zbigniew Brzezinski and Cyrus Vance within the Carter administration, and ostensibly Anthony Lake and Warren Christopher in the Clinton administration.[54] NSC problems were also seen in the Reagan and Nixon administrations. In the latter, NSA Kissinger usurped many of the secretary of state's foreign-policy duties. Consequently, Mulcahy argues that the vice president could step in as a neutral foreign-policy voice to the president.[55] Unlike other cabinet members, he avers, the vice president has no parochial interest other than the president he serves. Likewise, C. Boyden Gray argues that the NSC operation has grown as a "policymaker" rather than coordinator, and suggests the vice president be used as a coordinator of the NSC.[56]

Advocates agree that the vice president is the only member of the president's foreign-policy team that has no department or agency that he must represent or be responsive to. Such entities can cause some players to have dual, clashing interests, i.e., the secretaries of state and defense must often uphold the interests of their departments as much as those of their president—or, at the least, they must sometimes play a delicate balancing act of trying to adequately serve two masters. On the contrary, some maintain, the vice president serves only one interest: the president. Hence, unfettered to any bureaucratic-parochial or selfish interests, he is a perfect candidate for being employed in one of the two aforementioned manners (or both).

This notion sounds good, and logical. It is well intentioned. But is it a smart idea?

Not really. Here is one reason. Recall a point made in analysis of policy recommendation 18. The vice president is less accountable than other staff members, primarily because he is difficult to fire due to the uniquely political reasons why he was chosen as the president's running mate. He was likely picked to win votes. The reason may or may not be ideological and almost certainly is not based on total agreement on foreign policy. A presidential candidate does not pick a running mate because he agrees with him across the board on foreign policy, nor should he. On the other hand, as noted by one vice president's chief of staff, "The national security advisor . . . really should be your guy on foreign policy. The guy you agree with on foreign policy. He is your eyes and ears and arms. I think there's a big advantage to having the national security advisor chair those interagency committees."[57] One might also add that a vice president is rarely chosen because of his policy coordination and management skills, an obvious prerequisite for chairing an NSC committee or subgroup, interagency committee, or crisis-management group.

Also apropos, again, is the fact that vice presidents have their own political futures (this was an issue with recommendations 12, 17, and 18). Almost half of the last twelve vice presidents have assumed the presidency. Most make clear their desire to run for the presidency in the future. When it comes to carrying out certain foreign-policy tasks, a politically driven vice president may act in a manner that helps him but hurts the administration, such as may have occurred with vice presidents Mondale and Bush; despite both being generally model vice presidents, their political interests were at times their Achilles heel. Once more, imagine a situation where the president *is* forced to relieve the vice president of his duties, due to the fact that the latter has failed to perform adequately in managing something as important as a major NSC committee or crisis-management group. Such a move might produce a political fall out among the party faction the president initially sought to assuage when he selected his vice president as a running mate during the election campaign. Obviously, in this case, the president would have made a poor decision in deciding to use the vice president as he did. As Natoli notes, "While a president can get rid of staff and cabinet members, not so easily does a vice president exit."[58]

When asked about the vice president chairing a major NSC committee, crisis-management group, a Senior Review Group, or even a smaller group like the SALT verification panel (as well as assisting the State Department—Gray's suggestion), Kristol commented:

It's difficult to know. As a former vice president's chief of staff, I'm sympathetic to getting the vice president more involved. But if I were the president's staff I would rather avoid having it get that complicated. The vice president's staff would get involved. Then the vice president's press secretary wants to get good press for the VP. And suddenly it just gets too complicated.

The Mulcahy argument seems to suggest that a "turf-free" vice president's lack of a classical bureaucratic-parochial interest would allow him to handle certain problems better than other members of the president's foreign-policy team. However, as shown in recommendation 18, the vice president frequently clashes with these other players. And they typically react in a protective manner, noting that it is *their* job to handle that particular function. If this is true for the State Department, why would it not be true for other major executive-level groups? Would the NSA, NSC staff, secretary of state, or whoever runs the group not have a similar reaction? Of course they would. As proof, one need only look at the one case where such recommendations became a reality: Vice President Bush.

As vice president, Bush, in an unprecedented move, became the chairman of Reagan's crisis-management group, called the Special Situation Group. Lest anyone think the notion of a vice president as the White House crisis manager is merely a fuzzy theoretical idea postulated by detached academics or hair-brained presidents, it is worth noting that in addition to Reagan and Bush, the move was also supported by Baker, Meese, and Deaver. At the time of the move, Secretary of Defense Caspar W. Weinberger advocated it for reasons like Mulcahy's. Weinberger was pleased with the decision not only because he felt Bush was "thoroughly knowledgeable and experienced," but also because he believed the change would permit all information and ideas to get to the president without the bias of the State Department, DoD, CIA, or any other agency.[59]

Even more important were the results of the Bush move. Overall, we remember his chairmanship positively—and rightly so: He seems to have done an effective job.

The Special Situation Group first met on September 1, 1983 as a result of the Soviet shootdown of the Korean Air Lines passenger plane, KAL 007. An example of the group in action took place during the Grenada situation in October 1983. As a crisis manager during the Grenada crisis, Bush seemed very dynamic and proactive. He quickly assembled and coordinated the necessary staff and was able to effectively interact with the president, McFarlane, and Shultz in Georgia. According to accounts, he proposed, listened to, and evaluated others' ideas. He discussed these ideas over the telephone with the president's team in Georgia. Constantine Menges, an NSC staffer who worked closely with the vice president and was occasionally highly critical of him, said that, "During Grenada, Bush was superb." The vice president's performance during the Grenada crisis led Menges to conclude that a President Bush equipped with a competent staff of experts from outside the career services and using "his own sensible instincts" could preside over an effective foreign policy.[60]

However, despite his admirable performance in his role as crisis manager, Bush's experiences in that capacity also demonstrate the potential conflict that such a duty can cause due to bureaucratic infighting and the vice president's stepping on the toes of other senior administration personnel who traditionally maintain those posts. A perfect example was Secretary of State Al Haig's reaction. Reagan (in his words) decided to name Bush "chairman of a special group within the NSC that would help me manage affairs during an international crisis." During the March 24, 1981 announcement of the move, White House spokesman James Brady said Bush, as part of the NSC system, would "coordinate and control all appropriate federal resources in responding to emergency situations both foreign and domestic." In an actual crisis situation, Bush would only chair the team in the absence of the president. Importantly, however, he would "also engage in forward planning for emergency responses, develop options for presidential consideration and take the lead in the implementation of those decisions."

Why did Reagan make the move? For one, "In the past," the president later recalled, "the president's national security advisor had generally served as chairman of the White House crisis-management team. But Haig didn't like or trust National Security Advisor Richard Allen. I had discussed the matter with the top three staff people in the White House, Jim Baker, Ed Meese, and Mike Deaver, and we'd come up with the plan giving the responsibility to George Bush." In part, Reagan felt the move would "deal with Haig's unhappiness over Allen." Also, he made the move because he "thought it was prudent—and important for the country—for the vice president to play as large a role in the affairs of the administration as possible; I didn't want George, in the words of Nelson Rockefeller, simply to be 'standby equipment.'"

Yet, the Bush move still didn't satisfy Haig, who, according to Reagan, was "extremely upset" with it. The president recalled a telephone call with Haig in which the secretary of state was "going through the roof, saying he didn't want the vice president to have *anything* to do with international affairs; it was *his* jurisdiction, he said, and he told me he was thinking of resigning." The secretary of state felt his turf was being threatened.[61] Further infuriating Haig was the fact that he felt the secretary of state should chair the group. In a matter of poor judgment—which also demonstrates some of the unforeseen ugly off shoots of such innovations—Haig immediately publicly questioned the White House plan, telling a House Foreign Affairs subcommittee that he regarded the possibility of Bush getting the position with "a lack of enthusiasm."[62] Reagan eventually cooled Haig off by assuring him in a written, circulated statement that "the secretary of state is my primary advisor in foreign affairs."[63]

Many assessments of this episode tend to portray Haig as an egotistical brat who was complaining because he could not have his way. Haig, however, had a point. Duncan L. Clarke notes that all administrations have mechanisms for managing crises: the Executive Committee (under Kennedy), the Washington Special Action Group (Nixon-Ford), the Special Coordination Committee (Carter), and Reagan's Special Situation Group, to name a few. These bodies are properly located in the White House, since serious crises will command presidential attention. Since the Eisenhower administration, these groups have been chaired by the NSA or a high-level official from the State Department, such as the secretary of state—the latter of which Haig noted at the time. In recent years, the NSA has had the role. The vice president in the Reagan administration stands out as a notable exception. While Haig received negative publicity for his remonstrations against the Bush appointment, few recall that Secretary of State Cyrus Vance also argued unsuccessfully that he should chair the crisis-management group in the Carter administration.[64] Haig was not acting childishly.

Not surprisingly, Bush later wrote of the turf problem and the fact that even a vice president was not exempt from clashes with bureaucratic-parochial interests. He stated:

> The general rule in taking on any executive project is: never assume responsibility for something without the authority to carry it out successfully. The vice president's authority in any executive area comes from the White House, but the lines are sometimes blurred. Since Washington is a turf-conscious environment—never more so than at or near the center of power—a vice president perceived to be stepping over a line could be on a collision course with the White House staff or some Cabinet member.[65]

Vice presidents learn the turf lesson early. "Wherever I might go, somebody has primary jurisdiction, and that's one of the problems with being vice president," noted Vice President Quayle. "Anything you do, you're going to be getting into somebody else's domain."[66]

Finally, in a largely unknown example, some forty-plus years ago there was another attempt to give a vice president a major role with a key White House foreign-policy group. At the beginning of the second Eisenhower term, Herbert Hoover, Jr., an undersecretary of state who chaired the OCB, was planning to resign his chairmanship. As noted earlier, the Operations Coordinating Board was one of the two primary subgroups of the NSC, charged with ensuring that government agencies carry out NSC policy recommendations approved by the president. Obviously, chairmanship of the OCB was an important role in foreign and security policy. Protocol established that the next undersecretary of state, Christian Herter, would automatically fill the position. Yet, Vice President Nixon's internal supporters pushed to have him take over the seat. Herter was willing to waive his rights to the position in favor of Nixon. This started a minor skirmish within the administration. Eventually, Eisenhower and Dulles decided against Nixon taking over the post. Ike's rationale for his action is quite instructive, especially considering that he had been extremely open in allowing Nixon a strong foreign-policy role. (In contrast, one would not be surprised by a President Johnson rejecting such a role for his vice president, since he had constrained the role of his vice president in foreign policy anyway.)

As noted in chapter 3, Ike was revolutionary in allowing his vice president maximum latitude in foreign policy. At that point in history, Nixon's vice-presidential duties in foreign policy were unprecedented across the board. Yet, Eisenhower believed that taking over the OCB was beyond the scope of what the vice president should do. "The vice president has statutory constitutional duties," he said. "It would be impossible as a matter of practice to give, within the executive department, the vice president specified duties because if you happen to have a vice president who disagrees with you, then you would have . . . an impossible situation. . . . I don't know of any vice president that has ever been given the great opportunities to participate in difficult decisions, conferences, and every kind of informative meeting that we have than Mr. Nixon. But I decided as a matter of good governmental organization that it would not be correct to give him a governmental position in the executive department."[67] Eisenhower, a very sympathetic and path-breaking president as far as granting meaningful duties to his vice president, was in essence drawing a line at which his vice president could not cross. Perhaps we should take the advice of Ike, one of the master organizers in the history of the presidency.

So, should the vice president chair a major NSC or crisis-management group?

There are key benefits to the chairmanship beyond just keeping the vice president busy. The substantive foreign-policy role would boost his image internally and externally. It would also give him key foreign-policy experience, knowledge, management, and coordination. In the end, the experience would likely benefit him in the event of a necessary succession.

But would the chairmanship help the administration's and nation's foreign policy? That, of course, is what matters most. Often, it may depend on the situation. Yet, as noted, a president typically does not pick his vice president because they are completely compatible in foreign policy. For such compatibility he looks to his choice for NSA or secretary of state. Likewise with the issue of foreign-policy management and coordination. President Bush, for his NSA, picked Brent Scowcroft, who agreed with Bush on foreign policy and had plenty of experience and knowledge in foreign-policy management and coordination. Why should Bush then have turned to his vice president to take up those duties on the crisis-management front when he had Scowcroft? Remember, this is foreign and defense policy: often, the issues at hand, especially during crisis situations, involve the lives of human beings. This is not an area to toss around abstract ideas without fully contemplating their consequences.

Some might counter by correctly noting that in recent years the NSA has become too politicized and has neglected his management and coordination duties. Fair enough. But if such occurs, the solution is to straighten out the NSA or bring in a new one, rather than having the vice president step in, which would add a whole new series of dynamics that could go wrong.

So, then, if such a role is rejected, does the vice president lose crucial foreign-policy experience, knowledge, management, and coordination that might someday aid him and the nation in the event he assumes the presidency under emergency circumstances? Not necessarily. He still could chair NSC and cabinet meetings in the president's absence. Over a four-year period, he would also have hundreds of opportunities to observe the president, NSA, secretary of state, and others in managing and coordinating foreign policy. Of course, nothing beats personal hands-on experience, but he still would attain valuable experience by observation. Foreign-policy knowledge and insights will be gained via the vice president's presence at all NSC and cabinet meetings, morning intelligence briefings, weekly meetings with the president, receiving of all papers that go to the president, presence and counsel of his own defense and foreign-policy advisors, trips abroad, and so on.

Some may justifiably inquire why I would reject giving the vice president the ability to chair an administration's crisis-management group when the only precedent—Bush heading up the group in the Reagan administration—appears to be a positive one operationally (aside from Haig's complaints). Yet, the fact is that such a move seems unnecessary and invites more problems than solutions. Once again, what happens if the vice president performs inadequately? He may either be fired or talked into "stepping down." However, there lies the potential for political fall out that could hurt the president. And speaking of politics, evidence shows how the vice president's actions are often politically motivated. Finally, the NSA should take such a position because he, rather than the vice president, is picked for his foreign-policy management and coordination skills. This is not to say that a vice president could not adequately fulfill such a task, but only that it is unnecessary and potentially problematic.

Training for the Presidency

Clearly, involving the vice president in aspects of foreign policy is not a simple cut and dry move that reaps nothing but a cascade of benefits. Hopefully these pages have shown that some of the past recommendations made should have been analyzed more carefully.

While many of the foreign-policy activities explored over these pages had certain virtues, as well as negatives, it is worthwhile to note that all of them have had one particular overriding benefit, whether intended or not: They have helped train the vice president to be president. In some cases, this had a payoff within the administration, in which the vice president was forced to assume presidential duties at least temporarily. In other cases, it at least seemed to provide valuable down-the-road training that aided the vice president later when he became president through his own victorious election campaign for the White House. At the very least, perhaps the most inarguable aspect of this study is that some level of increased foreign-policy involvement by the vice president helps the second-office holder gain crucial preparation that would help rather than hurt him if he was forced to assume the presidency. While we can argue about certain roles that he should or should not assume, it is clear that the foreign-policy experience he gains as vice president would only benefit him in the event the 'unthinkable' happened to the commander in chief. In this sense, the activity vindicates Danny Adkison's point that the vice presidency is, if nothing else, a sort of apprenticeship for training and preparing the occupant to one day become the president.

Most, if not all, of the past reforms and suggestions examined in this chapter—particularly early ones made by Truman and Eisenhower—have the intention of preparing and, even, training, the vice president to take over the ship of state if he is needed. To that end, judging from the five vice presidents profiled, the post-World War II changes appear to have achieved that purpose. Such is certainly the most important, consistent, and noteworthy goal of all the reforms. It is worthwhile to examine the evidence of this achievement.

Consider some of the following from previous pages, such as this remark by Steve Gillon on Vice President Mondale, which perhaps unintentionally makes the point:

> Despite the setbacks, these years [as vice president] marked an important evolution in Mondale's development as a national leader. He immersed himself in foreign-policy issues, read diplomatic telegrams, attended NSC meetings, consulted with various experts, and made more than a dozen foreign trips. As a result he developed a more sophisticated view of complex international issues, learned how the bureaucracy worked, and received crucial diplomatic experience. Combined with his knowledge of the legislative process and his understanding of the political aspects of making foreign policy, Mondale emerged with a new confidence and skill in the art of international diplomacy.[68]

This passage leaves little doubt that this particular vice president, as a result of his extensive foreign-policy involvement, was more trained for the rigors of the presidency than he otherwise would have been in the pre-Truman days, in which many if not most of the second-office holders did not perform anything resembling the aforementioned activities.

Likewise, citing Bush's vice-presidential experience, as well as his background before 1981, NSC staffer Constantine Menges aptly notes, "One could hardly design a more ideal preparation for a future president than the professional experience of George Bush."[69]

There are also examples from the Nixon vice presidency, such as his first trip overseas—a 38,000-mile, seventy-two day round-the-world trip in 1953, in which Eisenhower utilized him as an emissary. This trip appeared to begin an odyssey into foreign affairs that would intrigue Nixon throughout his public career and afterwards as a private citizen. "His task had been to help convince our Asian friends that the United States was as fully concerned about their needs and dangers as we were about Europe," recalled Eisenhower. "It had been a highly successful mission. Through his observations and conferences, the Vice President had acquired knowledge and understanding of the areas visited, valuable to us in the formulation of our policies." Eisenhower's comments reflect on the personal education the foreign-policy duty offered to Nixon. Ike in general talks about how Nixon's vice-presidential experiences helped train him to be president. "During my first administration, Mr. Nixon had become well acquainted with the duties of the Departments," wrote Eisenhower. Eventually, the president "believed Nixon to be the best prepared man in government to take over my duties in any emergency."[70] Later, in a September 3, 1957 memo giving Vice President Nixon a stepped up foreign-policy role, Ike said to Nixon: "In addition you have gained an understanding of our foreign problems that is both unusual and comprehensive."[71] Eisenhower explained how Vice President Nixon's experiences helped prepare him for the presidency:

> [I]t was my conviction that Dick Nixon, by reason of his unique preparation for the Presidency, unmatched in our history, would be a worthy nominee of the Republican party. In addition to his earlier service in the House and Senate, his years in the Vice Presidency had given him extended opportunities to study the workings of the federal government, to meet world leaders, to gain an understanding of domestic and international conditions. He had traveled widely, knew our defenses, had shown an unusual grasp of foreign policy and economic affairs.[72]

Informed but much more distant observers agreed with Ike. "As he approached the 1960 presidential nomination and election," wrote Marie Natoli, "Nixon could point to his proven activity and expertise in the field of foreign affairs."[73] She added: "Nixon traveled to all reaches of the globe, and in doing so was widely covered, attracting both domestic and world attention. Besides giving him a very active Vice Presidency, this role immersed him in foreign affairs, clearly helping to prepare him for one day assuming the presidency. It is no wonder that when Nixon eventually did become president his foreign-policy achievements were so extraordinary."[74] Similarly, Sidney Warren commented: "As a roving representative of the president on numerous assignments abroad, he was constantly in the public eye.... Numerous meetings with foreign leaders and regular attendance at sessions of the National Security Council afforded Nixon an unusual opportunity for 'on the job' training in foreign policy and national security problems."[75]

In Nixon's own words, the training process he underwent in his new office was a "liberal education in what goes on in the world."[76] His trip to Moscow gave him insights into the Soviet people and Khrushchev that he unquestionably would not have otherwise ascertained. A passage on Khrushchev written by Nixon in *Six Crises* illustrates the personal education he received. "In the person of Nikita Khrushchev, 'Communist man' at his most dangerous best," wrote Nixon, "I had seen Communism in action—not just in theory." On the Russian people, his walks through the streets of Moscow, Leningrad, Novosibirsk, and elsewhere provided him with a crucial perspective: "The masses of the Russian people, as distinguished from the elite few who make up the Communist hierarchy, are truly friendly toward the United States. They remember our help in World War II, they know at firsthand the terrible destruction of war and desperately want peace."[77] Such insights would serve him well throughout his career, educating him into the foreign-policy "expert" and senior "elder statesman" that he would be considered for years to come, even begrudgingly among many of the most ardent Nixon haters.

Nixon's Khrushchev experiences provide a model example of political learning that might later have been helpful. After watching Kennedy in the Bay of Pigs debacle, Nixon later said that, if he were president, he would not have permitted the invasion to fail, that he would have committed the necessary forces in the first place, and that Khrushchev would not have had the chance or encouragement to put missiles in Cuba later. Some will argue that this is "armchair quaterbacking" by a politician detached from the heat of the battle. However, Nixon's judgment on how Khrushchev would have acted was based on his acquired understanding of the man—gained during his vice-presidential years. "If the United States had dealt with Castro effectively at the Bay of Pigs," said Nixon, "Khrushchev would not have miscalculated a year later in the missile crisis. Khrushchev, like all aggressors, all dictators, interpreted indecision as weakness. The way to avoid miscalculation is to never give them a moment when they think you're weak."[78] In part, he was correct. As JFK famously remarked during the Cuban Missile Crisis, he felt Khrushchev was testing him to see if he had "guts."

Nixon himself was cognizant of how his trips abroad as vice president helped him politically as a national presidential figure who could appeal to a broad base of voters beyond just the Republican party. He wrote: "My trips to Caracas and Moscow had provided an opportunity for me to appear [as a representative to all the American people]. And it was only after these trips that my strength rose the necessary level above that of the party."[79]

Even if using the vice president in foreign policy may not make a difference in the administration's achievements *at the time*, such activity can provide the occupant with substantive foreign-policy experience that could prove valuable in a succession situation. Natoli hit it on the head when she wrote: "The presidency is such a unique institution that it can justifiably be argued that the only training ground for it is the presidency itself. Nonetheless, the vice presidency is the closest we can come to having someone waiting in the wings should the need arise."[80] At the least, using the vice president in foreign policy helps in that respect.

Conclusion

The vice president is a "member" of the president's foreign-policy team simply by nature of the fact that he is a statutory member of the NSC. In this sense, he is at least assured somewhat of a foreign-policy role.[81] Yet, as noted throughout this study, while Truman's changes should always guarantee that a vice president will never be left in the dark in foreign policy, the second-office holder's ultimate involvement, influence, and ability to be taken seriously, will likely always be dependent upon he and the president he serves.

One need only point to the most recent available comparison: While vice presidents Quayle and Gore are near equals in many foreign-policy duties, the latter has been somewhat more influential in terms of advising the president and other players. The difference was not so much the two vice presidents—both of which came to the office with similar foreign-policy experience and equal desires to play roles in global affairs—but the presidents they served. While both presidents Bush and Clinton were very much sympathetic to involving the vice president, Gore faced a situation where he had far more room to move in foreign policy than his predecessor. A term that fits in this situation is the "idiosyncratic variable." James Rosenau aptly notes that each policymaker has his own idiosyncrasies that effect the way his administration operates and performs. This has ramifications for how the vice president is used by a president in foreign policy. This study shows that the foreign-policy role and ultimate level of involvement of a particular vice president is dependent upon the unique set of circumstances in which he finds himself—from the president he serves to the foreign-policy team he is a part of. Key among those circumstances are the idiosyncrasies of both he and his president. The idiosyncratic variable is especially fitting in understanding how presidents like FDR, Eisenhower, and Clinton used, or did not use, their vice president. Because of this variable, vice-presidential roles in foreign policy, and elsewhere, will always necessarily vary somewhat. This is why any credit to Gore (or other vice presidents) must also go to the idiosyncratic variables that sparked his enhanced foreign-policy role and the influence that accompanies it.

As further evidence, consider the Reagan-Bush relationship, influenced by Reagan's idiosyncrasies on how he used his vice president. Vice President Bush said that once Reagan made his vice-presidential selection, he viewed the Reagan-Bush ticket not simply as a convenient political alliance but as a "partnership," saying, "We would run and serve together as team." Bush carefully added that there was never any doubt which of the two was the senior partner. "But as president," wrote Bush, "Ronald Reagan—more than any president before him—broke down the barriers between the nation's two highest elective offices.... He [went] out of his way to bring his vice president inside the White House circle, and our trust and friendship had grown each passing day." Reflecting a theme illustrated among the presidents and vice presidents in this study, Bush himself said it best: "Given the right president, it's possible for the right vice president to have an impact on administration policy."[82] Reagan proved this through the substantive tasks he assigned to his vice president. Each of the vice president's in this study upheld this Bush credo, especially the two who most helped lay the framework: Nixon and Mondale.

Granting the idiosyncrasies, how should a vice president be used in foreign policy?

While there is a limited literature on how to best incorporate the vice president into the president's broader national-security system or structure, when it comes to the separate (and large) literature on how the president could best improve the operation of his NSC or use of his National Security Advisor (NSA), many scholars—despite countless suggestions—often fall back to a common conclusion that may have implications for using the vice president: the president should do what works best for him, although a degree of structure is important.[83]

Eisenhower, whom history has reevaluated as man of admirable organizational skills—including the way he ran his NSC—has some reasonable advice on how to best use the vice president in foreign policy. His suggestions fit the pattern of advice offered by many NSC experts. "No specific organization is sacrosanct in its details," Ike stated, "it is established and used by humans and it can be changed by them. Indeed, at times this may be necessary because of changing conditions or even by the entry of a new personality." As with the NSC, Ike is suggesting that a president use his vice president in a manner that works best for him. Ike believed the use of the vice president in foreign policy has its limits, but he also felt that it had its possibilities. "Thus, for example," said Eisenhower, "my use of Vice President Nixon as a member of advisory bodies and as a personal representative in many affairs, both domestic and foreign, created an organizational precedent in American history."[84]

With that in mind, it is worth driving home one of the more important findings of this study—one that goes against the wisdom of many suggestions for reform. Many reformers of the vice presidency note that the occupant is an ideal candidate for numerous foreign-policy roles because he "represents no institutional interest, and he lacks an independent power base."[85] In part, this seems true. But, in reality, the fact that most vice presidents want so desperately to be president in practice means that certain vice presidents end up having selfish interests that are nearly "institutional." So many vice presidents have become president or aspired to it and run for it—about the only post-World War II exception is Alben Barkley—that personal political self interests are almost an institutional element of the modern vice presidency—in practice if not in theory. I term this the vice president's "succession constituency." Again, Bush, for example, botched a critically important element of Reagan strategy in Saudi Arabia because of a selfish-political interest regarding the oil industry. Likewise, Mondale's actions were often dictated by politics. In sum, any consideration of how to involve the vice president in foreign policy must take into account this political factor.

One way to avoid the political self-interest problem might be to pick a vice president who is somewhat of an elder statesman or congressional veteran but has no personal presidential aspirations—someone who is simply ending out his political career. Finding such a person is admittedly difficult in a field in which unrestrained ambition reigns supreme—although Truman seemed to find one in Alben Barkley. Yet, Barkley himself demonstrates a problem with this notion. He did not fully exploit Truman's changes to the vice presidency. As a result, the first foreign-policy-active vice president was not Barkley but his successor, Richard Nixon. Ironically, picking a vice president without political self interests could lead to the selection of someone who is disinterested and not as helpful. The political self-interest issue can actually serve as a motivator leading to an engaged, ambitious, and fruitful vice president—like Nixon, Mondale, Bush, Quayle, and Gore. Hence, the political self-interest factor is a double-edged sword: It can be a good motivator with decidedly positive offshoots—Bush in Western Europe, Nixon in Moscow—but also act as a self-serving issue that takes away from the president's broader goals—Bush in Saudi Arabia, Mondale in South Africa. Regarding the former, it is worth noting that perhaps the best cases of the vice president being used in foreign-policy missions contained the following elements: It involved an area or issue in which the vice president at hand was knowledgeable, highly interested, and motivated to do a bang-up job that would benefit not only himself but also the administration. Also in these cases—again, Bush in Western Europe, Nixon in Moscow—the vice president was more of an educated and engaged spokesman who served his mission abroad as an assessor, conveyor of information, and fact finder, as opposed to a negotiator. He then was typically briefed by the president upon his return, only to do his bargaining and evaluating behind closed doors at home.[86]

The lesson is clear: The vice president can be very helpful to the president in foreign policy, but the president must be careful where he inserts him.

Equally important, the best reason for keeping him involved in foreign policy remains the reason Truman sought to involve the vice president in the first place: to be able to adequately assume the presidency. We must always keep our eye on that ball. Any other foreign-policy activities that seek to offer anything to the vice president aside from that central goal may often be either icing on the cake or fluff—that is what each president and administration must decide.

In conclusion, to paraphrase the NSC reformers, I would conclude that when it comes to using the vice president in foreign policy, there is no ideal structure, although some structure is important. This is evident in the table presented at the beginning of this chapter, in which there are a number of "musts," "rejects," and "potentials." The musts and rejects would suggest my attempt to define that seemingly arbitrary "ideal structure," whereas the "potential" that varies by administration allows for the flexibility of the president to mold the pattern that works best for him, his vice president, his team, and his nation's foreign policy.

To reaffirm, there are certain things that a vice president can do in foreign policy, and perhaps should do, irrespective of the particular administration. Likewise, there are things he should not do. At the least, I hope this work has proven that moves designed to enhance the vice president's foreign-policy role—for the better of U.S. policy—should be considered more carefully. This is, after all, important stuff we're dealing with.

Notes

1. Marie D. Natoli, *American Prince, American Pauper* (Westport, Conn.: Greenwood Press, 1985), pp. 183-85; and Natoli, "The Vice Presidency in the Third Century," in James P. Pfiffner and R. Gordon Hoxie, eds., *The Presidency in Transition* (New York: Center for the Study of the Presidency, 1989), p. 404.

2. Earl Mazo and Stephen Hess, *Nixon: A Political Portrait* (New York: Harper & Row, 1968), p. 207.

3. Interview with Joe DeSutter, former military aide to both vice presidents Quayle and Gore, via telephone from Washington, D.C., December 18, 1996.

4. Steven M. Gillon, *The Democrats' Dilemma: Walter F. Mondale and the Liberal Legacy* (New York: Columbia University Press, 1992), p. 180.

5. Paul C. Light, "The Institutional Vice Presidency," *Presidential Studies Quarterly*, Vol. XIII, No. 2, Spring 1983, p. 198.

6. "Interview with Bush: White House Leaks: 'We Have Been Undisciplined,'" *U.S. News & World Report*, December 14, 1981, Vol. 91, No. 24, p. 20.

7. Jimmy Carter, *Keeping Faith: Memoirs of a President* (Toronto: Bantam Books, 1982), p. 40.

8. George Bush with Victor Gold, *Looking Forward* (New York: Doubleday, 1987), p. 222.

9. Interview with Jon Glassman, former Deputy NSA to Vice President Quayle, in Washington, D.C., at State Department, May 24, 1996.

10. Carter, op. cit., p. 40.

11. Gillon, op. cit., pp. 181-82.

12. Zbigniew Brzezinski, *Power and Principle: Memoirs of the National Security Advisor, 1977-1981* (New York: Farrar, Straus, Giroux, 1983), p. 33.

13. Marie D. Natoli touches on the issue of legislative assistance by the vice president in Marie D. Natoli, "The Vice Presidency in the Third Century," pp. 404-07.

14. Interview with Bill Kristol, former chief of staff to Vice President Quayle, via telephone, May 28, 1996.

15. Ben W. Heineman, Jr., "Some Rules of the Game: Prescription for Organizing the Domestic Presidency," in "The Vice Presidency in the Third Century," in James P. Pfiffner and R. Gordon Hoxie, eds., *The Presidency in Transition* (New York: Center for the Study of the Presidency, 1989), pp. 45-53.

16. Gillon, op. cit., p. 291; and *New York Times*, January 21, 1981.

17. *Christian Science Monitor*, March 3, 1981.

18. Hamilton Jordan, *Crisis: The Last Year of the Carter Presidency* (New York: G. P. Putnam's Sons, 1982), p. 391.

19. Heineman, op. cit., p. 52.

20. Mondale was the first vice president to have defense and foreign-policy advisors, which was among the other changes that enabled his staff size to balloon significantly. In the case of Gore, *Roll Call* reported that his Senate staff was 18 percent larger and cost 21 percent more than Vice President Quayle's four years earlier. Light, op. cit., p. 198; and "Gore's Growth," *The Washington Times*, December 7, 1993.

21. Alexander Moens, *Foreign Policy under Carter: Testing Multiple Advocacy Decision Making* (Boulder, Colo.: Westview, 1990), p. 44; and Light, op. cit., p. 198.

22. Light, op. cit., p. 198.

23. Interview with Kristol.

24. Interview with Glassman.

25. C. Boyden Gray, "The Coordinating Role of the Vice Presidency," in James P. Pfiffner and R. Gordon Hoxie, eds., *The Presidency in Transition* (New York: Center for the Study of the Presidency, 1989), p. 429.

26. Finlay Lewis, *Mondale: Portrait of an American Politician* (New York: Harper & Row, 1980), p. 254.

27. The issues in this section open other interesting questions, some of which are beyond the scope of this study. For instance, why didn't Bush and others play more politics? Perhaps it was due to their strong loyalty. If that is the case, are the examples herein just occasional slips in which they let down their "loyalty" guard? Additionally, where is the boundary or limit at which the president refuses to tolerate such behavior? Research herein suggests the threshold is rather low; consider, for instance, how Reagan reprimanded Bush on Saudi Arabia, how Bush reprimanded Quayle on the Gorbachev remarks, and how Mondale was removed from some South Africa duties because of his gaffes. Finally, a much more open question—one that is very difficult to answer—is whether presidents attempt to force other behavior from their vice presidents. One would think that the reprimanding from the likes of presidents Reagan and Bush would be an indication that chief executives do in fact try to force changes in such behavior.

28. Constantine C. Menges, *Inside the National Security Council* (New York: Simon & Schuster, 1988), p. 272.

29. Martin Anderson, *Revolution* (San Diego: Harcourt Brace Jovanovich, 1988), pp. 259-60.

30. Interview with Carnes Lord, former NSA to Vice President Quayle, via telephone from Medford, Mass., December 11, 1996

31. Typically, with the exception of the NSA and deputy NSA, the vice president's defense and foreign-policy staff is paid by the Pentagon, not the White House. Interview with Joe DeSutter.

32. A separate issue concerns a vice president's ability to get past staff members (from pre-vice-presidency days) into key areas of the executive branch. Mondale, in particular, benefited in this way. Alexander Moens notes: "David Aaron, Mondale's former assistant in the Senate, became deputy director of the NSC. Mondale was alerted by him to upcoming issues and frequently walked the few steps to Aaron's office for information." Mondale's own staff, such as Chief of Staff Dick Moe, became integrated with the president's. Carter called Moe "one of my most valuable advisors." Similarly, also helping Vice President Bush's role was the fact that Reagan brought some Bush people onto his own staff. Especially important among these people was James Baker, who formed a key part of the triad surrounding the president—Meese, Deaver, and Baker. See John Dumbrell, *The Carter Presidency: A Re-Evaluation* (Manchester and New York: Manchester University Press, 1993), p. 38; Moens, op. cit., pp. 44-45; Carter, op. cit., p. 40; and Natoli, "The Vice Presidency in the Third Century," pp. 421-22.

33. Light, op. cit., pp. 198-99.

34. Interviews with Kristol and Glassman; and Dan Quayle, *Standing Firm: A Vice-Presidential Memoir* (New York: HarperCollins, 1994), pp. 88-89.

35. Carnes Lord confirms Glassman's role in this regard. Interview with Lord; Quayle, op. cit., pp. 146 and 161-62; and Interview with Glassman.

36. Interview with Carnes Lord; and Interview with Jon Glassman.

37. Interview with Glassman.

38. Interview with Joe DeSutter.

39. While Quayle's NSAs were members of the equivalent of the Deputies Committee in the Bush White House, they were not as influential or active in the committee as Gore's NSA. Ibid; and Michael K. Frisby and Barbara Rosewicz, "Gore, Adding Efficiency Study to His Portfolio, Has Carved Out a Significant Role for Himself," *Wall Street Journal*, March 4, 1993, p. A16.

40. Marie D. Natoli, "The Vice Presidency in the Third Century," p. 422.

41. In a grandiose fashion, Gerald Ford has advocated moving the vice president "right into the West Wing of the White House as the chief of staff of the whole administration." See *Time*, November 10, 1980, p. 30. I reject this recommendation, but don't focus on it in this study because it deals with far more than just foreign policy.

42. For an analysis of the relationship between the two most recent vice presidents (Quayle and Gore) and their secretaries of state, see Paul Kengor, "Vice-Presidential Involvement in Foreign Policy: A Tale of Two Vice Presidents and Their Secretaries of State," *Political Science Quarterly*, forthcoming in 2000.

43. The following paragraphs on Gray's argument are taken from, Gray, op. cit., pp. 425-29.

44. Interview with Kristol.

45. An issue for future consideration is how the president can in fact "fire" or relieve his vice president from certain duties—obviously, in a delicate, politically viable manner. Also, there are likely other options that the president could consider if he feels the need to discharge his vice president from a certain task, such as moving him into other assignments. Surely, there are alternatives that would allow him to iron out this problem in ways that help minimize the damage. (This section does not consider such options because its intention is to evaluate Gray's recommendation and the problems it poses, not to try to provide a host of solutions for a president faced with such problems.)

46. Ibid.

47. For examples of clashes between Quayle and Baker, see Quayle, *Standing Firm*, pp. 37, 69, 97, 183-84.

48. Interview with Joe DeSutter.

49. Interview with Carnes Lord, former NSA to Vice President Quayle, December 11, 1996.

50. Interview with DeSutter.

51. For an example of Quayle and Baker clashing in the area of space policy vis-à-vis the Soviet Union, see Quayle, *Standing Firm*, pp. 183-84.

52. Kevin V. Mulcahy, "Presidents and the Administration of Foreign Policy: The New Role for the Vice President," *Presidential Studies Quarterly*, Vol. XVII, No. 1, Winter 1987, p. 129.

53. Robert E. Hunter, *Organizing for National Security* (Washington, D.C.: Center for Strategic and International Studies, 1988); and Duncan L. Clarke, *American Defense and Foreign Policy Institutions: Toward a Sound Foundation* (New York: Harper & Row, Ballinger Division, 1989).

54. Elizabeth Drew, *Meet the Press*, NBC-TV, October 30, 1994.

55. Mulcahy, op. cit., p. 129.

56. Gray, op. cit., p. 424.

57. Ibid.

58. Marie D. Natoli, "The Vice Presidency in the Third Century," p. 422.

59. Bernard Gwertzman, "Haig Opposes Plan for New Bush Role But Reagan Moves," *The New York Times*, March 25, 1981, p. A6.

60. Menges, op. cit., p. 382.

61. Ronald Reagan, *An American Life* (New York: Simon & Schuster, 1990), pp. 255-56; and Alexander M. Haig, Jr., *Caveat: Realism, Reagan, and Foreign Policy* (New York: MacMillan, 1984), pp. 141-50.

62. Gwertzman, op. cit., p. A1.

63. Reagan, *An American Life*, pp. 255-56.

64. Clarke, op. cit., p. 20; and Gwertzman, op. cit., p. A1.

65. Bush, *Looking Forward*, p. 232.

66. David S. Broder and Bob Woodward, "Facing Limitations in an 'Awkward Job,'" *Washington Post*, January 8, 1992, p. A14.

67. William Costello, *The Facts about Nixon* (New York: Viking, 1960), pp. 244-45.

68. Gillon, op. cit., p. 249.

69. Menges, op. cit., p. 381.

70. Dwight D. Eisenhower, *Waging Peace: The White House Years, 1956-1961* (Garden City, N.Y.: Doubleday, 1965), pp. 6-8.

71. Mazo and Hess, op. cit., pp. 207-08.
72. Eisenhower, *Waging Peace*, p. 590.
73. Marie D. Natoli, *American Prince, American Pauper*, p. 159.
74. Marie D. Natoli, "The Vice Presidency in the Third Century," p. 416.
75. Sidney Warren, *The Battle for the Presidency* (Philadelphia: Lippincott, 1968), p. 299.
76. Costello, op. cit., p. 233.
77. Richard M. Nixon, *Six Crises* (New York: Doubleday, 1962), pp. 274 and 287.
78. Jules Witcover, *The Resurrection of Richard Nixon* (New York: Putnam, 1970), p. 48.
79. Nixon, *Six Crises*, p. 304.
80. Marie D. Natoli, "The Vice Presidency in the Third Century," pp. 409-11.
81. This means that even a vice president who prefers domestic policy over foreign policy (such as might have been the case with a Vice President Jack Kemp) would still be assured at least somewhat of a foreign-policy role.
82. Bush, op. cit., pp. 222 and 227.
83. As noted earlier regarding the NSC, see Clarke, op. cit., p. 3; Michael R. Beschloss and Allen Weinstein, "The Best National Security System: A Conversation with Zbigniew Brzezinski," *Washington Quarterly*, No. 1, 1982, p. 71; National Security Act of 1947, 50 U.S.C. Sec. 402(a); Philip A. Odeen, "Organizing for National Security," *International Security*, Vol. 5, No. 1, Summer 1980, pp. 112; I. M. Destler, "National Security Advice to U.S. Presidents: Some Lessons from Thirty Years," *World Politics*, 1977, pp. 143-76; I. M. Destler, "National Security Management: What Presidents Have Wrought," *Political Science Quarterly*, Vol. 95, No. 4, Winter 1980-81, especially p. 582; and Robert E. Hunter, *Organizing for National Security* (Washington, D.C.: Center for Strategic and International Studies, 1988).
84. Eisenhower, *Waging Peace*, p. 631.
85. Mulcahy, op. cit., p. 129.
86. This was developed in conversation with Paul Hammond, September 27, 1996.

Bibliography

Abrams, Elliott (1987). "Development of U.S.-Nicaragua Policy." Washington, D.C.: U.S. Department of State, Bureau of Public Affairs, Editorial Division.
Abrams, Elliott (1986). "Permanent Dictatorship in Nicaragua?" Washington, D.C.: U.S. Department of State, Bureau of Public Affairs, Editorial Division.
Abrams, Herbert L. (1993). "Shielding the President from the Constitution: Disability and the 25th Amendment." *Presidential Studies Quarterly* XXIII(3).
Adams, C. F., ed. (1850-1856). *The Works of John Adams.* 10 vols. Boston.
Adkison, Danny M. (1983). "The Vice Presidency as Apprenticeship." *Presidential Studies Quarterly* XIII(2).
Adler, Jerry (1991). "The War Within." *Newsweek V(117).*
Adler, Jonathan (1994). "Imagine Dumping Bill." *Newsweek,* XXIV(23).
Allen, Thomas B., and Norman Polmar. (1995). *Code-Name Downfall: The Secret Plan to Invade Japan and Why Truman Dropped the Bomb.* New York: Simon & Schuster.
Allison, Graham T. (1971). *Essence of Decision: Explaining the Cuban Missile Crisis.* Glenview: Scott, Foresman and Company.
Alm, Richard (1986). "Alarm Bells over Cheaper Oil; While Consumers Cheer Plummeting Prices, Vice President Bush and Others Are Warning Enough Is Enough." *U.S. News & World Report,* 100.
Alperovitz, Gar. *Atomic Diplomacy: Hiroshima and Potsdam; the Use of the Atomic Bomb and the American Confrontation with Soviet Power.* New York: Vintage.
Alperovitz, Gar, and Sanho Tree (1995). *The Decision to Use the Atomic Bomb and the Architecture of an American Myth.* New York: Knopf.
Ambrose, Stephen E. (1984). *Eisenhower: Volume II, The President.* New York: Simon & Schuster.
Anderson, Martin (1988). *Revolution.* San Diego: Harcourt Brace Jovanovich.
Aronson, Bernard W. (1991). Statement of Bernard W. Aronson, Assistant Secretary of State for Inter-American Affairs. "Fiscal Year 1992 Foreign Assistance Request for the Western Hemisphere." *Hearings before the Subcommittee on Western Hemisphere and Peace Corps Affairs of the Committee on Foreign Relations, United States Senate, First Session, 102nd Congress* (April 18).
Bailey, Kenneth D. (1994). *Methods of Social Research.* 4th edition. New York: The Free Press.
Barkley, Alben W. (1954). *That Reminds Me.* Garden City, N.Y.: Doubleday.
Barnes, Fred (1993). "More Gore." *The New Republic, 209(23).*
Barnes, Fred (1991a). "White House Watch: Quayle Alert." *The New Republic, 24(21).*
Barnes, Fred (1991b). "White House Watch: Brilliant Pebble." *The New Republic,* April 1.
Barone, Michael, and Kenneth T. Walsh (1991). "His Place at the Table." *U.S. News & World Report, 110(19).*
Bayh, Birch (1968). *One Heartbeat Away.* New York: Bobbs-Merrill.
Bedard, Paul (1994). "Talking Like Candidate, Quayle Starts Book Tour." *The Washington Times,* May 6.
Berke, Richard L. (1994). *New York Times Magazine,* February 20.

Berke, Richard L. (1993). "Prodded by Gore, Kazakhstan Signs Arms Accord." *The New York Times*, December 14.
Bernstein, Carl (1992). "The Holy Alliance." *Time*, February 24.
Beschloss, Michael R., and Allen Weinstein (1982). "The Best National Security System: A Conversation with Zbigniew Brzezinski." *Washington Quarterly, 1*.
Beschloss, Michael R., and Strobe Talbott (1993). *At the Highest Levels: The Inside Story of the End of the Cold War*. Little, Brown.
Bledsoe, Ralph C. (1989). "Policy Management in the Reagan Administration." In James P. Pfiffner and R. Gordon Hoxie, eds., *The Presidency in Transition*. New York: Center for the Study of the Presidency.
Boyer, Peter J. (1994). "Gore's Dilemma." *The New Yorker, 70(39)*.
Breslau, Karen and Bob Cohn (1994). "Al Gore: Talk a Lot, and Carry a Big Stick." *Newsweek*, October 31.
Broder, David S. (1977). "Mondale Begins Tour in Brussels." *The Washington Post*, January 24.
Broder, David S., and Bob Woodward (1992). "Facing Limitations in an 'Awkward Job.'" *The Washington Post*, January 8.
Broder, David S., Bob Woodward, and David Greenberg (1992). "Quayles and Bushes, Almost Like Family." *The Washington Post*, January 8.
Brown, Warren (1976). "Mondale Assails Foreign Policy As Tainted by 'Watergate Era.'" *The Washington Post*, September 11.
Brzezinski, Zbigniew (1983). *Power and Principle: Memoirs of the National Security Adviser, 1977-1981*. New York: Farrar, Straus, Giroux.
Bueno de Mesquita, Bruce (1985). "Symposium." *International Studies Quarterly, 29*.
Burke, John P., and Fred I. Greenstein (1989). *How Presidents Test Reality: Decisions on Vietnam, 1954 and 1965*. New York: Russel Sage Foundation.
Bush, George (1987). "Prelude to Retaliation: Building a Governmental Consensus on Terrorism." *SAIS Review 7(1)*.
Bush, George (1985). "Nicaragua: A Threat to Democracy." *U.S. Department of State Bulletin, 85(2098)*.
Bush, George, with Victor Gold (1987). *Looking Forward*. New York: Doubleday.
Butler, David (1979). "SALT II: And Now for the Battle." *Newsweek, 93(21)*.
Cannon, Lou (1982). *Reagan*. New York: G. P. Putnam's Sons.
Carter, Jimmy (1982). *Keeping Faith: Memoirs of a President*. Toronto and New York: Bantam.
Clarke, Duncan L. (1989). *American Defense and Foreign Policy Institutions: Toward a Sound Foundation*. New York: Harper & Row, Ballinger Division.
Clines, Francis X. (1983). "The Vice President: No Comment on the Future." *The New York Times*, February 25.
Collier, David (1995). "Translating Quantitative Methods for Qualitative Researchers: The Case of Selection Bias." Review Symposium, *American Political Science Review, 89*.
Cooper, Matthew (1994). "A Tale of Two Letters." *U.S. News & World Report, 117(22)*.
Costello, William (1960). *The Facts about Nixon*. New York: Viking.
Crossette, Barbara (1995a). "Gore, at U.N., Says Nuclear Powers Are Fair on Weapons Treaty." *The New York Times*, April 20.
Crossette, Barbara (1995b). "South Africa Emerges as a Force for Extending Nuclear Arms." *The New York Times*, April 23.

Cutler, Robert (1956). "The Development of the National Security Council." *Foreign Affairs, XXXIV.*

d'Estaing, Valery Giscard, Yasuhiro Nakasono, and Henry Kissinger (1989). "East-West Relations." *Foreign Affairs, 68(3).*

de Toledano, Ralph (1960). *Nixon.* New York: Duell, Sloan, and Pearce.

Destler, I. M. (1977). "National Security Advice to U.S. Presidents: Some Lessons from Thirty Years." *World Politics.*

Devroy, Ann (1990a). "Bush Prepares Mission to Iraq as Final Bid to Preserve Peace." *The Washington Post*, December 1.

Devroy, Ann (1990b). "Quayle Cites 'Moral Costs' of Waiting." *The Washington Post*, November 30.

Devroy, Ann, and Stephen Barr (1995). "Gore Bucks Tradition in Vice President's Role." *The Washington Post*, February 18.

Dolan, Anthony (1992). *Undoing the Evil Empire: How Reagan Won the Cold War.* Washington, D.C.: American Enterprise Institute.

Dorman, Michael (1968). *The Second Man.* New York: Delacorte.

Dowd, Maureen (1991). "Quayle Aims at Protests, A la Agnew." *The New York Times*, January 24.

Dowd, Maureen (1990). "U.S. Rebuffs Iraq on the Palestinians." *The New York Times*, December 2.

Drew, Elizabeth (1994). *Meet the Press with Tim Russert.* NBC-TV, October 30.

Duffy, Michael (1991). "Is He Really That Bad?" *Time*, May 20.

Dumbrell, John (1993). *The Carter Presidency: A Re-Evaluation.* Manchester and New York: Manchester University Press.

Einhorn, Robert (1985). *Negotiating from Strength: Leverage in U.S.-Soviet Arms Control.* New York: Praeger.

Eisenhower, Dwight D. (1965). *Waging Peace: The White House Years, 1956-1961.* Garden City, N.Y.: Doubleday.

Eisenhower, Dwight D. (1963). *Mandate for Change, 1953-1956; The White House Years.* Garden City, N.Y.: Doubleday.

Erlanger, Steven (1994). "Gore Upbeat after Talks with Top Russian Leaders." *The New York Times*, December 17.

Etheredge, Lloyd (1985). *Can Governments Learn? American Foreign Policy and Central American Revolutions.* New York: Pergamon.

Evans, Rowland, and Robert Novak (1986). "Oil Blooper." *The Washington Post*, April 9.

Falk, Stanley L. (1964). "The National Security Council under Truman, Eisenhower, and Kennedy." *Political Science Quarterly, LXXIX(3).*

Fenno, Richard F. (1989). *The Making of a Senator: Dan Quayle.* Washington, D.C.: Congressional Quarterly.

Frisby, Michael K., and Barbara Rosewicz (1993). "Gore, Adding Efficiency Study to His Portfolio, Has Carved Out a Significant Role for Himself." *The Wall Street Journal*, March 4.

Gaddis, John Lewis (1989). "Hanging Tough Paid Off." *Bulletin of Atomic Scientists, 45.*

Garland, Susan B. (1994). "The Teflon Vice President." *Business Week*, October 24.

Garthoff, Raymond L. (1994). *The Great Transition: American-Soviet Relations and the End of the Cold War.* Washington, D.C.: The Brookings Institution.

Gelb, Leslie H. (1993). "Foreign Affairs; Where's Bill?" *The New York Times*, March 11.

George, Alexander L. (1980). *Presidential Decision Making in Foreign Policy*. Boulder, Colo.: Westview.

George, Alexander L., and Timothy J. McKeown (1985). "Case Studies and Theories of Organizational Decision Making." *Advances in Information Processing in Organizations*, 2.

Getler, Michael (1983a). "Bush Will Confer in Geneva with Soviet Negotiators." *The Washington Post*, January 28.

Getler, Michael (1983b). "Bush Emphasizes 'Moral Position' of Reagan Arms Control Plan." *The Washington Post*, February 8.

Getler, Michael (1983c). "U.S. Is 'Deadly Serious' on Arms Reduction, Bush Tells Soviets." *The Washington Post*, February 5.

Gillon, Steven M. (1992). *The Democrats' Dilemma: Walter F. Mondale and the Liberal Legacy*. New York: Columbia University Press.

Goldman, Peter (1979). "The Hard Salt Sell." *Newsweek, 93(8)*.

Goldstein, Joel K.(1982). *The Modern American Vice Presidency*. Princeton: Princeton University Press.

Gordon, Michael R. (1990). "Quayle Says Delaying War Would Increase Risks." *The New York Times*, November 30.

Gore, Al (1991). "Defeating Hussein, Once and for All." Op-ed, *The New York Times*, September 26.

Gore, Al (1992). *Earth in the Balance*. Boston: Houghton Mifflin.

Gore, Al (1993a). "From Red Tape to Results: Creating a Government That Works Better and Costs Less." *Report of the National Performance Review*, September 10.

Gore, Al (1993b). "Ecology: The New Sacred Agenda." *New Perspectives Quarterly, 10(1)*.

Gore, Al (1994a). "Forging a Partnership for Peace and Prosperity." *U.S. Department of State Dispatch, 5(2)*.

Gore, Al (1994b). "The Cairo Conference: Defining an Agenda of Hope, Opportunity, and Progress." *U.S. Department of State Dispatch, 5(35)*.

Gore, Al (1994c). "International Conference on Population Development." *U.S. Department of State Dispatch, 5(38)*.

Gore, Al (1994d). "The Rapid Growth of the Human Population." *Vital Speeches of the Day, 60(24)*.

Gore, Al (1994e). "Partnership with S. Africa." *U.S. Dept of State Dispatch, 5(44)*.

Gray, C. Boyden (1989). "The Coordinating Role of the Vice Presidency." In James P. Pfiffner and R. Gordon Hoxie, eds., *The Presidency in Transition*. New York: Center for the Study of the Presidency.

Gray, Gordon (1959). "Role of the National Security Council in the Formulation of National Policy." *Organizing for National Security, II*.

Greenstein, Fred I. (1990). "Ronald Reagan—Another Hidden Hand Ike?" *PS: Political Science & Politics, XXIII(1)*.

Greenstein, Fred I. (1982). *The Hidden-Hand Presidency: Eisenhower as Leader*. New York: Basic Books.

Griffith, Pat (1993). "Gore Has Revolutionized the Role of the Vice President." *Pittsburgh Post-Gazette*, December 26.

Gugliotta, Guy (1991). "Quayle Vows Swift Stroke in Gulf War." *The Washington Post*, January 1.

Gwertzman, Bernard (1983). "U.S. Called Ready to Consider Shift on Missiles Plan." *The New York Times*, February 14.
Hatch, Louis Clinton (1934). *History of the Vice Presidency of the United States.* Revised by Earl L. Shoup. Westport, Conn.: Greenwood.
Heineman, Ben W. Jr. (1989). "Some Rules of the Game: Prescription for Organizing the Domestic Presidency." In James P. Pfiffner and R. Gordon Hoxie, eds., *The Presidency in Transition*. New York: Center for the Study of the Presidency.
Hersey, John (1946). *Hiroshima*. New York: A. A. Knopf.
Holmes, Steven A. (1992). "Gore Lashes Out at Bush on His Iran-Contra Role." *The New York Times*, September 4.
Holsti, Ole R. (1969). *Content Analysis for the Social Sciences and Humanities*. Reading, Mass.: Addison-Wesley.
Hoxie, R. Gordon (1989). "The National Security Council: Introductory Survey." In James P. Pfiffner and R. Gordon Hoxie, eds., *The Presidency in Transition*. New York: Center for the Study of the Presidency.
Hoxie, R. Gordon (1980). "Staffing the Ford and Carter Presidencies." *Presidential Studies Quarterly, X(3)*.
Hoxie, R. Gordon (1977). *Command Decision and the Presidency*. New York: Reader's Digest Press.
Humphrey, Hubert H. (1974). "Changes in the Vice Presidency." *Current History, (67)*.
Hunter, Robert E. (1988). *Organizing for National Security*. Washington, D.C.: Center for Strategic and International Studies.
Ibuse, Masuji (1969). *Black Rain*. John Bester, trans. New York: Bantam.
Ifill, Gwen (1993). "The Vice President; In Selling His Boss's Domestic Program, Gore Is Also Selling Himself." *The New York Times*, February 19.
Jackson, Senator Henry M. (1959). "How Shall We Forge a Strategy for Survival." *Organizing for National Security, II*.
Janis, Irving L. (1982). *Groupthink*. 2nd edition. Boston: Houghton Mifflin.
Janofsky, Michael (1994). "Gore Criticizes North's Remarks on U.S. Military Preparedness." *The New York Times,* October 12.
Jervis, Robert (1984). *The Illogic of American Nuclear Strategy*. Ithaca, N.Y.: Cornell University Press.
Jones, Gordon S., and John A. Marini, eds. (1988). *The Imperial Congress: Crisis in the Separation of Powers*. New York: Pharos.
Jordan, Hamilton (1982). *Crisis: The Last Year of the Carter Presidency*. New York: G. P. Putnam's Sons.
Karol, K. S. (1970). *Guerrillas in Power: The Course of the Cuban Revolution*. New York: Hill and Wang.
Kauss, Clifford (1991). "Top Bush Advisers Called In to Meet on Iraq Strategy." *The New York Times*, January 2.
Kearns, Doris (1976). *Lyndon Johnson and the American Dream*. New York: Harper & Row.
Kelly, Michael (1992). "Where Clinton Stood on War with Iraq." *The New York Times*, July 31.
Kengor, Paul (1998). "Comparing Presidents Reagan and Eisenhower." *Presidential Studies Quarterly, XXVIII (2)*.
Kengor, Paul (1997). "The Foreign Policy Role of Vice President Al Gore." *Presidential Studies Quarterly, XXVII(1)*.

Kengor, Paul (1994). "The Role of the Vice President during the Crisis in the Persian Gulf." *Presidential Studies Quarterly, XXIV(4).*
Keohane, Robert, Gary King, and Sidney Verba (1994). *Designing Social Inquiry: Scientific Inference in Qualitative Research.* Princeton: Princeton University Press.
Kissinger, Henry (1979). *White House Years.* Boston.
Krauthammer, Charles (1991). "Dan Quayle's Bum Rap." *The Washington Post*, May 10.
Lebow, Richard Ned (1987). *Nuclear Crisis Management: A Dangerous Illusion.* Ithaca, N.Y.: Cornell University Press.
Ledeen, Michael (1993). "This Political Pope." *The American Enterprise, 4(4).*
Lewis, Finlay (1980). *Mondale: Portrait of an American Politician.* New York: Harper & Row.
Lewis, Paul (1990). "U.S. to Postpone Debate on Zionism." *The New York Times*, September 16.
Light, Paul C. (1984). *Vice-Presidential Power.* Baltimore: Johns Hopkins University Press.
Light, Paul C. (1983). "The Institutional Vice Presidency." *Presidential Studies Quarterly, XIII(2).*
Lijphart, A. (1985). "Comparative Politics and the Comparative Method." *American Political Science Review, 65.*
Lockwood, Dunbar (1994). "U.S., Russia Agree to Phase-Out of Nuclear Weapons Reactors." *Arms Control Today, 24(6).*
Luxenberg, Alan H. (1988). "Did Eisenhower Push Castro into the Arms of the Soviets?" *Journal of Interamerican Studies and World Affairs, 30(1).*
Macilwain, Colin (1995). "New 'Security Role Urged for Science,'" *Nature, 374(6522).*
Maddox, Robert James (1995). *Weapons for Victory: The Hiroshima Decision Fifty Years Later.* Columbia: University of Missouri Press.
Magnuson, Ed (1983). "D-Day in Grenada." *Time, 122(20).*
Martz, John D., ed. (1995). *United States Policy in Latin America: A Decade of Crisis and Challenge.* Lincoln: University of Nebraska Press.
Mathews, Tom (1993). "Dan Quayle's Crisis Duty." *Newsweek, 116(13).*
Mazo, Earl, and Stephen Hess (1968). *Nixon: A Political Portrait.* New York: Harper & Row.
McCullough, David (1992). *Truman.* New York: Simon & Schuster.
Melloan, George (1993a). "Al Gore's Seven Seals and What They Cost." Op-ed, *The Wall Street Journal*, July 12.
Melloan, George (1993b). "Global View: Congress Is Scuppering Missile Defense." Op-ed, *The Wall Street Journal*, December 16.
Menges, Constantine C. (1988). *Inside the National Security Council.* New York: Simon & Schuster.
Meyer, Cord (1980). *Facing Reality: From World Federalism to the CIA.* New York: Harper & Row.
Millis, Walter, with Harvey C. Mansfield and Harold Stein (1958). *Arms and the State: Civil-Military Elements in National Policy.* New York.
Moens, Alexander (1990). *Foreign Policy under Carter: Testing Multiple Advocacy Decision Making.* Boulder, Colo.: Westview.
Morrow, Lance (1991). "The Strange Destiny of a Vice President." *Time*, May 20.

Motley, Langhorne A. (Tony) (1984). "Democracy in Latin America and the Caribbean." *U.S. Department of State Bulletin, 84(2091).*
Mulcahy, Kevin V. (1987). "Presidents and the Administration of Foreign Policy: The New Role for the Vice President." *Presidential Studies Quarterly, XVII(1).*
Natoli, Marie D. (1989). "The Vice Presidency in the Third Century." In James P. Pfiffner and R. Gordon Hoxie, eds., *The Presidency in Transition.* New York: Center for the Study of the Presidency.
Natoli, Marie D. (1988a). "Harry S Truman and the Contemporary Vice Presidency." *Presidential Studies Quarterly, XVIII(1).*
Natoli, Marie D. (1988b). "The Vice Presidency: Stepping Stone or Stumbling Block?" *Presidential Studies Quarterly, 18(1).*
Natoli, Marie D. (1985). *American Prince, American Pauper.* Westport, Conn.: Greenwood.
Natoli, Marie D. (1982). "Perspectives on the Vice Presidency." *Presidential Studies Quarterly, XII(4).*
Natoli, Marie D. (1980). "The Vice Presidency: Gerald Ford as Healer?" Guest Editorial, *Presidential Studies Quarterly, X(4).*
Natoli, Marie D. (1979). "Abolish the Vice Presidency?" *Presidential Studies Quarterly, IX(2).*
Nixon, Richard (1990). *In the Arena: A Memoir of Victory, Defeat and Renewal.* New York: Simon & Schuster.
Nixon, Richard M. (1978). *The Memoirs of Richard Nixon.* New York: Grosset & Dunlap.
Nixon, Richard M. (1962). *Six Crises.* New York: Doubleday.
Novak, Robert D. (1994). "Nixon and Hiss." *The Washington Post*, April 28.
Oberdorfer, Don (1991). *The Turn: From the Cold War to a New Era.* New York: Poseidon Press.
Oberdorfer, Don (1978). "U.S. Studies Soviet Attack: Vance May Reveal Reaction." *The Washington Post*, June 18.
Odeen, Philip A. (1980). "Organizing for National Security." *International Security, 5(1).*
Parrington, Vernon L. (1930). *Main Currents of American Thought.* New York: Harcourt, Brace.
Pipes, Richard (1995). "Misinterpreting the Cold War." *Foreign Affairs*, January/February.
Pipes, Richard (1984). "Can the Soviet Union Reform?" *Foreign Affairs, 63(1).*
Pomper, Gerald M. (1972). *The Performance of American Government: Checks and Minuses.* New York: The Free Press (as cited by Marie D. Natoli [1980], "Vice Presidential Selection: The Political Considerations," *Presidential Studies Quarterly, X[2]*).
Quayle, Dan (1994). *Standing Firm: A Vice-Presidential Memoir.* New York: HarperCollins.
Quayle, Dan (1991a). Office of the Vice President. "Prepared Text of Remarks by the Vice President, 48th Tactical Fighter Wing, U.S. Air Force." Deployed, Saudi Arabia, January 1.
Quayle, Dan (1991b). Office of the Vice President. "Prepared Text of Remarks by the Vice President, Los Angeles World Affairs Council." Los Angeles, Calif., January 8.

Quayle, Dan (1991c). Office of the Vice President. "Prepared Text of Remarks by the Vice President to Military Families." Fort Bliss, Tex., February 6.
Quayle, Dan (1991d). Office of the Vice President. "Prepared Text of Remarks by the Vice President, The Mid-America Committee." Chicago, Ill., March 13.
Quayle, Dan (1990a). Office of the Vice President. "Prepared Text of Remarks by the Vice President, The Washington Institute for Near East Policy." April 30.
Quayle, Dan (1990b). Office of the Vice President. "Prepared Text of Remarks by the Vice President, Seton Hall University." South Orange, N.J., November 29.
Quayle, Dan (1990c). Office of the Vice President. "Prepared Text of Remarks by the Vice President, Foreign Policy Research Institute Conference." Washington, D.C., December 18.
Quayle, Dan (1989a). "Text of Remarks by the Vice President, National Defense University Symposium, Department of Defense." L'Enfant Plaza—Monet Room, November 17.
Quayle, Dan (1989b). "SDI and Its Enemies." *Policy Review, 50.*
Quayle, Dan (1987a). "Should Congress Approve the ABM Treaty Controversy?" *The Congressional Digest, 66(11).*
Quayle, Dan (1987b). "Upgrading Our Cruise Missiles: Imperative for the 1990s." *Armed Forces Journal International, 125(1).*
Quayle, Dan (1987c). "Missile Woes." *The Washington Post*, July 14, 1987.
Reagan, Ronald (1990). *Ronald Reagan: An American Life.* New York: Simon & Schuster.
Ripley, Brian (1993). "Psychology, Foreign Policy, and International Relations Theory." *Political Psychology, 14(3).*
Risse-Kappen, Thomas (1991). "Did 'Peace through Strength' End the Cold War?: Lessons from INF." *International Security, 16(1).*
Robbins, Carla Anne (1993). "Gore's Success in Foreign Policy Role Depends on Commitment from Clinton." *The Wall Street Journal*, December 13.
Rosenau, James N. (1981). *The Study of Political Adaptation.* New York: Nichols
Rosenthal, A. M. (1992). "Saddam and Gore." *The New York Times*, July 28.
Rothenberg, Randall (1988). "In Search of George Bush." *The New York Times Magazine*, March 6.
Safford, Jeffrey J. (1980). "The Nixon-Castro Meeting of 19 April 1959." *Diplomatic History, 4(4).*
Safire, William (1993a). "Who's Got Clout." *The New York Times*, Sunday Magazine, June 2.
Safire, William (1993b). "Gore Flattens Perot." *The New York Times*, November 11.
Santini, Maureen (1986). "Knee-Deep in Troubled Waters." *U.S. News & World Report, 100(15).*
Schlesinger, Arthur M. Jr. (1973, 1974). "The Vice Presidency: A Modest Proposal." Appendix to *The Imperial Presidency.* Boston: Houghton Mifflin.
Schneider, Keith (1992). "Reagan-Pope Plan to Topple Warsaw Is Reported." *The New York Times*, February 18.
Schweizer, Peter (1994). *Victory: The Reagan Administration's Secret Strategy That Hastened the Collapse of the Soviet Union.* New York: Atlantic Monthly Press.
Sciolino, Elaine (1993). "Clinton Reaffirms Policy on Yeltsin." *The New York Times*, December 16.

Sciolino, Elaine, and Todd S. Purdum (1995). "Al Gore, One Vice President Who Is Eluding the Shadows." *The New York Times*, February 19.
Seaman, Barrett, and Strobe Talbott (1986). "An Interview with the Vice President (George Bush, Iran Arms Deal)." *Time, 128.*
Seib, Gerald F. (1988). "Bush's Role in Policy Is Difficult to Discern Reagan Officials Say." *The Wall Street Journal*, March 31.
Shalnev, Aleksandr (1994). "United States." *Current Digest of the Post-Soviet Press, 45(50).*
Shenon, Philip (1991). "Quayle Draws Ovation on Visit to the Troops." *The New York Times*, January 1.
Shultz, George P. (1993). *Turmoil and Triumph: My Years as Secretary of State.* New York: Macmillan.
Shultz, George (1986). "Nicaragua: Will Democracy Prevail?" *U.S. Department of State Bulletin, 86(2109).*
Sickels, Robert J. (1974). *Presidential Transactions.* Englewood Cliffs: Prentice-Hall.
Simpson, Christopher (1995). *National Security Directives of the Reagan and Bush Administrations: The Declassified History of U.S. Political and Military Policy, 1981-1991.* Boulder, Colo.: Westview.
Sirgiovanni, George S. (1994). "Dumping the Vice President: An Historical Overview and Analysis." *Presidential Studies Quarterly, XXIV(4).*
Smoke, Richard (1987). *National Security and the Nuclear Dilemma.* New York: Random House.
Smothers, Ronald (1990). "Quayle, in Sharp Attack, Accuses Some Democrats of 'Playing Politics' on the Gulf." *The New York Times,* December 11.
Solberg, Carl (1984). *Hubert Humphrey: A Biography.* New York: W. W. Norton.
Solomon, Burt (1991). "War Bolsters Quayle's Visibility . . . But Hasn't Increased His Stature." *National Journal, 23(9).*
Spiegel, Steven (1977). "Carter and Israel." *Commentary*, July.
Stathis, Stephen W. (1982). "Presidential Disability Agreements Prior to the 25th Amendment." *Presidential Studies Quarterly, 12(2).*
Taylor, Paul (1986). "Furor over Remarks Fails to Dismay Bush." *The Washington Post*, April 14.
Thompson, Kenneth W. (1995a). "The Reagan Presidency: Interview with Frank Carlucci." *Miller Center Journal, 2.*
Thompson, Kenneth W. (1995b). "The Reagan Presidency: Interview with Frank Carlucci." *Miller Center Journal, 2.*
Thompson, Kenneth W. (1994). "Richard Nixon: The Man & the Political Leader." Interview with Bryce Harlow, *Miller Center Journal, 1.*
Thomson, Harry C. (1980). "The Second Place in Rome: John Adams as Vice President." *Presidential Studies Quarterly, X(2).*
Truman, Harry S (1955). *Year of Decisions.* New York: Doubleday.
Tullai, Martin D. (1985). "Speaking of the Vice Presidency. . . ." *American History Illustrated, 19.*
Tyler, Patrick E. (1995). "The U.S.-China Slide." *The New York Times*, May 23.
Tyler, Patrick E. (1994). "Visit by Gore to China Is Under Study." *The New York Times*, December 20.
Ullmann, Owen (1994). "Who Has Clinton's Ear Now?" *Washingtonian, 29(4).*

Vance, Cyrus (1983). *Hard Choices: Critical Years in America's Foreign Policy.* New York: Simon & Schuster.
Vinocur, John (1983a). "Bush Says Reagan Arms Offer Stands." *The New York Times*, February 3.
Vinocur, John (1983b). "President Urges Soviet to Agree to Missile Curb." *The New York Times*, February 1.
Vinocur, John (1983c). "Bush Says the U.S. Is 'Deadly Serious' on Weapons Curbs." *The New York Times*, February 5.
Vinocur, John (1983d). "Bush, in London, Challenged by Nuclear Foe." *The New York Times*, February 10.
Vinocur, John (1983e). "Bush Finds Allies Open on Arms Pact." *The New York Times*, February 11.
Walsh, Kenneth T., and Michael Barone (1990). "The Vice President's View: 'It's an Awkward Job.'" *U.S. News & World Report*, 110(19).
Walsh, Kenneth T., and Matthew Cooper (1993). "A Vice President Who Counts." *U.S. News & World Report*, 115(3).
Walsh, Lawrence E. (1994). *Iran-Contra: The Final Report.* New York: Random House.
Weber, Robert Philip (1990). *Basic Content Analysis.* 2nd edition. London: Sage.
Weinraub, Bernard (1977). "More Open U.S. Diplomacy Is Message of Mondale's Trip." *The New York Times*, February 1.
Wiarda, Howard J. (1992). *American Foreign Policy toward Latin America in the '80s and '90s: Issues and Controversies from Reagan and Bush.* New York: New York University Press.
Wicker, Tom (1996). "Richard M. Nixon, 1969-1974." *Presidential Studies Quarterly*, *XXVI(1)*.
Will, George F. (1994). "Some Bravery, Even More Melancholy." Op-ed, *The Washington Post*, April 24.
Williams, Juan (1983). "Bush to Go to Europe for Talks." *The Washington Post*, January 9.
Witcover, Jules (1992). *Crapshoot: Rolling the Dice on the Vice Presidency.* New York: Crown Publishers.
Woodward, Bob (1994). *The Agenda: Inside the Clinton White House.* New York: Simon & Schuster.
Woodward, Bob (1991). *The Commanders.* New York: Simon & Schuster.

Editorials/Unauthored Articles and Published Interviews

American-Arab Affairs, 33 (1990). "Text of Remarks by the Vice President to the American Israel Public Affairs Committee on June 11, 1990."
American Legion Magazine, 120 (1986). "Terrorism: Special Report."
Armed Forces Journal International, 127(7) (1990). Interview with John G. Roos and Benjamin F. Schemmer, "An Exclusive AFJI Interview with Vice President Dan Quayle."
Business Week, April 1, 1991. Interview with Lee Walczak and Douglas Harbrecht, "A Talk with Dan Quayle: 'Washington Loves a Free Lunch.'"

Bibliography

Business Week, October 20, 1986. "Washington Outlook: Now the Right Is Taking Potshots at Star Wars."
Christian Science Monitor, March 3, 1981.
Editorials on File, 1983. "Bush Urges 'Zero Option' in Tour of Western Europe."
National Journal, June 10, 1981.
Presidential Documents, 21 (1985). "Magazine Publishers Association."
Public Papers of the Presidents, I (1987). "Reagan, Remarks and a Question-and-Answer Session with Southeast Regional Editors and Broadcasters."
The Department of State Bulletin, LXXVI (1967). "Vice President Mondale Visits Europe and Japan."
The Economist, January 8, 1994. "Lexington: The Tortoise of Foggy Bottom."
The Economist, September 10, 1994. "Lexington: Reinventing the Vice Presidency."
The Nation, 256(7) (1993). Editorial, "Dump this Nominee."
The New York Times, January 13, 1991. "Remarks in Congress during Last Hours of Debate."
The New York Times, August 3, 1994. "Gore, in Ukraine, Expresses Support for Economic Change."
The New York Times, September 29, 1977.
The New York Times, December 21, 1980.
The New York Times, October 16, 1976.
The New York Times, January 23, 1977.
The New York Times, January 24-31, 1977.
The New York Times, October 15, 1988.
The New York Times, June 18, 1978. "Excerpts from Pravda Commentary on Relations between Soviet and the United States."
The New York Times, December 31, 1990. "Quayle Meets with Saudi Royalty and Seeks More Aid for Military."
The Wall Street Journal, April 14, 1992. Editorial, "No Willie Horton."
The Wall Street Journal, November 9, 1993. Editorial, "Al Gore's Big Knockout."
The Washington Post, June 10, 1994. Editorial, "The Vatican vs. The VP."
The Washington Post, October 16, 1976.
The Washington Post, January 24-31, 1977.
The Washington Post, June 18, 1977.
The Washington Post, February 13, 1983. Editorial, "George Did It."
The Washington Post, January 2, 1991. "Quayle Sees Kuwait Emir on Funding."
The Washington Times, December 7, 1993. "Gore's Growth."
U.S. Department of State Bulletin, 83(2072) (1983). "Vice President Bush Visits Europe."
U.S. Department of State Bulletin, 84(2083) (1984). "Vice President Bush Visits Latin America."
U.S. Department of State Bulletin, 86(2111) (1986). "Vice President Bush Visits Persian Gulf."
U.S. Department of State Bulletin, 83(2072) (1983). "Vice President Interviewed on 'Face the Nation'" (excerpts).
U.S. Department of State Bulletin, LXXVI(1982) (1977). "Vice President Mondale Visits Europe and Meets with South African Prime Minister Vorster: Remarks during the Visit and News Conference Following His Meeting with Prime Minister Vorster."

U.S. Department of State Bulletin, 78(2017) (1978). "Vice President Mondale's Address to the Israeli Knesset."
U.S. Department of State Bulletin, 85 (1985). "Vice President's Visit to Moscow: News Conference."
U.S. Department of State Dispatch, 5(1) (1994). "Fact Sheet: Gore-Chernomyrdin Commission."
U.S. Department of State Dispatch, 5(38) (1994). "The Crisis in Haiti."
U.S. Department of State Dispatch, January 7, 1991. "Gulf Crisis Update."
U.S. News & World Report, February 18, 1991. Interview with Stephen Budiansky, "The Gulf War: The Real Target?"
U.S. News & World Report, December 14, 1981.
U.S. News & World Report, 91(24) (1981). "Interview with Vice President George Bush: White House Leaks: 'We Have Been Undisciplined.'"
U.S. News & World Report (1992). Triumph without Victory: The Unreported History of the Persian Gulf War. New York: Random House.
U.S. State Department Bulletin, March 1983.
Walsh, Kenneth T., February 18, 1991. "Quayle on Hussein: 'He Is Totally Irrational,'" *U.S. News & World Report*.
White House, Office of Vice President, March 27, 1995. "U.S.-Kazakhstan Agreements."

Television and Radio Broadcasts

ABC News PrimeTime Live (1994). "Standing Firm." Interview Transcript, May 5.
American Enterprise Institute, Washington, D.C., Brian Lapping Associates for Discovery Communications, Inc. (1992). "The Gulf Crisis: The Road to War" (video tape).
Facts on File (1954). Nixon television broadcast, March 13.
Meet the Press with Tim Russert (1993). "Vice President-Elect Al Gore" (television program), NBC-TV, January 17.
National Public Radio (1993). "Vice President Al Gore Travels to Mexico City." *Morning Edition* (radio program), December 1, program n1228.
This Week with David Brinkley (1993). "Turmoil in Russia" (television program), NBC-TV, March 28, program n596.
This Week with David Brinkley (1995). ABC-TV. June 25.

Personal Interviews

Interview with Bill Kristol, former chief of staff to Vice President Quayle, via telephone, May 28, 1996.
Interview with Carnes Lord, former NSA to Vice President Quayle, via telephone from Medford, Mass., December 11, 1996.
Interview with Joe DeSutter, former foreign-policy and national-security adviser to both Vice Presidents Quayle and Gore, via telephone from Washington, D.C., December 18, 1996.

Interview with Jon Glassman, former Deputy NSA to Vice President Quayle, in Washington, D.C., at State Department, May 24, 1996.
Interview with Tony Motley, via telephone from Washington, D.C., December 18, 1996.
Interview with Tony Motley, via letter from Washington, D.C., January 9, 1997.

Index

ABM Treaty, 174
abortion, 141, 248-49
Acheson, Dean, 223
Adams, John, 14, 36-37
Adkison, Danny M., 5, 10, 17, 37, 296
Africa, 2, 5, 64, 108-13, 115, 118, 247-48, 272-73, 276, 284
Agnew, Spiro, 9, 30, 39, 192, 195, 249, 271
AIPAC (American-Israel Public Affairs Committee), 102, 179-80, 288
Air Force, 62, 108, 142, 171, 195, 276, 280
Albright, Madeleine, 214, 230
Allison, Graham, 9, 11
Ambrose, Stephen, 45, 53, 56
Andropov, Yuri, 149-50, 152, 154
apocalyptic, 245
Aquino, Corazan, 189
Argentina, 30, 58, 60, 64, 143, 187-88, 202, 274, 281
Aristede, Jean-Betrand, 240-41
Armed Forces Journal International, 175
Army, 171, 280
Aronson, Bernard, 188, 281
Arrow project, 178, 181
Article II, Constitution, 45
Australia, 174

Baker, James, 21, 34, 102, 114, 128, 131, 134-36, 169- 72, 182, 197, 249, 272, 280, 288, 291-92
Balkans, 3, 225, 230-32, 250, 279, 282
Ball, George, 28
Baltimore Sun, 165
Barkley, Alben, 24-26, 38-39, 72, 301
Barnes, Fred, 172, 197, 200, 224, 239
Barone, Michael, 172
Begin, Menachem, 95, 103-05, 107- 08
Bentsen, Lloyd, 166
Berger, Samuel, 225, 230, 282
Berke, Richard, 214
Berlin Wall, 96
Book of Revelation, 245

Bosnia, 216, 225, 230-31, 233, 251, 282
Boyer, Peter, 10, 219, 221, 224, 238, 240, 274
Brazil, 58, 96, 187-88, 202, 274, 281
Brezhnev, Leonid, 95, 149, 154
Britain, 151, 153, 187
Broder, David, 37, 39, 167, 170, 172, 183, 190
Brokaw, Tom, 227
Browner, Carol, 245
Bulgaria, 25, 174
Bush, George, 2-4, 6, 8-9, 14, 18-20, 22, 26-27, 29-31, 34, 37, 39, 42, 52, 85, 126-57, 165-79, 180, 182-83, 185, 187-88, 190-93, 195-97, 199, 201-04, 214-18, 226-29, 231, 240, 249-50, 263-67, 269, 270-71, 275-77, 280-81, 283-86, 288, 291-93, 295, 297, 300-02
Business Week, 165, 189, 194, 228

Cambodia, 231
Camp David, 95, 103-04, 106-08, 118, 182, 186
Carter, Jimmy, 3, 4, 14, 22, 33-35, 54, 84-89, 92-118, 128-29, 157, 167, 183, 215, 226, 264-69, 272-73, 276, 280, 286-87, 290, 293
Castro, Fidel, 2, 29-30, 39, 42, 45, 50, 54-57, 72-73, 226, 263, 276, 299
CENTO, 21-22
Chechnya, 233
Cheney, Dick, 19, 170, 172, 182, 190, 197, 199, 268
China, 53, 90, 100, 127, 214, 245
Christopher, Warren, 21, 35, 92, 95, 115, 191, 214-15, 223-24, 227, 231, 235-36, 247, 249-52, 272, 290
Churchill, Winston, 14, 23-24, 186, 264
CIA, 30, 48, 55-56, 58, 61, 66, 87, 127, 138, 139, 147, 173, 182, 225-26, 281, 292
Clarke, Duncan, 34, 40, 47, 293

Clinton, William Jefferson, 4, 10, 16, 21-22, 30, 35-36, 88, 170, 214-41, 245, 249-50, 252, 270, 279, 281, 290, 300
Cold War, 4, 22, 26, 57, 111, 138, 183-85, 248
communism, 56, 63, 298
Congress, 17, 19, 30, 45-46, 52-53, 67, 85, 94-95, 97, 100, 137, 141, 143-45, 166, 173-74, 182, 191-96, 202, 223, 227, 229, 250, 267
Conservatives, 166
Constitution, 16-17, 19, 21, 45-46
Croatia, 231-32
Cuba, 42, 54-57, 72, 115-16, 276, 299
Cutler, Robert, 47-48, 89, 92, 269
Czechoslovakia, 25, 174

Democratic Leadership Council, 219
Democrats, 20, 53, 97, 126, 165-66, 182, 190-94, 216, 219, 220, 222, 226-27, 250, 281, 283
Department of Defense (DoD), 176
Desert Storm, 172, 189, 196, 239, 288
DeSutter, Joe, 170-71, 191, 201, 225, 250, 282, 288
Dodd, Christopher, 191
Donatelli, Frank, 182
Donovan, Robert J., 53, 92
Duffy, Michael, 39, 172, 187
Dukakis, Michael, 126, 166, 216
Dulles, John Foster, 46, 48-49, 52, 55, 58, 65-67, 69, 294

Earth in the Balance, 241, 245
Eastern Europe, 24, 172, 174, 227, 288
Egypt, 100, 103-06, 108, 176, 187
Eisenhower, Dwight, 4, 14, 20, 21, 26-27, 36, 42-56, 63, 65, 66, 70-73, 89, 136, 157, 169, 265, 293-94, 296-97, 300-01
El Salvador, 143-45, 156, 231
environment, 29, 99, 104, 223, 225, 233-34, 241, 245-46, 248, 251, 278, 293

Fahd, King, 2, 126, 139, 140-41, 189, 262, 275
Falk, Stanley L., 47

fascism, 241
Fenno, Richard, 166, 179
Ford, Gerald, 20, 34, 39, 94, 101, 127
France, 151, 187
Fuerth, Leon, 225-26, 251, 253, 281-83

Garner, John Nance, 23, 37
Gates, Robert, 170, 173, 182, 191, 199
GATT, 223
Gaza Strip, 102, 179, 272, 288
Gearan, Mark, 221, 252
Gephardt, Richard, 134, 194, 250
Germany, 24, 38, 94, 152, 187, 227, 241, 245
Gillon, Steven, 4, 95, 97-99, 104-05, 107, 110, 114, 117, 269, 287, 296
Glassman, Jon, 87, 168, 171, 173-74, 188-89, 191, 266, 275, 280-81
Goldstein, Joel K., 27, 39, 53, 192, 203
Gorbachev, Mikhail, 2, 149, 165, 169, 171-72, 288
Gore, Al, 2, 4, 10, 14, 22, 26, 29-31, 39, 84, 88, 158, 165, 170, 203, 216, 214-53, 264, 269-74, 278-79, 281-82, 299, 302
Gore-Chernomyrdin Commission, 2, 214, 233, 274, 278
Gore-Mbeki Commission, 39, 214, 247, 278
Gore-Mubarak Commission, 214, 278
GPALS, 200, 201
Gray, C. Boyden, 3, 10, 126, 263, 275, 283-91
Greenstein, Fred, 47
Grenada, 126, 135-36, 156, 292
Gulf War, 4, 97, 176, 180-81, 191, 197, 203, 268, 272

Haig, Al, 28, 34, 131, 135, 138, 157, 249, 272, 292-93, 295
Haiti, 225-26, 229, 240-41, 250-51
Hatch, Louis Clinton, 10, 16, 36
Heineman, Ben W., Jr., 3, 10, 268-71
Herter, Christian, 48, 55, 294
Hess, Stephen, 4, 50, 61-62, 64, 71
Hitler, Adolf, 38, 110, 186
Holocaust, 241
Hoover, Herbert, 48, 294
Horton, Willie, 216

Humphrey, Hubert, 9, 20, 27-28, 30, 39, 57, 66, 86, 93, 103, 108, 203
Hussein, Saddam, 22, 176, 178, 180, 182, 184-85, 192-94, 199-200, 217-19, 226-27, 274, 281

Indiana, 166
Indochina, 2, 51-52, 73, 126, 263, 272
International Monetary Fund (IMF), 226
Iran, 35, 40, 95-96, 134, 136, 140, 178, 180, 184, 218, 228, 235, 252, 275
Iran-Contra, 35, 40, 130, 215, 229
Iraq, 30, 140, 176, 178, 180, 181, 185, 186, 187, 189, 195, 198, 199, 200, 202, 217, 218, 226, 227, 237, 251, 252, 274, 281
Israel, 95, 99-108, 172, 176, 178-81, 184, 197-98, 202, 216, 287-88

Jackson, Karl, 37, 114, 171, 250, 280
Japan, 24, 38, 96, 174, 187, 189-90, 202, 245
Jerusalem, 103-04, 107, 178-79
Job Training Partnership Act, 166
Johnson, Lyndon, 9, 14, 20, 27-28, 30, 36, 57, 93, 103, 108, 203, 280, 294
Jordan, 92, 94-97, 105-06, 227, 265

Kemp, Jack, 166
Kennedy, John F., 9, 14, 34, 57, 69, 73, 116, 126, 132, 166, 167, 189, 266, 293, 298
Khrushchev, Nikita, 42, 45, 50, 54, 64-70, 73, 110, 233, 298
King, Larry, 2, 126, 139, 140-41, 189, 227, 238, 240, 262, 275
Kiriyenko, Sergei, 236, 252
Kissinger, Henry, 35, 97, 105-06, 108, 127, 167, 170, 250, 287, 290
Kitchen Debate, 233
Kohl, Helmut, 152
Kozyrev, Andrei, 235, 252
Krauthammer, Charles, 199
Kremlin, 65, 113, 116, 139-40, 150, 275
Kristallnacht, 241

Kristol, William, 10, 98, 170-73, 191, 197, 200, 203-04, 250, 268, 286, 288, 291
Kurdish refugees, 184, 218
Kuwait, 182, 184-89, 194-95, 198, 200, 202, 217, 229, 274, 281

Latin America, 4, 22, 42, 50, 51, 54, 56-59, 63-64, 66, 73, 126, 130, 143-46, 166, 171, 174, 188, 202, 204, 270, 275, 280-81
Lewis, Finlay, 4, 100, 104, 106-07, 112-13, 277
Light, Paul, 3, 10, 22, 37, 39, 93, 215, 280
Lord, Carnes, 168, 171-72, 183, 188, 200, 279-80, 288
Los Angeles Times, 95, 190

Malta, 169
Malthus, Thomas Robert, 248
Mandela, Nelson, 248
Mann, Thomas, 214
Marcos, Ferdinand, 60
Marshall, Thomas R., 20, 170, 250
Mazo, Earl, 4, 50, 61-62, 64, 71
Mbeki, Thabo, 214, 248, 278
McCarthy, Eugene, 18
McCurdy, Dave, 229
McCurry, Mike, 221
McLarty, Mark, 221, 223, 230, 238-39
Melloan, George, 245
Mexico, 126, 145, 147, 188, 226, 238
Middle East, 4, 8, 95, 99-108, 118, 166-67, 172, 174-76, 179-85, 197, 223, 280, 286-88
Millis, Walter, 47
Mitchell, Andrea, 217, 227
Mondale, Walter, 2-4, 6, 8, 14, 26, 28-30, 36, 40, 42, 52, 54, 84-118, 126, 128-29, 133, 134, 137-38, 142-43, 167, 171-73, 214-15, 252, 263-73, 276, 280, 286-87, 291, 296-97, 300-02
Monroe Doctrine, 23
Moscow, 38, 42, 52, 64-67, 69, 71, 109, 116, 135, 138-40, 149, 153, 171, 214, 221, 226, 233-34, 236, 252, 272, 278, 288, 298-99, 302
Mulcahy, Kevin, 3, 5, 10, 11, 35, 40,

73, 86, 263, 284-85, 289, 291

NAFTA, 223, 238-40, 245
National Defense University, 177
National Security Act of 1947, 7, 14, 22, 32, 34-35, 40
National Security Advisor, 104, 173, 199
National Security Council, 25, 26, 32, 35, 38, 47, 49, 87, 89, 106, 130, 263, 286, 289, 298-99, 302
National Security Strategy, 177
NATO, 22, 90, 96-97, 150-51, 153, 223, 232
Natoli, Marie D., 3, 10, 16-17, 19, 23-26, 36-39, 71, 84, 117, 128, 262-63, 291, 298-99
Navy, 43, 171, 175-76, 280
Neel, Roy, 221
New Democrat, 219, 241
New Orleans, 171, 288
Newsweek, 39, 172, 195
Nixon, Richard, 2, 4, 6, 9, 14, 20, 26-30, 34-36, 39, 41-73, 94, 110, 126, 142-43, 149, 167, 169, 233, 263-64, 269, 272, 276, 286, 290, 294, 297-301
North Korea, 26, 226-27
North, Oliver, 137, 229

Operations Coordinating Board (OCB), 48-49, 72-73, 294
Open Door, 23

Palestinians, 179, 218
Patriot (cruise missile), 174, 176, 178, 181, 200-02
Peretz, Martin, 226
Perez, Carlos Andres, 187, 274, 281
Perot, Ross, 219, 227, 238-39, 245
Persian Gulf, 8-10, 29-30, 39, 140, 165-66, 173-78, 182, 184, 186, 189-90, 195, 201-02, 216-18, 220, 229, 240, 250, 267, 270-71
Pershing II (missile), 150, 151, 155
Peru, 60
Philippines, 204
Pipes, Richard, 132, 138, 157
Poland, 24, 25, 38, 138, 174, 227, 245

Policy Review, 89, 177, 201
Pomper, Gerald M., 16, 36, 272
Pope John Paul II, 248-49
population growth, 223, 248, 251
Potsdam Conference, 24
Powell, Colin, 92, 106, 170, 172, 182
Primakov, Yevgeny, 237, 252

Quayle, Dan, 2, 4, 8-10, 14, 18-20, 22, 26, 29-30, 37, 39, 52, 87, 97, 98, 101-02, 131, 158, 165-204, 214-16, 225, 240, 249, 264-77, 279-82, 285-86, 288, 294, 299, 302
Quinn, Jack, 220

Reagan, Ronald, 3-5, 14, 20, 29, 34-35, 38, 40, 111, 117, 126-57, 166, 175, 201, 228, 265, 269, 275, 78, 289-95, 300-01
Republicans, 20, 45, 190-91, 230, 286
Rockefeller, Nelson, 39, 34, 86, 134-35, 293
Rogers, William, 46
Rome, 36, 153, 248
Roosevelt, Franklin D., 2, 14, 21-24, 26-27, 43, 86, 173, 264, 300
Rosenau, James, 21, 37, 300
Rouge, Khmer, 191
Russert, Tim, 40, 227
Russia, 30, 37, 214, 223, 225-26, 232-37, 245, 251-52, 272, 274, 278, 280, 282

Sabato, Larry, 215, 224
Sadat, Anwar, 103-05, 107
Safire, William, 220, 239
SALT, 3, 5, 90, 95, 100, 113-18, 134, 267, 289, 291
Saudi Arabia, 30, 126, 137-41, 185-89, 202, 262, 270, 275, 301-02
Sawyer, Dianne, 199-200
Schlesinger, Arthur, 17-18, 36
Schweizer, Peter, 140-41
Scowcroft, Brent, 30, 34, 170, 172, 173, 182-83, 266, 295
Scud, 178, 180, 197-98, 200
SEATO, 22
Serbs, 225, 231, 282
Seton Hall University, 183

Sickels, Robert J., 16, 36
Simpson, Alan, 168
Sirgiovanni, George, 4, 10, 37, 39, 71
solidarity, 132, 138
Solomon, Burt, 172
Somalia, 225, 227
South Africa, 2, 5, 84, 100, 108-13, 118, 126, 138, 142, 214, 247-48, 263, 270, 272-73, 276, 278, 302
South Korea, 26, 227
Soviet Union, 24, 50, 54, 57, 65, 67-68, 73, 95, 96, 100, 111, 113, 114, 116, 132, 135, 138-40, 148, 151-53, 155, 169, 175, 180, 200, 227, 237, 238, 274-75
Stalin, Joseph, 14, 23, 24, 37, 264
State Department, 3, 22, 48, 55-56, 58, 66, 93, 102-03, 105, 108-09, 113, 115, 146-48, 157, 165, 169, 171-72, 174, 179, 191, 198, 226, 263, 272-73, 275, 280, 283-93
Stathis, Stephen W., 46
Strategic Defense Initiative (SDI), 174, 178, 201, 216
Sullivan, Marguerite, 221
Summers, Lawrence, 245
Synar, Mike, 222, 239
Syria, 176, 181, 187

Tel Aviv, 178
Thailand, 174
Thatcher, Margaret, 153
The Economist, 151, 216, 220, 222
The New Republic, 200
Thomson, Harry C., 16, 36
Time, 37, 39, 187
Toledano, Ralph de, 4, 45, 53
Truman, Harry S, 2-3, 7, 10, 14-15, 20, 22-30, 32, 35-36, 38-39, 43, 47, 53, 86, 92, 117, 130, 157, 169, 173, 183, 262, 264-65, 279, 289, 296, 299, 301-02
Tudjman, Franjo, 231-32

Ukraine, 226, 237-38, 274
Unabomber, 243
United Nations, 26, 101, 110-11, 127, 153-54, 179, 194, 230-31, 273

Uruguay, 59-60
USSR, 65, 148

Vance, Cyrus, 89-90, 92, 95, 100-01, 104-06, 108-09, 111-13, 115-18, 167, 249, 266, 271, 287, 290, 293
Vatican, 132, 248
Venezuela, 30, 61-62, 126, 145-47, 188, 202, 274
Vietnam, 28, 30, 57, 94, 103, 108, 115, 175, 189, 192, 195-96, 219, 229, 271

Wallace, Henry A., 23, 37
Wall Street Journal, 223, 239, 245, 250
Walsh, Kenneth, 40, 172
Washington Institute for Near East Policy, 180
Washington Post, 37, 39, 110, 150, 153-54, 167, 176, 199
West Bank, 102, 106, 179, 272, 288
Western Europe, 5, 126, 138, 148, 150, 152, 154, 227, 275, 285, 302
White House, 2, 4-5, 7, 9, 14, 17-18, 20, 23, 27-28, 31-32, 34-36, 46-47, 53-54, 62, 66, 87, 89, 93-103, 108, 111-12, 114-18, 128-35, 141, 143, 145-46, 150, 155, 157, 169, 171-72, 179, 182, 187-88, 190, 194-95, 200, 202, 214, 220-26, 229-31, 233, 239-41, 245, 249, 251, 253, 263, 266-67, 273, 275, 277-79, 282, 286, 289, 291-96, 300
Wilson, Woodrow, 20
Wolfowitz, Paul, 199
Woodward, Bob, 37, 39, 167, 170, 172-73, 183, 190, 221
World Bank, 226, 245, 284

Yalta, 23-25
Yeltsin, Boris, 169, 171, 233, 235-36, 252, 288
Yitzhak, Shamir, 197, 227

Zedillo, Ernesto, 238
Zhirinovsky, Vladimir, 233

About the Author

Dr. Kengor is associate professor of political science at Grove City College, a small, Christian, liberal arts college located one hour north of Pittsburgh. He received his doctorate from the University of Pittsburgh's Graduate School of Public and International Affairs, where he focused on foreign/security policy, the presidency and vice presidency, and international political economy. He has a master's degree in international affairs from the School of International Service at The American University, where his concentration was defense/foreign policy, the vice presidency, and U.S.-Latin American relations. His focuses are international affairs and the presidency.

Kengor served on the editorial board of *Presidential Studies Quarterly* (the leading academic journal on the presidency) from 1997 to 1999. He has published a number of articles and book reviews in the quarterly, including articles on Presidents Eisenhower and Reagan as well as articles on Vice Presidents Quayle and Gore. His article on Quayle and Gore and their secretaries of state was published in the summer 2000 issue of *Political Science Quarterly*. Kengor recently contributed an article to the oral history series on the Clinton presidency at the University of Virginia's Miller Center of Public Affairs. He is currently working on a book on President Ronald Reagan's personal role in his administration's effort to undermine the Soviet empire, titled *What Reagan Knew*.

In 1991-1993, Kengor served in the Political–Military Affairs program at the Center for Strategic & International Studies (CSIS) in Washington, D.C., where he did policy analysis on Iraq, nuclear weapons proliferation, and other issues. He still does occasional work for CSIS and regularly lectures on Iraq and Saddam Hussein's weapons programs. Kengor also does research on trade issues, such as NAFTA. He has published NAFTA work in *Economic Development Commentary* and for think tanks such as Heritage Foundation, Allegheny Institute for Public Policy, Mackinac Center, Wisconsin Policy Research Institute, James Madison Institute, Texas Public Policy Foundation, Goldwater Institute, and others.

Kengor has been published in the *Los Angeles Times, Buffalo News, Christian Science Monitor, Defense News, Detroit News, Houston Post, National Review, Pittsburgh Post-Gazette, Policy Review, Roll Call, St. Louis Post-Dispatch, Washington Times, Weekly Standard*, and many others.

He lives in Grove City, Pennsylvania, with his wife, Susan, and two sons, Paul and Mitchell.